ETHICS AND EXPERIMENTS

most are Europe / US — less useful more ethical. (handwritten margin note)

talk about need for experiments (handwritten note)

For most of political science's history, discussions about professional ethics had nothing to do with human subjects. Professional ethics involved integrity in the classroom, fair tenure and promotion rule, and the careful avoidance of plagiarism. As most research was observational, there was little need for attention to how scholarly activities might directly affect the subjects of our work. Times have changed. The dramatic growth in the use of experiments in social science, especially overseas, is generating unexpected ethical controversies. The purpose of this volume is to identify, debate, and propose practical solutions to the most critical of these new ethical issues.

A leading team of internationally distinguished political science scholars presents the first examination of the practical and ethical challenges of research with human subjects in social science and policy studies.

- Part I examines contextual challenges provided by experiments conducted overseas—questions of culture, religion, security, and poverty.
- Part II examines questions of legal constraints on research, focusing on questions of foreign review of international experiments.
- Part III tackles the critical issues in field experiments, including deception and consent, impact on elections and careers, the boundaries of the public officials' exemption, and the use of partner organizations to avoid Institutional Review Body (IRB) review.
- Part IV considers strategies for the future, including training and education, IRB reform, institutional changes, and norm development.

Scott Desposato has held positions at the University of Zurich, the University of Arizona, as well as the Harvard Academy, and is currently Associate Professor of Political Science at the University of California, San Diego, USA. His research interests include American and comparative elections, institutions, voting behavior, and methodology.

Routledge Studies in Experimental Political Science

Edited by Kevin Arceneaux, *Temple University* and Cindy D. Kam, *Vanderbilt University*

Advisory Board: Howard Lavine, University of Minnesota; Joshua Tucker, New York University; Rick Wilson, Rice University; and Elizabeth Zechmeister, Vanderbilt University

Experimental methods are now firmly established within political science and are widely employed across its diverse empirical subfields to study important political phenomena. The logic of experimentation makes it an appealing and powerful methodological tool that enables scholars to establish causality and probe into the mechanisms underlying observable regularities. Experiments, because of their transparency, also enable researchers to communicate their findings to a broad audience. Although highly technical knowledge is not necessary for understanding the gist of experiments, experiments must be designed, administered, and analyzed with care and attention to detail.

The **Routledge Studies in Experimental Political Science** series was developed to publish books that educate readers about the appropriate design and interpretation of experiments and books that showcase innovative and important applications of experimental work.

1. **Ethics and Experiments**
   Problems and Solutions for Social Scientists and Policy Professionals
   Edited by Scott Desposato

ETHICS AND EXPERIMENTS

Problems and Solutions for Social Scientists and Policy Professionals

Edited by Scott Desposato

Routledge
Taylor & Francis Group

NEW YORK AND LONDON

First published 2016
by Routledge
711 Third Avenue, New York, NY 10017

and by Routledge
2 Park Square, Milton Park, Abingdon, Oxon, OX14 4RN

Routledge is an imprint of the Taylor & Francis Group, an informa business

Library of Congress Cataloging-in-Publication Data
Names: Desposato, Scott, editor of compilation.
Title: Ethics and experiments : problems and solutions for social scientists and policy professionals / edited by Scott Desposato.
Description: New York, NY : Routledge, 2016. | Series: Routledge studies in experimental political science ; 1 | Includes bibliographical references and index.
Identifiers: LCCN 2015030889 | ISBN 9781138909151 (hbk) | ISBN 9781138909168 (pbk) | ISBN 9781315694139 (ebk)
Subjects: LCSH: Social sciences—Research—Moral and ethical aspects. | Political science—Research—Moral and ethical aspects.
Classification: LCC JA86 .E83 2016 | DDC 174/.93—dc23
LC record available at http://lccn.loc.gov/2015030889

ISBN: 978-1-138-90915-1 (hbk)
ISBN: 978-1-138-90916-8 (pbk)
ISBN: 978-1-315-69413-9 (ebk)

Typeset in Bembo
by Apex CoVantage, LLC

To the memory of Richard Dale Desposato, an ethical man.

CONTENTS

Series Editors' Foreword   *xi*
Preface   *xiii*

1   Introduction   1
    Scott Desposato

PART I
Contextual Challenges for Experimentalists   **23**

2   The Ethics of Exclusion When Experimenting in
    Impoverished Settings   25
    Kim Yi Dionne, Augustine Harawa, and Hastings Honde

3   Ethics for Experimental Manipulation of Religion   42
    Richard A. Nielsen

4   Religion, Experiments, and Ethical Concerns   66
    Rebecca Morton and Jonathan Rogers

5   Prison States and Games of Chicken   81
    Jesse Driscoll

PART II
Local Ethical Review When Conducting Experiments Internationally

97

6 The Value and Challenges of Using Local Ethical Review
   in Comparative Politics Experiments   99
   Jennifer L. Merolla and Raul Madrid Jr.

7 Ethical Challenges in Comparative Politics
   Experiments in China   113
   Xiaobo Lü

8 Local Review: Confronting the Brazilian Black Box   128
   Saul Cunow and Scott Desposato

9 Ethical Perspectives in Countries Without an Institutional
   Review Board: The Case of Mexico   139
   Rosario Aguilar

PART III
The Ethical Challenges of Field Experiments

149

10 Obligated to Deceive? Aliases, Confederates, and the
    Common Rule in International Field Experiments   151
    Michael Findley and Daniel Nielson

11 Considering the Political Consequences of Comparative
    Politics Experiments   171
    Joshua R. Gubler and Joel S. Selway

12 Information and Power: Ethical Considerations of
    Political Information Experiments   183
    Brigitte Zimmerman

13 Conducting Research With NGOs: Relevant
    Counterfactuals From the Perspective of Subjects   198
    David W. Nickerson and Susan D. Hyde

14 Manipulating Elites   217
    Edmund J. Malesky

15 Field Experiments on Elected and Public Officials: Ethical
    Obligations and Requirements   227
    Christian R. Grose

PART IV
Strategies for Moving Forward   239

16 Human Subjects Protection and Large-N Research:
    When Exempt is Non-Exempt and Research is
    Non-Research   241
    Mitchell A. Seligson

17 Ethics and Research in Political Science: The
    Responsibilities of the Researcher and the Profession   255
    Elizabeth J. Zechmeister

18 Journal Editors as Ethics Sheriffs   262
    Rick K. Wilson, William Mishler, and John Ishiyama

19 Conclusion and Recommendations   267
    Scott Desposato

List of Contributors   290
References   292
Index   308

SERIES EDITORS' FOREWORD

The Routledge Studies in Experimental Political Science series was created to provide an outlet for a diverse and growing stream of experimental research in the discipline. The experimental method, uncommon 25 years ago, is now firmly established in the discipline's collective toolkit. The experiments employed by political scientists are every bit as diverse and varied as political science itself. We see experiments conducted in laboratories, administered in surveys, and embedded within real-world settings. They address topics ranging from physiological and psychological processes to the workings of governments. As political scientists continue to push the boundaries of what experiments do, where they are implemented, and with which target populations, we must remember to pause and ask hard questions about the *ethics* of our practices. Consequently, we are pleased and proud that the inaugural book in our series does just this.

In this comprehensive volume, Scott Desposato has assembled an exemplary set of essays from prominent scholars focusing on increasingly complex and vexing ethical issues for social scientists and policy professionals. This volume reflects a sea change among social scientists and policy professionals. The "identification revolution" has pushed scholars to design and implement experimental manipulations to provide causal leverage on their research questions. Innovations in transportation and telecommunications have facilitated the globalization of experiments in places that bear little to no resemblance to the artificial, sterile laboratories populated by the ubiquitous college sophomore. In these places, the linguistic, cultural, and power disparities between the researcher and the subject may be enormous. The local conventions may be unfamiliar to the researcher, and the formal rules that govern experimental research may be nonexistent, insurmountable, or somewhere in between. The increasing adoption of field experiments in the United

States and abroad highlights critical issues of informed consent, deception, and fairness.

These collected essays promise to provide students, scholars, and policy administrators with food for thought as well as practical advice on a wide range of ethical challenges that arise in experimental research. As the essays in this volume suggest, while formal review boards, journals, funding agencies, and mentors can provide guidelines for ethical research, ultimately it is each researcher's obligation to recognize, reflect upon, and respond to these ethical challenges.

Kevin Arceneaux, Temple University
Cindy D. Kam, Vanderbilt University

PREFACE

I am neither an ethicist nor an experimentalist, and my work on this project is as much a surprise to me as to my colleagues. Ultimately, it is the result of asking too many questions. At a granting agency review panel four years ago, some of the proposed experiments seemed to be pushing the envelope of acceptable design, and the question of ethics came up repeatedly. Eventually, Erik Herron suggested that I stop asking questions and do something. The result was a conference held at the University of California, San Diego, in the spring of 2013. Funding for that conference was provided by the National Science Foundation (# SES-1251510) and was the beginning of this volume.

The original conference had a limited focus constrained by the narrow bounds of my own knowledge: experimental research conducted by political scientists internationally, in the field we know as comparative politics. That origin is clear in presentation throughout the volume. It has become apparent to all involved, however, that the questions are not just about experiments, not just about international or comparative politics, and appropriate for more than just political scientists.

Many of the topics apply to non-experimental work. For example, violence does not distinguish between methodologies, and research in dangerous contexts is risky for all scholars operating in these environments, as well as for their subjects. These topics are also certainly not exclusive to non-US cases. Researchers in the United States could confront any of these questions. Indeed, recent controversies on field experiments have centered on studies conducted within the United States. Finally, most of the issues are not narrowly limited to the field of political science. The questions of context and local review apply broadly to all the social sciences—indeed, to any research involving human subjects. Similarly, the debates

When do ethical issues overlap with other topics

over field experiments—their potential impacts and spillovers, and the lack of informed consent—apply to studies conducted by scholars from other disciplines.

This was my first conference and edited volume and both would have been disastrous without the support of many scholars and staff. I owe thanks to all who helped make the conference a success, including UCSD students Michael Davidson, Ileana Gutierrez, Andrew Janusz, and Devesh Tiwari. Christina Butler deserves recognition for outstanding administrative support. In addition, Tanya Sukkari, Erica Yun, Ching Lee, Linda Liu, Kaitlin, Kelleher, Grace Park, and Jordan Hsu provided assistance with data collection.

The scholars who contributed to this project have been brave and generous. Some were advised to avoid this discussion and not attend the conference. Others advised me of their discomfort at where their participation had taken their thinking—but they have all pressed on. They have also been remarkably willing to talk openly and frankly about these issues, with insight and intellect, and without judgment. We have different opinions on many issues, but all contributors have my utmost respect and friendship.

My friends and colleagues at the University of Zurich have provided an amazing research environment that has only improved all my work, including this volume. Special thanks to Marco Steenbergen and Francis Cheneval and the research group at the Center for Ethics for encouragement and insightful comments. This project started at UCSD, and I am grateful for those faculty there that have supported this project, especially Clark Gibson, Jesse Driscoll, Gerry Mackie, and Michael Caligiuri. Many other friends and colleagues have been generous with their time, ideas, and encouragement, especially Alex Hughes, Matthew Hitt, Franchesca Nestor, and Trisha Phillips.

Erik Herron deserves the blame and credit as the puppet master behind this project (in a good way). He came up with the idea of organizing a conference and encouraged me to pursue funding and putting together this volume. He anticipated many of the costs and challenges of asking these questions and provided sage advice and unwavering support at critical junctures.

Kathryn Dove, a UCSD graduate student, has provided stellar support from beginning to end. She was invaluable in organizing and running the conference, recruiting and directing additional research assistants, tracking down and checking details, and organizing the contributions.

Seonghui Lee, a post-doc at the University of Zurich, has done an outstanding job of helping me edit, manage, and compile the manuscript. She read and provided critical and useful comments, helped with additional data collection, and is a Jedi master of LaTex.

My children, Gabriela, Luke, Sebastian, and Mikaela, have generously granted me time to work on this instead of the more important things in life. My lovely wife Jenifer has held us all together and supported this project from the beginning. For this and more, I am always grateful.

Scott Desposato, Zurich, March 2015

1

INTRODUCTION

Scott Desposato

For most of our discipline's history, discussions about professional ethics had nothing to do with human subjects. Professional ethics involved integrity in the classroom, fair tenure and promotion rules, and the careful avoidance of plagiarism. As most of our work was observational, there was little need for attention to how our research might directly affect the subjects of our work.

To the extent that political scientists did have any contact with human subjects, they were almost all respondents in surveys, and the major challenges involved preserving their anonymity. As for experiments, they were few in number, limited in scope, and conducted in carefully controlled environments with little risk of any negative consequences to subjects, researchers, or surrounding communities. In almost all cases, these were laboratory experiments. The treatments being administered were quite simple and apparently harmless, and the primary risk to human welfare was that a college sophomore-subject would become bored.

Today's world is fundamentally different. The field is seeing an explosion in the use of experimental methods for political science—indeed, a revolution in the way we study politics. From just a handful of experiments 20 years ago, experiments have reached 25% of publications in some journals. Given the popularity of experiments among graduate students, that percentage is likely to increase. Furthermore, these experiments are not just simple lab games conducted on US college campuses. They include survey and field experiments conducted in virtually every country on the planet.

This revolutionary shift in the nature of our research has many benefits for our progress as a field, but it also involves research with real risks and real injustice, some anticipated and mitigated, some ignored, and some completely unexpected. The rise of field experiments means that thousands of subjects

are participating in experiments that have substantial impacts on their lives—without any knowledge or consent. Differences in legal environments across countries mean that many experiments conducted overseas are illegal in the host country. Cultural differences mean that even simple, safe economic game experiments conducted entirely in laboratories may violate religious norms against gambling. In some cases, experiments are affecting entire political systems, through election results, party organizations, or by changing politicians' allocation of time and resources.

It is especially troubling that most experiments that are generating controversy are conducted overseas in less-developed countries. Of course it may be that experiments are less expensive overseas than in the United States or Europe, and it may also be that the challenges these countries face are especially pressing and deserve the focus of experimentalists. But it is also the case that in less-developed countries, subjects are more likely to comply and less likely to complain. Investigators working in these countries often enjoy a position of power that they would not encounter if trying to run a study in Rancho Santa Fe or Chevy Chase.

There is a growing awareness of these issues and increasing attention to questions of ethics in political science. There is also a great deal of diversity of opinion on what is ethical and what is not. Yet the discussion remains a sidebar, a postscript to be talked about in between panels rather than during presentations.

The types of issues we are confronting are in most cases new and do not fit into existing frameworks. Although Institutional Review Boards[1] (IRBs) typically have extensive experience with medical trials, they are not qualified to offer guidance on Brazilian campaign laws, Malawian views on the unfairness of random sampling and unequal compensation of subjects, or risk of political violence in the former Soviet Union. Our leading professional associations have virtually nothing to say about the ethics of research with human subjects. And our training rarely involves more than a legalistic look at the history of IRBs. The state of the discipline is effectively a "Wild West" when it comes to experimental research, especially overseas—and many prefer the "make your own rules" environment this provides.

Our field needs to directly engage the nature of the research we are conducting with human subjects and develop some consensus on appropriate standards of behavior. Ignoring the questions and controversies has real risks of harm and injustice to subjects and bystanders, as well as potentially serious repercussions for the entire field.

The first step in this process is dialogue, and that is the purpose of this volume. Our goal is to identify the most common types of ethical issues that scholars are likely to encounter when conducting experiments, especially overseas; to propose practical strategies to mitigate risk and ethical dilemmas; and to debate the bounds of ethical behavior—because on many of these questions, there is substantial disagreement within our ranks as to what is appropriate and what is not.

The focus in this volume is on political science experiments conducted internationally, especially in developing countries, because these provide, as we will see, a "perfect storm" for generating ethical problems. But as recent events have confirmed, the issues raised herein also apply to experiments conducted in the United States and Europe, as well as to experiments in economics, sociology, public policy, and other social science fields. Experiments have proven to be a method with little respect for disciplinary boundaries, with many fruitful cross-disciplinary partnerships and studies.

In the rest of this introduction, I explore the new ethical challenges for political science. I begin with a discussion of the history of experiments in our field and the changes brought by the experimental revolution. I then provide examples of the origins and nature of experiments that are generating controversy. I discuss the risks to research and the field associated with our current path and then present a plan for the volume.

1.1   The Experimental Revolution

In some ways, as human beings, we are always experimenting. Technically, an experiment simply involves manipulating the world or our experience of it in some way in order to gain knowledge. We might expose ourselves to new foods, clothes, hot stoves, or just try letting our fields lie fallow for a year from time to time, to see what happens. Indeed, children may be the great experimentalists, as any parent knows after watching their offspring consume dirt, toys, and anything else that isn't bolted down.

For scientific experiments, again we manipulate some aspect of the world, but the difference is in methodology and aims. The researcher uses careful protocols to eliminate contamination and confounding variables and assure accurate measurement. The aim is to test a narrow and specific hypothesis about a theorized relationship. Again, formal experimentation is also not particularly new, with scientists using experiments since at least the 1600s and, by some measures, much earlier.[2]

Political science is a young discipline, and the history of experiments in political science, with important exceptions, is fairly limited. Political science as a discipline has, for most of its existence, been an observational field. We observe and reflect on revolutions, elections, protests, wars, campaign strategy, and voting behavior. For both qualitative and quantitative scholars, our empirics were generated by nature with us as mere observers. Our interaction with human subjects was for many years limited to respondent interviews in surveys, and elite interviews with politicians or other political actors. For these studies, our ethical concerns were primarily with protecting respondent privacy, when appropriate. There were few other risks to subjects, if any—perhaps they might suffer boredom or a paper cut.

Although political scientists have been conducting experiments for nearly 100 years, for most of that period, experiments were relatively rare and exposed subjects to few risks. Estimates of exactly how many experiments were conducted before 1990 range from a few dozen to several hundred, depending on how one counts. These include rare early field experiments, like Gosnell's (1927) Chicago turnout treatments, as well as others on persuasion and campaign messages (Lund 1925, Rice 1929, Hartman 1936). These studies, however, were the exception rather than the rule. Experiments were very rare until their gradual adoption after World War II to study group dynamics and political psychology.[3] Most of these experiments from 1950 until about 1990 were restricted to a fairly narrow part of the discipline. In sum, while there is clearly a long history of experimentation in political science, that history is also quite thin. Experiments were, for most of our discipline's history, secondary to other types of research. They were relatively infrequent, limited to certain subfields, and rarely published in the broad field journals.

Most early experiments were very low-risk. Subjects played simple bargaining games in laboratories, read vignettes (or later, watched videos) in class and answered short questionnaires, or were randomly assigned different enumerators in survey experiments. Many experiments were conducted on college campuses with participants compensated financially or with extra credit in their classes. Subjects were typically informed and consenting, even if only implicitly.[4] If there was some deceit as to the nature of the study, subjects were usually debriefed post-treatment. One analysis of social science lab experiments conducted over 20 years and involving 100,000 subjects found just one adverse incident report: a case of a subject upset because he was bankrupt in an experimental game and had no way to earn any more money (Plott 2013).[5]

However, over the last 20 years there has been a dramatic change in the frequency, type, and context of experiments conducted by political scientists, and this change is generating ethical challenges and real risks to subjects. To demonstrate this change, I worked with a group of research assistants to collect data on the numbers of experimental and non-experimental published research. Others have collected data showing an increase in published experimental research (Bositis and Steinel 1987, Druckman et al. 2006, McDermott 2002, Morton and Williams 2010). However, these analyses are either fairly dated, limited in journals examined, or without information about the location or type of experiment conducted.

With the help of undergraduate and graduate assistants, I compiled a dataset of published experiments from 1990 to 2013, with a limited sample of earlier years: 1960, 1970, and 1980. Several features of the data collection deserve mention. First, rather than just count the number of articles as previous scholars have done, my team examined and recorded every article and its length—experimental and non-experimental. As the number of articles per journal has changed over time, an increase or decrease in published experiments may be misleading unless it is measured as a proportion of all articles. Second, experiments were coded as laboratory, field, or survey experiments, although these categories are fairly crude and sometimes difficult to apply in practice. Third, the country (or countries) where the study was conducted was recorded in each case. Fourth, the set of journals included the flagships—*American Journal of Political Science* (AJPS), the *American Political Science Review* (APSR), and the *Journal of Politics* (JOP)—as well as five other journals. Two of the others are from international relations: *International Organization* (IO) and the *Journal of Conflict Resolution* (JCR). Two were from comparative politics: *Comparative Politics* (CP) and *Comparative Political Studies* (CPS). The last was an American politics journal, *Political Behavior* (PB).

Figure 1.1 shows the percentage of articles using experiments published in all of the sampled journals from 1960 to 2013, by journal. The dots show the percentage of published articles using experiments in each year sampled; the line shows the smoothed relationship. A similar analysis using the percentage of pages instead of the percentage of articles yields very similar results.

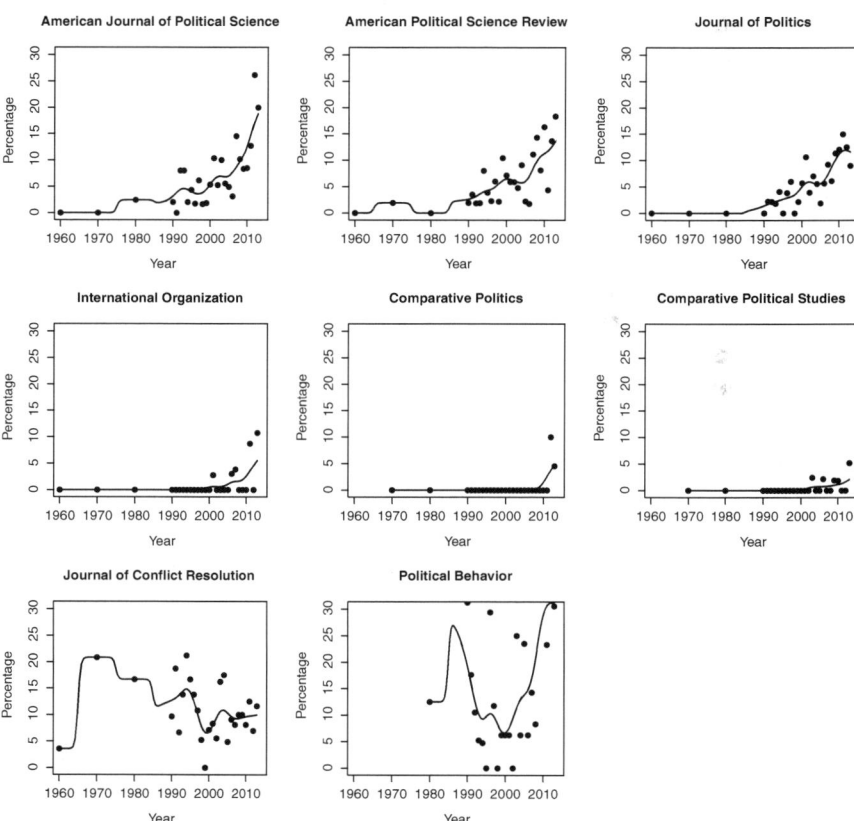

FIGURE 1.1 Growth in Published Political Science Experiments

Each of the leading field journals (JOP, APSR, and AJPS) shows the same general trend; few experiments before 2000, and a significant increase in subsequent years. Experiments were extremely rare before 1990 in the top journals (note again that only decennial volumes were sampled from this earlier period). Not a single experiment was published in any of these top journals in 1960; just one in 1970, and one more in 1980. Subsequently, there is a remarkable and continuing increase in experimental research starting in the 1990s, and accelerating after 2000. Across the 1990s, the average percentage of experimental articles in the three flagship journals was just about 3%; from 2000 to 2010, that rate doubled to 7%. And in just the first three years of the next decade, the average doubled again to over 14%. For AJPS, that percentage reached a new high in 2012 when 17 experiments, representing over 25% of all articles, were published.

Experiments were rare in most subfield journals. Prior to 2000, we found no experiments in sampled years from IO, CP, or CPS.[6] Since 2000, there has been a slight rise in experimental research in these three journals, although less dramatic than the trends in the flagship journals. In *International Organization*, we found no experiments prior to 2001, just three from 2001 to 2010, and five after 2010.

The comparative politics journals have embraced experimental research especially slowly. For *Comparative Political Studies*, we only found six experiments in all years surveyed. In *Comparative Politics*, we found no experiments until 2012, when two articles of 22 published included experiments. Although the frequencies remain very low, there is a clear trend of increase in recent years. This is surprising because, as we will see, many experiments in the flagship journals are in fact comparative politics.

The exceptions to the rule are in two subfield journals: *The Journal of Conflict Resolution* (JCR) and *Political Behavior* (PB). JCR has a long history of publishing experimental research, starting with early work on strategic interaction. In 1970, 18% (5 of 27) of articles reported on experimental research. The trend since then has in fact been slightly downward. In 1980, the percentage of experiments was 15%, and has slipped in each subsequent decade: 11% in the 1990s, 10% in the 2000s, and just under 10% during 2010–2013. JCR's early prominence in published experiments is consistent with Bositis and Steinel's 1987 findings, and reflects the early adoption of laboratory experiments to test game theoretic arguments, especially in international relations.

Political Behavior, the other exception to the rule, was not founded until 1979, but experimental research was relatively common immediately; over 10% of articles used experimental methods in 1980. Through the 2000s, experimental research was frequent and common in the journal, although publication rates varied widely year to year. Starting in the late 2000s, a more stable and consistent trend of increase appears and continues through 2013.

The growth in political science experiments has been accompanied by changes in the types and locales of research. Table 1.1 shows annual rates of experimental publications by type of experiment. Each experimental article was coded as a laboratory, survey, or field experiment (or more than one). The average number of each type per year was calculated from the sampled journals and years, aggregated by decades.[7]

Early experiments from the sample were primarily laboratory experiments. Indeed, the *only* experiments found in 1960 and 1970 were in laboratories. These were conducted in the United States with strict protocols. Subjects were informed, consented, and debriefed. Most treatments were sterile and safe, with no expected possibilities of spillovers outside the treatment or of risk of serious harm to subjects. The rates of laboratory experiments were relatively steady from 1970 through the 1990s at about 7 articles per year, but increased gradually from 1990 to 2010 with about 14 articles per year in journals surveyed in the 2010s.[8]

More recently, the field is shifting away from the laboratory and into survey and field experiments. No survey experiments were recorded in my sample in 1960 or 1970. In 1980, the rate was just one article per year from sampled journals. Their frequency has more than doubled every decade since then. They are now the most common type of experiment, at a current rate of 24 articles per year from sampled journals (about 6% of all publications and more than half of all experiments). No doubt part of this has to do with technological change and expense; the Internet makes original research much less expensive, in some cases costing just pennies per respondent. It also makes deployment of survey instruments to some overseas populations much easier.

In terms of types of experiments being conducted, the other change is the increasing use of field experiments. Although the first political science experiment may have been a field experiment (Gosnell's study mentioned above), for most of

TABLE 1.1 Annual Rates of Experimental Articles, by Type of Experiment

Year	Type of Experiment		
	Laboratory	Survey	Field
1960	1.0	0.0	0
1970	6.0	0.0	0
1980	7.0	1.0	0
1990	7.4	3.6	0.1
2000	10.6	7.1	2.0
2010	14.3	24.0	7.5

Note: Figures are the annual rates of experimental articles for each decade, calculated from sampled journals and years. Note that every year from 1990 onward was sampled, but previous years only include decennial volumes of journals due to resource constraints.

the last hundred years these were extremely rare. More recently, field experiments have been rediscovered and have grown tremendously in popularity. These are experiments conducted in the "real" world, with treatments administered to subjects as part of their natural environment. In many cases, subjects are completely unaware that they are participating in research projects. The goal of these studies is to enhance external validity and learn about the effects of treatments in practice, rather than just in an artificial laboratory environment. These are the least used of experiments—not surprising given that they are often expensive and require substantial infrastructure—but have grown tremendously in recent years.

There were none recorded prior to 1990, and just one over the period 1990–1999, for an average publication rate of 0.1 per year, representing about 0.04% of all articles, and just 1% of experimental articles.[9] The number of field experiments published annually increased to an average of two annually in the period 2000–2009, a twenty-fold increase, and more than tripled again by 2010. In this latest period, field experiments had grown to 16% of published experiments, or about 2% of all published articles. This change is particularly impressive given that many field experiments require deployment of substantial resources, and may take years to develop.[10]

In addition, many of these experiments are now being run overseas, in very different contextual environments. Whereas early experiments were almost entirely based in the United States, experiments today are being exported to almost every country. Consider Figure 1.2, which shows the location of published experimental work over the last decades.[11] In the 1990s, experiments published in the top journals were limited to "the usual suspects" with just a few exceptions. By 2013, published experiments just from those journals surveyed have been conducted in over 30 countries. Given the many other outlets for research, it is likely that this figure severely understates the globalization of experimental political science.[12]

Finally, all evidence is that the use of experiments in political science will grow. One predictor of the future is the type of research that current graduate students are conducting. One place to observe the research of our future stars is in the topics of National Science Foundation dissertation improvement grants. While the NSF does not release applications, nor does it release information on unfunded applications, it does release a title and abstract for each funded award. We searched on "experiment" and "experimental" in both the titles and abstracts, and coded any matches as having experimental components.

Figure 1.3 shows the percentage of experimental political science awards by year since 1978 (the earliest date in the NSF data). The trend echoes the patterns observed in the journals. There were very no experimental dissertation awards before 1988. In the 1990s, experimental awards increased quickly and averaged over 15% of awards in that decade. The percentage of these awards has continued to grow, exceeding 40% in several recent years. The general trend is one of rapid increase, suggesting that future generations of scholars will increasingly adopt experimental methods and that they will play a larger and larger role in the field.

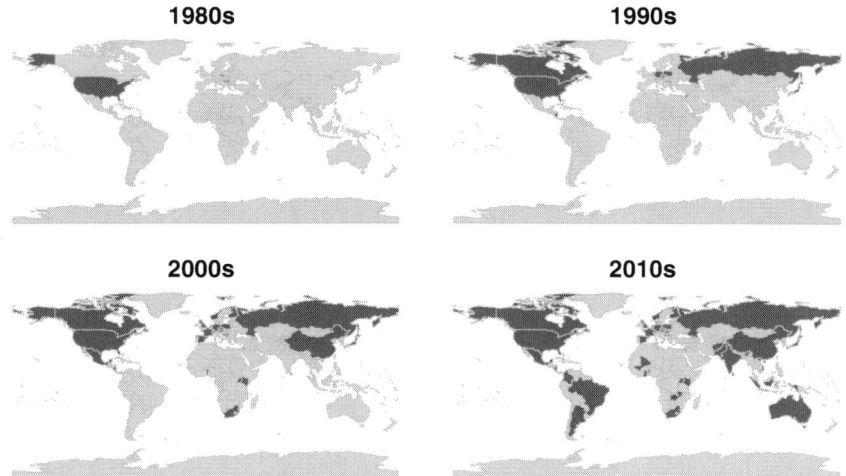

FIGURE 1.2 Distribution of Published Political Science Experiments

Note: Shaded countries are those where an experiment was conducted by the end of each period, again drawing only on sampled years and journals. Some borders are approximate based on mergers and cessations, especially post 1990.

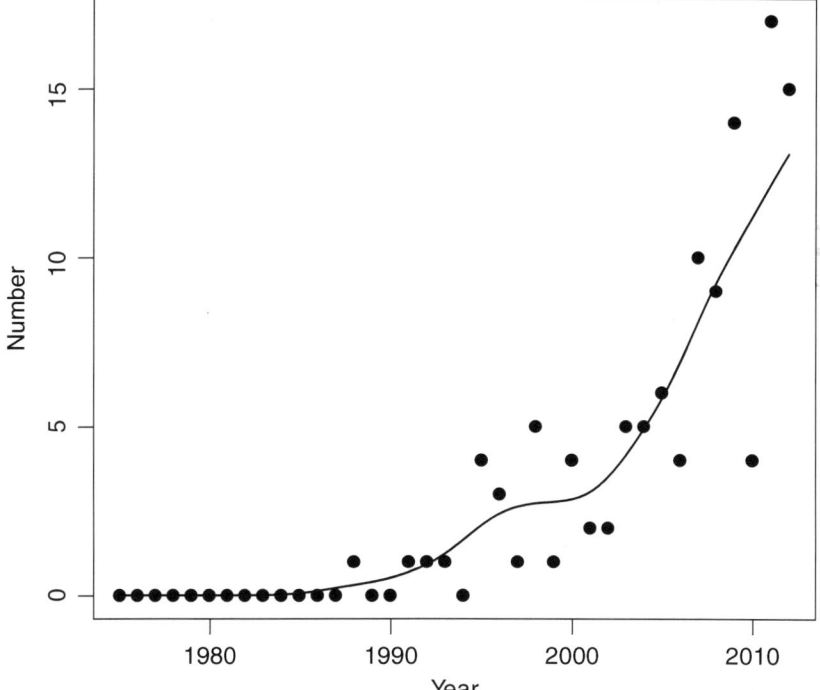

FIGURE 1.3 National Science Foundation Experimental Dissertation Grants

Note: The graph shows the percentage of NSF dissertation grants awarded in political science that included a reference to "experiment" or other terms in the award title. Data calculated from National Science Foundation (2014).

This data certainly understates the total number of published experiments and countries that have hosted them. Most experiments—indeed most research—are published in outlets other than the journals sampled herein. Regarding the NSF data, most dissertations (and indeed most scholars) do not receive NSF funding, yet many graduate students conduct experiments. Social scientists based outside the United States globally are engaging in more and more experimental research, with scholars in Europe, Latin America, Asia, and Africa conducting their own experimental projects, many of which are published in their associations' journals and are not on the radar of American political scientists. The new experimentalism represents a dramatic shift, its pace is accelerating, and it is a global phenomenon.

The methodological shift toward experiments has many laudable features. Most importantly, we can identify causal effects as opposed to correlations with the random assignment of treatment and control. Without randomization, scholars have three alternatives. One is that they give up on talking about causation. A second strategy is to talk about causation, but make ridiculously heroic assumptions. A third strategy is to make slightly less heroic assumptions and run more complex models (claiming to have found an exogenous instrument, for example). Randomization of treatments improves on each of these strategies, eliminating confounding variables (at least in expectation) and empowering scholars to reach causal conclusions.

In addition, experiments let scholars zero in on mechanisms of interest by controlling and generating the treatment, rather than relying on the world to generate variance of interest. With observational data, we often must rely on proxy measures for quantities of interest, and may only observe the blunt inputs and outputs of a causal chain—say, development level and corruption reports. Alternatively, the real world may not generate the variance in explanatory variables that we need for our study. With experiments, we can test for the effects of specific mechanisms in the chain, not just look for correlations between roughly measured endpoints of that chain, contributing to richer and more precise theory building.

For the scientific community, experimental research is often more suitable to real replication and retesting, with new data and new observations. Previously, replication meant rerunning an old dataset and trying to "break" the results. Effectively, replication was merely checking computer code for accuracy and testing the robustness of the models. With experiments, replication means testing the same mechanism on a different sample, to validate the results as more than Type I error or a design feature.

Combined, the experimental revolution promises to make the field more relevant, to empower advances and theory building, and to help political science contribute more effectively to ongoing policy debates. It will also help the field communicate with other scientific disciplines.

The experimental revolution is not without cost or critics. Some questions are difficult to study experimentally, and to the extent that experiments are fashionable, we may be distracted from important and relevant questions because we cannot easily manipulate treatments. Some treatments are poorly defined and dosages difficult to measure. For example, many experiments have examined the impact of positive and negative advertisements, yet it is not entirely clear how we should define a negative message. These limitations, however, are challenges that experimentalists will meet, and solving them will help us refine theories and hypotheses and design better experiments that lead to more advances. All these are challenges that scholars can solve and respond to, and these are *not* the topic of this volume.

1.2   Ethical Challenges

The growth of experimental research in political science has many obvious benefits, but it has also generated some unexpected challenges and controversies involving the ethics of human subjects research. In some cases, these reflect utterly unexpected situations encountered by scholars in the field. In other cases, these challenges reflect disagreement over the appropriate bounds on political science experiments. Generally, however, ethical issues in political science experiments have three origins. One is in the use of experiments in entirely new contexts, where seemingly innocuous treatments may be traumatic, offensive, or even dangerous. The second reflects the challenges and requirements of completing ethical review when running experiments overseas. The third is in the rise of field experiments that often treat uninformed and unconsenting subjects, sometimes with broader impacts on surrounding communities. These categories are neither exhaustive nor mutually exclusive, but they capture many of the problems scholars have encountered and provide a useful way to structure discussion. I will discuss each and present some illustrative examples.

First, the increasing use of experiments overseas means that many features of the local environment make treatments that seem trivial and ordinary in the United States troubling or even dangerous. Simple games of political and economic experiments may violate norms, create anxiety among subjects, and generate backlash from the broader community. In some countries, simply asking questions about politics in a survey experiment may be a dangerous activity that risks harm to subjects, enumerators, and investigators. In contexts of severe poverty, even modest compensation of subjects may generate conflict between participants or divide an entire community. In addition, different legal frameworks mean that some treatments and experiments that would be straightforward in the United States are illegal in other countries. Political speech by private citizens is unconstrained in the United States but highly restricted in other countries. Consider several examples, below.

Scholars in many countries have gone into the field with a simple survey experiment or similar study. A typical study asks standard political science questions,

questions that we have been asking for more than 50 years. Anonymity of subjects is assured by not linking any identifiers. The host country has constitutional guarantees of freedom of speech and thought that make the study entirely acceptable. Yet it turns out that just talking about politics risks repercussions for subjects and enumerators. In practice, enumerators in a number of countries have been kidnapped and on occasion faced lynch mobs. Subjects have been monitored by political bosses with threats of repercussions if their responses diverge from a party line. Some scholars are disturbed by this; others would note that the violence is part of everyday life in that country and is thus an acceptable risk to freely consenting subjects and to enumerators willing to do the work. Indeed, some would note that alternative employment opportunities might involve greater risk of violence than working as an enumerator. Is it possible and ethical to conduct research in countries with high levels of political violence? How can researchers protect subjects, enumerators, and themselves?

Simple economic games would seem some of the safest and most sterile of experiments. Most involve laboratory experiments in tightly controlled environments, with abstract treatments that have little obvious connection to the real world. One might plan a standard laboratory experiment and expect a safe and straightforward experience. But in some countries, there are religious prohibitions on gambling that would extend to many of the games that economists use in experiments. Subjects could suffer considerable angst as well as repercussions from their community. Scholars—and the entire discipline—could also face increased difficulty in recruitment and permissions to conduct studies. Is there any way to incentivize expected value calculations without violating norms against gambling? How should one proceed?

Many experiments that scholars are conducting are illegal in host countries. In some cases, treatments that would be legal in the United States are not in other countries. For example, Hidalgo, de Figueiredo and Kasahara (2011) may have violated research and political communication laws in Brazil by distributing 100,000 campaign flyers during an election. This might have been legal in the United States, but was illegal in Brazil, where political propaganda is highly regulated.[13] In other cases, scholars have administered treatments that would be illegal in any country. For example, Fried, Lagunes and Venkataramani (2010) hired confederates to commit traffic violations in front of police officers to test the impact of social class on bribery. Subjects were not informed, bystanders were exposed to risk of potential traffic accidents, and the investigators and their funders might technically be guilty of conspiracy to commit a crime in a foreign nation.

To some, these are examples of political scientists overreaching. Others might respond that providing more political information to voters is always a normative good, even if it is prohibited by local laws. Alternatively, traffic laws in Mexico City receive little respect from the local populace, so perhaps committing traffic violations is typical of everyday life and does not rise to the level of criminal activity. In addition, fighting corruption is an important task for our research, but corrupt officials would not knowingly consent to participation in our research. Does the important and illicit nature of the phenomenon justify the commission of crimes overseas? Must we respect the rule of law in host countries, or can we ever bend or break the rules?

Second, scholars are confronting dilemmas regarding appropriate procedures for local review. Local review is the process of having a research proposal reviewed by a foreign ethics agent before running an experiment in their country. Some countries have strict national regulation of all research and require an arduous review process, especially of research conducted by foreign scholars.[14] Many of the questions scholars confront involve the degree to which we must adapt to or confirm with local practices, culture, and law when conducting experiments in new environments. Sometimes this means that there is an elaborate and perhaps impossibly bureaucratic procedure for foreign scholars, involving years of paperwork. In other cases, this might simply be a rent-extraction program, with foreign officials requiring "donations" in order to have studies approved. In still other cases, authoritarian governments might ban experiments—or for that matter, all studies on politics—unless they provide knowledge that is useful to the regime. At the same time, many of our home IRBs do not explicitly require us to comply with foreign regulations or to have written permission from host governments to conduct our studies overseas.[15]

There are many excuses for just ignoring host countries' rules on research, which can slow or even prohibit some projects. Graduate students want to finish dissertations, junior faculty face tenure clocks, and everyone wants to publish their research first, but all are stymied by compliance with difficult local rules. In practice, most scholars are simply ignoring these rules, flying in on tourist visas, and executing studies "under the radar" in violation of host countries' laws. But do we have any ethical requirement to comply with local regulations? Does it matter whether we are studying a democracy or an authoritarian regime? Is it ethical to pay a bribe to an ethics commission to obtain an ethics approval?

The third source of ethical concerns is the increasing popularity of field experiments, due to issues of impact, deception, and informed consent. In particular, these experiments may have substantial impact on political systems and subjects, but those affected are almost never asked if they would like to join a study, or even told that they are in a study. Field experiments are conducted in the real world, not in a laboratory, and often involve assigning entire communities to treatment or control groups. In a laboratory, subjects are fully informed that they are participating in a study and must give their consent for the study to proceed. But, most critically in field experiments, subjects are often neither informed nor consenting. In many cases, they will never know they were part of a study at all. This deception is often required as subjects might not behave naturally or cooperate at all if they are fully informed.

[handwritten marginalia: "save seats? what are they? Are they real? spill effects"]

These types of treatments may have broad systemic impacts—affecting who wins elections, which communities receive public goods, or how hard it is to obtain welfare benefits, but subjects never gave us consent to treat them. These effects are magnified by the conduct of these experiments in less-developed countries, where political scientists' research resources, usually thought of as modest at best, are massive in comparison to the resources available to local actors. These experiments are generating questions about the deceit of subjects and the potentially large impact of projects on subjects and bystanders.

Field experiments do have many advantages; they provide opportunities to study democratic processes and avoid severe endogeneity problems that have plagued generations of scholars. Yet the treatments themselves may affect the processes being studied. For example, many field experiments simply provide factual information to voters during campaigns. That information might be about political candidates, about elected officials, or about budgets. Many would argue that providing human beings with more factual information about politics is always a normative good for accountability and representation. Yet, in the developing world, scholars with modest political science grants may have more resources than all the candidates and parties they are studying. Consequently, a voter information or campaign intervention could have a dramatic effect on voters and could change an election outcome. *[handwritten: Campaign finance ethics]*

Alternatively, publishing records of legislative behavior as part of an experiment has resulted in politicians spending more time in committee meetings and, presumably, less time with constituents.[16] Changing election outcomes or elected officials' behavior may affect millions—or hundreds of millions—of individuals who did not consent to our study. Do we have that right, and, even if we do, is it ethical? Alternatively, is the value of human knowledge such that any informational treatment is a normative good, regardless of details or impact?

Other experiments randomize the provision of public goods, often without informing subjects that they are participating in studies. Scholars have randomly made it more or less difficult to access welfare benefits and have randomized the distribution of health clinics, water treatment, and other benefits. These studies have generated valuable insights on means-based programs, on methods to contain HIV, and on clientelism. They also have resulted in real human costs—some subjects did not receive welfare benefits, some villages did not get a health clinic, and others did not get clean water. Almost certainly someone in a control village in some political science field experiment has died from lack of treatment—although she never consented to have health care or clean water randomized. And while we revel in a glowing reception for our study at a conference, our subjects still do not know that they were subjects or why they did not get a health clinic, they just know that their child is sick and they have nowhere to go.

These studies are easy to defend. Perhaps randomization is fairer than local politics in its distribution of scarce goods or perhaps we were merely consultants to a local government that did the randomization. Alternatively, perhaps we are distributing a good that none of the villages actually have—so the control group is not being directly harmed, similar to medicine's "standard of care" argument. Do the advantages of these field experiments justify the lack of informed consent? Does the use of partners to randomize really keep our hands clean?

More than a lack of informed consent, other field experiments deliberately deceive subjects in order to induce their participation in an experiment. For example, scholars send false resumes to employers to test racial bias in hiring (Bertrand and Mullainathan 2004), ask agencies if they would illegally incorporate a business (Findley and Nielson 2014), or ask legislators for help or for a response to a constituent inquiry (Butler and Broockman 2011).

These experiments require that subjects be unaware and unconsenting in their participation. In many cases, the design involves what I call "deception with implied benefit": The subject participates with some expectation of potential benefit. For example, an employer reviews a false resume looking for a new employee, a firm responds to a false inquiry hoping for new business, and legislator staffers answer email hoping to develop a reputation for constituency service. The only cost to the subjects is the time they invest in the exercise: reviewing the resume, responding to the business inquiry, or mailing the letter. Yet, should we view even a small amount of deceptively recruited time as unethical? And when magnified by a large sample size, does that change things? Bertrand and Mullainathan (2004) sent 5,000 fictitious resumes; if each were examined for, say 5 minutes, that is the equivalent of several months of unconsented and uninformed subject time.[17] Should we only consider individual costs, or should we account for the aggregate cost of a study? When is this level of deception justified? When is it fraud and theft?

One might respond that these are questions for IRBs to resolve, but there are at least two reasons not to outsource all ethical responsibility to IRBs. The first is that IRBs are not qualified to address many of these issues, nor is it their mission to do so. Contrary to popular belief, IRBs do not exist to provide judgment on the ethical qualities of a design. These are bureaucratic organizations whose primary purpose is to comply with federal regulations governing research using federal funds. Their stated mission involves the protection of human subjects, but practically, they exist to ensure that federal research money continues to flow to their universities. Before the federal government required university IRBs as a condition of funding, many universities had little or no ethical review of research. Their members do their best, but are constrained by their mission.

In addition, IRBs have little or no experience with the kinds of issues we are grappling with. Members' training and backgrounds are often in medical studies, or fields other than political science. They have never grappled with the potential risks associated with running surveys in Guatemala or the religious implications of asking Saudi subjects to play standard economic games. They aren't familiar with Brazilian campaign laws or with foreign IRB rules and, at most universities, do not ask about them. They rely on us—the investigators—to anticipate and identify the specific risks and convey them accurately.

The second answer is that, in many cases, there is no IRB review. Creative scholars have discovered a way to avoid IRB and execute experiments essentially unconstrained, with the "IRB End-Run." Basically, if scholars are merely advisers or consultants to an NGO, a government, or some other third party who conducts an experiment, then technically the scholar is not responsible for the treatment or its impact, and no IRB review is required. The scholar can publish with the data and never has to get his or her hands dirty with responsibility for the experiment.

Is this a problem? Scholars are regularly called on—even expected—to lend their expertise to the policy community. When they can help governments or NGOs evaluate and improve programs through experiments, why shouldn't they? And if the resulting data is useful for real research questions, why let it go to waste? On the other hand, this creates a very large loophole. If one can't get an IRB to approve a project—or one doesn't want to face any constraints—one need only convince a friend in the political or policy sphere to randomize a roll-out or a new program. In some cases, the third party may not fully understand the project or its ethical implications. And finally, at the extreme, a scholar could form a shell corporation and have it conduct randomizations on the scholar's behalf, perhaps while turning a profit. When are these partnerships appropriate, and when are they just IRB avoidance?

Many of issues are not entirely new to other fields—but political science offers some unique challenges that will require new solutions. For example, ethnographic scholars have extensively debated the appropriate degree of deception and consent in field and participant-observer studies, their impact on the communities they study, and confronting foreign ethical review committees. These debates, perspectives, and experience will be valuable for political science. At the same time, at least three features of political science experiments mean that we have new issues and challenges that are not addressed in the literature. The first is that political science is uniquely positioned to alienate powerful people. Our studies often can affect or even threaten political elites—the same actors that control access to funding often control our employment and regulate our research. Simple turnout or political recruitment studies are viewed suspiciously by US elites. Studies of corruption or clientelism by elites are personally and professionally threatening to government officials. This makes ethical review by local authorities when experimenting overseas especially complicated—as local authorities may be acting to protect themselves or their leaders, not to simply protect human subjects. Second, and related, in many cases, the normative value of our research is less clear. We understand that medical research has a potentially direct impact on human welfare. But the normative value of a negative advertisement's impact on vote choice, or flyers on turnout, is subject to debate. This leaves the discipline especially vulnerable to criticism from those threatened by our research. Third, while individually our treatments may be unintrusive, their aggregate effects can be massive. Political science experiments have the potential for massive numbers of subjects and massive spillovers, with potential effects on election outcomes, constituent-representative relationships, and entire political systems.

1.3 A Plan for Progress

The rise of experimental methods holds great promise for our discipline, but with it come new challenges. A prominent challenge is that our new use of human subjects has generated many unanticipated questions about the types of research we should be conducting. If there were agreement on all these questions, there would be no need for this volume—we would either condemn or condone collectively, and move forward. But there is substantial disagreement and uncertainty within the field on how to respond to questions and situations like these. For those that see real ethical problems in these studies, there is an obvious need for debate and discussion. The complex issues involved need to be explored and discussed in order to prevent harm to subjects and to protect our discipline. There is real harm coming to subjects as a result of inclusion in a study—they may face backlash in violent places, they may suffer random assignment into a group that does not have a health clinic, or they may see their entire political system altered by a treatment. There are also serious risks being borne by assistants and investigators in the pursuit of good hypothesis tests. It is particularly disturbing that many of the most controversial studies are being implemented in less-developed countries. While it is true that these groups perhaps most deserve attention as we seek policies to improve their welfare, these subject pools are also more likely to comply and less likely to complain. Scholars have significantly more power in these environments and a greater ability to affect the local political system with modest or even minimal interventions.

I have encountered some opposition to even having this discussion. Scholars see risk to the great promise and progress of experimental research. Indeed, scholars with whom I have discussed these issues have had a surprisingly uniform response to this project: "Don't shut us down!" There is fear that this debate will result in unwanted constraints on research agendas; talking about ethics is a threat.

The real threat, however, is sticking our heads in the sand and pushing forward. The consequences of ignoring these issues could be severe. Many studies hold the potential for real human tragedy, which we must strive to avoid. And besides the direct costs to subjects, a controversy involving a political science experiment could end access to subject pools or, potentially, to entire countries. Imagine the potential backlash from citizens and governments to an illegal, foreign-led field experiment that changes an election outcome, or that restricts citizens' access to public goods, or that involves the deliberate commission of crimes to test police response. Political science is already unpopular among leaders in the United States. Do we really need to promote similar attitudes in other countries?

A second criticism is essentially that this endeavor is a waste of time, since the great majority of research still involves extremely low or no risk studies where subjects are fully informed and consented and, indeed, the greatest risk to their welfare is a few minutes of boredom. This description is empirically accurate, but incorrect in conclusions. Yes, most studies are safe, and controversial studies are not frequent. But this description may have been even more accurate for medical studies during the 1950s and 1960s—for every Tuskegee there may have been 10,000 clinical trials with no adverse events. Even if rare, inappropriate experiments can cause real harm to subjects and to the field generally.

Finally, a third criticism is that this discussion requires a first-principles approach—beginning with a theory of ethics to guide the discipline, then deriving appropriate judgments for each situation we encounter. This sounds ideal in theory, but problematic in practice. General ethical guidelines already exist, most obviously in the Belmont Report and other declarations, and also in the voluminous literature on ethics in human subjects research. Even among dedicated experts, there is substantial disagreement as to what the foundational principles should be and how they should be applied. We are unlikely to stumble into this field as political scientists and resolve questions that ethicists have debated for decades.

These are just some of the questions that scholars are grappling with, and it would be presumptuous to expect that a consensus position could be developed in a single volume. But we can take a critical first step forward by identifying, debating, and proposing practical solutions for ethical and human subjects' issues that our field will increasingly confront. To this end, we have a set of contributors who will explore the most common problems the field is confronting and who also have very different opinions about what is ethical and how we should move forward. Some contributors are experimentalists, some are not, and there is a great deal of diversity of opinion regarding what are acceptable practices.

Our central goal is to explore both the practical and ethical sides of new challenges. Given controversy over a particular practice or context, we ask two sets of questions. First, is there some easy way to mitigate risk and eliminate the issue? Can we conduct the research and sidestep the issue? Scholars offer practical suggestions to dodge the quagmires and get the research done. Second, do we even need to worry about the issue? There is disagreement over whether some of these designs are ethical or not. Contributors explore the arguments and weigh in with diverse opinions that echo the diversity in our discipline.

The volume is organized into four parts. In Part I, contributors examine some of the contextual challenges provided by experiments conducted overseas—questions of poverty, religion, and security. In Chapter 2, Kim Yi Dionne, Augustine Harawa, and Hastings Honde examine the challenges of compensation in impoverished environments. Drawing on their own extensive experience conducting experiments in Africa, they describe the types of problems scholars may encounter with subjects in settings of poverty and inequality. In particular, unequal compensation and randomization, which might seem fair and objective to US-based subjects, were offensive to villagers for whom the experiment's nominal compensation was considered extremely high stakes. They propose several strategies they have used to eliminate such problems. In Chapter 3, Richard Nielsen examines the challenges of experiments on religion. Scholars are using religion as both an independent and dependent variable in experiments. Nielsen argues that both practically and ethically, we should avoid experiments that attempt to manipulate subjects' religiosity, and that we should limit our experiments in this area to measurement manipulations. In Chapter 4, Rebecca Morton and Jonathan Rogers examine the problem of experiments that violate religious norms, focusing on their own research in the Middle East. In particular, prohibitions on gambling by some religions make standard economic games offensive and impossible to administer. Morton and Rogers offer a series of alternative designs that can be deployed in these contexts. Chapter 5, by Jesse Driscoll, closes out the section by examining experiments in dangerous places. He discusses unexpected risks encountered by experimentalists and survey enumerators, strategies to mitigate those risks, and the responsibility of the researcher and especially graduate advisors to anticipate and adapt to dangerous situations.

Part II examines questions of legal constraints on research, focusing on questions of foreign review of international experiments. In some countries, review of foreigners' experiments is required; in others, there are no laws constraining researchers. In most cases, our home institutions never ask and most experimenters never comply. The first chapter in this section (Chapter 6), is written by Jennifer Merolla and Raul Madrid. They have conducted research in the United States and abroad, and Merolla has served on her home institution's IRB. They explore the dangers in relying solely on one's own IRB for ethical guidance, and identify local partners that may assure that a research design will be acceptable in the host country. The subsequent chapters provide brief case studies on a diverse sample of countries: China, Brazil, and Mexico. Chapter 7, on China, by Xiaobo Lü, examines the challenges and ethical issues surrounding research in China, where the government is likely to oppose most political science experimental work. He reviews the legal constraints on conducting research there, examines strategies available to scholars, and discusses the risks and ethics of each. In Chapter 8, Cunow and Desposato examine the review process in Brazil. There is a clear set of procedures for review in that country, but for non-Brazilians, review can take more than a year. They argue that international researchers should work with Brazilian scholars to improve the Brazilian review process and lower the cost of compliance. In Chapter 9, Aguilar examines the case of Mexico, where there are no clear local IRB guidelines and where scholars are administering treatments in the social sciences with essentially no constraints. She introduces a new ethics committee at her home institution and, drawing on recent experiments in Mexico, recommends that foreign scholars always seek some local approval.

Part III moves to issues of field experiments. Authors in this section tackle the critical issues in field experiments, including deception and consent, impact on elections and careers, the boundaries of the public officials' exemption, and the use of partner organizations to avoid IRB review. In Chapter 10, Michael Findley and Dan Nielson examine the role of deception in field experiments. They identify situations where deception is unavoidable and illustrate how it is essential to accurate measurement in many parts of the discipline. They discuss the morality of deception and propose a half-double rule of self-examination for scholars using these methods. Chapter 11, written by Joshua Gubler and Joel Selway, focuses on ways that political science experiments may intervene in existing political conflicts. They focus on three issues for comparative political experiments: the risks associated with unbalanced samples, the potential of experiments to affect ongoing political conflicts, and the possibility of repercussions to subjects. Their chapter includes a series of questions that scholars may use to assess the risk that their experiments will inappropriately affect studied political systems. In Chapter 12, Brigitte Zimmerman discusses problems associated with interventions in democratic processes and proposes development of short- and long-term assessments of costs and benefits. Finally, David Nickerson and Susan Hyde note that many political scientists are skirting IRB constraints entirely by offering consulting services to other actors who can act without constraints, then using the resulting "fresh data" for their publications. This framework creates perverse incentives for partnership and for manipulating NGOs or other actors into performing randomizations that scholars can then publish. They provide a framework useful for IRBs and scholars to assess whether such studies require review and to avoid natural conflicts of interest.

The next two chapters examine the public officials' exemption; research on public officials is exempt from IRB review. Edward Malesky examines the nature of this exemption and its boundaries, focusing on the definition of public officials. In the developed world, we often think of city politicians as elected officials; can we think of local chieftains as public officials and exempt them from human subjects protections? They may or may not have sought their positions; their positions may be hereditary or religious or even forced on them by a regime or other governing body. Malesky provides a tool to measure officials' degree of "publicness" to help scholars determine when treatments should be exempt and when they should not. Christian Grose then turns to the increasing research on public officials in the United States. He notes that while IRB rules are commonly interpreted as providing a blanket exemption for public officials, some boundaries on interventions are needed. He proposes a series of spheres of public officials' activity to distinguish between appropriate and inappropriate research activities.

Part IV of the volume examines possible strategies for moving the field forward. Mitchell Seligson offers a strong critique of the existing IRB as an appropriate framework for guiding political science research and the risks of "mission creep," in which an overzealous IRB intrudes inappropriately in research. Elizabeth Zechmeister shows how IRBs' lack of knowledge about international experiments can lead to errors of omission and commission. IRBs often overlook real risks to subjects and dwell on non-risky aspects of research. Zechmeister argues for increasing graduate training in human subjects protections, as well as research on the ethics of political science research. Finally, Rick Wilson, William Mishler, and John Ishiyama, the former editors of the *American Journal of Political Science*, *Journal of Politics*, and *American Political Science Review*, examine the role that journals should play in ethics. In the medical field, any research with human subjects requires certification of IRB approval or at least compliance with the principals of the Helsinki declaration. Should journals provide a similar or even more strict gatekeeping role in political science? They argue that journals have a limited role to play but can take some steps to reduce payoffs for aggressive interventions.

In the last chapter, I review the diverse positions of the authors on questions of ethical research. I argue that there is indeed a great deal of divergence of opinion, but that there is some widespread discomfort with some designs and practices. I explore some of the more divisive issues and propose a series of design modifications that will minimize controversy without disrupting promising research agendas. Finally, I conclude with a set of broad recommendations that the field should consider as we increasingly experiment with human subjects.

Notes

1 Institutional Review Boards are the committees that evaluate research protocols for ethics and/or for human subjects protections. They may also be referred to by many other names, but the term IRB is widely understood in the United States to refer to an ethics or human subjects protection committee. This abbreviation will be frequently used throughout this volume.

2 There is debate among historians about who was the first advocate of experimental methods. Interestingly, medicine was fairly slow to adopt experimental methods when compared with astronomy, physics, and chemistry. Ignaz Semmelweis' experiments on cleanliness and infection in hospitals in the 1830s were dismissed as heresy, and he was eventually confined in an asylum.

3 For a history of political science experiments, see Morton and Williams (2010), Bositis and Steinel (1987), Druckman et al. (2006), McDermott (2002).

4 Knowing participation in a research experiment is one form of implied consent. Many of these studies predated the adoption of strict human subject protection requirements, especially those of the Common Rule. However, even if there were no formal informed consent, subjects were aware that they were participating in research and their choice to participate could be considered a form of implicit or behavioral consent. There is always the possibility, of course, that some students were coerced or required to participate by faculty.

5 This does not mean that laboratory experiments are always low-risk. For example, the sociologist Milgram's (1977) laboratory experiments on obedience to authority are now widely cited as examples of unethical research for the psychological stress inflicted on subjects. However, most political science experiments involved abstract games or simple media studies with less risk of psychological harm.

6 One 1970 article in *Comparative Political Studies* makes reference to a future field experiment involving one control and one treatment village, but it is not clear whether that experiment was ever carried out or, if so, where it was published. See Agger et al. (1970).

7 Again, because only decennial years were sampled prior to 1990, this means that estimates prior to 1990 are based on a single sampled year. Further, post-2010 estimates are based on just four years, 2010, 2011, 2012, and 2013. This also implies greater variance in estimates for these years.

8 This pattern reflects the combination of a steady or even slightly declining rate of experiments in JCR, which has published primarily lab experiments, and the dramatic increase in experiments in the top three journals.

9 The one field experiment identified in this period would not even have counted as an experiment by some measures, as it did not randomize assignment to treatment and control; Larson's 1990 treatment was placing newspaper articles in a local newspaper, and their treatment and control groups were subscribers and non-subscribers, respectively.

10 Some field experiments, of course, may be as easy as sending resumes to employers, but many involve negotiations with government partners and lengthy protocol developments.

11 Note again that the 1980 map only shows data from 1980, not from the complete decade, due to resource constraints.

12 Indeed, many of the examples in this chapter and in others throughout this volume refer to work in press or published in other outlets.

13 To their credit, the authors sought an attorney's opinion before proceeding with the study and also chose their case carefully to avoid affecting the outcome of the race. More recently, the *Tribunal Superior Eleitoral* (the Brazilian Supreme Electoral Court) confirmed that field experiments with political propaganda would be illegal in Brazil.

14 In contrast, foreign scholars doing experiments in the United States have no need for local review of their projects—as private citizens they are free to randomize any legal activity without any local authority's oversight.

15 This is largely due to funding agencies. Note that it is unimaginable that a medical experiment would be carried out overseas without local government approval.

16 In medical studies, perhaps broad effects would be more permissible if there is consensus on their normative value. For example, if the effect were to broadly lower cholesterol in at-risk populations, that would improve human welfare. On the other hand, with political science, we do not always have a clear sense of the normative value of our dependent variable—are people better off with legislators spending more time in meetings? Can we say decisively that electing one candidate is normatively better than another?

17 Assume a work schedule of 40 hours per week. This equals 2,400 minutes per week. Subjects are spending $5 * 5,000 = 25,000$ minutes participating in the experiment, or just over 10 weeks worth of labor.

PART I

Contextual Challenges for Experimentalists

2

THE ETHICS OF EXCLUSION WHEN EXPERIMENTING IN IMPOVERISHED SETTINGS

Kim Yi Dionne, Augustine Harawa, and Hastings Honde

2.1 Introduction

As the other chapters in this volume demonstrate, the ethical issues that arise when social scientists conduct experimental research are wide ranging. Experiments involve risks of harm to participants and require protection of confidentiality and subjects' right to refuse or withdraw participation. Experiments can also provide benefits to participants, and, in fact, researchers are expected to ensure benefits outweigh risks. But what about the fairness or ethics of withholding benefits from populations excluded from participating in research?

In this chapter, we focus on the ethics of exclusion when social scientists conduct experiments in impoverished settings. We examine experiments of two types: 1) experiments conducted that test the impact of interventions aimed at improving the human condition and 2) research projects unrelated to measuring policy interventions but which use economics experiments to measure behavior. These research projects often exclude a portion of the impoverished population exposed to the research study, either as assigned to a "control" group in the former type of studies, or by non-selection in a random sample in the latter type. Often these research projects provide material benefits to study participants, meaning the excluded population is kept from receiving goods, services, or even cash. The question driving this chapter is: "What are the ethics of excluding the poor in the quest for random assignment or random samples?"

To study the ethics of exclusion, we try to identify relevant ideas and guidelines in the broader social science and medical literatures that examine the ethics of research involving human subjects. We also draw from our experiences collecting data for different research projects with experimental components over the last decade in Malawi. We discuss the challenges we have faced with community responses to randomized research to shed light on the question of fairness when excluding poor people from gaining advantage through research participation. We also provide an illustration of how we tried to address these challenges, drawing from a research project we conducted in rural Malawi in 2011 that included behavioral economics experimental games. The chapter concludes with some discussion of the "fairness fixes" that can be employed by researchers, along with the constraints and challenges.

2.2   Sample Selection: Randomization, Fairness, and Exclusion

Randomness in selection and/or assignment of research subjects is used by researchers to avoid selection bias,[1] "because a random rule is uncorrelated with all possible explanatory or dependent variables" (King, Keohane and Verba 1994, 124). Social scientists use randomization (in experiments, random assignment; in surveys, random sampling) as a tool to increase confidence in the impact of a treatment or in the potential generalizability of research findings. In social science experiments, random assignment permits unbiased comparisons between treatment and control groups "because randomization produces groups that, prior to the experimental intervention, differ with respect to both observable and unobservable attributes only due to chance" (Gerber 2011, 116). Similar to how random assignment in experiments eliminates biased differences between treatment and control groups, random sampling in survey research eliminates biased differences between the population of interest and the sample drawn from that population (Pollock 2012, 124). Random sampling and random assignment are tools used by researchers for *scientific* purposes, not *ethical* ones.

The central document guiding ethical treatment of human subjects in research, the Belmont Report, provides little insight on the ethical challenges associated with sample selection. First, the Belmont Report's section on *justice* asks the question, "Who ought to receive the benefits of research and bear its burdens?" The possibility that the burdens of research are unduly concentrated among the impoverished should raise an ethical concern if the motivation for researching in these populations is purely budget-driven and the research findings have no relevance for the populations under study. A reader of the experimental literature would be hard-pressed to find examples of researchers conducting studies in impoverished settings engaging in such activity. But the question about benefits and burdens is posed in such a way that imagines research participation as a burden, not a benefit. In the case of random selection into a study in which subjects are given inducement for participation, this frame of reference is unhelpful.

Second, the Belmont Report's section on respect for persons is loosely relevant to the question of fairness in sample selection in its recognition that some individuals may be incapable of self-determination. But the language of the Belmont Report delineates incapacitated people as ill, mentally disabled, or having "circumstances that severely restrict liberty" (The National Commission for the Protection of Human Subjects of Biomedical and Behavioral Research 1979). Only if we were to characterize impoverished populations as having restricted liberty would they fall into this category. Relatedly, particularly for research among vulnerable populations, the Belmont Report cautions against the provision by researchers of an inducement that reaches such a level that it would be considered an undue influence. However, what metric is available to researchers in calculating a fair inducement?

Beyond the Belmont Report, the literature on the ethics of clinical trials has not focused on sample selection but instead on informed consent or the risk-benefit ratio for participants. The broader ethical framework presented by Emanuel, Wendler and Grady (2000) asserts seven requirements in determining whether clinical research is ethical. To be ethical, clinical research must have social or scientific value; be conducted in a methodologically rigorous manner such that results are scientifically valid; select subjects using fair methods; minimize risks of research while enhancing benefits such that the benefits outweigh the risk; undergo independent review by individuals unaffiliated with the research to minimize conflicts of interest; accurately inform individuals of the purpose, methods, risks, benefits, and alternatives to the research so that these individuals can make a voluntary and un-coerced decision on whether to participate; and treat potential and enrolled study subjects with respect. Particularly relevant from this framework of ethical clinical research for our study is the third requirement: fairness of subject selection. Emanuel and colleagues specify that subject selection should not target stigmatized and vulnerable populations for risky research nor favor rich and socially powerful populations for potentially beneficial research. The study population should be selected based on the scientific goals of the study, not the convenience of studying a given population; the authors simply state, "Efficiency cannot override fairness in recruiting subjects" (Emanuel, Wendler and Grady 2000, 2704).

The limited scholarship on exclusion in randomized controlled trials examines how exclusion of subjects from analysis can introduce bias, impede generalizability of results, or create difficulties in data collection. For example, Doolittle and Traeger (1990) reported that random assignment to a control group to which services were denied led to refusals to participate in the National Job Training Partnership Act Study.

The expectation that researchers ensure benefits outweigh risks for the study population could also inform our discussion of the ethics in sample selection. The standard that benefits should not be less than subjects could expect in the absence of the experiment is met in any case where experiments provide a beneficial treatment that would otherwise not be available; the treatment group (or the induced-to-participate random sample) are unambiguously better off by participating, and the control group (or the randomly not selected population) are no worse off because of the study (Burtless and Orr 1986, 622). In fact, if service provision is constrained (e.g., by budgets), Burtless and Orr prescribe random assignment as an "ethical way to ration available services" (1986, 623).

2.3 Experiences Conducting Research in Malawi

Our earlier experience in non-experimental research gave us an appreciation for villagers' perceptions about the benefits of participating in research projects. In a previous research study in Malawi for which we all worked, it was not surprising to have a villager pose as a study respondent in order to receive the gift (inducement) the research project gave to study participants in exchange for the time spent during a survey interview. In one instance, an "imposter respondent," upon being found out, excused her action by saying, " . . . but we need the soap" (Adams et al. 2013). Essentially, the equivalent of two bars of soap were sufficient inducement for a rural villager in Malawi to say she was someone she was not: a respondent in our longitudinal cohort study.

Our experience with research associated with experiments, however, has been particularly challenging, and we attribute those challenges to researchers using cash inducements or incentives in poor, rural communities and distributing this cash in unequal—albeit randomly assigned—ways. This section illustrates the consequences of randomization in impoverished settings. It does so by highlighting examples of negative community reactions to five influential studies incorporating experimental research, all conducted in Malawi. The five research projects discussed below have been successful at examining major social problems and measuring the impacts of important policy interventions. To collect data necessary to evaluate in a convincing way the impacts of interventions, however, required randomization, meaning some of the population under study would not immediately benefit in a tangible way from the research.

It is important to note that in none of the research projects we discuss here were these negative community reactions a consistent issue. Nonetheless, the occasional negative reactions are still instructive. The effort here is not to question the studies, the subsequent research findings, or the choices made by investigators. These particular research projects are not exceptional in having met challenges in the field, nor were they conducted without careful thought to potential ethical problems that could arise (and all studies received clearance from researchers' home IRBs to conduct research with human subjects). We bring these examples to light to start a broader conversation about the ethics of experimentation, one that considers the risk of negative social outcomes when subsets of the population are excluded from benefits.

For each of the five experimental research projects, we provide a short description of the research purpose and randomization, followed by a narrative detailing negative community reactions to the research. Where applicable, we also describe the field team's responses. Names of people and villages have been changed to protect the confidentiality of study participants. As the examples show, the questions surrounding fairness in exclusion are not merely the luxury of an ethics thought experiment. Rather, not considering the potential drawbacks of exclusion can impose logistical challenges in implementing research.

An HIV-Testing Experiment in a Longitudinal Study

In a decade-long panel study,[2] an experiment was embedded that aimed to study the impact of incentivizing people to get tested for HIV (Thorton 2008). The experiment randomized individual incentives to learn HIV status, randomized the location of counseling centers where HIV results were available, and measured subsequent attendance at centers to obtain HIV test results (Thorton 2008, 1830). After being tested, participants were instructed to get their results two to four months later at a temporary counseling center, which was set a few kilometers from their community. The amount of cash awarded to each participant depended on the amount written on a bottle-cap drawn from a bag by the study participant; the amounts ranged from 0 to 400 Malawi Kwacha (MWK).[3] After a participant drew a bottle-cap, a research assistant recorded the amount on a voucher, which was given to the participant to bring when returning for his/her HIV test results for redemption.

Though the monetary incentives made no subjects worse off financially, in some cases the different potential amounts a respondent could receive created discord in the community. Some respondents who randomly drew a zero-Kwacha bottle-cap (and even some of those respondents who drew positive, but small amounts) were unhappy. Many did not turn up for the results[4] and some respondents even refused to participate in subsequent waves of the longitudinal cohort study. Even those respondents who drew a positive incentive but did not turn up in time at the temporary counseling center or lost their vouchers were unable to collect their incentives, and they also started to refuse to participate in a subsequent wave of the study. In some communities, there was a negative attitude towards the study; shifting blame away from study participants to the data collection team; the local interpretation of non-payment to subjects who misplaced vouchers or failed to get results on time was that the researchers were liars. One village in particular proved difficult in the 2008 wave of the study. Villagers who drew zero-Kwacha bottle-caps or who claimed to have not received the amounts they were assigned managed to influence other study participants not to take part in the study.

Usually field supervisors dealt with refusals on a case-by-case basis, explaining the stipulations of the earlier incentive experiment and its distinction from the broader cohort study. In the case of the village-wide refusal in 2008, multiple field supervisors convened a meeting at the village headman's compound to listen to the community grievances, try to better explain the earlier experiment's requirements for incentive payment, and express apologies for miscommunications or misunderstandings.

Conditional Cash Transfers in Zomba

The Zomba Cash Transfer Program was a randomized conditional cash transfer intervention targeting young women in Malawi that provided school fees and cash transfers to current schoolgirls and recent dropouts to stay in or return to school. Data from the study has been analyzed to measure the impact of these transfers on school attendance as well as on other outcomes of importance to school-age girls: age at first marriage, childbearing, sexual behavior, and the prevalence of sexually transmitted disease (Baird et al. 2010, Baird, McIntosh and Ozler 2011, Baird et al. 2012).

A stratified random sample of 176 census enumeration areas was drawn from one district in Malawi (Zomba) for inclusion in the study; half were assigned as treatment villages, half as control. In total, 3805 girls were selected into the study, 1951 in control villages; of the 1854 girls in treatment villages, only 1225 received cash transfers.[5] Girls selected into the treatment were provided with school fees and a monthly cash transfer for a period of two years whereas girls in the control group received nothing during this period of time.

The randomization within villages of some girls receiving transfers and others not generated challenges early in fieldwork. After discovering that some girls were benefiting monetarily from the project, some control households were unhappy with the research team and started avoiding them. The project encountered even more resistance from control villages in the last round of the study after people in these villages learned other villages in the study were receiving cash transfers. There were multiple refusals not only from girls in the study but also parents and guardians of these respondents. The attitude towards the study in the control villages changed and in some cases there were open insults made at the field teams conducting surveys. Although all survey participants were given small gifts for responding to the surveys (tablets of soap), some respondents in the control arm felt this was insufficient.

Other households not part of the study (neither treatment nor control study households) but within one of the study's enumeration areas also became involved. Rumors began in one of these communities that the research team was *opopa magazi*, translating to "blood suckers" in English. The rumor went that the research team was a Satanist group who came to the villages to look for human genitals. The rumor created confusion in the communities and difficulty for the research team.

One day when working in Mwayi Village, one of the authors went to the village chief to seek permission to conduct interviews in her village, and to our surprise, the chief refused.[6] She would not say at first why she refused, but after probing and reiterating the importance of the study, the chief said that the night before a group of angry young men invaded her house throwing stones and warning her that if she allowed the research team into the village, they would return to her home and burn it down. The chief said the whole village did not want to participate because they did not want people to see them associating with the survey team, or, as referred to locally: the bloodsuckers. The research team asked her to call an emergency village meeting for the villagers who were available. In less than an hour, more than 20 villagers arrived at the chief's home, and the survey supervisor (one of the authors) introduced the research team to them and started explaining the purpose of the research study. The villagers listened and immediately afterward some of the villagers who were sampled into the study invited the researchers to their homes to conduct interviews. The next day, the research team returned to the village to finish the remaining interviews and, upon arriving at the chief's house to greet her, asked if those young men did anything the previous night; the chief said that nothing had happened.

Such incidents are not uncommon for research teams working in rural communities when there are no social ties between the researchers and the study population and when there is no introduction of the study by means of a community meeting. Conducting a village meeting increases the time a research team is in the field (not collecting data), and is particularly challenging after research has already started. However, doing so was necessary in the case of Mwayi Village; otherwise, the whole village would have been dropped from the study. Village or community meetings prior to data collection are an investment against the risk of rumors in the community leading to study refusals.

Behavioral Economics Experiments on the Border

A recent study used a lab-in-the-field experiment to assess the relationship between national identification and interethnic trust (Robinson 2013). The study was situated along the border of Malawi and Zambia. A random sample of 32 villagers were drawn from each of 16 villages on the Malawi side of the border that ultimately yielded a sample of 508 Malawians, and a complementary group of 341 Zambians (not randomly sampled) also participated in the study. In the study, participants were asked to play trust games involving real money; by the end of the games, participants would take back home an amount ranging from 60 to 2000 MWK, in addition to the 500 MWK show-up fee.

Though participants were drawn from both sides of the border, the study's focus was on attitudes in Malawi; Zambian study participants were included as a comparison group. Thus, the Malawian study participants were drawn in a systematic way so as to be representative of the area in which the study took place. Prior to game play at the market, there were community meetings held in the Malawian villages from which the study sample was drawn and short questionnaires were administered to Malawian participants. The game play was explained to Malawian participants in detail at the end of these surveys, before giving the subjects invitation cards about the upcoming games to be played in the market. In contrast, potential study participants from the Zambian side of the border were just given an invitation card that indicated the time, date, and place of the game; these cards were distributed through chiefs in the Zambian villages.[7]

The experimental games started well and turnout was good from both sides of the border. However, when non-participants—particularly those from Zambia—learned that their fellow villagers were receiving money after playing the games, rumors began to circulate. Because these games were happening on a market day, participants would often spend the money they earned from the games at the market and then return home with more market goods than their fellow villagers. One rumor went that the money given to these study participants was from a Satanic group and everyone who participated and received the money were required to spend all of the money the same day at the market because if they didn't, taking the money home would bring ill fortune to the participant as well as the participant's household. Such rumors started affecting the number of participants coming to play the experimental games, primarily those coming from Zambia. The rumor was hastened one day in one of the Zambian study villages when there was a funeral of an elderly man that drew people from far away to pay their respects. At the funeral, one man whose village was not invited to participate in the research stood and warned the crowd that people should stop going to participate in the study where they are given money because the people who are giving the money are Satanists; he further warned that after two years, the area would experience a lot of deaths because of the money associated with the study. He told the crowd that he has never seen people receiving free money like those who had been in the study and he suspected a very serious hidden agenda behind this money. Because the funeral was so well attended by people from all over, this rumor about the research project traveled far and fast.

The next visit to the Zambian villages to invite participants for game play took much longer than anticipated and was a difficult day for the research team. After arriving, the team was surrounded by villagers who threatened physical harm. One of the chiefs aided them in getting away from the threatening group and then took the research team to all of the neighboring villages to conduct small meetings explaining to the villagers what the research team was doing. The chief also took the research team to the person who spread the rumor at the well-attended funeral so that the team could also chat with him about the study, its goals, and the study's funding source. The lesson learned from the experience working on the border was that chiefs could not be relied upon to sensitize their communities about the research project; even if chiefs were successful at distributing invitation cards to potential study subjects (and study participants arriving at the research site were fully briefed on the study before consenting to participate), community meetings help all villagers (not just participants) get firsthand information about the study and its goals and give villagers opportunities to ask questions of the research team in advance.

Community Based Rural Land Development Project

Malawi's Community Based Rural Land Development Project (CBRLDP) was a World Bank-sponsored initiative that purchased and redistributed land to nearly 15,000 smallholder farming households to address unequal land ownership. Beneficiaries were self-selected, formed in groups on a voluntary basis, but subject to predefined eligibility criteria that essentially required beneficiary households be landless or land-poor; CBRLDP targeted in particular the most vulnerable households chronically dependent on assistance for survival (Simtowe, Mendola and Mangisoni 2011, 17–18). Participation in CBRLDP required relocation, with some households moving to new districts. Beneficiary (treatment) households were given land, inputs, and money to settle down. Control households received no transfers.

Because beneficiaries were self-selected, evaluation of the intervention's impact employed a quasi-experimental design, in which CBRLDP beneficiary households were in the treatment group and were compared to a control group of three types: households in the area from which beneficiaries vacated, households in the area into which beneficiaries moved, and households not in the receiving or vacating areas. Differences in collecting data from these different populations were rather stark: It was easy to contact and question beneficiaries, but difficult to conduct research among those in the control group. For example, when the research team organized a focus group discussion in one of the control villages, the research team was chased from the village by a group of angry men, saying they did not benefit from the project. The men even threatened to damage the research team's vehicle if they refused to leave.

The transfer of resources to the treatment group and not the control group also created hostility between beneficiary and non-beneficiary households. For example, in one area of the intervention, control group respondents referred to beneficiaries as "Satanists." A more colorful rumor emerged in a different area of the study. According to the rumor, the Malawi government had agreed with people from the West to relocate people, give them land and inputs so that they could grow more crops and have a lot of food, which would eventually make the beneficiaries fat so that when they died, their remains could be taken to the capital city and be given to the Westerners for meat. Such rumors led to a number of beneficiaries abandoning their plots and moving back to their original villages, contrary to the intervention's goal.

Social Cash Transfers With a Phased-In Design

In response to widespread poverty and hunger, the Malawi Social Cash Transfer Scheme (MSCTS) was launched in 2006 to improve food security by targeting cash transfers to the country's most destitute households (Miller, Tsoka and Reichert 2011). Unlike cash transfers in other countries, the MSCTS did not have monitored conditions for transfers nor was it accompanied by programmatic benefits beyond the cash transfer, equivalent to roughly US$14 per month. To be eligible for the cash transfer, households had to be ultra poor, defined as being in the lowest economic quintile or having no assets or consuming only one meal per day, and labor constrained (Miller, Tsoka and Reichert 2011, 231).

Researchers studied the impact of the MSCTS using a longitudinal household survey comparing intervention and comparison households. Unlike other policy experiments described in this chapter, the comparison households in the MSCTS study were also beneficiaries of the cash transfer scheme; however, comparison households did not begin receiving their transfers until a month after endline data collection for the 18-month longitudinal survey was completed. Technically speaking, then, the comparison group in the MSCTS study was not excluded from receiving benefits; rather, their benefits were delayed.[8]

In collecting data for the MSCTS, the research team encountered current and future beneficiaries. The research team had particularly challenging experiences interviewing future beneficiaries; we highlight three examples. First, Samalani, a respondent in the "future beneficiary" group, was a disabled man who was popular in his village. Each of the three times the research team interviewed Samalani across the eighteen months of data collection, he complained that people were jealous of him because they thought that every time the research team's vehicle came to his house for interviews, he was receiving some money or other incentives; in fact, he received no inducement for participating in the study. In the final round, the research team went to his house, but did not find him at home at the time. Returning a second time three days later, the team discovered that he was laid to rest the previous day. On enquiring the cause of death, villagers shared that they believed Samalani was poisoned because other people thought that whenever the research team's vehicle visited his house, he was getting some incentives or cash transfer, not knowing that the cash transfer in the control area was delayed and Samalani would not benefit until a future date.

To reiterate, all MSCTS study participants were very poor; the study participants randomly assigned to the future beneficiary group were just as needy as those assigned to the current beneficiary group. After the initial interview of a woman in the future beneficiary group, an interviewer returned from the interview sobbing. Asked why, she just cried more. Later, the interviewer said that the condition of the woman that she was interviewing was very bad. She said that the woman had cervical cancer and had been sick for at least a year. Her condition was untreatable; the hospital prescribed only palliative care. Although she was discharged to go home, she was in poor health and lacked food and other necessities.[9] During the next wave of data collection, a different interviewer was sent to conduct the second interview. The respondent was still sick. Worse still, she lacked basic necessities. The second interviewer also returned from the interview crying because she felt so sorry about the respondent's condition. When the research team went to the respondent's home for the final round, she was dead. The research study benefited from the respondent's participation in the study; without her as a data-point in the analysis, it would have not been as clear that the social cash transfer had an impact on health. In contrast, the respondent did not benefit from participating.

In a child-headed household in the MSCTS, there was a blind boy who was living with his two younger sisters, both enrolled in primary school. The boy was not going to school because he did not have an opportunity to enroll in a special school for the blind. Instead, he walked to several villages, looking for piecework (*ganyu*). His blindness made it difficult to get piecework and so his two sisters would have to search for piecework to earn small amounts of cash for the household. There was no one in the area assisting these children. By the research team's final interview, both girls had dropped out of school and married because their brother could not get enough piecework to take care of day-to-day costs. The two girls got support from their husbands and their blind brother was left on his own. If these sisters were in the intervention villages, it is less likely they would have married at such young ages. This case highlights again how the study benefited from the information that was collected: The contrast of seeing how this child-headed household fared against those who received cash transfers helps to show that unconditional transfers can provide enough to keep children healthy and in school and reduce their need to seek work (Miller, Tsoka and Reichert 2010).

2.4 Critical Reflection on a Research Project in a Poor African Setting

In August 2011, the authors conducted a study on ethnic identity and social networks in rural Malawi that used behavioral economics experiments to measure cooperative behavior (Dionne Forthcoming). In this section, we provide some background on the study and choices we made in sample selection and the field logistics to highlight the challenges we faced in simultaneously promoting fairness and transparency. We also discuss the costs of exclusion for those Malawians in the study area not selected to participate.

The study was situated in rural areas of Zomba district. By car, the villages in our study would average 45 minutes drive to Zomba town, Malawi's fourth largest city. The great majority of that time spent in a car would be on unpaved, "dusty" roads. In rural Zomba, the 2010 Malawi Integrated Household Survey estimated 56% of the population lived in poverty according to local standards, which is slightly higher than the average district in Malawi (49%). This poverty translates into tangible outcomes. Children in Zomba, like in the rest of Malawi, are stunted, such that 20% of children in Zomba under five are three standard deviations below the median of the World Health Organization's Child Growth Standards (National Statistical Office [Malawi] 2011).

The study's goal to examine the relative influence of ethnic diversity on cooperative behavior required data collection from multiple villages, between which there were varying proportions of ethnic groups represented. The pilot funding for the research was sufficiently limited so that only a fraction of adults could be sampled from each village to participate in the study. Each village had between 200 and 300 adults.

Sampling: Aiming for Inclusion and Transparency

Though our original research design called for the study to draw samples from six villages, we reconsidered this configuration. Our budget was sufficient to cover the costs associated with a target sample size of 180 subjects. If we worked in six villages, we would only draw 30 subjects from each village, or 10 to 15% of the village population. If we worked in four villages, we could draw 45 to 50 subjects from each village and increase the proportion of villagers selected into the study per village up to as much as 25%. It happened that we learned only upon shortly before starting the research the particularities of the ethnic group proportions in the study area,[10] which illustrated to us that minimal additional analytical leverage would be attained by including more than four villages in the study. After deciding to reduce the number of villages in the study to four, we saw our team as faced with two options: increase the proportion of villagers in each village invited to participate in the study or keep the number of villagers per village constant. The first option would maintain the originally projected sample size (N =180), while the second option would reduce the overall sample size (N =120). The budget would cover either configuration, although the latter would result in savings by reducing the field costs associated with surveying an additional 60 adults and the potential earnings those additional 60 subjects could make in the course of playing the behavioral economic experiments.

We chose to maintain our originally budgeted sample size by increasing the number of villagers per village for two reasons. First, the particularly acute economic challenges faced by ordinary Malawians during the time of the study (Wroe 2012, Cammack 2012) made participation in our study even more attractive to potential study subjects and would yield tangible benefits to participants in a time of cash scarcity. Second, by increasing the proportion of participants per village, we increased the likelihood that each household would have a household member selected to participate. By increasing participation, we were less likely to run into issues of unfairness or envy felt between households in these communities. Because participants earned cash during our study, we recognized that participation might result in a neighbor's jealousy at a subject's newfound relative wealth. We recognized that bringing cash into rural and mostly poor villages could shift community dynamics and we did not want to leave social problems in the wake of our study.

We later invited the community to a village meeting.[11] One of the authors gave a 30-minute presentation that discussed the goals and process of random sampling[12] and the purpose and nature of the study. The community meeting is a useful tool, particularly because random sampling is a rather challenging concept to convey to an ordinary villager who can potentially become disappointed or even upset about not being selected. Conveying this is especially difficult during a conversation rushed because of other pressing data collection responsibilities. We preferred to discuss our study with participants publicly and in advance of the data collection to mitigate potential problems arising during the course of data collection. After the presentation was over, villagers asked questions and we answered them. The meetings in each village were well attended, and in one of the villages, the meeting was rather celebratory in nature, with groups of women singing and dancing when we arrived. In all villages, women sat separately from men, but questions and participation came from both sides.

Once it seemed the village had a good grasp of our proposed work, we drew the sample. In an opaque bag, we had the name of household heads from the village representing each adult living in the village, as collected during our census of households in the village the previous day. For example, if Abiti Jamusi's[13] household had three adults, Abiti Jamusi's name would be written on three pieces of paper in the bag. Volunteer villagers would blindly select from the bag one piece of wadded-up paper, which would be unfolded by the research supervisor and read aloud (usually twice), so the person—or another member of the household—would make him/herself known.[14]

The random sample was conducted publicly to demonstrate to all villagers the "fairness" of the study selection process. Our aim with the transparent sample selection was also to demonstrate to the village the universe of households selected to participate. Our previous experiences conducting research in rural Malawi are littered with accounts of ordinary villagers asking why they weren't asked to participate—asking why they aren't able to benefit from the what the research project had to offer its study subjects (Dionne 2014, Harawa, Honde and Mkandawire 2010).

Data Collection and Participant Earnings

When participants arrived at the field lab, they checked in and were verified using photographs taken during survey data collection. The subject was then given a show-up fee of MWK 200,[15] and directed to a facilitator team who would be leading his/her group in game play. Before playing, facilitators read instructions from a script and demonstrated play. Then, each player was given an envelope of his/her own to keep throughout the game play.

Using real money, participants played twelve games (six dictator games, three trust games, and three income allocation games). In the instructions for each set of games, participants were told they could keep or send money. To keep money, participants would put the money in their own envelope; to send money, the participant would place the money in an envelope attached to the game sheet.

Game play data was entered the same day. Play across all games and players in the village was later examined to calculate each player's earnings. Within a few days of play, the research team would return to the village to distribute participants' earnings one at a time and in private.

On average, a participant's payout was 320 MWK, in addition to the 200 MWK show-up fee, and whatever Kwacha they kept in their own envelope. In total, participation required no more than three hours of time, although this was spread over two days. The daily wage at the time paid by government public works projects was 100 MWK, but in no village where we collected data were there reports of recent or forthcoming public works projects that would offer this kind of temporary labor. In our sample, respondents reported annual incomes ranging from nothing to 300,000 MWK, with an average income of 21,975 MWK and a median income of 10,000 MWK.

Extrapolating from reported income, participating in our study would mean an average respondent forewent potential earnings of 85 Kwacha per day or 170 Kwacha total by participating in our study. In exchange, the average earnings subjects walked away with totaled 520 Kwacha. Participating meant the average villager made 350 Kwacha (or four days' average earnings) more by participating in the study than they might have earned by engaging in their normal activities. Taking these calculations a bit further, the villagers randomly not selected into the study had no opportunity to earn an extra four days' worth of earnings.

Social science experimental research is impossible without study participants. Our earlier research experiences made us mindful of how to incentivize our study population to participate in the research while also cautioning us about the potential pitfalls of infusing cash into a low-income area. Ultimately, our 2011 study was the first we had conducted together in rural Malawi in which we did not encounter a fieldwork delay because of a miscommunication or misunderstanding between the research team and the study population. We believe our proactive steps that promoted inclusion, transparency, and community communication were integral in shaping this outcome. Promoting inclusion and open communication were chiefly the ideas of Harawa and Honde, the Malawian authors of this chapter, who have been executing research projects for over a decade in rural Malawi. Our research project highlights the importance of local knowledge in implementing experimental research.

2.5   Conclusion

Experiments conducted in impoverished settings are often aimed at a greater good of furthering understanding about what works in improving the human condition. These research projects meet the conditions of the ethical principle that expected benefits should not be less than what subjects could expect in the absence of an experiment. Equally important to the same ethical principle, although populations are (randomly) excluded from receiving benefits associated with the experiments, they are no worse off because of the experiment's implementation.

Nonetheless, the examples shared here suggest even randomization cannot protect against negative community reactions that challenge our notions of fairness. We have offered a few fieldwork fixes that we believe can increase fairness. In fact, using random sampling gives everyone an equal chance to participate. However, random samples can be challenging to draw in developing country settings. In rural Malawi, drawing a random sample first requires conducting a census of the eligible population, which means additional resources are necessary for enumerators to walk door to door in the days prior to the random draw.

Random sampling without community awareness of what random sampling is or how it is implemented is insufficient in conveying fairness of study participant selection to the population living in the research site. Thus we also recommend sample selection by public lottery (as we did in Zomba) to increase transparency. The problem with the public lottery of sample selection is that it can reduce confidentiality of participation, raising other thorny ethical issues. Our intermediary solution to protect participant confidentiality was not to draw the participants during the community meeting, but to draw a number of participants from a named household (and to draw the specific participants at the household). Still, there are other questions that could be raised about a public lottery for sample selection. For example, does a lottery suggest there is something to be won by participating in research?

For interventions, researchers and policymakers could use a phase design like that of the MSCTS rather than creating pure control groups who will be excluded from receiving any benefits. Although benefits were delayed for the comparison group, these benefits were not delayed because of the researchers' insistence but because of the slow process involved in scaling up the provision of the cash transfers.

In addition to the aforementioned challenges, researchers and implementers face constraints in increasing the fairness and broadening inclusion in impoverished settings. Malawian research professionals largely devised the solutions we employed to increase inclusion and fairness. In contexts where there are few professional researchers available or where their contributions are limited to data collection and not research design or fieldwork approach, it will be challenging to forecast potential problems associated with local ethical frameworks or perspectives. Local knowledge is key in implementing research, particularly when monetary benefits are not universally transferred.

In this chapter, we have only begun to unpack the issues surrounding our motivating question: "What are the ethics of excluding the poor in the quest for random assignment or random samples?" Our assessment is that it can be unfair and even unethical to exclude some people in an impoverished community from research participation and compensation. Researchers from economically advantaged backgrounds should be particularly aware of and sensitive to their research project having a lasting impact beyond the project's scope or researcher's intentions. A research project in an impoverished setting is not an independent event, but interacts with local networks and those networks can be very strong such that a researcher's actions—even seemingly minor compensation strategies—can affect everyone in that network. Our proposed strategies for avoiding some of the challenges we have faced when collecting data point to the essential role of local knowledge in research design and implementation. Although we recognize the limits of our modest proposals, we hope and expect to learn from the experience of researchers going forward how to mitigate the challenges that arise in the unequal exchanges that structure the pursuit of knowledge.

Notes

1 See Geddes (2003), Chapter 3, for a detailed discussion on selection bias.
2 The panel study in which this experiment was embedded was the Malawi Longitudinal Study of Families and Health (MLSFH), a seven-wave longitudinal cohort study. The MLSFH studied how social networks influenced family planning choices and HIV/AIDS-related behavior as well as how individuals and households cope in a context of high morbidity and mortality (Kohler et al. 2013).
3 In 2004, when the experiment was conducted, US$1 = MWK 140.
4 Only 34% of respondents who received no monetary incentive showed up for their HIV test results, whereas those receiving any positive-valued incentive were more than twice as likely to show up at the temporary counseling center to learn the outcome of their HIV test (Thorton 2008, 1839–1840).
5 The remainder (629) were examined for spillover effects for living in villages where girls received transfers; we refer to these 629 subjects in this chapter as members of control households, even though they lived in treatment villages.
6 Seeking permission from local authorities to conduct research is necessary in rural Malawi, but largely perfunctory; in our years of conducting research, we have never been refused access from a chief if we sought permission before entering a village.

7 Prior to game play, the research team would meet the chief of the selected Zambian village, explain the research to him, and leave him the cards to distribute to interested men and women in the village.

8 During the midline survey in September 2007, UNICEF financed the provision of a food bucket valued at roughly US$9 for all comparison households (Miller, Tsoka and Reichert 2011, 231).

9 When households were observed to require assistance (e.g., healthcare) or if households asked for sources of assistance, the interviewers were trained to provide relevant information and/or an appropriate referral.

10 The 2008 census data on ethnic makeup at the level of enumeration areas was only accessible to the principal investigator upon arrival in Malawi.

11 We had met earlier with traditional leaders to discuss the nature of the research and gain access to the proposed study areas. With permission, the research team conducted a census of the number of adults aged 18–50 living in households in each of the four villages prior to the village meeting.

12 The research supervisor used an analogy drawing on the familiar: He asked how a visitor to the village might learn about the quality of the mangoes grown in the village (each village in the study had many mango trees, always visible from the location of the community meeting). He asked if such an inquiry would require eating all of the mangoes in the village. He asked whether eating from only one tree would yield a good answer. He equated our random sampling of the village population to a random sampling of mangoes, and it seemed reasonable to the villagers that we would draw people from some of the households but not include everyone in the study.

13 Abiti Jamusi is a hypothetical villager used for illustrative purposes, not related to any real person in our study area.

14 Within households, a household representative would draw a numbered card for each of the adults sampled, and whatever number was drawn would determine which adult in the household would be sampled into the study. For example, at Abiti Jamusi's household, each adult's name was written on a numbered list and if Abiti Jamusi's household had only one draw from the village sample, a research assistant would go to Abiti Jamusi's home and ask that she or someone else draw one of three cards. Whatever number was drawn would determine which person on that household listing, whether Abiti Jamusi, her husband, or her sister (listed as 1, 2, and 3, respectively) would be drawn. So, if #2 were drawn, Abiti Jamusi's husband would be the sampled participant.

15 At the time of the research, the Malawi Kwacha was officially exchanged at MWK 165 = US$1.

3
ETHICS FOR EXPERIMENTAL MANIPULATION OF RELIGION

Richard A. Nielsen

In this chapter, I explore the ethical boundaries of social science experiments that involve religion. I argue for a distinction: Experimental manipulations that allow *measurement* of an individual's religious beliefs, practice, or experience are generally ethical, while manipulations that *change* an individual's religious beliefs, practice, or experience are more likely to be unethical.

Is it ethical to change the religiosity of experimental subjects to learn how religiosity affects political attitudes and behaviors? This question is crucially important to the field of religion and politics, and comparative politics more generally. As the discipline of political science makes an experimental turn, fields where ethical experiments are infeasible will be at a structural disadvantage. Knowledge production within these fields is still as important as before; there is no reason to believe that the ability to ethically design experimental manipulations is correlated with the substantive importance of a given field. However, the inability to do ethical experiments may mean that (1) fewer researchers work on religion and politics because the field does not ethically allow certain approaches, and (2) it is harder to create new knowledge about the causal effects of religion. My conclusion is that meaningful interventions that change religiosity are likely to be unethical, corroborating earlier debates on psychology (Batson 1977, Yeatts and Asher 1979, Batson 1979).

Given the sensitive nature of religious experience (one of the topics not discussed in polite conversation!), I feel that I should briefly describe my religious commitments. I was born and raised a Mormon (the Church of Jesus Christ of Latter-day Saints, or LDS church), attended Brigham Young University, and spent two years as a Mormon missionary in Alaska and Canada. I am currently practicing, but not believing, meaning that I participate in the Mormon community and

Mormon religious rituals, but do not believe the foundational truth-claims of the religion. This background gives me a relatively rich ethnographic understanding of the experience of religious faith, the concerns of at least some segment of religious people, and the costs and benefits associated with changes in religiosity. Throughout this chapter, I appeal to religious examples. Because of my background, I am most confident in the examples based on Mormonism.

I begin in Section 3.1 by presenting a distinction between two ideal types of experiments involving religion: those that *measure* religious beliefs and those that *change* them. I argue that measurement experiments will generally be ethical (with respect to issues of religion), whereas experiments that change religiosity are less likely to be ethical. Section 3.2 provides three arguments to support my assertion that change manipulations are often unethical: (1) because individuals have a strong interest in forming beliefs about questions of ultimate value in non-manipulative circumstances, it is difficult to experimentally change religiosity without imposing a possible harm; (2) because religion makes untestable claims about harms and benefits, it is impossible to change religiosity without imposing a possible harm; and (3) it is impossible to provide adequate informed consent about changing subjects' religion without undermining the inferential value of the study. Section 3.3 discusses an experiment I proposed that raised the issues discussed here as well as evaluations of other experimental studies according to the criteria I suggest.

3.1 Measurement and Change Manipulations

In this essay, I am primarily concerned with experiments that test theories in which religion is an independent variable or mediating variable in some proposed causal mechanism. Both independent and mediating variables can be called *explanatory* variables because they are posited to form part of the explanation for some outcome of interest. I argue that experiments involving religion as an explanatory variable fall on a spectrum between two ideal types. The first ideal type uses experimental manipulation to elicit and measure religious beliefs, practices, or experience. The second ideal type uses experimental manipulation to change religious beliefs, practices, or experience. For ease of discussion, I refer to these respectively as *measurement manipulations* and *change manipulations*.[1] I draw a fundamental distinction between these two ideal types and suggest that change manipulations face ethical challenges that measurement manipulations do not. Figure 3.1 shows these two ideal types as ends of a spectrum with my placement of some possible experimental designs along the spectrum.

Measurement manipulations are those that use experimental manipulation to measure the level of some attribute of an individual, group, or environment. Table 3.1 includes examples of this type of manipulation. The key feature of this type of manipulation is that the researcher is not attempting to assign the subject

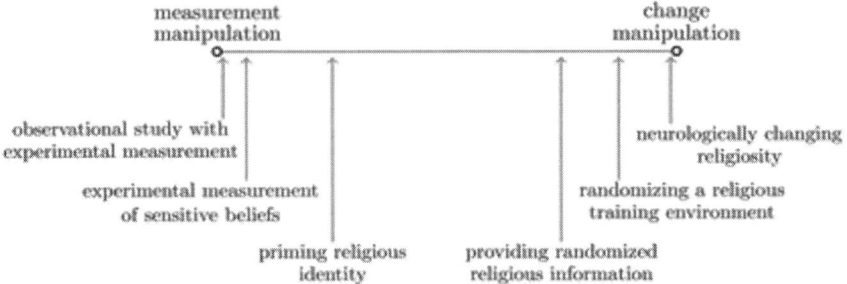

FIGURE 3.1 Spectrum of Research Designs From Measurement Manipulation to Change Manipulation

TABLE 3.1 Examples of Measurement Manipulations

(1)	Researchers randomize the contents of a survey to elicit responses to sensitive questions. (List Experiment)
(2)	In a survey setting, researchers randomize which individuals or groups are reported to support particular policies or actions. (Endorsement Experiment)
(3)	Researchers randomize elements of a fictional story to measure differences in responses.
(4)	Researchers use dictator games with confederates to assess altruism.

to a particular level of variable. Rather, the researcher is attempting to assess the "natural" level of a particular variable as unobtrusively as possible. This is not to say that these experiments do not change or intrude on subjects. Results from fields as disparate as anthropology and physics suggest that the act of observing changes the thing that is observed. However, the intent of measurement manipulations is to produce measurements that are maximally accurate and minimally intrusive. The results of measurement manipulations are desirable because they can reveal attitudes and behaviors that subjects are unwilling or unable to express directly in a survey or interview.

For example, in a list experiment attempting to measure racism in the American South (Kuklinski, Cobb and Gilens 1997), the researchers used an experimental manipulation to allow respondents to be honest about racism without revealing that racism to the survey administrator. Although there was an experimental manipulation, the intent was to be *less* invasive and more accurate than directly asking, "Are you a racist?"

Similarly, in an endorsement experiment attempting to measure support for the Taliban in Afghanistan (Lyall, Blair and Imai 2013), researchers asked respondents to rate various policies while randomizing whether respondents were told that the Taliban supported or opposed the policy. Because the policy was identical in each experimental condition, changes in the support following an endorsement by the Taliban were taken to signify implicit support for the Taliban that respondents might not be willing to openly express if directly asked.

It is possible that a measurement manipulation will change subject religiosity. In fact, because of the possibility that measurement inherently changes the thing that is measured, there may be no pure measurement manipulations. Even manipulations intended to minimize the intrusiveness of measurement may still induce changes. In the example of a list experiment on racism, the fact that a survey researcher has bothered to ask about racism may create new thoughts and attitudes in individuals who respond to the list experiment. Even if the researcher cannot tell what answers a respondent gives, the act of acknowledging racism in some domain could either decrease or increase feelings of racism. Likewise, while an endorsement experiment is intended to assess respondent support for an entity such as the Taliban without changing the respondent's beliefs and attitudes, the respondent may change his/her beliefs about either the entity or the policy to which the entity has been linked. It is impossible to know whether measurement induces these types of changes because this would require another measurement, which could also induce more changes. Thus, the closest we can confidently come to this logical end of the spectrum is that some experiments are primarily measurement manipulations.

Change manipulations do not simply measure some aspect of a trait or characteristic. Rather, they are designed to set that trait at a particular value so that the effect of the trait can be observed. This process of setting subject characteristics via experimental manipulation results in changes to the subject by definition. Table 3.2 gives examples of experimental designs with change manipulations.

In the physical sciences, it is possible for researchers to directly manipulate features of the object of study to estimate the effects of those features. Social scientists studying organizations can directly change aspects of those organizations (say, removing network ties or changing organizational structure). However, researchers who study individuals cannot generally directly set the beliefs

TABLE 3.2 Examples of Change Manipulations

(1) Telling subjects new information that affects their beliefs and attitudes.

(2) Manipulating a religious environment or experience to induce changes in subjects' beliefs and attitudes.

(3) Encouraging subject participation in a religious ceremony suspected to change religious commitment or identity.

or attitudes of individuals at a desired level. In the context of religion, this means that there is currently no way for a researcher to fix the religiosity of an individual at some level. Instead, researchers attempt to manipulate the beliefs and attitudes of humans by providing them with new information, by withholding information, by constraining a subject's environment, or by triggering some physical process that researchers believe is associated with an attitudinal change.

This means that there are no manipulations of religiosity that are purely change manipulations according to my definition. Researchers cannot be certain that they have set religiosity to a particular level. Instead, they can only randomize variables that affect religiosity and identify intent-to-treat effects of those interventions or use compliance information to estimate the effects of changes of religiosity in an instrumental variables set-up (where the randomized variable serves as an instrument for changes in religiosity).

In experiments on religion that identify intent-to-treat effects, the researcher can be thought of as testing the effects of an intervention that has religious side-effects. This type of research does not demonstrate any causal effect of religion without assumptions about compliance. Alternatively, experiments that use the manipulation as an instrumental variable for religiosity will necessarily have to measure religiosity following any manipulation. This means that pure change manipulations on religious beliefs and attitudes are not possible because the researcher cannot be confident whether religiosity was manipulated or the measurement has error. All this is a result of the inability of researchers to set the attitudes or beliefs of an individual to a specified level or category.

Thus, experiments on religion fall on a spectrum between pure measurement manipulations and pure change manipulations.

3.2 Change Manipulations of Religiosity Are Generally Unethical

My discussion of the ethics of experiments involving religion follows from my distinction between measurement and change manipulations. I argue that a pure measurement manipulation of religion is generally ethical unless it violates some other ethical principle of experimentation such as deception or harm to the subject. On the other hand, pure change manipulations of religion are unethical, even if other aspects of the experiment are ethical (subjects are fully informed, etc.). Because all experimental manipulations fall between these ideal types, I argue that the more an experiment approximates a change manipulation, the less ethically defensible it is likely to be.

An Argument From Interest in Forming Beliefs Without Manipulation

(a) People have a strong interest in forming beliefs, especially beliefs of ultimate value.

(b) People have a strong interest in forming these beliefs in favorable, non-manipulative circumstances.

(c) Change manipulations require that beliefs be formed under manipulative circumstances.

(d) Potential harm from such manipulations cannot be fully disclosed prior to manipulation and may not be reversible.

(e) Therefore the harm should be taken seriously and is often large enough to outweigh benefits of the research.

(a) People Have a Strong Interest in Forming Beliefs, Especially Beliefs of Ultimate Value

Human beings display strong interest in forming beliefs about themselves, other people, and the nature of humanity's physical and metaphysical surroundings. Beliefs of "ultimate value" are beliefs that deal with the metaphysics of human existence. These include beliefs about deity, the origins and purpose of human existence, whether aspects of an individual persist beyond death, and so on. While not all individuals seem equally driven to form such beliefs, virtually all individuals form beliefs to some degree and most hold these beliefs to be important.

(b) People Have a Strong Interest in Forming These Beliefs in Favorable, Non-Manipulative Circumstances

Individuals have a strong interest in forming beliefs about ultimate value in non-manipulated environments. Beliefs about "facts" are often passed on in manipulated environments (children learning multiplication tables in a classroom), but it can be problematic for someone to lead other individuals to hold beliefs about ultimate value through manipulation of their environment. Most modern conceptions of human rights enshrine such an interest in terms such as "freedom of thought" or "freedom of expression." This interest might also be perceptible in norms against censorship. While this interest in forming beliefs in non-manipulated environments exists for many types of beliefs, it is especially important for individuals forming beliefs about matters of ultimate value. This may be seen in the additional rights of "freedom of conscience" and "freedom or religion" that are additional to freedoms of thought and expression.

(c) Change Manipulations Require That Beliefs Be Formed Under Manipulative Circumstances

Manipulation is at the essence of experimental assignment of treatment and control. In order to experimentally learn about the effects of religiosity on attitudes or behaviors, religiosity must be randomly assigned, and this "assignment" requires manipulation. Thus, change manipulations that set a subject's religiosity to a value it would not have attained naturally are forming the subject's beliefs under manipulative circumstances. Any experiment that does not manipulate the subject's beliefs is, by definition, not a change manipulation. Because these beliefs are about religion, they are likely to involve beliefs about ultimate value. Manipulating such beliefs is very likely to run counter to subjects' strong interest in forming their beliefs about ultimate value in non-manipulated environments.

(d) Potential Harm From Such Manipulations Cannot Be Fully Disclosed Prior to Manipulation and May Not Be Reversible

Research in many settings requires subjects to form beliefs in manipulated environments. Most studies involving deception manipulate subjects' beliefs about the purpose of the research or the nature of the experimental task in order to maintain the validity of the experiment. This manipulation of beliefs is typically justified on the grounds that it can be corrected by debriefing subjects afterward to correct their misperceptions. Alternatively, it is justified by positing that subjects do not have a vital interest in knowing the information about which they were led to form incorrect beliefs. For example, it seems reasonable that subjects generally do not have a strong interest in knowing a researcher's precise hypothesis while participating in an experiment. Such knowledge can reasonably be withheld until after participation is complete because it is not generally vital to the subject to know and any incorrect beliefs can be easily addressed through debriefing.

Manipulating religious beliefs is problematic because there is potential for harm that cannot necessarily be mitigated through debriefing. Researchers cannot fully comprehend the harms that might come to respondents whose religiosity is manipulated, so they almost certainly cannot anticipate and mitigate these harms. Moreover, at least some manipulations of religious ideas and beliefs may not be fully reversible. Critical literature cannot be unread, doubt cannot be undoubted, and transcendent experiences are hard to shake, even if researchers subsequently inform subjects that these experiences were manipulated.

(e) Therefore the Harm Should Be Taken Seriously and Is Often Large Enough to Outweigh Benefits of the Research

If individuals have a strong interest in forming beliefs about ultimate value in non-manipulated environments, then change manipulations of religiosity will be difficult to justify on ethical grounds. There may be societal or scientific interests that trump this interest—it may on balance be ethical to manipulate the beliefs of religious terrorists to encourage pacifism—but such justification will require argument on a case-by-case basis. In general, subjects will rightfully have an aversion to experiments that manipulate their religiosity because of the value they place on forming their own judgments about things of ultimate value.

An Argument From the Ambiguity of Religious Harms and Benefits

(a) Religion makes untestable claims about harms and benefits.
(b) People with different beliefs can view identical treatments as clear harm or clear benefit.
(c) All treatments that meaningfully change religiosity will be a clear harm to someone.
(d) Such a claim of harm is not demonstrably false by (a).
(e) Therefore, the harm should be taken seriously and is often large enough to outweigh benefits of the research.

(a) Religion Makes Untestable Claims About Harms and Benefits

Religion makes claims about metaphysical facts that are generally not empirically verifiable. Most religions tend to make claims about the meaning of life, the terms of any pre-life experience or after-death experience, and the absolute morality of particular human actions. Many humans—particularly religious humans—find these questions to be of great importance, even though they are not typically susceptible to empirical verification.

Even when religious traditions generate falsifiable empirical claims, adherents often adopt methods of empirical investigation that allow for religion to retain meaning even if truth claims are, in a particular instance, apparently false. For example, religious groups whose charismatic leaders have made testable prophecies tend to remain faithful, even when those prophecies do not occur as the leader or group expected (Festinger, Riecken and Schachter 1956). Mormons argue that spiritual knowledge must be ultimately obtained through feelings of divine experience rather than through scientific study; some Mormon historians have become increasingly postmodern in their approaches to understanding aspects of Mormon history that seem to be in tension with theological claims of the church (Duffy 2008). The Kamajor secret society in Sierra Leone claimed to endow the power to withstand bullets following initiation and continued adherence to religious principles (Kelsall 2009, 129–137).[2] When adherents observed examples of society members succumbing to bullets, they believed that the individuals were not sufficiently scrupulous in their adherence to the requirements of the secret society, which included abstaining from sex and not eating pumpkin. All this is to say that many individuals have demonstrated that they find religious beliefs to be important and that they hold these religious beliefs to be largely outside of the realm of empirical verification.

(b) People With Different Beliefs Can View Identical Treatments as Clear Harm or Clear Benefit

Because of the incompatibility of competing religious claims, people with different beliefs can view identical change manipulations as clear harm and clear benefit. Any treatment that changes religiosity could be seen as a clear benefit by people whose religious ideal points are closer to the subject's post-treatment religiosity, while the same change will be seen as a clear harm by people with religious ideal points that are closer to the subject's pre-treatment religiosity.

(c) All Treatments That Meaningfully Change Religiosity Will Be a Clear Harm to Someone

Because of the exclusivity of many religious claims, there are proponents and opponents of almost all religious positions. Atheism, Buddhism, Christianity, Hinduism, and Islam (to name a few religious traditions in alphabetical order) are largely seen as incompatible and mutually exclusive by most adherents and detractors. Thus, for all meaningful religious changes that could be encouraged via treatment, there are some individuals who would view the change as religiously beneficial and some who would view it as harmful.

(d) Such a Claim of Harm Is Not Demonstrably False by (a)

These claims of harm cannot be tested because many of them rely on untestable claims about an afterlife. Many religions claim that eternal punishments exist in an afterlife for individuals who do not practice religion appropriately. If these claims are true, such infinite harm would certainly outweigh physically observable benefits following a particular course of action.

(e) Therefore, the Harm Should Be Taken Seriously and Is Often Large Enough to Outweigh Benefits of the Research

Without an ability to adjudicate between true and false claims of harm, social scientists that use meaningful change manipulations will be causing harm from the subjective view of the participant. If the perceived harms are substantial, then the potential harm to subjects is likely to outweigh the benefits of the research in many circumstances. At very least, experiments that attempt to change religiosity should explain why the potential metaphysical harms are small relative to the benefits of the research.

Scholars should be wary of their own judgments about which harms should be taken seriously. Natural scientists are more likely than the average individual to be agnostic or atheist (Larson and Witham 1998), and presumably social scientists follow suit. If academics are inclined against religion, they may tend to consider heavily the benefits of reduced religiosity and discount the harms. On the other hand, religious adherents are likely to feel the opposite: that the harm of becoming more religious is negligible relative to the harm of becoming less religious. Fundamentally, these individuals may simply not agree on the definition of a "harm." While damnation at the hands of a wrathful God seems like serious harm to some, contributing time, money, and energy to an organization with false claims about deity and discriminatory practices may seem like more serious harm to others. Because the truth claims of religions are not susceptible to empirical verification, this debate will not be resolved. This suggests that as scholars, we need to carefully consider harms that may be obvious to adherents but are not obvious to us because of our biases. Without an absolute standard for judging which change manipulations are ethical, there is strong reason to adopt the conservative position that scientific researchers should not do experiments involving change manipulations of religiosity without substantial justification.

Hypothetical Examples

To illustrate why the ambiguity of religious harms and benefits makes change manipulations problematic, I consider a series of potential experiments and how religious individuals might react to them. I discussed these thought experiments with three Mormons and I note their reactions to each, although they are hardly a representative sample of any religious population.

Imagine a study in which researchers at a national atheist group would like to improve the effectiveness of its materials for persuading Mormons. The group identifies a sample of Mormons and sends them mailings with elements of the mailings randomized. One year later, the researchers follow up with these individuals to measure the number of individuals who have decreased faith in the teachings of the Mormon church or left Mormonism. Perhaps not surprisingly, all three Mormons I talked with found this study ethically troubling.

However, consider an essentially identical study design: Researchers in the Public Relations department of the Mormon church would like to improve the effectiveness of its materials for persuading non-Mormons. The group identifies a sample of non-Mormons and sends them mailings with elements of the mailings randomized. One year later, the researchers follow up with these individuals to measure the number of individuals who have increased faith in the teachings of the Mormon church or have joined Mormonism. At this point, the three Mormons I interviewed typically said, "That sounds fine to me," and then a few moments later, "I see where you are going here." I then invited each of them to imagine that they were an atheist ex-Mormon who believed that the church was harmful and discriminatory rather than a practicing member of the Mormon church. Each agreed that their evaluation of the last two thought experiments would probably flip, with the deconversion experiment seeming ethical and the conversion experiment seeming unethical.

Although this example hinges explicitly on untestable metaphysical claims, experimental designs that present verifiable facts in an attempt to change religiosity are similarly problematic because they implicitly involve these same claims. For example, it might be possible to decrease the religiosity of Mormons by presenting them with particular pieces of true information about Mormon church history that do not square with the somewhat sanitized history that is taught within the church. Many former Mormon adherents credit their loss of faith to the experience of receiving such information.[3] However, it would probably be unethical to carry out an experiment that randomized exposure of this information to self-identified Mormons. Even if the historical information were entirely accurate, the resulting changes in religiosity are harmful from within the metaphysical framework of Mormonism and this potential harm should not be risked without substantial justification.

Now, I turn to hypothetical measurement manipulations and find that these are less problematic. Imagine a study in which university researchers identify a sample of religious individuals and a similar sample of non-religious individuals. The individuals in the study are randomly paired, sometimes with a co-religionist and sometimes not. The individuals play a dictator game to assess the generosity of one of the partners in each pairing. There is no randomization of religion. The manipulation is entirely to measure a particular outcome—altruism or cooperation—for each pairing. This strikes me as unproblematic, and the three Mormons that I discussed this example with agreed.

Adding an element of deception to a hypothetical measurement manipulation induced some concerns about ethics. Consider an experiment in which university researchers participate in online conversations with Mormons and act as if they are interested in learning about the beliefs of these Mormons. They request information about the Mormon church and invite the Mormon to share his/her personal feelings of belief (called a "testimony" in Mormonism). Each request contains some framing element that is randomized. For example, we could imagine that the name of the requester is randomized to be a name that is commonly associated with a certain ethnicity. The researchers then study differences in response rates and the content of the information provided by the Mormons in the study.

The three Mormons that I discussed this with had the gut reaction that this was unethical. I then asked them to imagine that the element of deception could be largely removed: that the Mormons would be adequately debriefed following the study. This led each of the Mormons I discussed this with to decide that the study was probably ethical. One of them—an academic economist— said "I wouldn't really want to do an experiment like this myself because of the amount of deception, but in other domains we tolerate this kind of minimal deception in experiments all the time." I argue that this experiment would be ethical from the standpoint of religion because it is primarily measuring religious response rather than changing religiosity. The ethical issues are issues of deception and informed consent rather than religion per se.

An Argument From the Impossibility of Informed Consent

(a)   People have a right to determine their own religious beliefs.
(b)   This requires informed consent of potential consequences of treatment.
(c)   Few individuals will consent to experimental manipulation of their religiosity and those that do are unlikely to be representative.
(d)   Therefore, we cannot experimentally learn about the effects of religion in most populations.

(a)   People Have a Right to Determine Their Own Religious Beliefs

Absent other considerations, individuals should have autonomy to choose their religious beliefs. Although these beliefs are often unverifiable, for adherents, the consequences of these beliefs are critical. In some religious traditions, individuals believe that they are determining the fate of their own eternal identity with these beliefs. In practice, no individuals are truly "free" to choose religious beliefs outside of the context from which they come. The strongest determinant of an individual's religious tradition is the religious tradition of their parents (Spilka et al. 2003, 115–116), suggesting that socialization and family dynamics constrain religious choice. In open societies, individuals face constant influences from peers to modify, change, deepen, strengthen, or relinquish religious beliefs. In general, such influences are morally defensible on the grounds that individuals should have freedom to associate (or disassociate) and communicate freely about matters they feel are important.

Social scientists as a class do not have the same rights to engage in such conversations. The fact that individuals are influenced by external forces when choosing their religious beliefs does not give social scientists the right to manipulate individuals' religious beliefs. While a social scientist as a private individual has rights to attempt to influence the religiosity of friend, the same social scientist does not have the inherent right to attempt to "set" the religiosity of the same friend to a particular level for scientific purposes without consent.

(b) This Requires Informed Consent of Potential Consequences of Treatment

I argue that informed consent is necessary for any experiment that intends to experimentally change religiosity because there is potential for harm to an individual who has their religious beliefs or experience manipulated for the sake of scientific inquiry. In Section 3.2, I considered metaphysical harms that cannot be definitively proven. Here, I consider physical and emotional harms for which evidence is readily available.

On a basic level, there may be harm to the subject if an experiment causes the subject's future self to adopt a level of religiosity that their current self would not like. I argue that this is true, *even if the subject's future self is satisfied with the new level of religiosity that they are assigned by the researcher.* This is because the right of an individual to choose their religious beliefs includes the right to fully determine one's own religious beliefs in the future. Such a change would generally only be ethical if participants were fully informed that their level of religiosity might be changed if they participated in the experiment and that they might or might not be happy with their assigned level of religiosity.

Individuals can often face harm from becoming more or less religious and they should generally be free to choose such harm for themselves. Examples of harm from decreased religiosity are relatively easy to list. For example, individuals that disassociate with the Jehovah's Witnesses may be shunned by family and friends. Likewise, Muslims who convert to other religions may face a capital sentence for apostasy under some interpretations of Islamic law. Similar social costs are imposed on apostates from a wide variety of faiths. More broadly, individuals who become less religious may experience a painful loss of community, a feeling of disorientation, alienation from social connections, mental illness, and other costs. There may also be benefits to decreased religiosity that potentially counterbalance these costs. Individuals may be controlled or manipulated within religious organizations, and may face sexual, physical, or emotional abuse as a result of affiliation with religious organizations. There is also potential harm in becoming more religious. Individuals have faced substantial religious persecution throughout history and still face human rights violations in some parts of the world. Individuals may also face mental illness as a result of increased religiosity, including tendencies toward obsessive-compulsive disorders and scrupulosity (Spilka et al. 2003, 511). Certainly, these harms do not happen to everyone who changes religiosity, but researchers cannot know *ex ante* which individuals will be harmed, so these should be serious considerations even if only a small portion of individuals are affected. At a minimum, the potential for these harms will generally require that experimental subjects give informed consent.

(c)   Few Individuals Will Consent to Experimental Manipulation of Their Religiosity and Those That Do Are Unlikely to Be Representative

Experiments on religion that use informed consent will only have subjects who knowingly agree to the possibility that a research will attempt to substantially change their religiosity based on randomized assignment to a treatment condition. What sorts of subjects will opt into such an experiment? The most obvious set are those whose attachment to their current and future religious identities is so weak that they are willing to allow their religiosity to be manipulated. I expect that there will be relatively few such individuals because most people seem unwilling to casually change their religious beliefs. A second set of individuals may believe that they are not susceptible to manipulation of their religiosity and agree to participate, but I believe these will also be relatively rare.

Neither of these types of individuals are representative of the adherents to a particular religious tradition or the broader population. It seems unlikely that most meaningful questions about the role of religion in politics could be answered using a sample of people who are willing to subject their religiosity to researcher manipulation, either because they are apathetic or extremely self-confident. After all, what does it mean to say that religion causes some outcome among a subgroup of people who are willing to determine their religiosity or religious beliefs according to a coin flip?

(d)   Therefore, We Cannot Experimentally Learn About the Effects of Religion in Most Populations

As a result, the necessity of informed consent means that even when manipulation of religion for experimental purposes is ethically defensible, it is likely to be impossible. Scholars will usually not be able to experiment on the population to which their theories apply, but rather the self-selected subset who would give consent. Perhaps there are some questions for which such a sample might be able to adjudicate between competing theories, but such cases seem unlikely. In general, social scientists care about the effects of religion precisely because it is a powerful, consequential force in the lives of individuals. Experiments on the small subset of individuals for whom religion is so inconsequential that they will allow it to be randomized are unlikely to be informative.

When Are Experiments That Change Religiosity Ethical?

Experiments that change religiosity may be ethical if researchers can show that there is direct benefit that comes to subjects or others from changing a religious belief or practice that outweighs untestable claim of harm. For example, militant Jihadists may believe that suicide bombings are a religiously encouraged activity, but research that discourages suicide bombing by manipulating religiosity will bring enough demonstrable benefit to both the subject and potential bombing victims that it is ethical (and perhaps imperative) to carry out the change manipulation. Even in this instance, much relies on the assumption that the researcher can apply a treatment that will only have ameliorative effects on radicalization. This is a problematic assumption. On one hand, if the assumption holds, then the experiment is unnecessary because we already know that the treatment will have deradicalizing effects. The experiment should be scrapped and a full-scale intervention should be rolled out. On the other hand, if we are not sure enough about the sanguine effects of the treatment, then we are unlikely to be sure enough that we are not causing harm to carry out the experiment. The benefits in such a setting are still likely to outweigh the risk, but scholars should be cautious.

Change manipulations of religion may also be ethical without direct benefits to participants if they occur in settings where the potential for harm is very small. For example, manipulations that are similar to circumstances in the daily lives of participants may be ethical because they pose no more risk to religiosity than the risk the subject faces from daily influences. In one study, Gervais and Norenzayan (2012) had subjects complete tasks that required analytical thinking and found that this decreased religious belief in the short term. In general, I argue that decreasing religiosity experimentally is problematic, but the tasks involved were to spend time looking at a picture of Rodin's statue *The Thinker* (control condition: a picture of the *Discobolus* of Myron) and a verbal fluency task in which treated subjects were given words such as "analyze, reason, ponder, think, rational" while control subjects were given words such as "hammer, shoes, jump, retrace, brown." Given that these seem like relatively innocuous treatments, the experiment does not seem problematic despite the finding that these tasks temporarily reduced religiosity.

Are Manipulations That Change Non-Religious Beliefs Ethical?

Religious beliefs are not the only kind of belief that social scientists might want to manipulate experimentally. For example, researchers might want to know whether making someone more politically liberal affects their political behavior or whether assignment to a civic education program increases belief that democracy is the best system of government. Do researchers face the ethical challenges outlined above when manipulating non-religious beliefs?

I argue that the differences between religious beliefs and non-religious beliefs are best viewed as differences of degree rather than differences of kind. The premise of my argument in Section 3.2 is that religious beliefs are generally not empirically testable. Neither are many political beliefs. The premise of the argument in Section 3.2 is that people have a right to determine their religious beliefs, in part because those beliefs have physical costs and consequences. Political beliefs also have costs and consequences, so informed consent is necessary and the subset of subjects willing to subject their political convictions to a coin flip may be small and unrepresentative.

It is primarily on the grounds of the argument in Section 3.2 that can we start to distinguish political and religious beliefs. Arguably, most political beliefs have less drastic metaphysical consequences than religious beliefs. Few people believe that they would face eternal punishment for changing their political beliefs than for changing their religious beliefs. This lessens the potential for harm considered in Section 3.2, meaning that experiments manipulating political beliefs have fewer costs to weigh against the benefits, so perhaps more experiments will be possible.

It is also possible that the argument in Section 3.2 may also provide some distinction between religious and political beliefs if some political beliefs are also more susceptible to evidence than religious beliefs. Political orientations tend to make at least some claims that are verifiable, and these claims can be linked back to philosophically defensible aspirations of individuals to autonomy, health, happiness, etc. Perhaps it is ethical to change political beliefs in ways that unambiguously expand the scope of human freedom and happiness.

Nevertheless, my argument raises serious questions about interventions intended to promote a variety of beliefs. If it is unethical to administer a treatment that turns a subject into an apostate who eventually faces death at the hands of their former religious community, then it seems similarly unethical to administer a treatment that turns a subject into a democracy activist who eventually faces imprisonment in a dictatorial regime, even if we believe that spreading democratic norms is good. These are extreme examples, but even when the potential consequences are far smaller, subjects should be warned about the costs and benefits of manipulations designed to change their beliefs. Many of them may opt out, perhaps making the experimental results unrepresentative to the point of uselessness.

3.3 Examples

The previous sections distinguished measurement manipulations from change manipulations and argued that the latter are likely to be more ethically problematic.

In this section, I discuss examples of experiments that have been proposed or published in light of the principles I have outlined. The first purpose of this is to see whether my framework offers useful guidance for considering the ethics of experimental manipulation in religious settings. The second purpose is to evaluate whether applying my framework to existing studies leads to judgments that are surprising or seem wrong.

I first consider a failed experiment proposal of my own that led to the arguments I have developed here. I then discuss other examples of experimental work.

A Failed Experiment Proposal

As part of a conference for "Experiments in International Relations" held in Park City, September 21–22, 2012, I prepared and presented an experiment proposal entitled "Why do Muslim clerics issue fatwas supporting militant Jihad?" The purpose of the proposed experiment was to test arguments I have made in other work[4] that Muslim clerics are sensitive to strategic considerations when they decide to express more or less extremist rulings in their Islamic legal rulings (fatwas).

I proposed to first identify a list of clerics who issue Islamic legal rulings over the Internet in response to questions from lay Muslims. I would then request fatwas from these clerics, hiding my identity so that the cleric would believe that they were simply answering yet another of the tens and hundreds of fatwa requests they answer daily. These fatwa requests would reference some current event and then ask for a ruling that had potential to be Jihadist or not. Specifically, I planned to ask clerics three questions on (1) the permissibility of participating in democracy (in the wake of the Arab spring), (2) whether it is permissible to participate in the Syrian uprising and whether it is a legitimate Jihad, and (3) whether suicide operations are permissible in the Syrian uprising. I would randomize the addition of several statements to the baseline fatwa request, intended to make clerics think of either the costs or benefits of issuing certain types of rulings. To cue the costs of being Jihadist, I would add "I know that in the past, some clerics have faced punishment or been imprisoned for speaking freely on issues like this one." To cue the credibility benefits that I theorize accrue to Jihadists, I planned to add "In the past, I and many of the other brothers have found that those who are willing to speak freely on this issue are the most trust-worthy of the clerics." Finally, to test whether the rulings of other clerics matter, I considered including "I have read the ruling by [CLERIC NAME] which rules on this issue as follows: [RULING]. What is your opinion on this matter?" These would have been compared to a fourth, baseline condition with just the fatwa request.

I then planned to collect responses from clerics and look at two outcomes: response rate and the content of the fatwas for those clerics that responded with fatwas. My theory would have found strong support if a reminder of the costs made clerics' rulings more democratically oriented and less prone to support violent activism of various kinds, while a reminder of reputation benefits of Jihad-ism would have the opposite effects.

Not surprisingly, the bulk of the comments I received about this proposal related to ethical concerns.

1.   What will an IRB say? And if an IRB approves, is it still unethical?
2.   Can we make this more ethical by only using de-radicalizing treatments?
3.   Could you openly invite the clerics to participate so that there is no decep-tion? Is informed consent through email a problem?
4.   Is there a possibility that anyone could be harmed or killed as a result of this research? Is there any way to justify the commissioning of texts that advocate violence? Commissioning potentially violent fatwas is a bad idea.
5.   Don't do this experiment because it could backfire publicly and threaten the entire experimental social science enterprise!
6.   Should we be randomizing other people's religious beliefs?

In my proposal, I had anticipated (and invited) virtually all of these critiques except the last—should scientists be randomizing other people's religious beliefs? I agreed that something seemed problematic with randomizing religious beliefs, and as a person with long-standing experience with religion, I felt sensitive to such considerations. On the other hand, this had not occurred to me, while basi-cally all of the other critiques had. I spent the remainder of the conference serving as something of an ethical baseline (Discussant of another paper: "I find this ethi-cally problematic, but not as problematic as that fatwa paper."), which naturally forced me to think seriously about both justifying and abandoning the project. This chapter is the result of my attempt to respond to the critique I had not anticipated: that an experiment involving religion was inherently problematic.

As I conceptualized it, my experimental proposal to elicit fatwas was essentially a measurement manipulation. I did not explicitly conceive of it in these terms— I had not yet developed either the terms or the concepts—but I believe this is why I was blind-sided by the criticism that I was randomizing religious beliefs. In my other work on Islamic fatwas, I use fatwas as a vehicle for measuring cleric ideology (Nielsen 2013). In doing so, I work from the basic assumption that their ideology is fixed at the time of writing, and that writing is an observable manifes-tation of ideology. I have not generally considered the possibility that the process of fatwa-giving *changes* a cleric's ideology, at least in the short term. Rather, the cleric already has an ideology that is latent until they are asked about a particular situation. Thus, I believed that fatwas could be used as a very authentic form of survey, and that my framing manipulations were akin to a survey experiment manipulation intended to explore different aspects of a fixed ideology rather than to actually change the religious ideology of the cleric in any way.

Most of the ethical concerns raised by participants at the conference seem to have been premised on the belief that my intervention might in fact be a change manipulation, either for the clerics themselves, or for their followers. It is possible that by asking clerics about violence and Jihadism, I might force them to think about issues more deeply and that they would come to more radical positions than they previously held. The framing experiment is certainly an attempt to temporarily focus the subject on a particular aspect of a decision; this itself could be viewed as a way of changing the subject's religiosity, depending on how one interprets the psychology of framing. If fatwas are effective at changing the opinions and practices of lay Muslims, then generating additional fatwas from artificial questions could actually distort "natural" Muslim orthodoxy and orthopraxy. Ethical concerns about the unintended consequences of eliciting texts that might justify violence are also founded partially on the idea that the experiment would be changing religious behavior rather than merely measuring it. Those concerned about deception were at least partly worried that pretending to be a co-religionist with a sincere request would be insensitive to the religious context and subtly change the religious experience of the cleric or lay Muslims.

I believe that there could be ways to eliminate the risks of violence and issues with deception and informed consent. If these other ethical issues were resolved, would it be ethical for a non-Muslim to participate in the practice of fatwa-asking and fatwa-giving for the purposes of social science research? I think this is an open question that hinges on whether I would be simply measuring cleric ideology, or whether the religious beliefs of clerics or lay Muslims would change as a result of the experiment. Put differently, would it bother clerics and followers to find out that a particular ruling was actually in response to the question of a social science researcher who had randomized parts of the question rather than a sincere religious seeker? My hunch is that this would actually not change clerics' or lay Muslims interaction with the text (in other words, it would not be blasphemous to do this experiment), but this is an open question.

Having described the specific project that prompted me to develop the ideas in this chapter, I now apply my framework to a series of studies to illustrate the usefulness of my distinction between measurement manipulations and change manipulations in religious contexts.

Measurement Manipulations

My framework suggests that experiments that primarily measure religiosity rather than changing religiosity to estimate effects are more likely to be ethical. Is this really so when I examine actual studies that appear controversial at first blush?

A seemingly hard case is the paper "The Economics of Faith: Using an Apocalyptic Prophecy to Elicit Religious Beliefs in the Field" (Augenblick et al. N.d.).[5]

In this paper, the authors examine a small religious group following Harold Camping, who prophesied that the end of the world would occur on May 21, 2011. The authors test whether "beliefs in the prophecy among Family Radio members [Camping's followers] are a matter of external profession rather than inner conviction," by offering them financial incentives of either $5 prior to May 21st or varying amounts up to $500 after May 21st. The amounts and probability of payment were experimentally manipulated to allow estimation of the discount rate of participants. As a comparison group, the authors gave the same choices to a sample of Seventh Day Adventists who similarly believe that the end of the world is "imminent" but did not believe that the end would come on May 21st.

The authors summarize their findings:

> The evidence indicates that the vast majority of Family Radio members held extreme beliefs even in the face of direct financial costs. Nearly all Family Radio subjects preferred $5 dollars today to any amount up to $500 payable after the Rapture, regardless of the probability of implementation. At the same time, the SDA members made choices consistent with time preference parameters estimated in laboratory studies (Frederick, Loewenstein, and O'Donoghue 2002). Taken together, these findings indicate that the Family Radio members held sincere and full beliefs in the prophecy, with little apparent elasticity. This finding underscores the role of sincere faith in the demand side of religion, and simultaneously rules out two alternatives: evidence-based beliefs, and faith-related activities that occur exclusively due to social factors.

I argue that my framework correctly illuminates why this study is ethical (at least with respect to issues of religion). Although the paper uses the word "experiment" over 80 times in reference to the research, the experimental portion of the research is simply an innovative way to measure the discount factors of two religious groups. There is nothing experimental about the actual assignment of religious beliefs. This means that the portion of the paper that essentially estimates the effect of a change in religious belief about the Camping prophecy is actually observational rather than experimental. Thus, in the framework I introduce, this paper is close to a pure measurement manipulation. Contrary to what I might have assumed from the title and abstract, I do not think this paper exploits a vulnerable religious group or attempts to tinker with "odd" religious beliefs for the purposes of social science.

Similar principles apply to a genre of studies that use experimental manipulations to measure cooperation between individuals and then test whether the religiosity of participants conditions their level of cooperation (Ruffle and Sosis 2007, Tan and Vogel 2008).

Temporary Change Manipulations

The other major category of existing studies are what I call "temporary change manipulations." These are typically framing experiments in which the experimenter attempts to cue religion by exposing the subject to text or images that will remind them of their religious identity rather than some other identity. This is arguably a change manipulation because the researcher is attempting to manipulate the religiosity of the respondent by making them temporarily more religious. However, in most of these studies, the authors appear to assume that this manipulation is temporarily *priming* religion by activating an already existing religious identity, rather than fundamentally changing the long-term religiosity of a person. These experiments thus occupy a middle ground between measurement and change manipulations as shown in Figure 3.1.

Generally, the treatments in these experiments are relatively minimal—an image of a religious figure or exposure to a passage of scripture—meaning that they pose no more risk to religiosity than other common influences in respondents' ordinary environments. I conclude that temporary change manipulations are ethical if they involve randomly assigning stimuli to which participants could reasonably be exposed in their regular activities and if the effects are likely to be temporary.

The major weakness of these studies is that they tend to overclaim when interpreting their results. For example, a recent working paper that uses a priming experiment is titled "The Effects of Religion on Social Cooperation: Results From a Field Experiment in Ghana" (Parra N.d.).[6] However, this experiment cannot identify the effects of religiosity unless it is meaningfully making respondents more religious. The treatment does not seem to do that. Rather, participants are primed with religious imagery—a picture of a Christian choir, a Muslim praying, the Ka'ba in Mecca, and a crucifix and prayer beads—and then participate in a dictator game to (experimentally) measure social cooperation. This priming intervention seems too weak to support claims about the "effects of religion." It is a stretch to extrapolate from the momentary burst of religiosity after viewing a religious image to estimate what would happen if individuals became more devout in the long-term. Under this interpretation, the experiment is likely to be ethical but limited in its relevance to understanding the social world. Alternatively, if the experimenter believes that such priming *is* inducing substantial or long-lasting changes in religiosity, then the ethics of the experiment should be questioned.

Experiments that prime religious identities are quite common, suggesting that scholars and review boards find them ethical.

Permanent Change Manipulations

I could find not published examples of permanent change manipulations—experiments where manipulations were intended to change participants' religious beliefs in a substantial and long-term way. This lack of examples probably supports my assertion that such experiments are typically unethical. It could be the case that finding opportunities to meaningfully change subjects' religious beliefs is more difficult than other types of experiments on religion, but I suspect that some opportunities are available. Scholars appear not to have taken those opportunities, suggesting the existence of a taboo.

3.4 Conclusion

In this paper, I have argued for a distinction between measurement manipulations and change manipulations in experiments involving religion. While neither ideal type is possible, the continuum from measurement to change is an important dimension for evaluating the ethics of experimental manipulation of religion. Manipulations that primarily measure the religiosity of an individual without changing it will generally be ethical, provided that they comply with other ethical criteria. Experiments that change the religiosity of participants may be less ethical. A middle ground exists with experiments that prime religious identities because it is not clear whether the manipulation is changing a subject's religiosity or merely increasing the salience of a stable religious identity without changing it. This probably hinges on a careful definition of religion and religiosity that I have failed to provide here.[7] My argument does point to a dilemma with these studies: Either priming interventions are not as informative about the effects of religiosity as some proponents suggest or they are possibly unethical.

I do not claim that the spectrum from pure measurement manipulations to pure change manipulations is the only dimension for ethical evaluation of experiments in religious contexts. I do think the distinction I introduce is instructive for thinking about the ethics of some experiments that are being carried out in the contemporary social sciences, but other distinctions may also be helpful.

There is no empirical way to establish that the arguments I advance here are the right way to think about the ethics of randomizing religion. I believe it supports my case that the types of experiments that I argue are clearly unethical are the same types of experiments that seem largely non-existent on the scholarly literature. I interpret this absence as partly the effect of a taboo, but it may have other causes. I am aware of some experiments in the planning stages that I would classify as permanent change manipulations. If these experiments proceed, the reaction to them will be instructive as to whether the ethical claims I make here resonate with social scientists more broadly.

However, we should be careful that we do not exclusively benchmark against the ethical beliefs of social scientists. Religious individuals and communities have important stakes in this debate and scientists are unlikely to automatically consider or represent these other views. One way to explore the ethics of religious experimentation would be to survey individuals outside of academia to find out the types of experiments that they would consider ethical. In fact, one could propose an (ethical?) experiment on the ethics of experiments on religion in which respondents of differing religiosity are presented with a brief summary of an experimental design where key parts of the description were randomized. In order to test my argument, such an experiment would need to vary the degree to which the religiosity of respondents would be manipulated to see whether religious and scholarly communities agree that change manipulations are less ethical. Note that this survey experiment would be ethical under my proposed framework, but might not be ethical under others.

My argument implies that it may be difficult to ethically learn about the effects of individual religiosity from experiments. The only way to experimentally test the effects of changes in religiosity is to change subjects' religiosity arbitrarily. Otherwise, subjects' observed levels of religiosity are endogenous to their own choices and are likely to be related to the outcome of interest through confounding variables. Experiments are not the only way to learn about causal relationships, but removing experiments from the toolkit of social scientists studying religion could be a real impediment to progress. Still, scholars cannot do unethical things simply because we would like to know more about the social world.

My fear is that these challenges will deter young scholars from working on issues of religion and politics. If experiments are privileged and professional rewards accrue to those who use them, young political scientists may naturally gravitate toward topics and questions for which conducting experiments is not fraught with ethical complications. Given the importance of religion in politics, this would be a real loss. My remedy is to propose that scholars should entertain unethical research designs—not in order to implement them (please do not!)—but because pondering an unethical design can often lead to ideas about how it could be made ethical. If scholars are too quick to reject some approach as unethical, a breakthrough that allows the research to proceed will never occur. This work may be more difficult, but ultimately the importance of understanding the role of religion in politics demands that we face the inherent ethical hurdles head-on rather than diverting our best efforts to more tractable topics.

Notes

1 I define experimental manipulation as a change to an individual, group, or environment as a result of actions by a scientific researcher. My definition has an embedded causal assumption: that the change would not have occurred without actions by a researcher. A second key distinction is that the change results from actions of scientific researchers, rather than individuals of other backgrounds.

2 Thanks to Rebecca Nielsen for bringing this example to my attention.

3 See http://www.whymormonsquestion.org/wp-content/uploads/2012/04/Survey-Results_Understanding-Mormon-Disbelief-Mar2012-1.pdf (accessed September 28, 2015).

4 See Nielsen (2013), accessible at http://dash.harvard.edu/handle/1/11124850 (accessed September 28, 2015).
5 Available at http://faculty.haas.berkeley.edu/ned/WaitingForTheEnd.pdf (accessed September 28, 2015).
6 Parra (N.d.) is available at http://www12.georgetown.edu/students/jcp29/ghana-exp3.pdf (accessed September 28, 2015).
7 Defining "religion" is not trivial. See Platvoet and Molendijk (1999).

4

RELIGION, EXPERIMENTS, AND ETHICAL CONCERNS

Rebecca Morton and Jonathan Rogers

4.1 Introduction

In broad terms, the effect of religion on politics is a question of great interest to social scientists, but one that has only recently seen an increase in experimental study. One of the principal reasons for the dearth of experimental studies is ethically based.[1] While it may be possible to experimentally manipulate beliefs, it may be wrong to do so. First, it may not be possible to obtain informed consent. Second, there are potential psychological, social, and even physical harms to subjects when beliefs are manipulated. In more extreme cases, particularly in areas of existing tension, it could be possible to induce civil unrest. Third, investigators risk placing their research team members and themselves in the way of harm, either physical or legal.

We address these ethical issues as they relate to four broad classes of experiments that involve religion:

- First, we consider experiments that attempt to measure the strength and sincerity of religious beliefs and relate beliefs to attitudes and behavior. In some circumstances, direct discussion of religious beliefs may be dangerous to both the subject and enumerator. Therefore, simply measuring beliefs can involve ethical concerns.
- Second, we examine experiments that use frames and primes to alter the weight that subjects place on religious beliefs. Doing so raises the possible dangers with measurement mentioned above, as well as the additional ethical issues concerning the use of deception by experimenters.
- Third, we discuss experiments that are designed to alter, rather than prime, religious beliefs (or the lack thereof). In these experiments, deception may be

nearly unavoidable and the subject may not be able to give informed consent to undertake the treatment.

- Fourth, we consider experiments where the intent may not be to study religion, but instead the research question studied may mean asking subjects to engage in activities that are in conflict with their religious beliefs. These activities may offend participants and also lead to prosecution, as well as harm the ability of other researchers to conduct future studies with a given population.

In this paper, we provide examples of each of these four types of experiments, consider possible solutions to ethical issues involved, and make recommendations for future experiments involving religion. Note that our review of the literature is not meant to be comprehensive, but rather we chose research cases selectively as illustrative examples. Before turning to our study of the literature, however, in Section 4.2 we present a basic overview of the ethical calculus we use in evaluating these issues.

4.2   Our Ethical Calculus

In order to make ethical judgments, it is necessary to have a basis for calculating what is ethical and what is not. We follow the analysis presented in Morton and Williams (2010). Specifically, we use a benefit/cost approach to evaluating the ethical concerns involved in experimentation with human subjects. The benefits from experimentation can be short and long run, and can benefit society as well as the subjects themselves (therapeutic benefits). Benefits to society are extremely difficult to calculate, especially in the social sciences. It is easy to speculate that a particular research project could lead to exciting new evidence on an important topic, but not easy to prove because if we knew the results of the experiment for society we presumably would not need to conduct the experiment in the first place!

Hence, in our view these benefits are not generally clear enough in social science experiments to justify significant harms to subjects and others likely affected by the experiment.

Possible benefits to subjects are also likely small in social science experiments because it is rare that a social science experiment provides direct therapeutic benefits. Moreover, it is the standard view that any payments (either "in kind" or monetary) that subjects receive from participation (so-called "collateral benefits") should not be counted as benefits because such payments might lead to an undue influence on subjects' behavior and could be used to support experiments that have little to no benefit for society but have high potential costs. Indeed, the Common Rule, the US Federal Regulations concerning human subjects research, prohibits Institutional Review Boards from considering cash payments or other things provided to subjects in return for participation as benefits from research. Payments may, however, be used to offset the opportunity cost of a subjects' time. Hence, in most social science experiments, our view is that the maintained assumption should be that known benefits are likely small or nonexistent and thus the key ethical issue should be how high are the costs.

The costs of experimentation can range from the opportunity cost of a subject's time to more serious psychological and physical harms. As noted above, collateral benefits can be weighed against the simple opportunity cost of time and thus we can compensate subjects for these costs, but not to mitigate or justify harms. Furthermore, these additional costs can also be borne not only by subjects, but by third parties who are related or working with subjects who are unwittingly affected by an experiment,[2] as well as experimenters and experimenters' assistants.

In most ethical evaluations of experiments, experiments are seen as acceptable even with little obvious benefit, if the costs or risks from the experiment are minimal. In order to evaluate whether risks are minimal, researchers need to consider a number of things: the magnitude of the harms, the likelihood of the harms, the standards by which the risks are evaluated, the anonymity provided to subjects, and the extent to which subjects have given their informed consent and/or are debriefed after an experiment. The first two aspects (magnitude and probability of harm) should be seen as working in tandem. That is, some things are highly unlikely, but if they occur they are significantly harmful; other things have a high likelihood, but if they occur are not that harmful. Hence both dimensions of harms need to be evaluated.

The typical standard for evaluation of whether a risk is minimal used for social science experiments is "daily life." If a risk is similar to that experienced by subjects in their daily life, then it is deemed minimal. But when we conduct experiments with subjects outside of our own culture or region, then whose daily life is relevant? If we draw subjects who are living in a precarious environment with serious everyday dangers does that allow us to subject them to equivalent dangers in our experiments? Or are there some things that are not allowed, regardless of the nature of the subjects' everyday life? Such reasoning might lead a researcher to conclude that the standard should be his or her own safe environment in order to be fair to the subjects. Note that we assume that as researchers we come from cultures with freedom of speech, expression, and religion, and regions without violent conflict.

Yet, suppose that an experimental manipulation we wish to conduct is typical and normal in our own daily life, but abnormal and unusual (and dangerous) in our subjects' daily lives. Then using our lives as the standard may be insufficient. It is our view that researchers should consider both. Is the manipulation they wish to conduct of minimal risk in their own lives *and* the lives of their subjects? If the answer is yes, then the manipulation is acceptable. If the answer is no to just one, then the experimenter should reconsider why he or she wants to conduct the experiment and how the experiment might be altered to make it minimal risk using either standard.

Finally anonymity, informed consent, and debriefing are important methods by which experimentalists can reduce risks when there are concerns that they may be more than minimal. Anonymity gives subjects privacy in their actions and may allow them to make choices that are outside of what they would do in their daily lives. This privacy makes their choices not as risky as they may potentially be if made in public. Anonymity requires that researchers give special protections to subjects in experimental designs and may mean that experimenters may not gather individual data but only aggregate data that would be impossible to match to specific subjects. Informed consent gives subjects the ability to choose for themselves whether to take an action that is not typical in their daily lives and debriefing gives them the opportunity to see the experimental manipulation for what it was. Informed consent requires that researchers cannot conduct an experiment with deception or nontransparent purposes or alternatively that experiments with deception and non-transparencies provide subjects with appropriate debriefings.

To summarize, in social science, the benefits we can estimate at the time we conduct an experiment are likely negligible and cannot generally justify experiments that involve more than minimal risks. Hence, the key determinant in evaluating a social science experiment is whether it is minimal risk. In determining this, the researcher needs to consider the types of harms that can occur as well as the probability that such harms can occur, and evaluate them against their own daily life as well as those of the subjects. The researcher should also consider the risks to nonsubjects (either through their connections to subjects or their connections to the researcher). When an experiment involves minimal risks for all those involved, then it is (usually) ethically justified. Anonymity, informed consent, and debriefings are important features in experimental designs that can help minimize risks when there are concerns that the risks are more than minimal.

We now turn to our four types of experiments on religion and the ethical issues involved.

4.3   Measuring Religious Beliefs

The strength and sincerity of religious beliefs are difficult to measure. Beliefs are personal, subjective, and open to interpretation. When asked directly whether or not a belief is sacred, a subject may respond that it is, simply because they believe such a response must be appropriate, regardless as to whether they truly hold the belief as sacred or not. When confronted with a real choice, however, they may not behave in a manner consistent with the belief being sacred. Sheikh et al. (2012), for example, give subjects pairs of diametrically opposed options such as "I believe in God" versus "I don't believe in God." On its face, one would consider the answer to be a sacred belief, but the authors go one step further. They ask subjects if there is a hypothetical dollar amount they could be offered to change their opinion. If the subject refuses to place a dollar value on their belief, then that belief is interpreted to be sacred.

As these dollar amounts are not paid, this choice is no different than a subject facing a question of her religious beliefs in daily life, as may happen in some cultures. However, if the experiment is conducted using subjects in an environment or culture where such a question is highly unusual or dangerous, then the experiment may involve more than minimal risk and may be unethical. For instance, in several countries with official state religions, apostasy (renunciation of a religious belief) is illegal. Particularly with the frame of a cash payment, even a hypothetical one, a respondent could misinterpret the question as an offensive challenge of his or her faith. Hence, the key factor in such an experiment is the extent to which these questions are not dangerous and are normal in the subjects' own environment and culture.

Similar to the study by Sheikh et al. (2012), Berns et al. (2012) also ask for hypothetical amounts subjects require to change beliefs. Before the experiment, subjects are told that at the end they will need to sign a statement of their personal values that reflects possible payments made to change their beliefs. However, the authors also actually pay subjects to "change" beliefs using a Becker, Groot and Marschak (1964) auction. That is, subjects were asked to name a price between 1 and 100 dollars for which they would be willing to "change" their beliefs. Subjects could also refuse to name a price. For each belief, a price was randomly drawn from 1 to 100, inclusive. If the randomly drawn price was higher than or equal to the price a subject stated that she would be willing to accept to change her belief, then the subject was paid her stated price and her statement of values was updated before signing. Refusal to name a price is again interpreted as considering the answer to be sacred, whereas the prices provided a measure of the strength of religious beliefs. At the end of the experiment, subjects were given a printout of their stated beliefs, including any new positions that they had been paid to take, and were required to sign it.[3]

Although doubt can be cast on whether subjects truly did change the beliefs for which they were paid, the experiment raises a number of ethical issues. The experimenters changed some subjects' beliefs and/or some subjects lied, either of which may place them at odds with their faith. We will deal with the ethical concerns of changing subjects' beliefs in Section 4.5 below. Here we first ask, assuming that the beliefs were not actually changed, whether or not it is unethical to induce subjects to lie about their beliefs. Again, in some cultures, such inducements can also occur in daily life. For example, subjects may wish to participate in a organized activity or receive a scholarship or other financial incentive for which membership is restricted to those with given religious beliefs; for instance, many Jewish young people participate in free trips to Israel, although some may question the strength of their beliefs in Judaism. However, such inducements may be seen as untoward and unusual in other cultures. So, again, the key factor is the extent to which these sorts of inducements occur in the subjects' daily lives, not just in our own.

Sheikh et al. (2012) conduct an additional study using a panel of Palestinian youths to test whether participation in religious rituals affects whether preferences are transformed into sacred values. Rather than examining whether subjects place monetary values on answers, they present well-known Palestinian positions (such as the right of return) and ask if subjects are willing to take a different opinion if it would be of great benefit to the Palestinian people. Presumably, less sacred beliefs are those that subjects are more willing to abandon to help their group. The experiment then tests the relative weight subjects place on their group identity, independent of their religious beliefs. Given that the subjects were granted anonymity and that the data has been kept private, the experimenters attempted to reduce the risks faced by the subjects in this particular experiment.

However, the same study could not necessarily be conducted in a region where subjects find it dangerous to openly discuss religion. Challenging religious beliefs or asking subjects if they are willing to change their beliefs could be interpreted as proselytization. Advocating a religion other than that officially adopted by the government is illegal in some countries. This type of experiment could place the enumerator in legal jeopardy or lead to violence if the act is reported to religious authorities or militia groups. Participants face the same dangers if their data becomes public, either intentionally, by confiscation, or by accident. Although informed consent and anonymity may help reduce these risks, they may still be sizable.

In these situations, it may be advisable to use indirect measures. Fair, Malhotra and Shapiro (2010) approach sensitive issues in Pakistan by asking non-controversial questions that closely proxy for the intended measure. For example, the type of school that respondents in the region would like their child to attend is taken as an indicator of the respondent's religious sect. As part of a related project, Blair et al. (2013) examine support for militant organizations, using an endorsement experiment. Directly asking about opinions toward such organizations can be dangerous, and it can also lead subjects to give what they believe will be the socially desirable response. To avoid this problem, the authors ask subjects about their opinions on a series of policy issues, but a subset of participants are told that policies are supported by a particular Islamist militant organization.

However, in this experiment there is a risk in the deception in which the experimentalists engage. Many experimentalists, such as ourselves, who come from the tradition of political economics, do not use deception in experiments, primarily for methodological reasons. That is, if subjects are deceived in a given experiment, then they may be less likely to want to participate in other experiments. More importantly, they may not believe what they are told in other experiments. Those who have been deceived may share their experiences with other potential subjects who have not been deceived and the use of deception could become common knowledge in a subject pool (see Morton and Williams 2010 for a discussion of deception).

In contrast, experimentalists who come from a political psychology background often engage in deception in their experiments because they believe that deception is the only way to evaluate the questions they are concerned with studying.[4] Is deception itself unethical?[5] In terms of daily life, deceptions certainly occur in almost all cultures and environments. But deceptions vary in terms of potential harms. So deception is not itself unethical, but some deceptions, which have high potential harms and greater than minimal risks, are unethical. What are the potential harms due to the deception in the Blair et al. (2013) experiment? Insofar as militant groups have known policy positions, researchers risk spreading misinformation about those platforms and affecting opinion by using incorrect labels. If respondents are told that a militant group supports a pro-social agenda, they may not believe it—but if they do, they may leave with a more positive view of the group. Alternatively, linking a pro-social policy with an extremist group may decrease support for the policy. Given the use of local enumerators to promote trust and the low levels of education among respondents, in this experiment it could be important to debrief subjects to remove any effects of misinformation from the deception.

4.4 Framing Questions and Priming Beliefs

A vast literature in political psychology uses various frames and primes to alter the weight that subjects place on attitudes and values. In this literature, it is useful to distinguish framing and priming from persuasion. Framing is the presentation of a stimulus in a manner that affects how it is interpreted by a respondent, while priming is presenting a stimulus in order to affect how a later stimulus is interpreted. Practically speaking, a survey question may be framed so that the respondent (consciously or unconsciously) is more likely to place additional emphasis on the concept of interest. For example "Do you approve of the job X is doing as President?" can be reworded to "Do you approve or disapprove of the job X is doing as President?" to remove any potential positive bias. Similarly, some survey-based studies present a piece of information (like a news article) and then ask a series of survey questions. The information is given so that subjects are primed to think about that information when forming answers.

In social science experiments, neither framing nor priming is intended to change the beliefs of the subject. Absent of the immediate context, the subject should be left unaffected. As a result, such experiments differ from the deliberate framing and priming present in some media, in that it does not intend to persuade.

Indeed, some studies make use of bias in the media (campaign ads, editorials, etc.) to observe its effect on attitudes.

One such example is Weber and Thornton (2012). The authors study whether the embedding of religious symbols in campaign ads primes religious traditionalism and also if providing information about the candidate reduces this effect. All subjects are shown a real campaign ad for a candidate running for a US Senate seat. Some subjects are given the ad, but without references to God or religious values (the control), while other view the original ad (the prime). Before seeing the ad, some subjects are shown a modified version of the candidate's website to provide policy information.

Subjects are anonymous and choose privately. Because the provided materials are true and naturally occurring, this experiment is perhaps the least ethically problematic type one can conduct on religion. However, some studies seek to avoid confounds by employing hypothetical candidates. Campbell, Green and Layman (2011) present information about candidates and then add (or not) religious labels and wording. This use is not misinformation, because the candidates themselves are fake. Similarly, Pepinsky, Liddle and Mujani (2012) ask subjects about hypothetical parties that may wish to implement Islamic law. There is no harm, because the nonexistent parties cannot be falsely labeled. In either case, subjects do not complete the study with any incorrect beliefs about real candidates or parties. The net effect could even be positive. McCauley (2013) presents persuasive videos to subjects in the Ivory Coast aimed at uniting Christians and Muslims. In all cases, persuasive speeches are made by professional actors who dressed and identified themselves as politicians from opposing parties or as Christian and Muslim leaders. Beyond the deception of using actors to present the arguments, there is minimal harm in presenting positive arguments that a real leader may or may not make.[6]

McCauley (2010), as part of a dissertation project, produces mock radio news reports in Ghana and Cote d'Ivoire, and manipulates whether ethnic or religious groups are mentioned. While it is unclear whether the news reports are deceptive, a focus group is used to make the reports as realistic as possible. The intent is not to prime positive or negative affect toward the group, but rather to manipulate the salience of religion or ethnicity. It appears that the news reports are well designed and the study also has the advantage of exploiting natural variation. Religious differences are more conflictual in Cote d'Ivoire than in Ghana.

In addition to answering survey questions, subjects then participate in a version of the Dictator Game. The subject is given an endowment of money and asked how much of that endowment she would like to anonymously give to a receiver. As a treatment, receivers are labeled with a first or last name (not both) that suggests the subject's religious or ethnic group identification. In this experiment, McCauley intended to give the money as promised and thus did not intentionally deceive the subjects. However, after conducting the experiment, he chose to instead give the money to charity to prevent wealth effects and the revelation of identities. In a small community, the dictator and receiver could quickly learn each others' identities, which could have negative social repercussions if the dictator had given little or create a sense of obligation if she had been generous. The conflict between the need to maintain anonymity and the need to avoid deception is a conflict that can often be avoided, with additional preparation. For example, the receiver could have been a real person located in a distant area or, alternatively, the dictator could have been tasked with how much to share with an ethnically/religiously oriented charity.

As a related issue, researchers must also be aware of how their studies may affect government or NGO initiatives. In regions of ethnic or religious tension, there may be active reconciliation programs. A researcher who deceives subjects could decrease the willingness of subjects to engage with these programs, especially if the researcher holds a governmental or NGO affiliation.

Finally, just as religious beliefs can be primed by researchers, they can also be primed by naturally occurring events or events out of the control of the experimenter. Religious calendars, for example, provide predictable times at which subjects are religiously primed by observances. Akay, Karabulut and Martinsson (2013) conducted a survey experiment in Turkey on Leylat alQadr (the Night of Power) during Ramadan and again on a day outside of Ramadan. They find some modest effects of religious festivals, but the important feature is the natural priming of beliefs. In situations where openly discussing religious beliefs could be dangerous to the subject or enumerator, the timing of studies could be sufficient to prime subjects. Indeed, charities have used this fact to increase donations and organize campaigns around when contributors are either required or otherwise predisposed to give. There is no deception or overt persuasion. This method is a potentially excellent way of unobtrusively obtaining primed subjects, without the experimenter providing the prime.

4.5   Manipulating Religious Beliefs

Rather than seeking simply to prime religious beliefs, some experiments take an additional step and attempt to alter those beliefs (as in the Berns et al. 2012 experiment discussed in Section 4.3). Some may contend that this task is unethical for researchers to attempt. The researcher cannot know the true state of the world as to the existence or nonexistence of a higher being or beings. As such, any change of a subject's faith could cause harm. However, all people may encounter challenges to their beliefs in everyday life. In some societies, there is open debate on religion, but everywhere in the world subjects experience events that cause them to doubt their beliefs (or reaffirm them). Thus, the experimenter is often putting the subject through no more risk than she would experience outside of the experiment in many cultures and environments.

As an example, Gervais and Norenzayan (2012) test for the link between analytical thinking and religious disbelief. Subjects are put through tasks that subtly require or induce higher level thinking, and then researchers measure the religious beliefs of subjects. While the long-term effects of study participation on subjects are likely minimal, the implication is that if critical thinking causes an increase in disbelief, then putting subjects through analytical exercises could change their beliefs. However, higher level thinking cannot be considered a harm to subjects (it is, after all, something that we would like to encourage in our students).

Making the manipulation more obvious, Shariff, Cohen and Norenzayan (2008) expose subjects to arguments against the existence of God, in the form of an essay from Richard Dawkins, a noted skeptic. Subject religiosity is then measured using an Implicit Association Test (IAT) and self reports. Again, the risk to subjects is no different from reading a newspaper or watching television in many cultures as long as subjects are allowed and able to leave the experiment and not participate (much as they may turn off the television or not read an article whose content they find distasteful). The net effect of exposure to criticism may be for subjects to question their beliefs, but this effect is not the responsibility of the researcher. The subject could just as easily choose to ignore the argument, which is simply the stated opinion of a well-known figure. However, it may be the case that in some cultures and environments such exposure may not be available or normal in everyday life, in which case the experiment may be unethical because it does not meet the standard of what may occur in the subjects' own daily life (and it may be dangerous for subjects to be given such materials or to be seen with such materials).

It is more ambiguous when researchers provide knowingly false information. Gebauer and Maio (2012) provide subjects with fabricated articles. One states that astrophysics has proven the existence of God, while the other informs subjects that astrophysics cannot provide such proof. The former is certainly deceptive, although the latter may be as well. The authors attempt to mitigate this potential harm with funnel debriefing to prompt subjects to express skepticism in the information provided.

Assuming that subjects are exposed to such material in their daily lives, then the ethical question in this case is limited to the use of deception and whether debriefing is sufficient to remove the harm. Unlike studies that provide biased or false political information that can be remedied with a balanced or factual counterpoint, a study of this type could lead subjects to question their beliefs. A subject may learn that the information was false, but she may also have observed how easy it would have been for her to forsake her beliefs. She may even have given a price she was willing to accept to agree to change a belief (Sheikh et al. 2012, Berns et al. 2012). This experience could be profoundly disturbing to some subjects. Care should be taken, particularly in situations or locations where directly questioning religious beliefs would be dangerous.

4.6 Experimental Tasks Variant With Beliefs

Finally, there are experiments where the intent is not to directly study religion, but where the religion or culture of subjects are at odds with the experimental task. Asking subjects to participate could cause offense and lead subjects to report the case to legal or religious officials. This risk may potentially rise and fall with proximity to religious holidays. Consider three tasks that are commonly employed in experimental economics: incentivized measures of risk preference, the Public Goods Game, and the Trust Game.

In Islam, it is *haram* (forbidden) to wager money in the hopes of winning a larger amount. Incentivized measures of risk preference like Multiple Price Lists (Holt and Laury 2002) often do precisely that. The task is for subjects to choose between a series of pairs of lotteries. Option A has a small gap between the high and low payoff, while the gap in option B is large. In each pair, one of the two is a relatively safe option, while the other is relatively risky. From pair to pair, the gaps between the expected payoffs of the two options are varied. Risk preferences are measured by the point at which subjects switch from option A to option B. The last pair of choices is between two certain outcomes, but each of the previous choices requires the subject to participate in lotteries. In most experimental laboratories, and even some in the Middle East (Bohnet, Herrmann and Zeckhauser 2010), the use of lotteries is not a problem, but issues could arise in the field.

An alternative is to use non-incentivized measures. It is always possible to at least indirectly ask subjects whether they consider themselves to be more risk-seeking or risk-averse. The tradeoff is that we are often interested in measures of behavior, rather than stated attitudes.[7] Incentivized lotteries are preferred, particularly in economics, as they involved observed behavior. One possible solution is to ask about behavior the subject would engage in outside the lab. An example might be how subjects choose between commuting options. Would they select a means that will surely get them to their destination in one hour or would they attempt an alternate route that could take thirty minutes in a best-case scenario, but could take three hours in heavy traffic. This task could be incentivized (essentially framing the incentivized lotteries as a choice made in everyday life) and tailored to the location of the experiment, using local routes and modes of transportation.

Another possibility, used by Rogers (2014), is to implement incentivized measures (like Multiple Price Lists and the Bomb Risk Elicitation Task), but with the subject never facing personal stakes. The subject does not risk any of her own money and does not directly benefit from a fortunate outcome, but rather makes choices that impact how much money the experimenter will donate to charity. Insofar as warm glow is a component of the utility function, risk choices made for charity may be a practical, although imperfect, substitute.

The prohibition against lotteries can also make for more inherent difficulties in incentivized experiments using randomization. That is, if subjects are randomly assigned roles or otherwise affected by random draws and these randomizations affect their payoffs, then the entire experiment may be considered problematic for some subjects. It is possible to interpret a fortuitous outcome of randomization as having engaged in and won a lottery. Because randomization is one of the two main methods by which experiments provide causal inferences (the second method is control, see Morton and Williams 2010), designing experiments that do not have this problem can be difficult. One method used by Linardi et al. (2014) is to make these choices in advance and to write them on a white or chalk board prior to the experiment. The choices are then covered by opaque pieces of paper and revealed to subjects when the time is necessary. Subjects are simply told that the choices have been made in advance and will be revealed later. The danger with this method is that the experimenter loses some control over the subjects' subjective beliefs on the likelihood of different choices; the presumption is that subjects implicitly believe that these choices have been made randomly.

Beyond matters of risk, the Public Goods Game and Trust Game may also be deemed be *haram* in some areas, depending on how they are interpreted. Researchers have been able to conduct them in the past (Johansson-Stenman, Mahmud and Martinsson (2009)), but the possibility of doing so depends on the population. The issue is *riba* (interest). In Islam, an individual may not increase their capital without providing a good or service.[8] In each of these games, subjects are asked to contribute an amount that is then multiplied by an efficiency factor and shared with another subject (or several others). Because the efficiency factor is arbitrarily imposed and involves no real production, it may be interpreted as unclean interest.

One solution, related to Rogers (2014), is to give the option for subjects to donate proceeds to charity. In spite of the prohibition on earning interest, there is an Islamic finance industry. Some financial products do include a degree of interest, but any earnings are purified by a donation to charity. It is also permissible to engage in profit or loss sharing investments as well. By permitting subjects to donate earnings, a researcher may reduce the risk of subject refusal. Again, care should be taken to remain in accordance with local laws and customs. In most cases, problems for both researchers and subjects can be avoided by properly obtaining informed consent and by seeking the relevant local approvals.

4.7 Conclusion

Whether an experiment is or is not ethical depends on the researchers' answers to two questions:

- Is the experiment ethically designed and executed?
- Is the topic one on which experiments can be conducted?

The first question requires preparation and care. It is our contention that ethical studies can be designed to examine almost any topic of interest, if the researcher is clever. The design stage is the most important stage in an experiment because it is in the design of the experiment that a researcher uses random assignment and control to tease out causal inferences not possible using naturally occurring data. The better the experimental design, the easier and less messy the analysis of the data. Similarly, the more effort a researcher spends on the design in considering ethical issues, the less likely the experimenter will find his or her work questioned on its ethics ex post. Creating an ethical experimental design may involve using proxy measures and non-standard approaches such as framing lotteries, but it may also involve exploiting natural variation. All studies require a degree of compromise in design, particularly if the research topic is sensitive or even forbidden to openly discuss. There may be a tradeoff among validity, ethics, and cost, but it is the duty of the researcher to strike the proper balance.

We also believe that in the design of an experiment, deception should be avoided wherever possible. As discussed above (and in another chapter in this volume), there are methodological reasons for avoiding deception and in economics it is standard throughout the discipline to avoid deception. Although we do not argue that deception in experiments is in itself unethical, in studies on religion it is important to avoid doing harm that can not be reversed by debriefing. Risks to subjects and experimenters should be no greater than what they would experience in everyday life, which is culturally dependent. Challenging the religious beliefs of subjects may be acceptable in some societies, but elsewhere in the world, it may lead to legal sanctions or physical confrontation.

The second question, if it is ethical to experimentally study religion, is open to some debate. While measurement of beliefs and their effects on behavior generates little objection, the active manipulation of beliefs through framing, priming, and persuasion can be construed as fundamentally wrong (Batson (1977)). Yeatts and Asher (1979) respond that where true experiments are possible, it would be unethical not to perform them. If researchers believe that religious beliefs produce benefits or harms to subjects, then the gold standard of study is true experimentation. While we, the authors of this chapter, do not pretend to be the final authority on whether a given study is or is not ethical, we can provide practical guidance to researchers attempting to design studies. As there is still the afore-discussed debate as to whether or not it is ethical to experiment on religious beliefs, no design will be immune from criticism, but researchers should do their best to meet the following criteria:

1.   The experiment exposes subjects and enumerators to no more than minimal risk. The acceptable level of risk to both is either that which the subject would face in her daily life, or that which the researcher would face in her own, whichever is less.
2.   Subjects do not leave the experiment with misinformation.

3. Subjects are not psychologically or socially harmed by the experiment.
4. Subjects are only asked to complete tasks for which they have given informed consent.
5. Researchers do not negatively affect the ability of future researchers to conduct studies.
6. Researchers do not negatively affect the ability of governments and organizations to provide public goods.

In the end, researchers are responsible for making defensible choices in the design and execution of their work. However, researchers do not make these decisions alone. Many institutions have the equivalent of human subjects committees or higher authorities and peer review systems, which also evaluate the ethical issues involved. Ultimately, we must consider the well-being of all involved. As direct benefits to subjects of social science studies are negligible, the potential for harm must be carefully considered. We cannot allow ourselves to forget that, in the eyes of some subjects and their societies, souls are at stake.

Notes

1 A second principal reason is methodological. Experimentation relies on random selection and random assignment. While random selection from a population is possible, the random assignment of religious beliefs is not. However, random assignment of subjects to various frames and primes can change the weights that subjects place on religious beliefs, as demonstrated by McCauley (2013), Pepinsky, Liddle and Mujani (2012), Campbell, Green and Layman (2011), and Weber and Thornton (2012), and at least temporarily alter those beliefs, as demonstrated by Gervais and Norenzayan (2012) and Shariff, Cohen and Norenzayan (2008).

2 As an example, if a subject receives information, she may pass it along to a third party and cite the experimenter as the source. The third party would be less able to assess the information's validity and would be unavailable for debriefing. Alternatively, a subject may be psychologically affected by an experiment, which in turn has a negative effect on his or her work or family life.

3 It is not clear if there were repercussions for not signing the document.

4 It is our view that in many cases deception can be avoided through clever experimental designs that researchers fail to consider. That is, one typical experiment with deception in political psychology is to provide subjects with some information about supposed "real" candidates to allow for the researcher to vary that information systematically. But an alternative approach is to have one "real" candidate and then a set of ones who are "hypothetical" but only one dimension different from the "real" choice. Subjects are told the probability that the candidate they evaluate is the one that is "real" but not whether that candidate is actually the "real" one or not. In this way, the experimenter measures subjects' evaluations without deceiving the subjects. See Morton and Williams (2010) for further discussion.

5 Of course, there is a long debate about whether deception might be ethical in situations where the truth can lead to harm, or whether lying itself is a breach of trust in human relations. Our question here is limited to whether deception is unethical in experiments.

6 Another chapter in this volume deals with the ethics and pitfalls of deception.
7 For a discussion of the difference between experiments in political economy and those in political psychology, see Dickson (2011).
8 Speculation in commodities is also forbidden and could lead to complaints in market experiments, but a cursory search reveals no examples of field research where such speculation has been a problem.

5

PRISON STATES AND GAMES OF CHICKEN

Jesse Driscoll

> You are going to get a 23-year-old Azeri kid mutilated, and afterwards I don't know how you are going to live with yourself.
>
> David Laitin, to the author, August 2008

Authoritarian governance practices represent an important research frontier for comparative politics graduate students. Certain regimes rule through a mix of surveillance, fear, and violence. Many researchers in the subdiscipline agree that there are normative reasons to know more about how these practices function. Experiments are one type of tool in a researcher's arsenal to understand the kinds of behaviors that political institutions incentivize. Scholars will continue to think hard about how to safely and responsibly conduct field experiments in challenging environments because they promise to provide our research community with greater traction on causal impacts.

This chapter is primarily addressed to the next generation of graduate students who are contemplating fieldwork in "hard authoritarian" regimes, and may be thinking about running experiments. The thrust of my argument can be easily summarized: You are basically on your own. If you choose to spend your time in graduate school living in dangerous places—and I believe that there are good reasons to do this—one of the consequences is that you will probably, with time, come to disdain the authority of the bureaucratic entities at your home institution tasked with helping you weigh risks. You will, with time, become *the* area expert on what life is really like in "your" particular poorly governed corner of the planet. No one—not even your dissertation chair or your other advisors—will be better positioned than you to evaluate the risks of whatever experimental interventions you are proposing. With that in mind, this chapter is organized around a few questions you should ask, with a bit of distance, before you commit yourself. They are not meant to be "gotcha" questions. They do not have easy answers. You should take some time to argue with yourself about them. To convey a sense of how conflicted I am on these questions, and how ambivalent I am about the possibility of a generalized rule-set or regime to incentivize good behavior, this chapter is written in the first person.

A secondary audience for this chapter is the community of mentors (and regulators) tasked with restraining the ambitions of the first audience. Most experimental research interventions have historically sold themselves as positive-sum enterprises: Everyone wins, but a control group may win less. However, at the current moment it is reasonable to think out loud—not just in anonymous referee reports, but also in public meetings—whether this analogy actually holds when our research questions concern raw power in the form of zero-sum distributional politics backed by guns. There may be different stakes associated with accidents and miscalculations, and not just for study participants, requiring different ethical frames. This chapter draws attention to two different kinds of analogies that are sure to invoke moral discomfort for most audiences: *prison states* and *games of chicken*. Research designs that involve cooperation with state authorities in order to build state capacity can be compared to constructing social science–enabled police states, or "prison states" (the catchier moniker). At the other extreme, research designs that eschew cooperation with the state and instead work with NGOs to encourage low-intensity confrontation with state authorities are open to the charge of irresponsibly encouraging "games of chicken" against undemocratic regimes, with any serious costs borne by locals. In their most extreme forms, these paired criticisms suggest that some states are so badly governed that conducting any social scientific research at all should be discouraged. By giving voice to these considerations, I hope to inoculate the discipline against extremist articulations of persuasive reactionary arguments.

5.1 The View From 2015: Confessions From the Experimental Frontier

I am neither an ethicist nor a particularly rabid experimentalist. I spent most of my time in graduate school working on questions related to violence and civil war settlement. In practice, this meant spending a great deal of time living in the former Soviet Union (namely, Georgia, Tajikistan, and Kyrgyzstan), and more recently working closely with the Somali-speaking population of San Diego. The research design of my first book project involved extensive ethnographic research and long-form interviews with former combatants in Georgia and Tajikistan.[1] In 2012, I was the principal investigator for the first representative survey of the city of Mogadishu in 25 years.[2] These observational research designs required calculated risks with my own safety, the safety of my research team, and my human subjects. I weighed risks as best I could. I sought advice from trusted friends and mentors and the Institutional Review Board (IRB). I ultimately opted to not publish certain data and to abandon certain research projects when I deemed things were getting too dangerous. I do not think anybody has been hurt as a result of my research, and I am glad for that.

The subdiscipline of comparative politics is a competitive and psychologically trying subfield of political science. It has historically valued the labor of young scholars who learn difficult languages, travel to uncomfortable places, live for long periods of time far away from loved ones, and eventually bring back data from under-studied parts of the planet. We "walk the walk," serving as living reminders that if one really wants to know more about the world outside the ivory tower, at some point it becomes necessary to shoulder the burden of going there. Fieldwork is often lonely, as researchers cultivate the self-reliance necessary to engage for months (often years) in distant (often hostile) political environments. Gratification for empirical data collected is often delayed years or decades. But more than the other subfields of political science, comparative politics dangles the promise of getting inside other cultures. We respect and reward efforts to creatively break down the subject-object distinction across language barriers. We tell our students to leave the comfort of the academy, get their hands dirty, and see for themselves how theories interact with the messy details of the real world. The rise of the experimental paradigm suggests that they will be increasingly rewarded for attempts to tinker with the world they find.

Search committees and tenure committees tend to place great value on demonstrations of scholastic aptitude. Scholars who take questions of identification seriously and demonstrate a "go-get-it-done-then-get-it-published" attitude are, as an empirical matter, more likely to rise successfully through the ranks than academic laborers who become enmeshed in moral quagmires and delay publication of work. I am sorry to report that the implication of this may actually be a prisoner's dilemma for professionally vulnerable untenured researchers. Even controlling for subfield, some researchers are going to be more risk-acceptant and others more risk-averse. And so long as the discipline continues to reward entrepreneurialism and creativity, it may simply be the case that the risk-acceptant young researchers have a competitive advantage in the marketplace of ideas. And perhaps—just perhaps—that is as it should be.

The primary institutional entity tasked with serving as a check on the ambitions of graduate students is the Institutional Review Board (IRB). The IRB derives its moral authority from the claim that it protects the interests of research subjects. The IRB has the authority to evaluate researchers' ethical intuitions, despite the fact that the researcher will almost always have a comparative advantage in the "ground truth" of the research site.[3] I believe that everyone involved in this process has the best intentions. But it is a mistake to pretend that there is interest convergence or incentive compatibility where none actually exists.

Professionally vulnerable young scholars are explicitly told that they will make no progress up the tenure ladder if they do not produce work that lands in top outlets. This makes for a host of "motivated misperceptions" when it comes to assessing risks. If cowboy behaviors are modeled by professionally successful faculty, the lessons will leak to graduate students. The IRBs tasked with limiting university liability, by contrast, are inherently conservative. This can make for an adversarial relationship. Little about checking in with an IRB that only convenes once per month is incentive-compatible for scholars attempting to improvise solutions in rural areas of a developing country.

I currently work at a policy school that credentials terminal MA students. Many are interested in working in the field of international development, and their intuitions seem to be that so long as foreign aid flows from the core to the periphery—in the name of security or charity—the justifications for those aid flows will be articulated in a results-oriented language. Very few of our students matriculate to PhD programs, but our methods sequence—which is state of the art—leaves very little doubt in the minds of our students about what they ought (normatively) to be doing: They should be randomizing what interventions they can, when they can, as best they can. Our best students take these skills and ethical intuitions to very well-funded actors that *do not have IRBs*—investment banks, multinational corporations, advertising conglomerates, Internet start-ups, democracy promotion NGOs, the US military, and the like. The world outside of the ivory tower moves pretty fast. A lot of people in the future are going to get into the business of convincing constituencies in embassies, militaries, and the NGO community to randomize programming. The unexpected results of gradual experimentation will almost certainly teach us all a great deal about the world.

So in summary: I really do believe that there are normative reasons to keep experimenting, and no obvious way to put brakes on the train. Given this constraint, the following two sections are meant to draw attention to ways that the experimental ethos might interact with authoritarian practices in a way that that pose ethical challenges for researchers.

5.2 Four Questions

I think that a decentralized regulatory regime—one in which everyone asks themselves difficult questions as they course-correct in the field—is superior to the feasible alternatives. It is not clear that a centralized regime to gauge the ethics of research is either feasible or desirable. When one multiplies the number of research institutions by the myriad possible combinations of field sites, dependent variables, and experimental methodologies, and complicates the picture further by acknowledging the vast diversity of leverage-able personal networks and potential second- and third-tier harms, we are suddenly in a space that is so vast that it hardly seems useful to generalize about best practices. Abkhazia is not Somaliland.

The best practices of doing research on elections in Afghanistan may not travel even as far as Tajikistan, let alone Kenya or Russia. India's military is not Mexico's municipal police force. Internet monitoring works differently in Turkmenistan than in China. Democracy promotion NGOs work very differently in Burma than their counterparts do in Bahrain. The basic norm governing the scope and scale of interventions at the research frontier certainly seems to be: "Let the area specialists, who can gauge risks best, figure out what they think they can get away with and try to get published afterwards." The magnification of the possible harms emerging from field experiments would not serve the interests of the discipline. Most experimental interventions tend to be very small, and cannot possibly do much harm. Large interventions are almost always randomizations of practices that happen all the time, or are representative of the kinds of things that were probably going to happen anyway. No one has any idea how to assess the probability of a black swan-style "nuclear" failure.[4] The people who are potentially threatened in a "black swan" scenario, where everything goes as wrong as it could possibly go, could easily be people who are not subjects.[5]

For graduate students reading this, let me make the point as explicitly as possible: It is *your* job to assess these risks and stop the project if these risks are serious—not the job of the IRB. The IRB framework is not always going to be able to help you sort through these questions (and, as a community, we should not try to force them to do any more work than they already are). Conducting scholarly work in authoritarian environments on politically sensitive topics while staying safe requires keeping one's eyes open and responding flexibly to highly local and contextualized variables. To their credit, many individuals who work at IRBs will readily admit that they do not have a clue about those kinds of details. So: You are basically on your own. Be really honest with yourself. You have a long memory.

Will Your Findings Legitimize Authoritarian Behaviors or Perpetuate Bad Government?

I have spent much of the last five years working on a series of projects that assess welfare outcomes in Somalia. The stakes of this research project are high, and we have found many willing allies. But these allies usually wanted something from us: They wanted evidence that what the Somali government was doing was working. And when they noticed that the evidence did not seem to support this theory, but that we were continuing the research anyway, their partnership became more and more costly.[6] I mention this particular story only to draw attention to a familiar fact: Doing work in authoritarian or badly governed societies requires taking advantage of the idealism of people who see themselves engaged in public goods provision or charity. And when we "sell" projects to these local partners, we are often tempted to pretend as if we share their assessment of an ideal outcome. (Otherwise why would we be there?)

If we are truly honest with ourselves, one of the of the important reasons that field experiments have gotten so popular is born from a logic of pure pragmatism: They are a technology that facilitates a positive-sum exchange relationship between academics (who desire original datasets) and practitioners (who want to be able to report to constituencies that they are *positive* that the programs are working). This exchange relationship can be easily overlooked if one focuses strictly on the philosophy of science arguments supporting the experimental tradition in social inquiry.[7] This pragmatic rationale also has a mercenary variant. One begins by simply noticing, as a matter of fact, that the World Bank is probably not going to stop making loans or discontinue commissioning papers. Development economists arrive to this ongoing conversation armed with the confidence that their methods produce the only kinds of answers that count. What this means, in practice, is that even if influential political science departments coordinated to put a halt to experiments because of shared ethical considerations, *the experiments would not stop and might not even slow down.* And the truth is that clever identification strategies are a more valued currency in the discipline today than in the past. Articles in the *American Political Science Review* and the *American Economics Review* do not look as different as they did two decades ago. There are real, measurable rents to being the kind of political scientist who can pinch-hit as an economist. I could be wrong, but I doubt this observation will have become obsolete any time soon.

There are many outcomes that are interesting to social scientists but that cannot be experimentally studied without cooperation from state organs (e.g., taxation; economic redistribution; the orderly production of justice; efficient counterinsurgency; the collection of social intelligence, using technologies like the census; and the functioning of the education, prison, or pension systems). In a well-functioning society, it is difficult to imagine even an observational study of most institutions without state permission. Sometimes states are principals, scholars are agents.

And none of this is a problem, really, until we notice that many states function quite a bit like prisons. One can imagine a spectrum. On one end you would find places where citizens basically elect their government and slowly shape its institutions. On the other end you would find places where the governing authority is analogous in most ways to a prison warden.[8] It is important to notice that at both ends of the spectrum, the state not only experiments but also observes—often archiving vast quantities of citizen data without their permission. The rapid proliferation of computer and smartphone technology is expanding the state's ability to do these things. As social scientists, many of us badly want these data. Such desire will lead some of us into talking ourselves into helping states—even the bad ones—to collect and analyze more data. Now: If a student hopes to someday be a principal investigator working on political violence, part of her graduate school training ought to include a serious probing of her own threshold for dealing with the agents of state security bureaucracies. My threshold is high. I invested many hours lobbying to randomize the placement of police cameras in the city of Newark. I spent two weeks with no security living in the unrecognized state of Abkhazia, attempting to secure political permissions from elites in the unrecognized government to conduct the first representative household survey since the Soviet era. Both projects would have involved substantial cooperation with "the state." Both would have involved populations that could not easily opt out of the study.[9] We have ethical intuitions that study populations that cannot easily "opt out" of the study—especially prisoners—are somehow deserving of different protections than regular subject pools. It is difficult for a researcher to extract herself from the background-level of coercion in a prison by blithely invoking the language of informed consent, once the ghosts of the Zimbardo experimental subjects have been summoned forth.[10]

As social scientists, there are reasons to be wary of the top-down, "eyes of the sovereign" perspective. The entire conversation about randomizing scarce public goods is implicated by this line of thought. It is vulgar, somehow, for the foreign observer to assume a "right to treat." But when matters of life and death are at stake, and the state is badly governed, it is not always clear that there is a local domestic moral authority to legitimize the enterprise. In some cases it is possible to argue that any findings that could serve to legitimize certain very bad states, or make these very bad states more efficient and effective at controlling their populations ("in the name of order, in the name of development, in the name of making the trains run on time . . . ") is morally compromising. When the PI doubts her own ability to publish or publicize non- or negative findings on the intervention, political compromises are being made. Every researcher is responsible for finding her own threshold of comfort for self-censorship, of course. But we would do well to notice that the hard-won ethical intuitions that IRB professionals have developed about the experimental paradigm are calibrated to the harms that can arise for subjects that reside on college campuses.

I do not have strong ethical intuitions on whether there are some states that are just *so badly governed* that we should not study them at all. The truth is there are many states with ruthless security services, whose leadership is desperate for foreign aid and hungry to validate certain outcomes for impatient donors. What "informed consent" is supposed to mean when the study is backed by a state of this kind is by no means clear.[11] In the third round of telephone call-backs to respondents residing in Somalia—individuals who had been read lengthy Somali-language consent scripts multiple times—at the end of a survey we asked respondents who they thought we were. Some of the responses were very funny and self-aware ("What do you think I am, stupid? You're researchers from a university in California! You made me sit through a three-minute script explaining that to me!"). Some were equally self-aware, but not at all funny (e.g., "You're working for the US military—you just don't realize it." "You're going to probably sell this to a NGO who is trying to decide whether or not to send aid.") An intuition that the researcher is in league with the prison warden is likely a source of bias in much of the data generated by surveys and experiments in certain places.

How Will You Publish If There's No Effect—Or, Worse, If Your Results Are "Signed Wrong"?

If the experiment is well designed and implemented with integrity, non-findings ought to be publishable. Our science is young and our theories have low predictive power. But the reality is that our discipline has a poor track record with the publication of non-findings. And today there are a lot more scholars planning RCTs than there are slots in top field journals. This means well-identified papers that are not *quite* meshing with where the gears of interest are at the time of submission will be rejected at top outlets and ultimately land in journals with low impact factors. Sometimes this is going to occur because of completely insincere ethical hand-wringing, and sometimes because of completely unjustifiable parochial interests (" . . . But what would it *mean* if our interventions were having *no effect at all*?"). The temptation to weaponize the language of ethics in the service of old-fashioned interest group politics is very real.[12]

The only field experiment I have personally overseen was conducted in Georgia in 2008, in collaboration with another then-graduate student (Daniel Hidalgo, now an Assistant Professor at MIT). In brief, it was an information dissemination RCT, intended to lower the cost of election-day malfeasance reporting. The randomization protocol worked exactly as we expected it would, and the subjects behaved in ways that were consistent with our theoretical priors. If we had stuck to our pre-committed data analysis plan, we would have written up an optimistic narrative of citizen empowerment. However, the experimental design forced us to confront an unexpected downstream effect of the intervention: For every person contacted, two people stayed home on election day. When we "went fishing" for heterogeneous treatment effects, the most plausible narrative to explain the mechanism was fear. Many Georgian citizens, especially in rural areas where the political machine was contested, were alienated by the study. We speculate that they found the increased attention to their district unnatural.[13]

For myself as a researcher, it the experiment represented an important turning point in my relationship with Georgia as a field site. I had imagined myself to be working in solidarity with NGOs against a state apparatus—but many of the subjects clearly assumed that I was working for (or with) the state. And I don't really think that the problem was a lack of local knowledge: I knew enough about shady Georgian electoral practices to design an experiment that successfully disrupted those practices. But the motives for doing this were suspect for a large percentage of the study population. Ultimately the study found its way into print.[14] But noticing that our experimental interventions were interacting with authoritarian legacies really did open a can of worms. It became clear that our donors had no idea what they were supposed to do with these findings, and that there actually is no consensus in our discipline on what should happen if experimental outcomes turn out to be normatively bad and/or genuinely unexpected.

I am not sure anyone hearing this story thinks that we ought to have stuck to our data analysis plan and wound a self-congratulatory yarn about how we increased citizen activism, just burying the unexpected suppression finding. But I am still not 100% sure how we should have reported the suppression finding. This really does bother me sometimes.

Is Your Experiment Mostly an Excuse to Engage in Confrontational Activism?

Thomas Schelling famously compared bargaining in the shadow of violence to a game of chicken, where two cars speed towards each other to see who swerves first. Most of the time at least one player swerves. But sometimes players both miscalculate the resolve of their opponent and a tragic collision occurs. In game theory, it demonstrates the idea that there are circumstances in which each player prefers not to yield to the other, but both structure their strategies to avoid the worst possible outcome that occurs when neither yields. So far, when social scientists have worked in solidarity with local activists—on election monitoring and on "get out the vote" campaigns to help opposition candidates—it has been state security entities that have swerved. We should not expect this to continue indefinitely.

My early graduate school experiences with the IRB emphasized that scholarly work can be akin to a diplomatic passport. As members of a scholarly community, we get visas, we get a number of invisible social protections, and we are expected to methodically conduct the research we set out to conduct. While this model works well for historians working in archives, it does not work nearly as well for political scientists working on contemporary party politics, contemporary voting behavior, or contemporary counterinsurgency. I am afraid that it works less well the longer a political scientist stays in the field, makes friends, and begins to see herself in solidarity with her subjects. If a scholar is inclined to fly into a country, stay for two to three weeks, conduct a few elite interviews, eat at nice restaurants, and then fly home, the diplomatic immunity model works fine. But if the researcher engages in sustained fieldwork over many years—learning local languages, unraveling the ironies of local political representation, allowing herself to cultivate empathy with human subjects and "go native"—at some point it occurs to the researcher that she might be able to actually effect social change. Once they feel that they *can* cause change, some of our students will decide that they *should* cause change. Many of us are interested in processes of social mobilization, party formation, and opposition voting, and continue to struggle with the question of whether we ought to do more than just watch on the sidelines.

Many professional political scientists self-selected into the discipline because of an interest in understanding how political structures change. Political science attracts students interested in sustained thinking about the constraints on political change, but also in testing theories about how systems can adapt to perturbations.[15] Particularly in graduate school, when the time horizons stretch out towards infinity, many choose dependent variables that can be squared with the kinds of changes they would like to see in the world. Advisors often encourage this attitude, up to a point.

But the impulse to tinker can be dangerous. A colleague once proposed putting up pro-Aliyev and anti-Aliyev stickers in randomly selected neighborhoods of Baku (the capital of Azerbaijan) and measuring how long it would take for them to get taken down. We hoped the research project would reveal something about expectations of regime autosurveillence without drawing attention to shady election practices (which we both agreed would be too dangerous to study). Over several weeks, I slowly operationalized the idea. Having sketched a formal research proposal, I finally shared the idea with my advisor, David Laitin. After careful consideration and 40 minutes of back-and-forth to reveal that I had done my due diligence on issues of identification and research design, he finally paused, looked me in the eye, and delivered the quote that provides the epigraph to this chapter. I stopped immediately and I am glad that I did. But the sequencing of events is telling and representative of the way that scholar-NGO collaborations actually unfold: First I came up with something that was do-able and interesting, then I thought about relevant literatures, next I began to plan the logistics of getting local permissions and implementation allies, then I consulted with a trusted advisor, and, had I proceeded with the project, only at the end would I have begun the process of reverse-engineering a self-righteous moral justification for IRB paperwork. I doubt that I am the only one for whom this is true.

In the best-case scenario, the rise of RCTs and the experimental ethos can serve as a tool for researchers to get a lot of early advice, interface early and often with advisors and home IRB institutions, learn the relevant local laws, acquire local allies across the spectrum of relevant civil society actors about best practices, and pre-commit to data analysis plans. But, in the context of games of chicken, all of this early work *must also be understood as a mechanism for locking-in one's commitment*. With a large organization mobilized, tenure clock pressures, and a donor waiting for results, the PI could easily come to see herself as fully committed to a confrontation with the authorities. In the worst-case scenario, certain of us will be complicit in blurring the line between anti-regime activism and the march of science. In the event of tragedy, I suspect it would take hours, not days, for certain conservative voices to opportunistically rush to claim in hindsight that "anyone could have predicted" the risks. The language of "playing God" will be invoked. "Nazi doctor" analogies are sure to follow. It would be bad for the entire discipline.

There are two kinds of disadvantages to these sorts of confrontational projects. The first have already been alluded to: As a community, we may be overdue for a high-profile incident in which we will not be able to falsify the hypothesis that it was the researchers' intervention that *caused* someone to be injured. Just off the orderly equilibrium path that we observe in authoritarian regimes, there is more violence than most people can easily conceive. Large-scale field experiments in badly governed states are already interacting with local political equilibria in ways that are well beyond our capacity to predict. My hunch is that if a cascade of unexpected events ends in violence, it will be due to the entrepreneurial labor of a very bright, ambitious, and idealistic young scholar: Someone vulnerable and hungry, trying to get out ahead of the curve, fighting the tenure clock, who has only selectively internalized the advice that has been heaped upon him or her, but who *earnestly believes* that they are working on behalf of a brutalized population that needs helping, that their position is functionally unique, that their labor is changing the world for the better.

But a second disadvantage is in many ways just as serious. Affiliation with activists risks gradually eroding our political neutrality, even without a "black swan" crisis.[16] The observer status that undergirds the diplomatic passport analogy (above) is worth preserving. My university business cards did not give me diplomatic immunity or unlimited access, but they weren't exactly cheap talk, either. When I was understood to be a neutral, scholarly observer, I think I received more access and better data. Affiliations with activists or NGOs who are "against the state" can have liabilities. A simple one is the possibility that the side you are on may change—either because the political environment changes or because your ideological predilections change. You may be compromised without your assent. (Field notes can be confiscated. Emails can be read without your knowledge or permission.) Working on politically sensitive topics invites scrutiny about your true motives—and that scrutiny can have real, tangible, negative effects on the lives of your interview subjects. I eventually stopped working in Tajikistan completely because I could not, in good conscience, answer these questions to my own satisfaction. When we can credibly present ourselves as scholars, and not activists or spies, we are at our safest—and so are our human subjects. It is very important to remember that.

Are You Really Planning to "Go Native," or Are You Collecting Exotic Passport Stamps?

Imagine a spectrum. At one end, you have non-American graduate students who have gravitated to the subdiscipline of comparative politics in order to write credibly about their home societies. They do not need to "go native"— they *are* native, and cannot jettison this status. These scholars enjoy substantial comparative advantages over their American counterparts in terms of fieldwork start-up costs: They already speak the language(s), know the history, have a "feel" for how to get things done, and may already have a network of contacts that will help them collect data. At the other end are pure technologists. These academics would never be confused with having any interest at all in going native. They may have no real knowledge of the language spoken by the experimental subjects or even be able to produce a credible map of the country. But they *do* know exactly what the paper needs to look like in order to appease reviewers, and the value of replicating experiments in different settings.

Where do you lie on this spectrum, vis-à-vis your current field site? Do you really see yourself as someone who will be back here in 5, 10, or 20 years? Or are you, in your private moments, very very uncomfortable and counting down the minutes until you can go home? If you don't exactly know, it is good to be able to admit that. Your answer will probably change with time. But it is important to appreciate that the kinds of experiments that you will consider worthwhile—worth writing grants and recruiting labor for—are different depending on where you are on this spectrum. Performances of "going native" are an unattractive result that may be inevitable in your mid-20s. As a rule: You should never forget who you actually are, because your study population certainly won't. If you are really planning on going native, it may make more sense to self-censor certain opinions so that you can go-along-and-get-along over the long haul. By contrast, it may *only* make sense to engage in confrontational activist politics in a society that you have embraced as your own. Experimentally demonstrating uncomfortable social facts is, after all, an important facet of how political science works. But you should notice, for your own ability to sleep at night, that as one gets closer to opposite ends of the spectrum *the same RCT* can be described as urgently necessary or a stupid stunt; *the same experimental study* can be described as normal science or a gratuitous waste of valuable energy.

In my experience, it is easier to talk people into collaborative research if you can credibly present yourself as someone with a real stake in getting the local story right. But once you secure local collaboration, it is very tempting to simply "parachute in" for the minimum amount of time necessary to get your name on the paper. Different approaches work for different people, but I will warn you that locals, at least in my experience, become very cautious—and very nationalistic on behalf of their co-nationals in the "control group"—when they feel that they are being experimented on. One of my graduate students, who had spent years living in Kyrgyzstan, was rebuffed in her efforts to organize a randomized roll-out of Internet service to rural areas. I have no doubt that she was capable of articulating (in fluent Russian) the canonical justifications for a lottery: a scarce public good, more transparent mechanism of selection, and all the rest. But the phrase that she kept hearing was *ne-naturalnaya*: not natural. I am speculating, but my guess is that that her Kyrgyz interlocutors understood why it would be good for this PhD's career if she could manipulate the provision of a public good to real people, but still thought the whole arrangement being proposed was . . . *nenaturalnaya*. As Jarvis Cocker observed: "Everybody hates a tourist, especially one who thinks it's all such a laugh."

5.3 Conclusion

In a decentralized self-regulating environment, academic advisors and senior scholars will have to shoulder the responsibility of policing this new frontier. Indeed, this is just an acknowledgement of a burden that they already bear. Projects are already being judged by the ethics of the research design. What is missing now is for academics to push their students to articulate an ethically defensible frame for their ongoing research. "I had IRB for this" is not going to be a sufficient answer at all. In contrast, students ought to be expected to articulate a positive case for their interventions into the lives of their subjects. (And note that this is not exactly the same thing as saying what most people currently say, which is "Well, it was going to happen anyway, so there was no additional harm to randomizing.") Senior scholars have a comparative advantage in the production of credible "area studies" wisdom—an intuitive sense for what makes some studies worth the risk, and others less so. But ultimately the arguments must be voiced by the graduate student as she learns what it means to be a PI. Senior scholars can play the guiding role, perhaps with some gentle assistance from junior scholars and allies in the IRB.

If trends persist, there is a non-zero probability that an experimental social science intervention will alter facts on the ground enough to literally change who gets shot and who does the shooting. If this happens, the discipline will confront the big question that this essay has danced around: Are there certain kinds of inputs that we simply should not randomize? If the applications of a certain kind of violence are inevitable, but the efficacy is in question, is there not a case for randomization? How about using social media, or collaboration with state security services, to apply different kinds of fear-inducing treatments to populations? It is fine to laugh all of this off as something akin to a movie plot, but if randomnistas are not wrong on the philosophy of science, isn't limiting the size or kind of intervention arbitrary? On the one hand, I suspect that many in our community would balk at endorsing the kinds of large-scale social engineering projects that Soviet social scientists engaged in.[17] On the other hand, when pressed, I am forced to admit that I would like to know many things that we do not know but are forced to act as if we do in order to make policy at present, such as whether or not UN Peacekeepers need to be armed.[18] Policy entrepreneurs would rush to assert they know the answer already, but they may be mistaken in their belief that their observational data can provide insights that are actually analogous to having run a proper experiment with a real control group.

Some of us may decide that research is too dangerous to sign off on, or too damaging to the interests of the study population (particularly for populations that cannot easily opt out of the study). If we articulate these concerns loudly and publicly, agents of risk-averse universities may find themselves obligated to stop the science. But in general there are not many mechanisms to hold risk-acceptant colleagues to risk-averse standards, even in the same department at the same institution. In the short term, I do not see any reason that referee reports, combined with old-fashioned naming and shaming at academic meetings, cannot steer our ship. Disagreements should be aired. In this give-and-take, graduate students will have the chance to hear different points of view and then vote with their feet, "forum shopping" for advisors who are optimally paired with the students' risk profile. In the worst-case scenario, our discipline may balkanize into do-ers and scolders. I have no doubt that the discipline will survive.

I firmly believe that inquiry into the ugly facets of politics, such as political violence, civil war, intergenerational poverty, and racial discrimination, is normatively defensible. Most of us believe that the rigorous application of the scientific method to social diseases provides a host of direct and indirect goods to liberal society. All of the potential disadvantages sketched above could easily be outweighed by the social benefits associated with pushing the frontiers of social science research. And all of the potential disadvantages sketched above could easily be outweighed by the creation of transnational civil society linkages, enabled by technology and a great deal of volunteerism from within our discipline. Many of us will continue to do experimental science while imagining that in the future citizens in badly governed states will feel a bit more protected, and governments a bit less likely to act with impunity, because of our labor. It is a reassuring sentiment, even if the evidence is mixed.

Notes

1 Driscoll (2015).
2 Driscoll and Lidow (2014).
3 IRB practices have evolved in a way that are designed to shield research institutions from legal liability, and tend to be staffed with people who want to help researchers think through potentially negative downstream consequences of their projects. The scholar must submit to a set of lengthy trainings, occasionally change the research design, and in general provide evidence that the PI has thought about a standardized battery of questions. As a quid-pro-quo, it is the institution that will be liable if anything goes wrong, not the researcher.
4 "Black swan" events are a catch-all metaphor for a high-profile cascade of unforeseeable events. Taleb (2007) developed the theory of black swan events, suggesting they are characterized by rarity, extreme "impact," and retrospective (though not prospective) predictability (xvii–xviii). The thrust of the work, in my reading, is summarized well on page 77: "We worry about the wrong 'improbable' events." In this essay, a black swan nuclear event is a high-profile cascade of terrible events that could be traced to a social science PI.

5 They could be the experiment's implementers, who end up jailed for high treason. They could be people who are just at the wrong place at the wrong time during the violent outbursts that take place in the wake of a contested election.

6 I was once asked point-blank by the head of the Somali Youth League of San Diego: "Are we putting together a predator drone list?" I explained that we were not—we were coding the identities of public figures in Somalia. I do not know if he really believed me.

7 And for the record: These arguments are very persuasive and self-replicating. No matter how many times critics repeat the assertion that they are a passing "fad," I doubt randomized control trials (RCTs) are actually a passing phenomenon the way critics wish that they were.

8 The correlation with the off-the-shelf democracy and governance indices would probably be high.

9 Neither effort resulted in a study, but if they had I am certain that I would have talked myself into doing the research. I think it is also important to note for posterity that in the preliminary "scouting" stage of the research no one—no one at Yale, at Stanford, at Harvard, at UCSD, no one, not once—suggested that randomizing the placement of police cameras in Newark was anything other than a NATURE paper, or that the Abkhazia work would be anything but historic.

10 It is unlikely that any individual social scientist is having a uniquely negative impact on the study population, but it is also not clear exactly where it is appropriate to construct the rhetorical "analogous to a prison population" boundary. Are citizens living in certain authoritarian police states (e.g., Pyongyang) analogous, in some way, to a prison population? How about native populations living on reservations? How about populations of refugee camps? How about populations living under military occupation by a country that is known to monitor cell phone and email communications?

11 This is only to say that there are certain frontiers of comparative politics where I anticipate that it will be very difficult for researchers to live up to the best practices articulated in Green and Gerber (2002, 829): to "aspire to leave no footprints . . . like visitors to nature preserves."

12 "Of course I'm ethical. So are my friends. You want to be my friend, don't you?" Cumulatively, this is probably going to lead to a lot of frustration in the next generation of scholars, many of whom are investing a great deal of energy, and doing everything they are being told they are supposed to do, but still aren't going to get the recognition they feel they deserve. I expect crocodile tears as these arguments filter through the sieve of department, subdisciplinary, and disciplinary politics. The tone and tenor of anonymous referee reports probably matter as much as anything in determining the future of field experimental research in comparative politics.

13 Although I felt genuinely guilty about this for a while, I managed to remain focused on the fact that if we had not conducted the work experimentally we would never have even *known* about the troubling downstream finding. The guilt finally passed when it sunk in that doing a pre-election voter attitude survey—e.g., just showing up to ask questions in randomly sampled Georgian villages—had a voter suppression effect that was analogous to distributing information. No one thinks that we should stop doing surveys in Georgia and allow elite pontification from the capital to replace systematic data on public opinion.

14 Driscoll and Hidalgo (2014).

15 Many members of our community put our training to work to do things other than just publish papers. Many political scientists consult. Many more volunteer their labor to political parties, write op-eds, blog, or "do politics" in a way that Max Weber would have immediately recognized.

16 All political scientists are guilty, to lesser or greater degrees, of being disingenuous about our actual political neutrality. We simply present ourselves and our research differently at different times. As I have struggled with the ethical dilemmas discussed in this chapter (and others not discussed), it has been extremely comforting to know that my home institution has "had my back." I am increasingly appreciative of how shared cultural understandings of what professors *are* shielded me while in the field. Some of my subjects understood this better than I did at the time.

17 Recall that the Soviet Union was administered by a class of fully self-aware social scientists, confident that there was no normatively defensible alternative to testing their theories. They were very interested in development, order, and social transformation, just as we are.

18 I am extremely grateful to Don Green for articulating this point in this way. The short discussion in Green and Gerber (2002, 828–831) is highly valuable.

PART II

Local Ethical Review When Conducting Experiments Internationally

6

THE VALUE AND CHALLENGES OF USING LOCAL ETHICAL REVIEW IN COMPARATIVE POLITICS EXPERIMENTS

Jennifer L. Merolla and Raul Madrid Jr.

It is common knowledge among social scientists that research involving human participants needs to be reviewed by the Institutional Review Board (IRB) at an individual's university before any data collection can proceed. A more complex issue that arises for individuals conducting comparative politics experiments is whether some type of local ethical review should also be acquired. Local ethical review is a review that takes place in the locality or institution where research is set to take place. For comparative politics experiments, local ethical review would entail getting reviewed in the country where the experiments are to be conducted. In some cases, the IRB at one's university may require such an approval. In other cases, it may not be required by one's institutional IRB, but may be required in the particular country where the study is to be conducted, or the researcher may think it is desirable.

This chapter first reviews the status quo with respect to what domestic Institutional Review Boards typically require for comparative politics experiments, drawing from discussions with IRB professionals. The chapter will then discuss why some type of local ethical review may be desirable. It will then assess the extent to which local ethical review is used by systematically looking at published papers that employ comparative politics experiments. The chapter will then discuss the challenges of obtaining local ethical review, and how one might go about getting some form of local ethical review in different contexts. In closing, we will discuss whether journals and funding agencies should consider including local ethical review of comparative politics experiments as a requirement for publication and funding.

As a point of disclosure, one of the authors on this paper is approaching this topic both as an academic who conducts politics experiments and also as a faculty member who has been on her university's Institutional Review Board for almost five years.

6.1 The Status Quo

In 1991, a federal policy for the protection of human subjects, known as the Common Rule, was adopted across 15 federal departments and agencies. According to this policy, any research involving human subjects that is funded by any of the 15 governmental agencies needs approval from an Institutional Review Board. Most universities extend the requirement of IRB approval for all research being done at the institution that involves human participants, not just research that is federally funded.[1]

The majority of federal funding for political science comes from the National Science Foundation (NSF), one of the agencies covered in the Common Rule. One of the requirements for receiving funding from the NSF is to demonstrate that IRB approval has been received when working with human participants. This is very straightforward for work being done within the United States, but what are the requirements for those doing experiments abroad? Below is an excerpt from the NSF's website:

> The US institution administering the research has the primary responsibility, normally codified in an Assurance, to ensure that the project complies with US regulations. The Common Rule §101 (h) discusses foreign human subjects regulations and procedures for substituting them for US regulations. When an appropriate foreign Institutional Review Board exists the regulations foresee involving it in reviewing the research. The US institution's IRB chair determines that the procedures prescribed by the foreign IRB afford protections that are at least equivalent to those provided in the Common Rule.
>
> This regulation is most germane to biomedical research, as few foreign countries apply human subjects regulations to social and behavioral science. In many foreign countries IRBs deal only with biomedical research and will refuse to extend their purview to cover social and behavioral science. In other foreign situations there will be no analogue to an Institutional Review Board and the concept may be irrelevant. When this situation occurs, the US institution remains the responsible authority and the services of a foreign IRB might not be necessary.[2]

The NSF clearly provides some general guidelines, but the ultimate burden for a decision on local ethical review is placed on the Principal Investigator's (PI's) home institution. As an illustration, for an NSF-funded, multi-country study looking at terrorist threats and support for democracy—conducted by one of the

authors on this paper along with Elizabeth Zechmeister (Vanderbilt University)—
the NSF only requested documentation of IRB approval from the collaborators'
home institutions before releasing funds.

Because local ethical review of comparative politics experiments is recommended but not required by the NSF, domestic IRBs may not require Principal
Investigators to get some form of local ethical review. The lack of clear guidance
in federal guidelines, coupled with the decentralized nature of IRBs, means that
there is likely to be variation in whether some form of local ethical review is
required by one's Institutional Review Board before conducting experimental
studies abroad. In the case of the NSF-funded study noted above, which entailed
conducting survey experiments in eight countries, the domestic IRBs involved
did not require the PIs to obtain local ethical review.

In further conversations with an IRB staff member at our home institution (Claremont Graduate University), questions were asked about the norms
for reviewing social science research being done outside of the United States.
The staff member indicated that there are no formal requirements by the US
government for local ethical review for social science work being done outside
the United States. The staff member also noted that the training for Institutional
Review Board professionals in this domain is ambiguous because much of the
focus is on biomedical research.[3] Given a lack of clear guidance, each institution
develops its own norms for dealing with such protocols. At Claremont Graduate University, whether local ethical review is requested by the IRB depends on
the level of risk in the study. For studies with minimal risk, the IRB consults
with a country expert within the United States. If a minimal risk study is being
conducted at an educational institution abroad, the Institutional Review Board
requests IRB approval or some type of approval letter from that institution. If a
study is deemed to involve high risk, then the IRB requests some form of ethics
review within the country to be studied, and will often help the researcher in
finding an IRB to review the protocol. In countries without any ethical review
process for social science research, the IRB usually has an expert within the country review the protocol.

Of course, this only speaks to the nature of Claremont Graduate University's
IRB, and how it handles protocols for research conducted abroad. The decentralized nature of IRBs means that each institution will likely handle this in a different way because there is no clear guidance in federal guidelines (see Seligson 2008
for a discussion of some of the problems of decentralization). Furthermore, even
the determination of risk and the type of review required for a given protocol is
likely to vary across institutions. In the study mentioned earlier with Zechmeister,
CGU's Institutional Review Board deemed that it had to go to the full board for
review, while Vanderbilt's IRB decided it should be expedited. The main point of
difference was with how the two IRBs treated the newspaper articles that were
created and edited together based on real newspaper articles. Because the articles

were edited together, CGU's IRB thought it should be considered a study containing deception, which goes to the full board, while Vanderbilt's Institutional Review Board did not, and instead used expedited review.

While the status quo requirements are vague with respect to local ethical review for comparative politics experiments (or any politics research conducted with human participants abroad), the requirements are better specified for research funded by other agencies, such as the National Institute of Health (NIH). Any research that is funded by the NIH abroad needs to have IRB approval both at the Principal Investigator's home institution, as well as within the country where the proposed study will be done. Of course, the level of risk is generally higher with NIH-funded studies compared to the type of studies being done in comparative politics.

Another important aspect to the status quo is that the laws in some countries require foreign researchers to go through an ethical review process. For example, as will be discussed more in depth in later chapters in this section, this is the case in countries such as Brazil and China (see Chapter 8 by Cunow and Desposato, as well as Chapter 7 by Lü, in this volume).

6.2 Why Get Some Type of Local Ethical Review?

In this section, we will first discuss the experience of sitting on an Institutional Review Board and reviewing studies that are to be conducted outside of the United States, by way of the purview of one author on this chapter. Second, we will discuss examples whereby local ethical review might help issues surface that fall under the radar of domestic IRBs. Third, we will discuss how local ethical review might help counter what some consider "overzealous" IRBs.

Because sitting on an Institutional Review Board is an interesting and unique experience that was afforded to one of the authors on this paper, it is useful to attempt to re-create a typical conversation that takes place once a protocol comes in that proposes to do research abroad. One protocol that came to the full board for review came from a student who was proposing to do interviews with people who protest in Istanbul, Turkey. The student was not proposing to do interviews at protests, but rather, sought to recruit people who have participated in protests. Such a study is not an experiment, but still falls under the purview of the IRB because it involves human participants. Some might question why such a protocol would go to the full board for review in the first place. One reason is that the IRB staff in this particular instance did not feel that they had enough expertise with Turkey to know whether talking about protest experiences might be dangerous in the country, so they felt it best to bring the study to the full board. They were not able to get a country expert to review the protocol before the full board meeting, so all the board had to go off of was the protocol itself.

During the discussion, questions were raised about whether or not participants would be put at risk by talking to the student about experiences with protests, or if sharing information with the student about their views toward the Turkish government might also put participants at risk. Others questioned whether or not the student would be put at risk by simply conducting such interviews. Due to the fact that one of the authors on this paper had experience doing research in Turkey, questions were posed directly to the author about risk factors for both the student and the participants of the study. Yet, because said author only had experience conducting a survey experiment in Turkey (that was contracted through a local firm), and only had modest exposure to Istanbul, it was determined by the board that a decision would be deferred until an expert within Turkey could review the protocol. The review of the protocol was therefore very brief, about five to ten minutes, because no one had answers to the questions raised.

The conversation that took place stands in stark contrast to protocols that are reviewed that propose to collect data with human participants in the United States. It often takes the Institutional Review Board a half hour or more to discuss such protocols. The obvious problem in dealing with protocols overseas is that IRB board members do not necessarily have knowledge about the norms, customs, culture, and government institutions in the given country. Without such knowledge, it can be difficult to assess whether a given protocol upholds the Belmont Principles of respect for persons, beneficence, and justice. The short example given about Claremont Graduate University's IRB illustrates that domestic IRBs simply may not be able to give a comparative politics experiment the same level of review that they can for studies being done domestically. As we will discuss below, given this lack of knowledge, IRBs may either let things that may be problematic for human subjects fly under the radar, or they may overreact to a protocol that genuinely poses minimal risk.

With respect to the first situation, even when domestic Institutional Review Boards are doing their due diligence, as most surely do, they may not be aware of issues that may pose problems from a human subjects standpoint. One example is the use of survey questions that have been validated in many studies, but have primarily been used in the United States and other western countries. Because the questions have been used so often, it may not even occur to scholars conducting the studies and domestic IRBs that the questions may be problematic in the given country context. Such a problem occurred when Merolla and Zechmeister conducted a study in Turkey. They adapted some questions that had been used to assess opinions about civil liberties restrictions for Muslims in the United States to Kurds in Turkey. Neither IRB from either of their institutions raised any issues with this battery of questions. For that matter, the Institutional Review Board at Koc University in Turkey, which also reviewed the protocol, did not raise any issues with the questions. However, individuals at the survey firm requested that they remove the battery of questions because it might put their interviewers, and by extension participants, at risk with respect to getting the attention of the local police. In this instance, local ethical review, which was obtained, did not even catch the potential concern with respect to human subjects protection. Another example is whether studies with elected officials should be exempt in other countries. If the domestic political situation in a country is unstable and elected officials may be at risk if they take stances against the government, such studies should likely get a higher level of scrutiny than they would in the United States, but domestic Institutional Review Boards may not be aware of these issues. Compensation might also pose a potential problem of coercion if researchers are offering a high level of compensation for a given country's context. Domestic IRBs may not know enough about the local norms to determine whether the amount could potentially be coercive.[4]

At the same time, domestic Institutional Review Boards may also overreact to a protocol that poses very minimal risk. As Seligson (2008, 478) discusses, some IRBs have treated pregnant woman as a protected class and insist that surveys begin by asking females if they are pregnant. Such questions not only might make it more difficult to recruit respondents, but seem out of place for a public opinion survey. The protocol discussed above in which the student proposed to conduct interviews with protestors in Turkey likely fits into this category, as well. A similar protocol being conducted in the United States would likely not go to the full board for a number of reasons: 1) protestors are not generally considered a protected population; 2) the study was not taking place during a protest; and 3) it did not involve deception. With that in mind, an argument could be made that protestors should be considered a class with protected status in country contexts where they would be at risk from the government. Claremont Graduate University's Institutional Review Board did not have enough knowledge about acceptance of protests and protestors in Turkey to be able to make this determination and went the safer route of full board review. In Zechmeister's piece for this volume, she discusses other examples of IRBs not understanding enough about the country context such that they overreact to minimal-risk studies. These examples only fuel perceptions among many in the academic community that IRBs are overzealous and go outside of their purview (see discussion of this as well in Seligson 2008 and Yanow and Schwartz-Shea 2008).

However, all of these examples also attest to the fact that domestic Institutional Review Boards are limited in their ability to review research that is done outside of the United States. Even if we, as researchers, have the best intentions with respect to human subjects protection, we are so close to our research that we may not be able to see potential problems that may arise. Therefore, some type of local ethical review is desirable to ensure that our research does obtain the level of review that is important for meeting the Belmont principles. This, of course, does not come without costs. Adding a layer of local ethical review means that it takes much longer to conduct research abroad. In some countries that require foreign researchers to undergo ethical review by the bureaucracy, the process is very inefficient, and it can take almost a year to get a study approved.[5] Before delving into the topic of how scholars can obtain some form of local ethical review, we address how researchers doing comparative politics experiments talk about IRB review in their published research, and whether they obtain local ethical review for their studies.

6.3 How Do Scholars Report About the IRB Process?

To get a sense of the extent to which those doing comparative politics experiments seek out some form of local ethical review, we turn to a content analysis of a sample of published work in the field. To do this, we looked up all articles published between 2008 and 2013 that contained an experiment and were conducted outside of the United States. We reviewed articles from the *American Political Science Review*, the *American Journal of Political Science*, the *Journal of Politics*, *Comparative Political Studies*, *Comparative Politics*, and *Political Behavior*. We then coded for whether the article discussed domestic Institutional Review Board approval as well as some form of local ethical review.

Figure 6.1 displays the number of articles with comparative politics experiments from 2008 to the end of 2013. The first important point is that the number

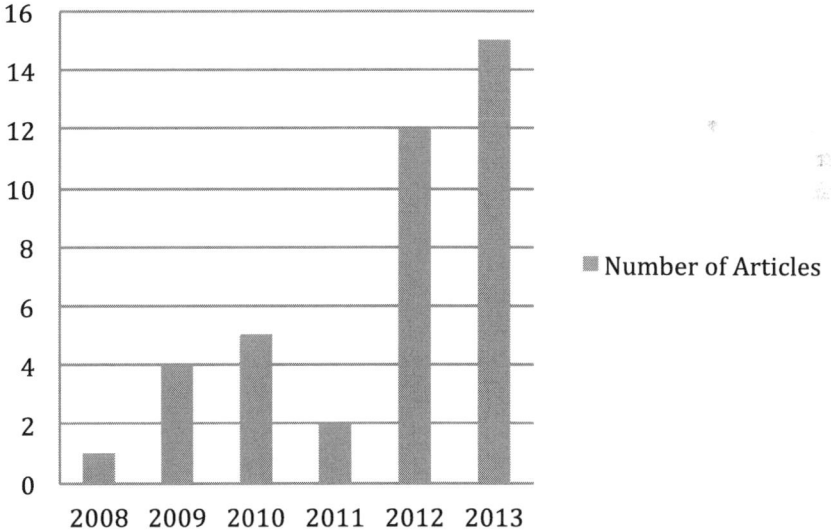

FIGURE 6.1 Number of Articles Using Comparative Politics Experiments, 2008–2013

Note: This is the total number of articles that use comparative politics experiments in the American Political Science Review, American Journal of Political Science, Journal of Politics, Comparative Political Studies, *and* Political Behavior *in this time frame.*

of comparative politics experiments published in these journals has increased substantially over time. In 2008, we only found one comparative politics experiment published in the *Journal of Politics* (Gibson 2008). By 2012, that number increased to 12, and by 2013, there were 15 articles that appeared in these journals. This number will likely increase even more over time given the increasing interest in experimental research abroad.

If we look at whether the articles mention that the study has domestic Institutional Review Board approval, it appears that this is the exception rather than the rule. In only six of the 39 articles do the authors mention that the study has domestic IRB approval.[6] Of those studies that discuss IRB approval, five mention this in the acknowledgments or a footnote (Dunning and Harrison 2010, Lü, Scheve and Slaughter 2012, Baldwin 2013, Samii 2013, Lyall, Blair and Imai 2013), while the sixth has an extensive discussion in the first appendix (Paluck and Green 2009). With respect to obtaining local ethical review, only one article explicitly discusses local ethical review, and that is the Paluck and Green piece. It should be noted that the risk level in this latter piece was much higher than most other studies (with the exception of the Baldwin piece, which included face-to-face interviews in Zambia) in that it was looking at the effects of a reconciliation program in Rwanda over the course of a year. A high percentage of participants knew someone who had been killed in the genocide and the interviews asked some sensitive questions. In the appendix, Paluck and Green (2009, 639) note:

> We sought ethics reviews for the proposed study protocol in Rwanda and in the United States from Yale's Institutional Review Board (IRB). Because there was no official IRB in Rwanda at the time, we reviewed our design with several Rwandan academics, with international researchers who had experience conducting surveys or program evaluations in Rwanda, and with advocacy and human rights groups in Rwanda, including prison advocacy groups. Yale University's IRB reviewed and approved the entire research design, including the unobtrusive behavioral measurement.

Just because articles do not mention IRB approval does not mean that scholars are not obtaining Institutional Review Board approval at home and/or abroad. Because most journals in political science do not require IRB approval for publication, scholars may not necessarily include this information in the published article. Given norms across research institutions, it is likely that most of these studies had at least domestic IRB approval. In order to gather more information about the level of review that individuals obtained in their studies, we contacted all of the scholars from the sample of articles. Most of the lead authors, with the exception of eight, responded to our inquiry. The responses cover about 3/4 of the articles pictured in Figure 6.1. All of the scholars who replied had obtained

IRB review/approval from their home institution, as we suspected would be the case. Some of the studies were deemed to be exempt.

There was more divergence in whether some type of local ethical review was obtained. In five of the studies, four were field experiments being conducted primarily by the researchers, and one was a survey experiment, but scholars were nonetheless able to obtain permission from government officials to conduct the study in the country. Review by a local Institutional Review Board was not always possible because the countries did not have an IRB.[7] In an additional ten studies, formal local ethical review was not obtained (nor required by one's domestic Institutional Review Board), but all of the studies were survey experiments that posed minimal risks and were conducted by local survey firms, some of which had requisite survey permissions. In many of these cases, scholars noted that they consulted not only with the firms about any sensitive issues that might arise from the survey, but also with scholars inside of the given country, as well as experts outside of the country. There was only one study that did not have any form of local ethical review, but that study was working in close partnership with an NGO and also had minimal risk for participants.

In sum, there is very little discussion about ethical review in published work, whether that pertains to domestic review or local ethical review. While this content analysis was focused on studies in comparative politics experiments, we suspect this is also the case for experimental studies in the United States. Part of this lack of discussion is likely related to the fact that most journals do not require evidence of IRB approval and if they do, they do not necessarily require authors to disclose this information in the article. In a search of the journal websites for all of the journals reviewed in this paper, only two of the five had a discussion of ethical review in the submission guidelines (or instructions for authors after acceptance). The *American Political Science Review* notes in the submission guidelines: "For experiments, provide full descriptions of experimental protocols, methods of subject recruitment and selection, payments to subjects, debriefing procedures, and so on. In any case involving human subjects, the editors may require certification of appropriate institutional review and/ or conformity with generally accepted norms."[8] In a conversation with one of the authors of the articles reviewed for this paper, the scholar indicated that the *American Political Science Review* required evidence of the IRB exemption for the study, but this is not discussed in the article itself. *Political Behavior* has adopted a requirement of reporting Institutional Review Board approval, noting: "Manuscripts submitted for publication must contain a declaration that the experiments comply with the current laws of the country in which they were performed. Please include this note in a separate section before the reference list."[9] This is a more recent change to the submission guidelines. In every other journal we reviewed, there was no mention of reporting IRB approval in the respective guidelines.

There is also variance in whether scholars seek some type of local ethical review. Our limited discussions with other scholars working in this area suggests that part of the variation is due to the nature of the research being done (especially the level of risk), the presence or lack thereof of ethical review boards in the country they are doing research in, as well as variation in what domestic Institutional Review Boards and funding agencies require. In the next section, we turn to some challenges in obtaining local ethical review.

6.4 The Challenges of Obtaining Local Ethical Review

Given the issues outlined earlier with domestic Institutional Review Board review of comparative politics experiments, some form of local ethical review should be obtained by researchers, even if it is not required by their domestic IRB. While local ethical review via a formal Institutional Review Board process sounds nice in theory, in practice it can be very difficult to obtain such a review. In this section, we discuss ways in which scholars may obtain some form of local review, even if it is not through a formal IRB process in another country.

The easiest situation is usually when a scholar is conducting an experiment in a country that has some type of ethical review process for social science research. If an ethical review process is present at universities, one can try to collaborate with scholars within the country and have their institution review the protocol. It is often in the interest of the researcher to collaborate with scholars within the country anyway to gain more local knowledge for the project. Furthermore, subjects may be more willing to participate if they know people from their own country are involved in the study. If collaboration is for some reason not possible or desirable, it can be more of a challenge to obtain local ethical review. Institutions will not necessarily be willing to review a protocol for a study that is not being done by their employees or being conducted at their institution. The country may not have other types of IRBs, such as community IRBs or commercial IRBs. In this type of situation, scholars may not be able to get a local Institutional Review Board to review their study and may need to seek alternative forms of review.

At the same time, it can be very costly to obtain local ethical review, even in countries that have such a process, and there may be other ethical issues that arise in obtaining such a review. For example, Brazil requires foreign researchers to undergo an ethical review process through the government bureaucracy. This process can take many months and can even extend to over a year, and after this whole process, the study may not even be approved (see Chapter 8 in this volume for more discussion of the case of Brazil). In other contexts, researchers may need to pay a bribe to get their study reviewed, which opens up a host of other ethical issues. The actual human subjects review in such a context is likely colored by whether a researcher pays a bribe or not, which is highly problematic.

Another challenge researchers may face is in countries that do not have any ethical review process for social science research. In these cases, scholars might seek letters of approval from the appropriate institutions. For example, if a study is being done at an institution of higher learning, scholars might get an approval letter from the chair of a department or dean of a college. If the study is being conducted outside of an educational institution, scholars might get letters of permission from government officials. This is essentially what some of the scholars we talked with did for their research in some of the countries that did not have Institutional Review Boards for social science research. That being said, it is not clear how carefully the given individual is reviewing the study for human subjects concerns.

In cases where scholars cannot obtain local ethical review via an Institutional Review Board, there are a few alternative options. If a study is high risk and the country does not have an IRB, scholars can try to help individuals in the country set up an IRB, either through educational institutions or within the community. Some scholars working with NIH grants abroad have helped set up Institutional Review Boards in countries that do not have them. For example, a colleague working in the school of global and community health at Claremont Graduate University helped a community in Sri Lanka and several villages in China set up an IRB. There is no requirement that the IRB be housed at an educational institution, so this is a feasible process. However, the process can take some time to set up. In the case of Sri Lanka, it took about three months to get the Institutional Review Board started, while it took about six months in China. This may not be too much time for someone with a National Institutes of Health grant, which is typically five years, but may be too long for political scientists, whose grants from agencies like the National Science Foundation typically are two years. Graduate students doing comparative politics experiments have an even shorter time window. To properly get local ethical review could add an additional year to finishing their dissertation project. Furthermore, this might be asking too much of a study that carries minimal risk, and would normally fall under expedited or exempt review.

In the event that setting up an Institutional Review Board is not feasible, scholars (as well as IRBs) can try to obtain less formal types of review. First, scholars or IRBs can ask experts both within and outside of the country to review the proposed protocol. These individuals will be more attuned to potential issues within the given country. This is essentially what many of the scholars doing survey experiments in comparative politics have been doing. Some additional safeguards that are recommended by Bhat and Hegde (2006) for non-clinical health related research that may be useful to consider for social science experiments include local oversight and involvement of subjects. In the first case, Bhat and Hegde (2006, 539) recommend: "Research on humans should be designed and conducted in conjunction with a subject advocate, preferably one who is knowledgeable of the culture and customs of the participants, and with the scientific basis and methods associated with the study." They note that this person should not have a high level of influence with the study population; otherwise, participants may feel coerced into doing the study. As an example, these individuals might be representatives from nongovernmental organizations who are not involved in the research. While it may not be appropriate to have a subject advocate involved in the design of a social science study, it may be desirable to have them review the study and be present while the study is being conducted. With respect to the involvement of subjects, Bhat and Hegde (2006, 536) suggest:

> Ideally, subjects should not be limited to serving as the source of data but should also participate in voicing issues that need to be considered in study design and in gauging the importance of the results to the study population; representatives from the sample population should be presented with the study proposal for their input before the start of data collection. Our study was designed with the input of villagers, and the proposal was presented to and approved by village representatives before data collection. Furthermore, representatives of the sample population worked closely with and guided researchers during data collection on site.

This is a suggestion worth considering in the design of social science experiments abroad. We did not ask the scholars we contacted if they used a subject advocate in their studies. It may be a bit more complicated to involve a subject advocate if a study is using deception. If this is the case, the researchers can disclose the study design to the subject advocate and ask that the person not share that information with the study participants prior to and while the study is being conducted.

At the end of the day, whether and what type of local ethical review one should seek out will depend on what is feasible in a given country context, what funders and journals require, what one's home IRB requires, the level of risk of the study, and one's own judgment about the appropriate type of review. At the very least, it is wise for scholars conducting comparative politics experiments to at least have local experts reviewing the study instruments. Of course, individuals in political science may not be sensitive to human subjects issues that arise from our own research, so review by a human subjects advocate within the country may be a further safeguard.

6.5 Conclusion

There is wide variation in the use of local ethical review in comparative politics experiments. This variation is certainly understandable, for many of the reasons noted above. Many countries simply do not have ethical review boards for social science research,[10] and our funding timeline may be too short to place the burden of creating IRBs on researchers, especially for studies that are minimal risk. In countries that do have processes in place for ethical review, such as Brazil, it may simply be inefficient to go through the governmental bureaucracy, as Cunow and Desposato explain in Chapter 8 in this volume. Likewise, in Lü's Chapter 7 of this volume, there is a discussion about conducting research in authoritarian regimes, where undergoing ethical review may simply not be practical. There are, however, many sensible alternatives to a local IRB review, which many scholars already undertake in their research.

Moving forward, we should do more to encourage disclosure of the ethical review process in published research. It is fairly standard in other fields to have some indication that a study has Institutional Review Board approval, and many journals in other fields, such as health and psychology, require IRB approval to publish a piece. It would be good practice for those conducting research with human subjects both within and outside the United States to have some discussion of the ethical review process (even if it is in a footnote), and in the case of the latter, to note the type of local ethical review that was obtained. In order to create stronger norms, political science journals may want to require evidence of domestic IRB approval before publishing a piece, as the NSF requires IRB approval before releasing funds. Given the challenges of obtaining local ethical review, journals and funding agencies may not want to require evidence of local ethical review, but may want to ask authors/Principal Investigators to provide some discussion of the types of review they obtained within the given country context.

Notes

1 For a discussion of the history of human subjects regulations in the United States, see Morton and Williams (2010).
2 See the section, "How should IRBs deal with research in foreign countries?" on the National Science Foundation web page, "Frequently Asked Questions and Vignettes" at http://www.nsf.gov/bfa/dias/policy/hsfaqs.jsp#foreign (accessed September 28, 2015).
3 For more on the focus with respect to the biomedical field, see Morton and Williams (2010). The OHRP does provide a fairly extensive list of ethics rules and links to further information across many countries, although the focus of the list is on biomedical research: http://www.hhs.gov/ohrp/international/ (accessed September 28, 2015).
4 As Zechmeister notes in her chapter for this volume, they can also overreact and think too much compensation is being offered because they are not aware of local norms.
5 In the experience of one researcher in this volume, it took 293 days to undergo the review process that is required by Brazilian law. Many other researchers doing comparative politics experiments in Brazil do so without going through the ethical review process, which is technically against the laws of that country.
6 There are a few cases in which IRB approval is not relevant because the sample includes some natural experiments (four of the articles in Figure 6.1).

7 See, for example, the case of the Danish ethics system, which only requires ethical review for biomedical research. A more in-depth discussion can be found at: http://www.onlineethics.org/cms/8082.aspx and http://www.cvk.sum.dk/cvk/home/english.aspx (both accessed September 28, 2015).

8 See http://www.apsanet.org/apsrsubmissions. Reference is made to norms for the American Anthropological Association's code of ethics: http://www.aaanet.org/issues/policy-advocacy/upload/AAA-Ethics-Code-2009.pdf (accessed September 28, 2015).

9 See http://www.springer.com/authors/manuscript+guidelines?SGWID=0-40162-6-795225-0 (accessed September 28, 2015).

10 For a detailed discussion on a country that does not have ethical review boards, see Aguilar's chapter on Mexico (Chapter 9 in this volume).

7

ETHICAL CHALLENGES IN COMPARATIVE POLITICS EXPERIMENTS IN CHINA

Xiaobo Lü

7.1 Introduction

Students of Chinese politics have taken a new methodological approach in recent years by conducting experimental studies. These studies have generated numerous new insights into Chinese politics and comparative political behaviors. However, the Chinese government is keen to control the information flow within society in order to maintain regime stability. In particular, the government is anxious about social science research studies conducted by foreign scholars and organizations that could potentially be regime destabilizing. Consequently, conducting experimental studies in China raises a number of challenges for researchers, ranging from experiment logistics to research design. On many occasions, scholars face ethical dilemmas between satisfying the scientific standards in their studies and ensuring the safety of local collaborators, respondents, and even scholars themselves. These issues are particularly salient when studying topics that are considered politically sensitive to the Chinese government.

The difficulties of conducting research in this controlled information environment have not gone unnoticed. Several studies have made important contributions to our understanding of the challenges and strategies for studying politics in contemporary China.[1] For example, Manion (2012) provides an overview of public opinion research on Chinese politics in the last two decades. Tsai (2010) offers some valuable insights concerning quantitative and field research on politically sensitive issues in rural China.

However, issues related to experimental studies of Chinese politics remain largely unexplored. Although experimental studies inherit many existing challenges in traditional methods of data collection in China, they also generate some new issues. I argue that experimental studies differ from traditional studies primarily in two aspects: the data-generating process and the barrier of entry in data collection. Specifically, researchers who conduct experimental studies, particularly field experiments, not only are observers but also play a more active role in the data-generating process. Hence, the "treatments" in these studies could potentially generate unintended political behaviors that are not trivial in nondemocratic regimes. Meanwhile, the low barrier of entry in data collection (e.g., research costs, the degree of collaboration with local partners) may induce some researchers to overlook the safety concerns of those local collaborators who implement the data collection for them. If the trust between local collaborators and foreign researchers is broken, it may undermine future collaborative opportunities for other foreign scholars. Given the burgeoning experimental studies in political science outside of China in the last decade,[2] scholars have increasingly attempted to employ this new methodology in the study of Chinese politics, with various degrees of success. This paper sheds some light on tackling the ethical issues that scholars may encounter in this context.

Building on the insights in Manion (2012) and Tsai (2010), I begin by first briefly outlining the motives behind the Chinese government's restrictions on social science research involving data collection with foreign affiliations. Next, I discuss the potential risks facing respondents, local collaborators, and scholars in the context of China's regulatory regime. Specifically, many practitioners consider the enforcement of these regulations to be a gray area because the enforcement is arbitrary and inconsistent at best. I then examine experimental studies in the context of China's political environment and suggest some potential ethical issues that scholars may face. Given these challenges, I discuss several common practices concerning experimental studies in China and their practical trade-offs.

7.2 Understanding the Chinese Government's Motives

Governments in authoritarian regimes often have concerns about any activities involving social, economic, and political data collection in their societies. Governments in authoritarian regimes may fear the *process* and/or the *outcome* of studies that could shape mass political attitudes and engender political actions, which subsequently destabilize the regime. As the discussion below shows, however, the *process* of using non-experimental research approaches, to my knowledge, has generated little impact on political attitudes and behaviors of Chinese citizens to date. The *outcome* of these studies, on the other hand, could be regime destabilizing in the eyes of the government under some conditions. I further argue that the fear that regime destabilization might result from the outcome of the research (even though that destabilization is very unlikely) could induce the government to take action against the scholars and their Chinese collaborators, but *not* necessarily against the subjects involved in the study.

Broadly speaking, one may understand the Chinese government's restriction on social science research through the theories of censorship. As recently suggested by King, Pan and Roberts (2013), we can conceptualize the motives of the Chinese government's censorship in two categories: a *state critique* theory that emphasizes silencing dissidents, and a *collective action potential* theory that suggests governments repress the potential for citizens to collectively express their dissatisfaction toward the government. King, Pan and Roberts (2013) argue that the primary motives of the Chinese government's Internet censorship programs are to repress the potential for collective action, and they find supporting evidence in the analysis of social media in China.

If we follow this line of logic, we may consider collective action potential as the primary motive behind the Chinese government's restriction on social science research that involves data collection, particularly those studies conducted by foreign scholars or funded by foreign organizations. To my knowledge, however, we have not observed that the *process* of social science research engenders mass collective action against the government among Chinese citizens to date. There are several factors that can explain the low level of impact on collective action from the research process. First, the sampling strategy in many studies, particularly public opinion research, randomly selects respondents from a large pool of individuals. Hence, these respondents often do not know other participants involved in the project, and therefore are unlikely to organize collective action. Second, the survey or interview questions used are often subtle and not very sensitive, in large part due to the discretion of the scholars. These traditional data-collection methods may avoid engendering strong anti-government sentiment among subjects, which could potentially put the subjects at risk if they chose to take political action.

However, the government may remain concerned when research is conducted at sensitive times or in sensitive areas. For example, the Chinese government, especially local governments, often discourage research activities in unstable areas (e.g., Tibet and Xinjiang) or during sensitive times (e.g., post-riot, post-natural disaster, and during annual meetings of the national assemblies and Party congress). Furthermore, studies that challenge the legitimacy of the Chinese Communist Party, such as exposing high-level political elites' corruption without government approval, or raise issues concerning territorial integrity (e.g., Taiwan, Tibet, Xinjiang) are also considered sensitive.[3] It is worth noting that the process of social science studies has not provoked much social unrest in China to date, in part because most scholars have been careful in to design their research to avoid crossing red lines.

In the meantime, the outcomes of social science research, particularly those papers that are not published in Chinese, have not yet directly generated any anti-government activities among Chinese citizens. Specifically, it is very difficult for the outcomes of academic papers to generate significant impact on mobilizing opposition against the regime for two reasons. First, papers published in academic journals are not easily accessible to Chinese citizens because they often require institutional subscription. Second, even if these papers are accessible, most of them are in English and use social scientific methodologies and terminologies that present barriers to Chinese citizens' comprehension. In particular, those who are more prone to social unrest, such as peasants and migrant workers, lack the necessary language skills and scientific training to make any use of these papers.

If neither the processes nor the outcomes of social science research generate significant collective action potential among citizens to destabilize the regime, it is puzzling why the Chinese government maintains tight restrictions, at least in the regulatory regime. I highlight two conditions under which the outcomes of social sciences research could draw government's attention and potentially cause them to take action against scholars and local Chinese collaborators. First, when the research results are critical of the legitimacy of the Chinese Communist Party as the ruling party, they could attract the government's attention. This concern is compounded by those studies that are widely reported by foreign media outlets and social media venues. The Chinese government is wary of the content of media reporting, particularly those reports related to the quality of governance that could undermine regime legitimacy. For better or worse, media outlets and social media do a better job than academics when informing Chinese citizens about the state of governance in Chinese society. Consequently, research results reported in the media could shape political attitudes and, subsequently, generate political action.

Second, if Chinese dissidents and foreign governments or organizations use researchers' papers as the ammunition to criticize the government and the party, and as the means to mobilize other citizens against the government, they could draw the government's attention. The Chinese authorities are particularly worried about any organizations with mass mobilization capacity, which could potentially serve as an opposing force to challenge the monopoly of the Chinese Communist Party. As a consequence, the government will punish any activities that directly challenge the regime.

7.3 Understanding the Risks Under the Chinese Government Regulations

Because most research does not directly fuel the potential for collective action by citizens to express their dissatisfaction toward the government, the Chinese government does not censor social science research as tightly as they do media and the Internet. However, the inconsistency in censoring provides both challenges and opportunities to scholars. On the one hand, inconsistent censoring creates a significant gray area in which scholars do not know when and how the government might take action against them, because the government often selectively enforces the rules and regulations when deemed appropriate. On the other hand, the inconsistency in government enforcement provides leeway to enable scholars to collect data and answer some important questions that were not possible in previous research. In this section, I discuss specific Chinese regulatory regimes concerning social sciences research with foreign affiliation (i.e., funded by foreign sources or conducted by foreign individuals and entities) and their corresponding risks to respondents, local partners, and scholars.

The current regulatory regime concerning research projects with foreign affiliation is directed by the National Bureau of Statistics of China (NBS). The most relevant regulation is the *Measures for the Administration of Foreign Affiliated Surveys* (涉外调查管理办法, the *Measures* hereafter), which was issued by the NBS in 2004.[4] This document was a revision of the previous regulations established in 1999, and it aims to regulate market research (市场调查) and societal investigation (社会调查) activities funded by or in cooperation with foreign individuals, entities, and local subsidiaries of foreign entities outside of mainland China.[5] It defines market research as "activities collecting information concerning commercial products and services in the Chinese market." It defines societal investigation as "any activities such as survey, interviews, ethnographic observations, and any other approaches to collect, organize, and analyze information about the Chinese society."

There are two issues worth noting regarding this document. First, some first-time researchers may think the Chinese regulation only applies to public opinion surveys, but the definition above suggests that it has a broader interpretation. Specifically, the definition of societal investigation (社会调查) includes many approaches that are not considered standard survey methods, as reflected in the definition above. Second, the wording of "*any other approaches*" (其它方式) in the definition of societal investigation is purposely vague, thus giving the government flexibility to enforce this rule as it sees fit. Vague language is a general pattern in some Chinese laws, and the government flexibly interprets these regulations to serve its own purposes.

According to the *Measures*, data collection with foreign affiliation, as defined above, cannot be conducted without the approval of the NBS. There are several steps that organizations or individuals need to take in order to conduct market research or societal investigation with foreign affiliations in China. First, the local institutions or firms are required to obtain a permit from the National Bureau of Statistics of China prior to the study if the study involves interviewing subjects across provinces.[6] Similarly, if the study requires interviewing subjects within a province, the local institutions or firms are required to apply for a permit from the provincial Bureau of Statistics of China.

Without obtaining the permit from the government, no organizations or individuals can conduct data collection with foreign affiliation. In terms of the application process's timeline, the *Measures* indicate that NBS is obliged to approve or disapprove the application within 20 days, and this deadline could be extended by another 10 days if necessary. The permit remains valid for three years, and it is renewable. Second, even after obtaining the permit, the organizations are still required to apply for approval from the NBS when conducting any specific projects with foreign affiliations. The application includes a brief description of the study objectives, target population, and questionnaires, among many other requirements detailing the study. Again, the NBS and corresponding provincial statistical bureaus are obliged to approve or disapprove the project within 20 days, with a potential 10-day extension. While the application process appears to be straightforward, it is common knowledge among practitioners that studies concerning sensitive topics or during sensitive times could face a lengthy reviewing process, often resulting in rejection.

The *Measures* specifies the punishment for violating the regulations. It is worth noting that the associated risks for respondents, local partners, and researchers could sometimes exceed the *Measures* because of other Chinese laws and regulations, especially those concerning so-called "state secrets."

To begin, the *Measures* do not indicate any specific punishment or repercussions for the subjects who participate in studies that violate the regulations in the *Measures*. Furthermore, I am unaware of any individuals who have been fined or prosecuted by the government because of their participation. Hence, the risks to research participants are minimal as far as government harassment is concerned.

However, for scholars and local Chinese collaborators (e.g., survey firms, academic institutes, and Chinese scholars), violation of the *Measures* could result in a fine up to RMB 1,000 (approximately US$160) if the research is not for profit, and up to RMB 30,000 (approximately US$4,840) if it is for profit. Although the financial punishment is relatively small, the local organizations could lose their permit to conduct future market research and societal investigation. Losing the permit is the most severe punishment for Chinese local collaborators because it threatens their institutional survival. Meanwhile, Chinese scholars could face disciplinary action by their organizations, and they could be blacklisted by the government, undermining their career prospects.

Note that the *Measures* suggest that if research activities violate other Chinese laws and regulations, the individuals and local collaborators can face criminal charges. For example, the *Measures* prohibit research activities such as undermining Chinese sovereignty, stealing state secrets, provoking inter-ethnic tension, disturbing social safety and welfare, and violating other laws and regulations. Again, the vague language of "other Chinese laws and regulations" in the *Measures* gives room for government discretion regarding the definition of "violation."

Despite the harsh language in the regulation, the enforcement of these rules is not as universal as one would expect. To understand the pattern of selective enforcement, one could borrow insights from the "police patrols versus fire alarms" model on congressional oversight in the United States (McCubbins and

Schwartz 1984). Essentially, the selective enforcement is due to the fact that the Chinese government lacks the capacity to monitor every single market research and societal investigation study. As a result, the Chinese government's actions are likely to be *reactionary* rather than *proactive*, and the extent of their reaction is often based on media exposure, particularly by foreign media. However, the government is sometimes more proactive and vigilant in restricting societal investigation during sensitive times and on sensitive topics, and will enforce these rules and regulations more strictly.[7] For example, the Chinese government often has strict oversight of research activities during the annual national assemblies' meetings ("liang hui") or during political transitions at the higher levels of government and party organization. In addition, local governments may be more assertive when the studies could potentially expose the governance issues in their localities.

7.4   Experimental Studies in China and Potential Ethical Issues

In this section, I first highlight some examples of the existing experimental studies concerning Chinese politics. I then suggest two important differences in data collection between experimental studies and traditional methods. In light of these differences as well as the above discussion of government motives and potential risks, I discuss several potential ethical challenges that scholars conducting experimental studies could face.

Experimental studies of Chinese politics are burgeoning in recent years, and they have taken several different forms, primarily field and survey experiments. For example, Guan and Green (2006) conducted one of the first field experiments on door-to-door canvassing techniques in China. Hoffmann and Larner (2013) used field experiments to study the formation of nationalism among Chinese citizens. King, Pan and Roberts (2013) conducted a large-scale field experiment to detect the Internet censoring mechanism in China. Using survey experiments, Lü, Scheve and Slaughter (2012) studied the effects of inequity aversion on trade protection preferences and Lü (2013) investigated how unequal educational opportunity affects resentment toward income inequality. Finally, Gries, Peng and Crowson (2012) conducted a cross-country survey experiment of nationalism in both the United States and China.

Given the restrictions on research with foreign affiliation imposed by the Chinese government, scholars conducting experimental studies in China face similar issues as scholars who use traditional methods. Nonetheless, I contend that experimental studies differ from traditional research methods in two important ways: the data-generating process and the barriers of entry in data collection. Consequently, these differences could raise some new ethical challenges.

First, researchers in experimental studies play a more active role during the data-generating process, which could potentially provoke political behaviors that traditional research may not be able to. Previously, most foreign scholars relied mainly on three types of traditional data-collection approaches when studying contemporary Chinese politics: 1) government documentation and statistics, 2) public opinion surveys, and 3) interviews and ethnographic studies. Scholars using these methods function as observers with minimum intervention in the data-generating process. In other words, these data-collection methods have little ability to provoke political behaviors among the subjects or by the government.

Scholars using experimental methods, however, play a more active role during data collection, which could potentially generate greater impacts on social and political dynamics. By definition, experimental studies require scholars to invoke a "treatment" on the subjects in the experimental group and compare the outcome with that of a control group that does not receive the treatment. Current studies' experimental treatments range from minimum intervention, such as survey experiments that present different information to the subjects (e.g., Gries, Peng and Crowson 2012, Lü, Scheve and Slaughter 2012, Lü, 2013), to intermediate levels of intervention, such as field experiments that trigger different political behaviors in subjects (e.g., Distelhorst and Hou 2014, Guan and Green 2006, King, Pan and Roberts 2013). Take King, Pan and Roberts (Forthcoming) as an example, in which the experimental protocol attempts to reverse engineer the Internet censoring mechanism in China by randomly creating different social media texts on many Chinese websites and studying the extent to which these texts are deleted. While generating important insights, one could expect the Chinese government to revise their future censoring mechanisms in response to this study.

The second primary difference between experimental studies and traditional studies is that traditional studies have a higher entry barrier in data collection—namely, the need for a local partner and the research costs. Collecting reliable information concerning China's politics has been a great challenge to foreign social scientists since 1949, largely because of the complexity of Chinese society and the Chinese government's tight control of information. New opportunities arose for scholars after the establishment of diplomatic relations between China and the United States in 1978 as well as the subsequent economic reforms in China. Nonetheless, scholars still need to possess sufficient language skills and develop strong ties with Chinese domestic scholars, academic institutions, and even government officials in order to carry out their studies.

However, researchers using experimental studies may rely less on the assistance from local partners in China, if not eschewing their help completely. For example, researchers conducting survey experiments may only need to ask a few questions for their experimental treatments. Hence, survey experiments could be embedded into a larger, "omnibus" survey, and many local organizations, especially market research firms, offer these survey opportunities to make a profit. In this approach, the costs could be as little as a few thousand dollars to several thousand dollars, depending on the sample size and methods of interview (e.g., Internet, phone, or face-to-face). In addition, field experiments conducted over the Internet (e.g., Distelhorst and Hou 2014, King, Pan and Roberts 2013) may minimize the need for local partners. In contrast, a traditional large-scale survey, especially those with nationally representative samples, could cost more than ten thousand dollars. Furthermore, carrying out these kinds of studies requires strong collaboration among the foreign and domestic researchers and institutions.

These two unique features of experimental studies generate some ethical dilemmas for researchers to consider. First, the intervention of the experimental treatment could potentially provoke changes in political behaviors by some subjects. As a result, should scholars be responsible for the subsequent political actions taken by the subjects, and more importantly, the adverse responses from the Chinese government? Some may argue that the experimental studies are conducted on such a small scale that they could hardly generate any significant political impact. Furthermore, even if the subjects decide to take political action, one could hardly identify the experimental treatment as the only reason; these subjects may act regardless of the experiment. However, scholars have to be mindful about the potential adverse consequences of the experimental treatment, because ultimately the Chinese citizens and collaborators, not the foreign scholars, are subject to them.

Even if scholars are mindful about the potential adverse consequences, it is difficult to anticipate all of the potential issues *ex ante*, especially for foreign scholars who are not always aware of the most current political environment in China. Traditionally, foreign scholars resolve this issue by relying on Chinese domestic collaborators to gauge the political sensibility of their studies and the potential risks to the subjects and Chinese collaborators. As discussed earlier, however, scholars who conduct survey and field experimental studies may not develop strong ties with local collaborators. Hence, the probability of generating adverse consequences could potentially be higher in experimental studies. In other words, the low barrier of entry for some experimental studies compounds this issue because it may not require the scholars to possess strong language skills and/ or develop strong ties with Chinese researchers or institutions. While the lower barrier of entry for conducting research in China is an advantage for experimental studies, scholars could potentially generate some unintended consequences because of their lack of understanding of Chinese society.

Furthermore, even if researchers have strong ties with domestic collaborators, scholars could pass the ethical dilemma onto the Chinese collaborators by relying on them to make the judgment about whether a study generates too much risk. Broadly speaking, there are two schools of thought concerning this issue. On the one hand, some scholars contend that as long as the research protocol satisfies the Human Subject Committee's board of review, and if Chinese collaborators are willing to participate in the study, they explicitly or implicitly agree to the risks because they understand what they entail. As a result, the burden falls on the Chinese collaborators if they decide to participate in the project. On the other hand, others suggest that scholars should bear the full burden and may not conduct this kind of research if any potential risks emerge that might harm the local partners and/or respondents.

These are two extreme viewpoints, and I would argue that neither of them is completely appropriate in the context of conducting experimental studies in China. The problem with the first perspective is that some Chinese collaborators may not be fully informed about the risks involved, and it is unrealistic to assume they implicitly accept them. In particular, a significant number of commercial marketing firms have been founded in China in recent years. Because many of these firms are new to market research and seek profit maximization, they may not fully understand the potential risks involved, as their primary customers are domestic ones. Concerning the second perspective, if we strictly follow the regulations indicated in the *Measures*, very little, if any, research could be conducted within China's borders. Given the ambiguity of regulations and their inconsistent enforcement, it is difficult for scholars to gauge the risks involved *ex ante*. More importantly, the approval process could undermine the objectivity of the research because the government is inclined to disapprove projects that could expose governance issues.

Finally, scholars may still face a dilemma between the research design and Chinese collaborators' unwillingness to complete compliance for their own safety. Publishing experimental studies in academic journals outside of China has many standard practices, such as detailing the experimental protocol, revealing the institution that carries out the experiment, and sharing the data after the paper is accepted for publication. However, precisely because it is the outcomes rather than the processes of research that are likely to draw the Chinese government's attention, releasing information such as the identity of the Chinese collaborators could potentially jeopardize their safety. As a result, Chinese collaborators may not want to reveal their identities in the publication, and/or they may suggest unconventional ways to describe the data-collection process that conflict with commonly shared scientific standards.

7.5 Common Practices of Experimental Studies and Their Trade-offs

As the above discussion demonstrates, scholars could face various ethical dilemmas when collecting data through experimental studies in China. In particular, the regulatory regime in China suggests that the government is more likely to take action against the local Chinese collaborators than against foreign scholars. In what follows, I discuss four common practices of conducting experimental studies in China and their practical trade-offs. The upshot is that although in theory scholars could individually apply for the permit from NBS to conduct their research, these applications often face a lengthy process and significant barriers to approval. As a result, foreign researchers often seek collaboration with local partners in China.

Practice 1: Collaboration With Chinese Academic Institutions

Collaborating with Chinese academic institutions has been a traditional method for foreign scholars to conduct research in China in past decades. Scholars work closely with Chinese collaborators in academic institutions and think tanks and bear a significant share of the financial costs of the study. The primary advantages of working with Chinese academic institutions are their institutional knowledge and networks that facilitate the study's design and implementation. Chinese domestic academic institutions, particularly those well-established universities and think tanks, offer valuable local knowledge and extensive institutional networks to help foreign scholars navigate the complex and unclear regulatory regime in China. Furthermore, these institutions generally have the government permit and expertise to carry out research with foreign affiliation.

The disadvantages of this practice are twofold: barriers to entry and potential limitations in research design and data distribution. First, the barriers to entry to work with these academic institutions can be high because they do not easily commit to projects with foreign scholars and institutions without credible referrals. In addition, conducting a large-scale study in China with academic institutions can be expensive partly because these institutions have high overhead costs. This is particularly true when the study aims to draw from a national representative sample. Second, these institutions are often more reluctant to ask sensitive questions because they have greater concerns regarding the institution's long-term survival. Furthermore, some of the organizations have close ties with the Bureau of Statistics, and the Bureau may indirectly influence the research design. Finally, they may be reluctant to make the data publicly available, given their concerns that scholars could misuse the data in their publications, thus potentially undermining Chinese academic institutions' survival. As a consequence, foreign scholars may have to seek some compromises when working with Chinese academic institutions.

Practice 2: Collaboration With Commercial Marketing Firms

Public opinion research conducted by marketing firms has been increasing in China in recent years. The growth of marketing firms provides new opportunities for scholars to conduct public opinion and survey experiments. It is worth noting that many of these marketing firms are new to this research area and may not fully understand the potential risks involved. Consequently, scholars need to bear a significant share of the responsibility to inform these firms about the potential risks resulting from the regulations in the *Measures*. Scholars also need to make sure the local partners have the appropriate permit to carry out studies with foreign involvement.[8]

There are several advantages to working with marketing firms. First, the barriers to entry are generally low, because these firms are less selective when working with foreign scholars. Furthermore, working with them generally incurs lower costs than working with academic institutions. Second, studies can be implemented at a faster rate when working with commercial firms. Finally, scholars tend to have a greater degree of freedom in the research design and data distribution.

However, several caveats remain when working with marketing firms. First, upon learning of the potential repercussions, some firms may remain committed to a partnership. Scholars, however, may want to avoid some profit-seeking organizations that do not have much experience with foreign-funded projects, even if these organizations claim to fully understand the risks and are willing to be involved. Second, some firms often lack the capacity to design a proper sampling strategy, especially a nationally representative sample, to satisfy common standards in survey research. While this may not be a critical issue in experimental studies, it remains a concern if scholars attempt to obtain a nationally representative sample. In sum, scholars face a significant challenge when choosing reliable marketing firms to implement their studies in China, as well-established firms will generally have greater capacity than newer ones.

Practice 3: Independent Research Without Government Approval

Anticipating that the Chinese government will not approve the subject of their studies, some scholars may choose to conduct independent research without acquiring government approval or the required permit. In some cases, one or more scholars carry out the study by themselves without utilizing local collaborators. In other cases, they may bring a team of research assistants from outside of China or hire local residents to help them implement the study. Many of these scholars are either unaware of the regulations specified in the *Measures* or choose to ignore them.

The advantage of this approach is that scholars bear the full responsibility of the study without exposing local collaborators, eliminating the ethical dilemma regarding potential harm to local partners. Furthermore, scholars have a significant degree of freedom in designing and implementing the study, as well as post-study data distribution.

The disadvantage of this approach is that it violates the Chinese government's regulations, regardless of how unreasonable the regulations may be. The study could be undermined at any point during the implementation process if the authorities discover it and choose to intervene. In addition, while this approach may be appropriate for ethnographic observations and interviews as well as small-scale survey studies, the sampling strategy has significant limitations, particularly if the scholars aim to draw a national or local representative sample. For experimental studies, while generating a nationally representative sample may not be necessary, conducting independent experimental research may still face significant logistical and coordination challenges.

Practice 4: The Use of Internet

In recent years, scholars have explored new ways to conduct survey or field experiments through the Internet. These studies have been carried out by using Internet services (e.g., email, web pages, etc.) either on domestic Chinese servers or on foreign servers. In some studies, scholars use these venues to directly recruit participants for their studies. In others, scholars directly use the existing Chinese Internet portals to carry out the experiments. This new method has the advantage of relatively low costs and a high degree of freedom in research design, and they may not need any local collaborators to carry out their research. In addition, this method may allow some researchers to legally avoid acquiring government permits when conducting their research. Finally, scholars have complete control over data generation and distribution.

However, experimental studies through the Internet in China are very new, and scholars face several potential issues. First, it is difficult to obtain a nationally representative sample through the Internet in China. In particular, it is difficult to reach rural residents, who in most cases do not have Internet access. Second, if scholars rely on Chinese domestic websites to recruit participants or to conduct their experiments, they may implicitly involve local Chinese "collaborators" without their consent. The Chinese government could take action against these websites, whereas the scholars would bear few repercussions.

Discussion

The risks associated with the first and second strategies largely fall upon the local collaborators. In short, academic institutions or marketing firms bear the main responsibility if the studies generate backlash from the government. As a result, researchers have to think about how much risk they would place upon their local collaborators by carrying out the study. Furthermore, honest and open communication with Chinese collaborators is critical to ensure they understand the risks involved.

For the third and fourth strategies, in which no local collaborators are involved, the risks are ethical and practical ones: (1) Is breaking the law equivalent to "harm" and should we care in an authoritarian country? (2) Does breaking the law make it harder for other scholars to do work in China? Some would argue that breaking the law in authoritarian regimes is not "harm," particularly when the research outcomes could potentially have a positive impact on improving Chinese society. However, the primary risk of this approach is that may potentially endanger other scholars' opportunity to conduct future research in China. For example, if researchers opt for the third strategy, of conducting studies inside China without seeking government permission, and the study attracts significant government attention, the government could impose stricter visa policies for scholars' future visits. Finally, it remains possible that the Chinese government could pursue the researchers when they enter mainland China.[9]

7.6 Conclusion

In this essay, I discuss the challenges of conducting experimental studies in a controlled information environment, such as in China. I argue that although the Chinese government has imposed strict regulations governing social science research with foreign involvement, the enforcement of these regulations is rather scant and inconsistent. Hence, scholars face significant uncertainty with respect to the potential risks when conducting experimental studies in China. In addition, I suggest that if the government decides to take action, it is more likely to punish local collaborators, but not subjects or foreign scholars.

Scholars have attempted different approaches to overcome these restrictions, each of which has various advantages and disadvantages in terms of research design and risk-sharing among scholars and local collaborators. These strategies have been successful in generating insights for our understanding of mass political behaviors in an authoritarian regime context. The pillars of these successes are scholars' cultural sensitivities and the open and honest communication with Chinese collaborators in most cases. However, one can easily imagine that a single study could provoke the government to tighten the control of data collection with foreign affiliation. Hence, most scholars have been trying to avoid sensitive and controversial questions, or at least study these questions in an indirect way.

One could argue that scholars' cultural sensitivity is a form of self-censorship, which hinders our ability to answer important questions about authoritarianism (Holz 2007). This is a valid critique, and scholars should think about the greater social benefits of tackling these important questions. However, risking one's own career and safety to study important questions about authoritarianism may be worthwhile, whereas risking others' careers and safety in the process is unethical at the minimum. Ultimately, this is the key ethical issue we should consider when conducting research in an authoritarian context. As advocated in Wood (2006) and Tsai (2010), no research is more important than the safety of respondents and local collaborators. Researchers have to be mindful about the potential adverse consequences to Chinese collaborators and citizens in order to avoid killing the goose for the golden eggs.

Notes

1 A recent edited volume by Allen Carlson, Mary E. Gallagher, Kenneth Lieberthal, and Melanie Manion offers some excellent insights into research methods for studying contemporary Chinese politics (Carlson et al. 2010).
2 For an overview of recent development in experimental studies in political science, see Druckman et al. (2006) and Humphreys and Weinstein (2009).
3 The definition of "high-level" usually refers to cadres in the central government and party organizations.
4 An official version of the Measures can be found here: http://www.zj.stats.gov.cn/art/2008/5/13/art 93 689.html (accessed March 23, 2014).
5 "Foreign individuals and entities" refers to citizens and organizations outside of mainland China, including Hong Kong, Macau, and Taiwan.
6 The guidelines (in Chinese) for applying to the NBS for a permit can be found here: http://www.stats.gov.cn/tjfw/swdcgl/spcx/201401/t20140114_499382.html (accessed March 23, 2014).
7 Qiang Xiao, a scholar at University of California at Berkeley, regularly publishes the most recent censorship guidelines issued by the government at China Digital Times (http://chinadigitaltimes.net).
8 The National Bureau of Statistics of China publishes the list of organizations approved to carry out research with foreign involvement on their website.
9 For a recent example, see the case of Peter Humphrey and his wife, Yingzeng Yu: http://www.huffingtonpost.co.uk/2013/08/28/china-peter-humphrey_n_3827834.html (accessed September 26, 2013).

8

LOCAL REVIEW

Confronting the Brazilian Black Box

Saul Cunow and Scott Desposato

8.1 Introduction

Political scientists are increasingly adopting experimental methods for research in Brazil. These include both experiments conducted by scholars at Brazilian institutions as well as by foreign scholars, primarily from the United States (Hidalgo, de Figueiredo and Kasahara 2011, Turgeon and Rennó 2010, Dunning 2010, Boas 2012). These experiments cover a diverse set of theoretical questions about development, political parties, voting behavior, and media, but almost all share a single common feature: They did not comply with Brazilian ethical procedures.

Brazil does have a well-documented process for ethical review of experiments involving human subjects. Research ethics, norms, and procedures are established in a regulation issued by the National Council of Health, part of the Ministry of Health. The regulation applies to *anyone* conducting an experiment in Brazil, although it is often ignored by foreign social scientists.

In this chapter, we examine the procedures and practice of ethical review in Brazil. We draw on our own experience seeking review for an experiment we conducted in Brazil, in collaboration with Rosario Aguilar, author of Chapter 9 in this volume (Aguilar et al. 2015, Aguilar, Cunow and Desposato Forthcoming). In total, ethical review took over a year, and technically was never complete. The challenges of completing an ethical review in Brazil and conducting a fully legal experiment mean that compliance with Brazilian law could severely stifle most experimental research conducted there. How can scholars with legitimate low-risk projects proceed? And what should scholars do to avoid being "scooped" by less scrupulous colleagues?

We begin with a review of Brazilian law covering human subjects, then discuss our experiments and our experience with the human subjects review process.

Finally, we conclude with a series of recommendations for how scholars should proceed in the short and long term when conducting research in environments like Brazil's.

8.2 Brazilian Ethical Rules

Although most political scientists seem unaware that they exist, Brazil has a highly organized and centralized set of institutions for overseeing research ethics. The entire process is managed by the Ministry of Health, reflecting its origin and ongoing concern primarily with medical studies, as well as research on indigenous tribes. Within the Ministry of Health is a National Council of Health, which is an appointed body whose mission is "the deliberation, supervision, oversight, and monitoring of public policy in the area of health" (Conselho Nacional de Saúde 2015). One of their jurisdictions is establishing rules for human subjects research, most of which are in their Resolution 196/96. This resolution establishes a National Committee for Ethics in Research (CONEP), which has national authority for managing human subject review. CONEP occasionally reviews research proposals, but also certifies and supervises local ethics committees, called "Committees on Ethics in Research," or CEPs.[1] These local committees are usually based at universities and other institutes.

This resolution's status and authority is what would be called *Direito Administrativo* in Brazil, technically a form of regulation. It is broad and comprehensive. The resolution establishes rules governing research and the requirements for and nature of ethical review.

While our focus in this chapter is on the review process, we briefly draw attention to one unique feature of their rules: a prohibition on compensating subjects for participating in trials. Subjects can be reimbursed for travel costs or provided with meals or other benefits while waiting for appointments. Researchers might also be able to compensate subjects for lost income. But the cash payments offered to potential subjects in some countries are illegal.[2] Presumably, this prohibition is to prevent researchers from inducing Brazilians to participate in especially risky experiments, just as excessive compensation for risky trials is considered unethical in other countries. However, the prohibition on all compensation poses challenges to scholars seeking to incentivize behavior.[3]

Regarding review procedures, Brazilian rules state that, "Every study involving human beings must be submitted for review to a Committee on Research Ethics" (Conselho Nacional de Saúde 2000). Most simple studies can be reviewed by a local CEP, without referral to the national committee (CONEP). However, some studies require a second round of reviews by the national CONEP (more on that below).

Many social science departments in Brazil do not have local ethics committees, and historically research in political science has not required interaction with human subjects. With increasing experimental studies and public opinion surveys, some departments are beginning to establish local committees and seek certification from CONEP. If one's home institution does not have a CEP, the researcher must request referral to an appropriate CEP from CONEP, the national committee. The local committees may not refuse to review these proposals referred from CONEP.

The basic review is fairly straightforward, if cumbersome. A series of documents must be submitted in an online registry of scholars. The documents are referred to a local ethics committee (CEP), which can approve, request changes, or reject most studies. For a typical experiment from a US-based scholar, the one complication is identifying a local CEP to work with, as most US scholars do not have affiliations with local institutions. In this case, the scholar requests that the national committee (CONEP) refer the research proposal to a local ethical committee (CEP). The scholar can suggest and request a target institution; CONEP may grant that request or refer the proposal to a different institution.

For most types of studies, the CEP makes final determination and the research proceeds promptly. Some research protocols that are considered higher risk must face a second review by the national ethics committee, CONEP. More precisely, national review is required for any study involving human genetics; human reproduction; new/new to Brazil vaccines; new/new to Brazil medical equipment; new/new to Brazil procedures; indigenous populations; biosecurity; anything that a CEP wishes to refer to CONEP for additional review; biorepositories; and, most critically for our purposes, research with foreign participation. Foreign involvement means either that the research is funded internationally (by an organization outside Brazil) or includes scholars based outside Brazil. Although intimidating, the resolution does establish reasonable time limits for these analyses, some 60 days to review submitted proposals.[4]

Besides mandating a national review of the research, foreign involvement also triggers other requirements. The project must show substantial domestic (Brazilian) involvement, that results of the study will return to Brazil, and that there will be technology transfer, as appropriate. Again, these requirements reveal a focus on high-tech medical procedures rather than the simple lab or survey experiments common in political science. This focus on technology transfer and return of results seems to imply that political scientists must have a domestic partner to conduct the research.

The consequences of any violations of Brazilian ethical rules—including research without ethical approval—are determined after an administrative process, although most of the potential consequences will most directly affect Brazilians: One loses one's research rights and the ability to obtain fellowships for students, one is removed from the research association, and one cannot be a Principal Investigator. These consequences, as well as the administrative procedures for seeking ethical review, are directed primarily at Brazilian researchers, and the regulations do not appear to have anticipated foreign political scientists without local partners.

8.3   Our Experiment and Experience With the Brazilian Review Process

We have observed some ethical problems involving political science experiments overseas, and when we started planning a series of experiments to be conducted in Brazil we were determined not to make any mistakes. Our experiment was simple and extremely low risk—we describe it below—but still required a full review by Brazilian IRB. We enthusiastically engaged the process, prepared the documents, and submitted them for review. Three years later, we are less enthusiastic. The process would be amusing, if it did not nearly derail a research agenda in which we had much time and effort invested. But it has been a learning process.

Our study used a simple survey experiment where subjects were presented with hypothetical candidate profiles and asked to choose their most preferred one. The profiles consisted of names, photographs, short biographies, and brief policy positions on three issues. All of the information in the profiles was hypothetical— no information from any actual candidates was used. The experiment varied the ethnicity and gender of the candidates, their location on the ballot, and the total number of candidates. The dependent variable was the preferred candidate, or the refusal to choose a candidate.

The study focused on whether increasing the number of candidates affected subjects' preferences. Our hypotheses were derived from the literature in consumer choice, which has shown how giving subjects too many choices leads to their making worse choices—a form of information overload. In political science, Cunow (2015) has shown how choice set size affects voters' ability to choose a best candidates as well as their willingness to choose *any* candidate. We hypothesized that subjects choosing from just a few candidates would be more likely to choose based on policy positions. But when faced with long ballots and many choices, we expected subjects to be overwhelmed by the complexity of decision-making and fall back on racial heuristics.

Our design and protections were reviewed by the UCSD Institutional Review Board, which provided initial approval on May 6, 2010. The experiment was extremely low risk. The candidates were all hypothetical, imaginary people— some of their photos were even digitally altered so that they did not represent any single "real" individual. Respondents were only asked to evaluate the hypothetical candidates and provide some basic demographic information. No identifying or contact information about subjects was recorded. Subjects were given information about the study and voluntarily participated, and there were no adverse incidents. Moreover, at the time of the study there was no election taking place that could have polluted the results or that might have been influenced by our experimental stimuli or manipulations. The primary risk to subjects would be becoming bored, and even this would be difficult given the extremely short time period of the trials, which we expected to be less than five minutes.

Our study poses minimal risk to subjects, yet the Brazilian review process was long and bureaucratic. The timeline below summarizes major events in the review process. Approval for our project from the Human Research Protections Program at UCSD took 21 days from the day we submitted our application. Following this approval, we began the process of seeking local approval in Brazil. This process took 293 days (220 days for the first contingent approval) from the time we first contacted the National Research Ethics Committee (CONEP) to request information about the approval process.

April 15, 2010	Application submitted to UCSD Human Research Protections Program.
May 6, 2010	UCSD Human Research Protections Program approves study, 21 days after the proposal was submitted.
June 21, 2010	First email contact with the National Research Ethics Committee/Comissão Nacional de Ética em Pesquisa (CONEP) was made to request information about the approval process and whether it was necessary to seek approval for our project.
June 22, 2010	Received an email response from the CONEP. Requested assignment to a local Research Ethics Committee/Comissão Nacional de Ética em Pesquisa (CEP).
July 12, 2010	Received a referral from the CONEP to the Commitê de Ética em Pesquisa (CEP) at the Faculdade de Ciências da Saúde at the University of Brasília (UnB).
July 19, 2010	Emailed CONEP about part of application that did not seem to apply to our project.
July 21, 2010	Received response from CONEP about application question.
August, 2010	Scheduled date for meeting of the CEP and the University of Brasília.
August, 2010	A strike at UnB cancelled the meeting. When the CEP did meet, they refused to review our proposal, citing their backlog of projects to review. After several rounds of exchanges between the national CONEP and UnB CEP, we asked for reassignment to a new Ethical Committee. We were assigned to the Public Health School at the University of São Paulo.
September 15, 2010	Received a response from the Commitê de Ética em Pesquisa (COEP) at the Faculdade de Saúde Pública at the

University of São Paulo (USP) indicating their willingness to review our proposal.

September 31, 2010	Meeting scheduled for the COEP at USP.
October 7, 2010	Received response from the COEP at the USP indicating that our proposal could not be accepted because they had not received the referral from CONEP and because our cover sheet was outdated. This was the cover sheet we had downloaded directly from the CONEP's website.
October 21, 2010	We filed a new form with CONEP and requested referral from the CONEP to the COEP at the University of Saõ Paulo.
November 12, 2010	CONEP sends referral to COEP at the USP.
November 17, 2010	Proposal delivered by hand to the COEP at the USP.
January 28, 2011	Initial proposal given contingent approval by COEP at USP 200 days after the proposal was first referred to the CEP by the CONEP on July 12, 2010 and 220 days after initial contact was made with the CONEP on June 22, 2010.
February, 2011	We submitted requested revisions.
April 11, 2011	We received notification that our project had been approved by the COEP, 293 days after initial contact with CONEP on June 22, 2010.

Reviewing our years' work, part of the delay was our unfamiliarity with the process, and part of it was just bad luck—a strike at a university, for example, and a refusal by a local ethics committee to find time to review our proposal—in spite of a directive from the national Ministry of Health.

The process was especially frustrating because of the lack of communication at every step of the process. We would wait months for an update, and calls and emails were often unanswered. This was particularly discouraging when the end result was a refusal to review our proposal because of an expired cover sheet.

This lack of communication continued after the research project. For the next year, we emailed members of CONEP, asking for guidance, and inviting them to our workshop on ethics in political science. We never received any response. We also tried tracking down individual CONEP members through their home institutions, emailing them, and even "friending" and messaging them via Facebook. We never received any responses from them.

Ironically, while we labored to comply with the resolution governing ethical review for our research project, both local CEPs that were scheduled to review our proposal failed to comply with the required time limits for reviewing proposals as dictated by that same resolution. CNS Resolution 196/96 states that one of the duties of the CEP is "to issue written technical opinions, within thirty (30) days, clearly identifying the assay, documents studied and date of review" and to issue a judgment on the proposal or request modifications (Conselho Nacional de Saúde 2000, 24). Our review took far longer than thirty days as did communication from the CEP at the UnB indicating that they would not review our proposal.

Although our experience with the ethical review process in Brazil was particularly slow and frustrating, it does not seem to be entirely atypical. At an interdisciplinary conference in Washington, DC, one of the authors was told by a number of medical researchers that lengthy delays in the Brazilian review process are common. Indeed, one mentioned that large grants have expired unspent because of delays in the review process. An anthropologist at a prominent Brazilian university also indicated to the authors that lengthy delays, poor communication, and a lack of familiarity with research methodologies outside of the hard sciences on the part of the members of the CONEP often delayed or derailed research agenda in the humanities.

An additional frustration for us was that during the same period, other scholars executed and published similar experiments on candidate race in Brazil—without any local human subjects' review.

8.4 Conclusion

Our experience with the Brazilian review process was not exactly a positive one. Merely obtaining a partial approval was extremely time consuming and frustrating. We rarely had clear communications as to our proposal's status or what was needed to expedite and facilitate review. There was never any hint of corruption; it instead seemed that they were either incompetent or uninterested in reviewing our project. In addition, the review itself made no contribution to the safety or cultural sensitivity of our low-risk project; all our experiences with the Brazilian review process involved bureaucratic procedure.

What should scholars do in a country like Brazil, where the review process appears to be inappropriate for social science and where the regulatory body empowered to conduct review conveys indifference regarding social science proposals? Let's consider the issues at stake, and then examine several possible strategies.

The case against seeking any review in Brazil is compelling for many. The ethical issues associated with the extent of review sought in the Brazilian case are usually not about protecting individual human subjects or bystanders. Most political science experiments are very low risk and most are likely to have been reviewed already at scholars' home institutions. The process is lengthy, confusing, and time consuming. For a non-Brazilian, there are unlikely to be any legal or career repercussions from ignoring Brazilian regulations. The regulatory consequences appear more consequential for Brazilians than for foreigners.[5] Further, although many Brazilian and foreign scholars have run political science experiments in Brazil without obtaining required ethical approval, we know of no case where CONEP has asserted any authority or where there have been any consequences for scholars.

Not surprisingly, most scholars simply ignore the Brazilian review process and conduct experiments without local approval. This is clearly the path of least resistance. We are not aware of any other non-Brazilian political scientist who has even bothered to attempt the full review process, and many Brazilian scholars have also not sought ethical approval.[6] One scholar told us that we were "stupid" to seek approval.

Our experience with the national review committee in Brazil suggests their posture is one of bored indifference to our activity. They did not comply with their own rules regarding time limits for review, they did not provide transparent and updated information about how to complete the review process, and at least one local committee (the CEP at the University of Brasília) ignored a national directive to review our proposal. Our follow-up efforts to communicate with the National Research Ethics Committee (CONEP) were simply ignored. In other words, we tried to play by the rules, but no one else showed up to the game!

Many US-based scholars' home institutions have no rules that require compliance when operating in foreign countries. The UCSD IRB (Human Research Protections Program or HRPP) does not ask its researchers to obtain foreign approval or even whether their experiments are legal when conducted overseas. The main funding agency for US political scientists, the National Science Foundation, also does not ask award recipients for any proof of foreign review. Thus it appears that there are unlikely to be any consequences in the United States or in Brazil for foreigners running experiments without local review. For Brazilians, the IRB process is easier because their proposals do not need a national review, and the consequences of noncompliance are higher under existing regulations. Even so, in our experience, many Brazilian scholars are ignoring their country's ethical rules.

There is, however, a case to be made for compliance. Brazil is a consolidated and legitimate democracy. Their regulations are driven in part by negative experiences with anthropologists working with indigenous tribes, by fear of being guinea pigs for multinational pharmaceuticals, and concern that poverty will lead Brazilian citizens to bear the risks and costs of experiments while the benefits of learning accrue to those wealthy enough to afford first-world treatment. In this sense, Brazilian rules are designed to protect subjects, not prevent research or protect a regime.[7] As such, their rules deserve our respect, even if they are easy to avoid.

There are also potential benefits to compliance. The Brazilian review process might help assure that research is contextually appropriate and legal, especially for scholars from institutions with no IRB process or requirements at all. In addition, review may be valuable for protecting the broader community of political scientists. A controversial experiment conducted in Brazil without review could generate a backlash against all political science experiments in Brazil, especially those conducted by foreigners. A local review process could help assure that research designs are contextually appropriate and do not violate local laws or norms. It could also provide some legal cover if an experiment were to prove controversial.

Most experiments are unlikely to generate any controversy. But some may, and in those cases, compliance with local rules provides some legal cover protection against allegations of foreign imperialism. Hidalgo, de Figueiredo and Kasahara (2011) ran a field experiment during an election in Brazil in which they distributed over 100,000 campaign advertisements attacking prominent politicians in São Paulo. Their goal was to measure the impact of the advertisement on vote share, and they randomized treatments across voting districts. They did many things carefully—for example, choosing an election in which their treatment would not affect the result and consulting a lawyer. However, according to Brazil's electoral authority, the treatment was illegal under Brazilian electoral law. In addition, it was not submitted for ethical review in Brazil. A local review could have helped clarify the legal status of the study in Brazil and provided some protection in the event of any public controversy. At a minimum, a local review might deflect criticism away from foreign research in general. Yet compliance comes with a cost. If others' experience is like ours, full compliance with Brazilian rules will probably mean that the pace of research will slow considerably for non-Brazilian scholars or those in Brazil using foreign research funds.

How should the field proceed? Push forward and run experiments illegally, and hope we stay off the radar? Or attempt to comply with Brazilian regulations but suffer long, perhaps endless delays? We believe that there are constructive alternatives to this dichotomy, and we conclude with some recommendations.

First, we suggest not giving up just yet on CONEP and the Brazilian review process. As far as we know, we are the only foreign political scientists to ever attempt a full national review, and there is probably room for learning on both sides. If more political scientists were to attempt the full review process, one possible result is that the process itself would improve. Scholars would learn how to navigate the process, which committees were most appropriate for review, and what types of experiments should simply not be attempted. CONEP might respond favorably, learn about social science research, and adapt accordingly. This could lead to an improved and streamlined review process. Other social science fields do navigate the process successfully—published ethnographic research usually cites CONEP approval in addition to IRB approval from scholars' home institutions. In the short run, the obvious cost of full compliance is that initially, the pace of research might slow to a trickle for those attempting a full Brazilian review. In addition, our expectations for scholars' and CONEP's learning might be too optimistic.

Second, should foreign scholars continue to have difficulty communicating with CONEP or having their research proposals reviewed, perhaps local review by a Brazilian university committee would be sufficient. In the past several years, social science departments in Brazil are increasingly establishing their own ethics review committees (CEPs). In particular, the University of São Paulo has expressed a willingness to work with foreign scholars and provide ethical review at their CEP, and is developing a fast-track procedure for minimal risk studies. This should streamline the process and help scholars avoid the problems we experienced.

Third, some types of experiments may provide ways to avoid triggering the need for Brazilian review. For example, Internet-based survey experiments, when run on servers based outside Brazil, might be appropriate candidates for skipping local review.[8] These studies tend to be no more than minimal risk with informed and consenting subjects. Brazil is a democracy with rights of freedom of expression and many polling organizations, so questions about politics are not sensitive or risky. And technically, because the survey data is recorded on computers based outside the country, the study is not being conducted in Brazil. Perhaps studies like these don't need to wait a year for CONEP's approval. Similarly, third party interventions where scholars are merely analyzing data post-treatment need not trigger a CONEP review for foreign involvement.[9] The scholar is not causing or implementing the treatment—just analyzing the data after it has been generated. Such activities would not seem to require any Brazilian IRB process.

Lastly, Brazilian scholars in social sciences and humanities are currently engaged in a debate over the appropriate nature of ethical review for research in their disciplines. There is widespread frustration with their having to use burdensome and lengthy procedures that were clearly developed for medical and related disciplines. Review procedures are likely to change in the near future. We should support these efforts, share our knowledge about the strengths and weaknesses of our own IRB processes, and contribute to the development of appropriate institutions in Brazil.

The current generation of researchers may be forced to bear a disproportionate share of the costs of establishing better relationships with local ethics boards and clearer, more efficient procedures for foreign scholars. Research may be delayed and scholars risk being "beaten to the punch" by others who choose to ignore local ethical standards. This cost is especially high for scholars with short time horizons—graduate students and junior faculty—and the leadership here should be provided by those with tenure. However, investments today will yield easier processes and higher ethical standards for the field in the future. Efficient ethical review boards at universities in the United States have enhanced the integrity of research in the social sciences. Similarly efficient and thorough processes and high standards for work in comparative politics will surely yield similar dividends for the field in the future.

Notes

1 There is variation in names of ethics committees across institutions as well as acronyms. Most common are Comissão de Ética em Pesquisa (or Pesquisas), Cômite de Ética em Pesquisa, and Coordenadoria de Ética em Pesquisa.
2 One of the authors, not knowing this, ran an experiment in Brazil some years ago where subjects were compensated 10–20 reais per trial, or about $5-$10 at that time.
3 Our inquiries on how incentivized laboratory experiments might be conducted have gone unanswered.
4 The text notes that their responsibility is to "to approve, within sixty (60) days, and monitor the protocols of research in special areas . . . " (Conselho Nacional de Saúde 2000, 27), or in the original Portuguese, "Analisar, no prazo de 60 dias, e monitorar direta ou indiretamente, os protocolos de pesquisa nas seguintes áreas temáticas especiais . . . "
5 For example, one possible consequence is losing one's ability to serve as a PI in Brazil.
6 One example on Brazilian scholars' attitudes on their own ethical rules may be illustrative. One of us taught a class on experiments at one of Brazil's best social science research institutes, the Fundação Getúlio Vargas, and dedicated about 10% of the course to ethics of experiments. The audience was entirely Brazilian graduate students, who proved extremely engaged and capable. A year later, when we returned, many were conducting their own experiments. Some were quite elaborate. One student was conducting media studies of voters. Another student was conducting elite experiments, sending different treatment emails to randomly drawn legislators. Yet another was arranging meetings between community organizations and legislators to study how legislators would allocate their time to different community groups. The intellectual community there is rich and interesting, and these students were quickly moving forward with engaging ideas. But even after a course that covered ethical review requirements, not a single experimentalist from this class was even considering seeking ethical review.
7 See Lü's chapter on China (Chapter 7 of this volume).
8 This strategy is also discussed in Lü's chapter on China (Chapter 7 of this volume).
9 See the Nickerson and Hyde chapter (Chapter 13 of this volume) for additional discussion.

9

ETHICAL PERSPECTIVES IN COUNTRIES WITHOUT AN INSTITUTIONAL REVIEW BOARD

The Case of Mexico

Rosario Aguilar

9.1 Introduction

Political science research is limited by funding and should certainly be limited by ethics. As a political scientist trained in the United States in experimental methodology, I quickly learned about the role of the Institutional Review Board (IRB) in evaluating and approving my research. I had to take exams that proved I understood the ethical principles guiding research with human subjects and the historical reasons for their existence. As a political science scholar now working in Mexico, I started investigating the role of ethics reviewers in Mexico when I began applying for funding. I found there was no legal framework to regulate the ethical component of social science research. Thus, I started teaching my students the ethical concerns we should take into account when conducting fieldwork, as no one evaluates that component of our research. Because of my familiarity with the IRB procedures in the United States, I am well aware that the procedural issues we deal with as social scientists are not distinct from the biomedical ones. These differences between the social sciences and biomedical research methods and questions should evolve into different review processes (Seligson 2008, Singer and Levine 2003). In my experience going through IRB procedures at different universities in the United States, research in the social sciences can be significantly delayed if reviewers use the same standards to evaluate biomedical and social science research applications, where in most cases the latter's scope of intervention is not as broad as in the former.

This chapter seeks to open a discussion about the ethical concerns researchers should take into account when conducting experimental research in developing countries that have no ethical regulations for conducting social science research. We should think about the ethics review process as evaluating the ethics of the research but not the results.[1] I use the example of Mexico because it is where

I have conducted research and where I work. The structure of the chapter is as follows: The first section presents my experience conducting research in Mexico. The second section discusses the legal framework for researchers as well as what social scientists have done when seeking ethical approval for their research design. The third section concludes with suggestions for actions we should take to ensure our research abides by basic ethical principles in settings where they are not required.

9.2 Experimental Research in Mexico

In the last 15 years, experimental research has expanded in Mexico. Among the topics covered, scholars have looked at the effect of public programs on citizens' political, economic, or social behavior (i.e., Attanasio, Meghir and Santiago 2012, Behrman, Sengupta and Todd 2005, De La O 2013, Todd and Wolpin 2006); the causes and effects of corruption on government officials and/or citizens (i.e., Chong et al. 2015, Fried, Lagunes and Venkataramani 2010); compliance of government officials with the law depending on citizens' characteristics (i.e., Lagunes 2009); the effect of the perception of a threat on citizens' political attitudes (i.e., Merolla and Zechmeister 2009); and the effect of racial phenotypes on voters' electoral preferences (i.e., Aguilar 2009; Chapter 9 in this volume).

To date, scholars have relied on their own judgments regarding the ethics of the experimental design, recruiting process, and other procedures of their studies because there are no ethical committees working in Mexico. In this situation, the Belmont Report is a good initial reference for the ethical guidelines we should follow when conducting research (The National Commission for the Protection of Human Subjects of Biomedical and Behavioral Research 1979). The Belmont Report consists of three principles: respect for persons, beneficence, and justice.

The principle of respect for persons includes treating individuals as autonomous agents so they can decide whether or not to participate in our research. This principle also implies that we have to protect vulnerable individuals, such as children, the elderly, and inmates, who might not be able to give an autonomous consent. The principle of beneficence guarantees that people are not only treated with respect but also that researchers do their best to secure their well-being. This principle mandates that researchers avoid hurting participants in their research. At the same time, researchers should maximize potential benefits and minimize potential harm participants might derive from taking part in the study. According to this principle, we should ask ourselves about the value of our research, thus evaluating the risks and benefits of our study. If we ask people to participate in a study that may somehow affect their lives, even if minimally, we should ensure that the results of our research are valuable, not only for us but for society in general. In addition, we should determine how essential the experiment is and whether the data could be obtained by methods other than those involving people's participation. It is rare, although not impossible, for participants in political science experiments to derive benefits from our research; therefore, we should always seek to minimize any potential harm they might suffer because of their participation.[2]

The principle of justice aims for fairness in distribution or to adjudicate what each individual deserves. Thus, we should treat individuals equally unless our research justifies not doing so, remembering to minimize harm to all participants and nonparticipants alike.[3]

In my experience in developing research, running into ethical issues we do not initially think about is unavoidable, even if we go through an IRB. Researchers have documented and explored those issues in special cases, such as conflict zones (Paluck 2009, Wood 2006) and have also discussed the ethical requirements when conducting field experiments in general (De La O and Wantchekon 2011, Gerber 2011) or taking advantage of a natural experiment (Druckman et al. 2011).

In this section, I will present my personal experience as a researcher in Mexico. While I was conducting my dissertation research, I identified ethical issues in Mexico that I did not find when conducting the same research in the United States. In my research, I examined the political and social consequences of prejudice related to people's racial phenotypes among Mexican Americans and Mexicans. I conducted experiments in Chicago and Mexico City, recruiting participants from different settings. In Mexico City, I recruited people from shopping malls, markets, plazas, movie theaters, factories, offices, and coffee shops. In Chicago, I recruited people from churches and a Latino fair, all in the neighborhood of Pilsen (Aguilar 2009, Chapter 9 in this volume). I explained the purpose of my research to all subjects and asked for their consent. My explanation did not include telling participants I was interested in their evaluation of other people based on phenotypes, nor did I tell them that I would take their pictures to look at their phenotypes.[4]

In order to take subjects' pictures, I verbally debriefed them, explained the research purpose of the pictures, and assured them I would not make them public. This information was also explained in the debrief form. Most of the Chicago subjects agreed to have their pictures taken. In Mexico, most of the subjects permitted their pictures to be taken, but I was concerned that some were acquiescing because they felt pressured to do so. As an explanation, some of the subjects in the plaza and factories were low-income and dark-skinned individuals whose social status was lower than mine. Although I am Mexican, it was obvious that I had more economic means than they did, and I am lighter skinned. Both characteristics convey a higher social status. I solved this issue by spending more time talking to these participants and assuring them that they would receive compensation regardless of whether their pictures were taken.[5] In the end, all but one person agreed to have their pictures taken, and I attribute this, in part, to the rapport I was able to develop with them. However, I felt uncomfortable in these situations when I sensed that they perceived me as having some kind of power over them, and I worried that I was not respecting the participants' ability to make an autonomous decision.[6]

This experience of different relations of power between researchers and research participants is common when conducting comparative research. These differentials of power occur regardless of whether the researcher is a member of the society being studied (Sultana 2007). The power relation between the researcher and the research subjects tends to be more apparent when the researchers come from more economically developed societies than when they are dominant culture members of the society they are studying. Certain characteristics of these researchers, such as their socioeconomic status (i.e., social class and education), racial appearance, and nationality, are likely to convey greater privilege to the researcher in relation to the subjects. One way of reducing the negative impact of this differential of power is being transparent about the researchers' status, purposes, objectives, and research procedures (Fassinger and Morrow 2013). In this sense, it is important that research subjects understand their rights and feel free to decline to participate in a study.

For this reason, when designing experiments and recruiting participants in Mexico, as in other countries with high levels of inequality, it is a good idea to follow the principles of respect for persons, beneficence, and justice discussed in the Belmont Report (The National Commission for the Protection of Human Subjects of Biomedical and Behavioral Research 1979). As Mexico is a country with high levels of socioeconomic inequality and a diversity of indigenous groups that tend to overlap with the lower social class, we need to be vigilant that participants in our research never feel pressured to enter or stay in a study.[7] We also have to be careful to not put subjects at risk and to ensure that there is fairness in the distribution of costs and benefits to all subjects derived from the research.

There are other ethical and legal considerations we should take into account when conducting research in other countries besides the principles included in the Belmont Report. First, the Confucian principle of not doing to others what you do not want others to do unto you applies when conducting research in different countries. If there are research designs that would not be considered ethical in the United States or in another country, it is very likely they are not ethical elsewhere because ethical treatment and behavior are not relativistic. Ethical treatment refers to the way we should treat each other because of our shared humanity. Second, we should be familiar with the country's legal framework and abstain from breaking laws. For example, in the case of Mexico, the Electoral Law establishes that the National Electoral Institute (INE), electoral candidates, political parties, and local electoral bodies are the only ones that can promote the vote. In every election, the INE is responsible for setting the rules for non-governmental organizations (NGOs) to follow when organizing campaigns to promote citizens' electoral participation (Congreso de la Unión 2014).[8] Therefore, if researchers want to conduct a field experiment to examine the effect that "get out the vote" messages have on people's behavior on Election Day, they should follow the rules set by the INE. Even better would be to coordinate with the INE or with an organization already promoting the vote so the researcher would have the support of an actor involved in such an effort.

In the following section I discuss the status quo regarding regulations for social science research in Mexico, options for researchers in need of ethical approval, and plans in progress to create and institutionalize a review process.

9.3   Mexico: Laws and Ethics

In contrast to medical research, other types of research that involved the participation of individuals had not, until recently, been regulated in Mexico. In 2010, a new law regarding the collection, treatment, and protection of personal data changed this situation; researchers in both public and private institutions now have to follow this law if the information collected is used for nonpersonal purposes. In spite of this new regulation, I did not find any research institution, including mine, with clear processes to regulate the use of personal data in social science research.

As I was writing this chapter, I engaged in conversations with my institution's Centro de Investigación y Docencia Económicas (Center for Research and Teaching in Economics [CIDE]) authorities and with researcher Prof. Sergio Cárdenas from the Public Administration Division,[9] who needed an ethics certification for his research as it was being funded by a foreign foundation. We decided to embark in a process to 1) create an ethics committee that could review research proposals and 2) create a curriculum to teach the role of ethics in research to both our students and faculty members. We are in the process of developing these two goals.

In the search for ethics review committees in social science institutions, I found one private university, Universidad Iberoamericana, that mentions a review committee in the psychology department. In personal correspondence with Prof. Alejandra Domínguez from that department, I learned that the academic committee is more interested in the technical components of a proposal. Prof. Domínguez noted that the committee could also address any ethical issues, but this is not one of their responsibilities. Finally, this committee looks into psychological and biomedical research only, not political science (personal communication with Alejandra Domínguez, April 17 and 25, 2013).

In the case of the CIDE, Prof. Sergio Cárdenas, who is researching education and equality and has received grants from American foundations, has previously required an ethics review from a Mexican evaluator. Cárdenas started talking to faculty within his division to create such a committee that could review research proposals. As he needed a review of his work quickly, he contacted a professor from the Mexican National Institutes of Health who is a reviewer on an ethics committee within that Institute. The reviewer agreed to evaluate Cárdenas' research proposal and eventually certified it. The foundation agreed with this procedure (personal conversations and communication with Sergio Cárdenas, February 20, 2013). It is clear that we do not have a set of ethical regulations for conducting research within the social sciences in Mexico, and when we need an ethical review, we have to recruit the help of evaluators from the health sciences.

While regulation for the complete ethical treatment of subjects in social science research is missing, the 2010 Law for the Protection of Personal Data in Mexico regulates the process for collecting, treating, and storing personal data. The law applies mainly to people who collect personal data in the country. There are eight principles considered within the law (Ornelas Núñez 2013):

1. Legality: The use of the data collected should be within the country's legal framework.
2. Fidelity: The collection of data should be done through truthful means, without lying to subjects.
3. Consent: Treatment of the data requires their owners' explicit or tacit consent, except in the cases considered within this law. For this purpose, people receive a privacy notice explaining the reasons for collecting the data, its future usage, the rights they have over the data, and how it will be stored.[10]
4. Quality: The person responsible for keeping the personal data should make sure that the data is accurate and current for the purposes of its collection. After the complete use of the data, according to the privacy notice, the personal data should be destroyed.
5. Purpose: The use of the data is restricted to the uses specified in the privacy notice.
6. Proportionality: The use of personal data should only be necessary, adequate, and relevant in relation to the information included in the privacy notice. Furthermore, the responsible party should make every possible effort to spend as little time as possible using sensitive personal data.
7. Responsibility: The responsible party for storing and handling the data should make sure that the handling and storing of the data is always within the framework of the law.
8. Information: The responsible party has the obligation to inform, through the privacy notice, the subjects that are providing their data about the information being collected and the purpose of the data collection.

The law establishes as a general rule that we should assume tacit consent for most of the treatment of the data collected unless the nature of the data is financial or sensitive. The law sets different regulations depending on the type of data collected because the legislators considered that the use of financial or sensitive data could have a negative effect on their owners. The concern was that misuse of sensitive data could lead to endangering or discriminating against individuals. Examples of these data are people's racial or ethnic origin; current and future health status;

genetic information; religious, philosophical, and moral beliefs; political opinions; sexual orientation; and union membership (Congreso de la Unión 2010*a*).

According to the law, the nature of most data collected by political scientists is sensitive, so we must ask for expressed consent in order to collect it. Where there has been a previous process of disassociating the identifiable data of the person from the rest of the data, it is not necessary to obtain people's consent (Congreso de la Unión 2010*b*).

Consent is provided after the researcher gives or explains the privacy notice to the subject. According to the law, the privacy notice should include an explanation of the researcher's usage of the data, including the reasons for collecting the data. The website of the Federal Institute for Access to Public Information and Data Protection has a template researchers can follow to write the privacy notice.[11] The regulations establish that in order for the consent to be legal it should meet three criteria. First, the person giving the consent should not feel pressured or obliged to give it. Second, the person should have a clear idea of the researcher's purpose in collecting the data. Third, the person should have all the information included in the privacy notice and the consequences of consenting to give up personal information before the researcher uses that data.

The law also provides subjects the ability to access, change, cancel, or oppose the treatment of their data by the party responsible as long as it is contemplated within the law. Participants always have the right to stop the use of their data without having to justify their decision unless the data stored are not associated with participants' identifiable information. Thus, in cases where researchers do not store participants' identifiable information, such as name and address, with the rest of the data, the law ceases to apply to the information stored (Congreso de la Unión 2010*a*).

The privacy notice should clearly explain these options to the participants and provide researchers' contact information in case participants do not want researchers to use their data when research participants can be identified, such as in panel studies. In sum, participants should consent to provide their information in a study in a written, electronic, or verbal form. If the research design does not involve storing subjects' identifiable information with the data, then subjects cannot request the researcher to withdraw their data. In addition, the privacy notice should explain the reason for collecting people's data (Congreso de la Unión 2010*a*).

The law leaves open the option of presenting a consent form at the beginning of the study that does not inform completely or gives a different reason from the real one for conducting the study. In these cases, when explaining the real reason for conducting the study would bias the results of the research, researchers must debrief the participants, provide them with the privacy notice once the treatment is over, and give them the option of not including their personal data in the research.

If we consider the law and regulations regarding the collection, usage, and storage of personal information in Mexico, there are some experiments we cannot conduct without a person's consent. For example, it would be illegal to collect political data with identifiable information from subjects without their consent. If we are going to collect such data in a field experiment without the consent of the participants, then the data should be anonymous from the beginning.

The law requires researchers to securely store the data and destroy the data once they are no longer needed. The exception to this regulation is when the purpose of the data is scientific, historical, or related to public health. Because the data collected in political science research have a scientific goal, researchers do not have to destroy them. These regulations are similar but not identical to what most IRBs require from US-based researchers; thus, it should not be hard to follow them.

Finally, researchers wanting to conduct studies in Mexico could ask a Mexican-based researcher who has used similar research methods for an ethical review of the study for compensation. Thus, the study would have the support of both the US-IRB and a faculty member of the country in which the research will be conducted. This process could be improved when academic institutions create committees for ethical reviews of their own research projects. Then non-Mexican-based researchers could ask such committees to review their project and compensate them for their time and administrative work. As the number of researchers conducting behavioral studies in Mexico is increasing, it should not be hard to find a potential reviewer as such ethics committees become a reality.

9.4 Conclusion

Even though Mexico lacks ethical regulations regarding social science research, there are regulations regarding the collection, treatment, and storage of personal data that we should consider when doing research. For now, researchers wanting to conduct studies in Mexico can seek the support of a colleague working in Mexico. In the near future, I expect there will be at least an ethics committee at CIDE that can evaluate their research.

In addition to the law, the three general principles of the Belmont Report are sound guidelines to guide our research in the absence of ethics reviewers. Researchers should not embark on research that would be ethically unthinkable in other contexts, such as in the United States. Moreover, researchers should be aware of both the regulations for conducting research and the regulations on their topic of research within the country where they are working.

As foreign funds support research in Mexico, we see the need for some kind of ethical committee evaluating research projects. However, it is not only the need for ethical approval that guides the move in building this type of committee but the assurance that as researchers we are protecting and treating with respect, fairness, and beneficence the participants in our research. In field experiments, for example, it is almost always the case that participants do not know they are taking part in a study so they cannot give their consent. This fact raises ethical concerns regarding the respect for subjects' autonomy and decision to participate in a study. The challenges are even broader if the results change relevant outcomes, such as an election, that could have not only consequences at that moment in time but also consequences in the future because the results could affect the strength of the political parties in future elections (Desposato 2014). There are options we could consider for obtaining participants' consent or informing them of their participation in a field experiment. Before treatment, we could inform subjects of the possibility of participating in the research through the same means that we would treat them. Another option is to let subjects know of their participation in the research after the study is completed. Desposato (2014) and Humphreys (2014) discuss these and other options.

In my opinion, whenever possible, researchers should coordinate with the country's authority or other legitimate organizations when conducting research that might affect people's relation to the government, test the relationship between public officials and citizens, and look at the efficiency of the laws, in a broad manner, such as when conducting a field experiment. Usually, researchers conducting field experiments partner with authorities, candidates, or other actors so that all those involved in this procedure know about the research and the researchers can count on their support (De La O and Wantchekon 2011).

Another consideration that we have to take into account is our status as researchers vis-à-vis the status of our subjects. We need to ensure subjects are not feeling pressured to participate in the research because they are members of vulnerable groups (i.e., indigenous people, poor, elderly, illiterate) When in doubt about the ethics of our research design, we have to think about whether there are other possible ways of testing our theories outside experimental research.

I expect that the committee at CIDE will have, in general, fewer issues than the IRBs in the United States as it will be created to evaluate the ethics of social science research, not biomedical research. In terms of institutional incentives to guarantee our research is always bounded by ethics, I believe we should provide workshops to comparativists on ethical issues outside of the United States, regardless of their research method. Finally, journal editors might require some kind of approval from a committee or some reasoning for the authors to conduct their research in a certain way. This is not an attempt to turn editors into ethics evaluators, but it will force researchers to consider possible ethical concerns within their research that they will have to justify.

Notes

1 I am not implying that IRB approval is the same as ethical approval, as the IRB procedure is set by each university to protect it against legal problems resulting from research conducted by its academics. I thank Liz Zechmeister for this comment.

2 One might argue that participants who take part in studies that involve obtaining information about government officials or candidates derive a benefit from their participation because they can make a more informed political judgment. This type of benefit is qualitatively different from the benefit subjects derive from clinical trials, for example.

3 For example, in my research I was interested in comparing similar populations who live in and have been socialized into different contexts, so the ideal comparison for my study contrasted Mexicans in Mexico to US-born Mexican Americans. For that reason I did not recruit or let participate individuals who did not fit into these categories.

4 I needed their pictures to evaluate whether people judged more favorably other people who looked phenotypically like them.

5 I provided a compensation of MXN 50 (US$4.12) to subjects in Mexico City and US$15.00 to subjects in Chicago.

6 Other problems that could arise from this type of power relation between a researcher and research participants are the occurrence of social desirability bias, in which subjects try to please the researcher or subjects feel pressured to participate and their responses reflect a feeling of duress rather than a real reaction to the stimulus. If conducting the research in person, one possible solution to these issues is to ensure subjects understand that there are no right or wrong answers, that the researcher(s) will not be able to match the answer to the participant because it does not carry identifiable information (if that is the case), and that they can stop participating in the research at any time without penalty.

7 Mexico's GINI coefficient is 0.48. It is the most unequal country after taxes and transfers within the Organisation for Economic Co-operation and Development (OECD). It is located in the 15th percentile of the most unequal countries in the world based on available data on social inequality (World Bank 2015). According to the 2012 census data, 77% of the indigenous population lives under the poverty line (CONEVAL 2014).

8 The text of the General Law of Electoral Institutes and Procedures in Spanish can be found at www.diputados.gob.mx/LeyesBiblio/ref/lgipe.htm

9 CIDE is academically organized into divisions, which are the equivalent to departments in the US context. There are six divisions: Economics, History, International Studies, Law, Political Studies, and Public Administration.

10 We can think of the privacy notice as the part of the consent form that relates to the treatment of the data collected in the study.

11 The web address is http://inicio.ifai.org.mx/SitePages/Modelos-De-Aviso-De-Privacidad.aspx

PART III

The Ethical Challenges of Field Experiments

10

OBLIGATED TO DECEIVE?

Aliases, Confederates, and the Common Rule in International Field Experiments

Michael Findley and Daniel Nielson

During a research seminar, our colleague's face flushed red and his brow furrowed; he was visibly angry. He sputtered, "I am outraged that you had BYU students lie for you in this so-called 'research' project." Indeed, under the guise of fictitious identities, our undergraduate research assistants had approached thousands of corporate service providers around the world by email in an audit experiment to probe the efficacy of international law prohibiting anonymous incorporation. The criticism stung. All things equal, lying is morally wrong—and it is especially problematic at a religious university with a stringent honor code where personal integrity plays a prominent role.

But here is the rub: A type of "petty ethics" fixated on rules, stringent procedures, and blind devotion to narrow legalistic principles may ironically generate greater moral mistakes than minor deception in social science studies such as the type we deployed in our shell company experiment. Philosopher Immanuel Kant's concept of "moral rigorism" parallels the notion of petty ethics and underscores the difference between morality as the adherence to rules and duty in contrast to morality as the pursuit of human welfare.

After all, as bad as deception is as a rule violation of ethical conduct, a strong case can be made that money laundering, tax evasion, sanctions busting, transnational corruption, and terrorist financing—all serious crimes for which anonymous corporations often prove the most important financial vehicles—are significantly worse in terms of losses to human welfare. Despite the efforts of researchers and organizations such as the Financial Action Task Force, the World Bank, and the International Monetary Fund, no reliable data existed on the availability of anonymous shells. It seemed to us that the acquisition of reliable, unbiased data on the topic would need to necessarily precede meaningful policy remediation. Refusal to pursue the research might therefore prove much more questionable ethically than avoiding the study over qualms about deception. It is for this reason that both the Belmont Report, which outlined the modern ethical principles that guide human subjects research, and the US Department of Health and Human Services' Common Rule, which formally governs the domain, allow for the waiver of informed consent under certain conditions.

On the other hand, the human capacity for rationalization and justification is notorious (Tavris and Aronson 2007). Researchers have attempted to excuse a number of very serious violations of common ethical standards on the pretense that the value of the scientific knowledge outweighed the costs of the temporary suspension of moral decency. The Tuskegee sterilization experiments, the Guatemala syphilis experiments, and, most heinously, the sadistic Nazi medical experiments provide only the most egregious examples of a too-common tendency for researchers to justify their fixation on scientific problems and rationalize away the human costs.

In this paper, we explore the tradeoffs between the use of deception and fully informed consent in international field experiments. We propose a "half-doubled" rule of thumb that conscientious researchers might use informally to weigh the benefits of the anticipated scientific findings against the costs of a deceptive study. In the half-doubled rule, we recommend that researchers sincerely and as accurately as possible estimate the benefits to scientific knowledge and the costs to human (or organizational) subjects in the proposed research. Then, to partially account for justification biases, researchers would divide the benefits by half and, to adjust for rationalization biases, double the estimated costs to subjects. Only when the halved benefits outweigh the doubled costs would we recommend that researchers proceed with the deception research. Of course, such a rule would not be formal in any way but rather would serve as more of a self-integrity check on researchers' own eagerness to proceed with ethically sensitive research.

We also consider alternatives to deception, which we strongly recommend that researchers fully explore before undertaking a study that might involve dishonesty. One substitute design makes use of confederates who might sincerely undertake the activity at the heart of the research and for whom researchers can act as agents. The other alternative, of course, is fully informed consent. We explore all three approaches to field experiments by using examples from our own studies of anonymous incorporation, microfinance confirmation bias, and behavioral support for foreign aid.

10.1 Deception in Social Science Research

Acceptable standards for deception—"intentional and explicit misrepresentations before, during, or after an experiment" (Morton and Williams 2010)—in the social sciences require several considerations. These principles are thoroughly articulated in the Belmont Report and reiterated in the Common Rule. Most notably, the research should not involve any physical or emotional pain, the research cannot be carried out in another way, the benefits are significant, and the costs are minimal.

Specifically, the Common Rule (46.116 c and d) states that:

(c)   An IRB may approve a consent procedure which does not include, or which alters, some or all of the elements of informed consent set forth above, or waive the requirement to obtain informed consent provided the IRB finds and documents that:

   (1)   The research or demonstration project is to be conducted by or subject to the approval of state or local government officials and is designed to study, evaluate, or otherwise examine:
      (i)   public benefit or service programs;
      (ii)   procedures for obtaining benefits or services under those programs;
      (iii) possible changes in or alternatives to those programs or procedures; or
      (iv) possible changes in methods or levels of payment for benefits or services under those programs; and
   (2)   The research could not practicably be carried out without the waiver or alteration.

(d)   An IRB may approve a consent procedure which does not include, or which alters, some or all of the elements of informed consent set forth in this section, or waive the requirements to obtain informed consent provided the IRB finds and documents that:

   (1)   The research involves no more than minimal risk to the subjects;
   (2)   The waiver or alteration will not adversely affect the rights and welfare of the subjects;
   (3)   The research could not practicably be carried out without the waiver or alteration; and
   (4)   Whenever appropriate, the subjects will be provided with additional pertinent information after participation.

Some disciplines have also established internal rules about deception in research. The American Psychological Association (2002, 11–12) notes that deception should be avoided unless the use of such techniques is "justified by the study's significant prospective scientific, educational, or applied value and that effective non-deceptive alternative procedures are not feasible." It further establishes that deception is not used when subjects could experience "physical pain or severe emotional distress" and cautions researchers to, if possible, inform participants at the conclusion of the study in some way.

By articulating the conditions for the waiver of informed consent, both the Belmont Report and the Common Rule, as well as the APA, acknowledge that deception can indeed be used in social science research. And, as we detail below, many researchers have made use of the articulated exceptions.

10.2 Prominent Research in Which Aliases Prove Key

A survey of the social science literature finds several prominent examples using fictitious identities or aliases. And some of the most prominent among them were undertaken in economics, a field in which scholars are normally allergic to deception. Most of the prominent research using aliases appears in areas of discrimination, including revealed prejudice in labor and housing markets. Perhaps the best-known piece is the Bertrand and Mullainathan field experiment on labor market discrimination (2004). The researchers sent hundreds of resumes to Chicago- and Boston-area employers, randomly assigning each resume a false "Anglo" (Emily or Greg) or false "African-American" (Lakisha or Jamal) name. They found statistically significant evidence that the African-American names received half the number of callbacks from employers compared to the Anglo resumes. This topic of discrimination, of course, is very sensitive, and thus unbiased findings likely could not have been obtained without the use of aliases and the accompanying mild deception. And yet the research has clear and important implications for employment law and labor markets.

Further research in this vein builds upon the same experimental format, using false names or other fabricated identifying information. In a study of renter discrimination, Carpusor and Loges (2006) sent more than 1,000 alias emails to potential renters, randomly assigning each an Anglo, African-American, or Arab-American name. The emails with the Anglo names all received significantly more responses than the others. Very similar research—all using aliases—has been performed even more recently in Sweden and Spain (Ahmed and Hammarstedt 2008, Bosch, Carnero and Farre 2010).[1]

A novel new study from another Swedish author followed the Bertrand and Mullainathan hiring discrimination model but used pictures instead of names to test bias (Rooth 2009). With the job applications, Rooth randomly assigned normal pictures and doctored "obese" pictures of applicants and measured the response, finding that "obese"-pictured candidates received significantly fewer callbacks from employers.

Using a similarly deceptive design in political science, Butler and Broockman (2011) sent emails to state legislators using two different aliases: DeSean Jackson (the name most statistically associated with African-American origin) and Jake Mueller (statistically the most Anglo-American name). The DeSean Jackson alias received significantly fewer responses than Jake Mueller. This research is important in identifying racial discrimination in American politics and again would have proven difficult if not impossible without deception.

All of the research discussed above relied on deception, but the significant social implications of the findings arguably outweigh the costs of the deception involved. Because of the control over experimental conditions the method provides, the use of aliases has led to important discoveries that would not have been possible with other research approaches.

10.3 The Ethics of Using Aliases in Research

Though a fundamental debate exists between the ethics of using deceit in human subjects research, reviews show that the large majority of relevant studies—especially in experimental psychology, which almost exclusively relies on human subjects research—involve some form of deception. In the 1980s, 58% of psychological studies involved some form of deception, and this number steadily increased for decades (Singleton et al. 1988, 451). As discussed above, many field experimental studies continue to use aliases and deception in research, which has led to important knowledge about discrimination.[2]

Some argue that deception has individual and societal costs that are hard to quantify, meaning that it should be approached cautiously (Baumrind 1979). We agree with this sentiment. As a result, deception must be justified both by its value to informing scientific knowledge as well as by its relatively low level of potential harm to the participant (Singleton et al. 1988, 452). Furthermore, in important areas of research, small deceptions, such as using a false name to contact incorporation services, remain well within the threshold of appropriate social research, as they "place participants in a mental state where they will behave naturally" (Singleton et al. 1988, 452). Indeed, some important research may nigh prove impossible without deception.

10.4 Deception vs. Bias in Field Experiments

In particular, field experiments—where subjects typically do not know they are being studied and are thus behaving in their normal day-to-day routines—are thought to induce greater "ecological validity" so that experimental settings closely mirror real-world conditions (see Brewer 2000). Because subjects generally do not know they are being studied in field experiments, they presumably will not anticipate researcher desires nor alter their behavior from their typical actions because they are conscious they are being observed. Moreover, in field settings subjects typically evince significantly less self-selection and the attending biases than in lab experiments, field experimental contexts are usually not artificial, and the stakes involved in the studied action in the field tend to parallel the natural environment—all features that are difficult to achieve in laboratory settings (see

Levitt and List 2007*a*, *b*). However, in order to preserve such naturalism in field experiments, even if no other deception is used, researchers typically withhold knowledge that subjects are participating in a study. This, of course, is deceptive in its own right, albeit in a more passive way.

Is such deception—however passive—justified? In terms of the social-science ideal of achieving unbiased findings, the answer so far appears to be a tentative "yes." List (2006) found that subjects acted very differently in a laboratory experiment involving the trading of sports cards than the same class of subjects behaved when actually selling cards in a field experiment during a genuine trade show. Similarly, Gneezy, Haruvy and Yafe (2004) found that subjects behaved quite prosocially in the laboratory during a social dilemma but much less so when the same class of subjects confronted a very similar set of conditions in the field while dining at a restaurant. However, Coppock and Green (2013) found general agreement between lab and field experiments across a set of political science studies. It is likely that the correspondence between lab and field results varies depending on context and the degree of social desirability, but it is clear that at least some of Levitt and List's (2007*b*) concerns about ecological validity are borne out when the same questions are approached in both the lab and the field. From a social-science perspective focused on unbiased findings, then, some deception might be justified.

However, it is reasonable to ask what is the harm of lab experiments, especially when they avoid the ethical challenge of deception? Our answer would be that there often may be little harm other than the perpetuation of biased knowledge. It would merely add a few more decibels to the cacophony of noise in social scientific findings. Nevertheless, when social science is used to justify or formulate public policy, which is sometimes the case with political science studies, social-scientific bias might lead to significant real-world harm. This is especially so if a potentially corrective policy is foregone based on biased lab or survey findings—or worse, if a policy is pursued based on biased lab results that might actually lead to the opposite of the intended effect in the field. Here, the costs of biased results appear non-trivial and might vastly outweigh the costs of the minor deception required by the field experiment.

Christensen (1988) makes two important points on justifications for deception in research. First, he posits that subjects to deceptive research have both benefited from the process and generally have few qualms about being deceived for research purposes. Second, he makes an important moral-ethical argument that bolsters our point about "petty ethics" or moral rigorism raised in the introduction. He suggests that it may be more immoral to refuse to employ deception in research than it is to deceive in the study of important issues. He contends that the potential benefit to humanity outweighs the small potential cost of a minor deception.

To provide a concrete application of Christensen's principles, in medical trials doctors sometimes perform "sham" surgeries on patients—complete with incisions, sutures, and the non-trivial risk of infection, but no actual surgery—in order to differentiate the benefits of the surgeries from placebo effects (see Moseley et al. 2002). These false procedures occur with fully informed consent—patients know they may receive placebo surgery—but great pains are taken for the placebo group to hide the fact that subjects are receiving the sham procedure (saline solution is splashed to simulate lavage, the time spent in "procedure" is identical to the surgery, etc.).

Even though the study meets the strictest definition of informed consent, significant deception is nevertheless employed. And clearly the placebo procedure entails real risk to the patient. Yet such studies are vital to learning about the effectiveness of surgical procedures. Indeed, they have shown that routine knee surgeries provided no more pain relief or physical function than did the sham surgeries (Moseley et al. 2002). As bad as the sham surgeries are ethically (and we clearly see problems here), continuing to routinely perform actual surgeries with no meaningful benefits may be much worse. By contrast, the types of social science studies routinely undertaken in political science's cognate disciplines typically involve risks to participants that are much less grave.

10.5   The Half-Doubled Rule

Still, researchers should approach prospective studies involving deception very cautiously. By articulating a clear tradeoff between the benefits to science and the costs of deceptive research, both the Belmont Report and the Common Rule appear to endorse the questionable maxim that the "ends justify the means." Most moral people believe this proposition to be false on its face. But, of course, when pressed most people would also acknowledge that there are many circumstances where it likely applies.

For example, the morally correct answer to "Does this shirt make me look fat?" is likely something along the lines of "You look great," even if the objectively "true" answer to the question is "Frankly, yes." The misdirection involved is justified by the emotional harm the "true" answer might have caused. To take a more extreme example: Lying to the police—or to anyone—is morally wrong, but lying to authorities to protect refugees from genocide is unquestionably the correct moral choice. Telling the truth in this circumstance would count as moral rigorism in the extreme and would commit an unambiguous act of immorality.

Of course, this example begs the question of when does one individual's morality constitute immorality to another? And it puts researchers in a particular ethical bind. Because of common human cognitive biases, it is very likely that a given social scientist may simultaneously overestimate the value of the proposed research and underestimate the costs to human subjects.

Human subjects committees of institutional review boards will likely not provide a sufficient check on this tendency. Some IRBs, it seems, exist almost solely to vet proposed research for its perceived implications for legal liability and little more. Indeed, at many universities, lawyers from the universities' offices of legal counsel sit on the IRBs as *ex officio* non-voting members to advise on legal matters. A legal screen is not tantamount to an ethical screen.

Rather, it falls to researchers to self-regulate on ethical matters. We recognize that some may not elect to do so. But we suspect that many others are genuinely concerned about the ethics of their research and may appreciate guidance on how to make challenging judgment calls. Thus we propose the half-doubled rule to help guide researchers as they contemplate ethically sensitive research projects involving deception. The half-doubled rule is completely informal, intended merely as a rule of thumb for researchers to employ as a self-check when planning research.

The motivation for the rule stems from well-known human tendencies to rationalize choices and justify cherished beliefs (Festinger, Riecken and Schachter 1956, Festinger 1957, Aronson and Mills 1959, Festinger and Aronson 1960, Harmon-Jones and Mills 1999). While some people some of the time have the ability to admit their mistakes, update their beliefs, and self-correct, most people most of the time, when confronted with information suggesting that they behaved badly or believe mistakenly, tend instead to simply dig in. The engine that drives this tendency is what Festinger (1957) identified as "cognitive dissonance": "a state of tension that occurs whenever a person holds two cognitions (ideas, attitudes, beliefs, opinions) that are psychologically inconsistent, such as 'Smoking is a dumb thing to do because it could kill me' and 'I smoke two packs a day'" (Tavris and Aronson 2007, 13). Dissonance is uncomfortable and sometimes even agonizing, so when people encounter it they naturally seek to reduce it. The healthiest way to lessen dissonance is through self-correction. The smoker could quit. But the healthy way is often difficult, so an easier method is for the smoker to convince herself that smoking is not that bad—after all, she uses filtered cigarettes—or that it is worth the risk because it relaxes her (Tavris and Aronson 2007, 13).

Analogously, it is natural for researchers to feel dissonance when confronting the prospect of interesting and potentially important research that would likely involve deception. On the one hand, the prospect of a fascinating study proves enticing. But on the other, the research involves lying to people, which is morally wrong. We suspect that many researchers, ourselves included, are strongly tempted to opt for the psychologically easier path of justifying the research on its scientific merits while rationalizing the costs as worth it given the benefits.

The half-doubled rule provides a possible self-check on this tendency. Researchers might fudge the tradeoff between the costs and benefits in a way that works in favor of their preference to perform the study. After all, the current standards stipulated by the Belmont Report and Common Rule merely stipulate that the benefits of the study need to outweigh the costs. Yet, given that the judgment must be made prospectively, it seems likely that researchers—even unconsciously—might exaggerate the benefits and minimize the costs. Thus, in an informal way through the half-doubled rule, researchers can guard against this inclination by first performing an honest assessment of the costs and benefits of the research. Such a mental exercise involves prediction, which is always uncertain given the many unintended consequences that might result. This uncertainty should be acknowledged and estimated if possible, and researchers should ground the assessment of the costs and benefits—as much as possible—on prior research where the tangible costs and benefits can be quantified.

Once the estimate of costs and benefits are obtained and quantified (or, if possible, even monetized), using the half-doubled rule researchers would divide the benefits (including any benefits to subjects from participation in the research) in half and double the costs. We recommend that only when the halved benefits exceed the doubled costs should the researchers proceed with deceptive research. The re-weighting of costs and benefits—remembering that this is an informal rule of thumb used as a self-check by researchers—might help to adjust for the researchers' natural tendency to justify the value of the research and rationalize away the costs. Employing the half-doubled rule provides nothing more than an informal pre-assessment of the value of the proposed research vs. the costs of deception, but we hope it provides a starting point for discussions of how researchers might guard themselves against the proclivity for self-justification in social science.

It also provides a counter to a tendency by some to call for absolutely no deception in social science research whatsoever. While few take this extreme position, scholars with this view seem disproportionately likely to serve as reviewers at prestigious journals, especially in economics. In what follows we hope to show that the costs of deception in social science are sometimes very much justified by the benefits produced by the research. Indeed, eschewing deceptive studies of important social phenomena might well prove more immoral than undertaking research involving deception. We also discuss alternatives to deception and report our thinking in choosing among deception studies, confederate designs, and informed consent. We begin with our study of the availability of anonymous shell companies worldwide, which did involve deception.

10.6   The Case for Deception: Anonymous Incorporation

In 2012 we carried out a global field experiment on financial transparency. Specifically, we set out to address the extent and determinants of compliance with international incorporation law. As fuller descriptions are available elsewhere (Findley, Nielson and Sharman 2013*b*, 2014), we briefly describe the experiment here with an emphasis on the deceptive components. Following, we explicitly discuss why unbiased results could not have been obtained without aliases and how we arrived at the decision to use deception. Having established the necessity of the deception, we then consider whether the experiment justified such costs in the first place. We therefore offer some preliminary evidence of potential societal benefits that, we believe, outweigh the costs of deception.

In the experiment, we approached corporate service providers (CSPs)—businesses that specialize in setting up companies for other people—with insincere requests to set up anonymous corporations. Of course, an anonymous corporation would be in violation of international law, so we stopped well short of legal incorporation and only inquired after the documents required for forming a company. We were keen to learn who would violate rules requiring identity documents and how violations were dependent on the randomly assigned information we provided.

Treatments included informing subjects about international law, possible penalties, international norms, willingness to pay a premium for confidentiality, and domestic enforcement. Other experimental conditions varied the identity of the alias: In the placebo condition, the alias putatively originated from innocuous, minor-power OECD countries. In one treatment, the alias hailed from the United States. In another condition, the fictitious consultant claimed to come from a corrupt country and work in government procurement. And in the strongest treatment, the alias purported to hail from a country associated with terrorism and work for Islamic charities in Saudi Arabia. An example approach appears below.

Dear NAMECOMPANY,

I am an international consultant living in COUNTRY. My associates and I have been based in COUNTRY for some time and we have done extensive international work, especially in your area. After looking at the specific needs of our growing company, we were feeling that it would make sense for us to expand and to set up an international company. We would like to form a new company in your area as private individuals. We especially hope to limit taxes and reduce liability.

We were wondering what you require us to give in order to do this. We would like to form this corporation as privately as possible. TREATMENT What identifying documents will you need from us? We would also like to know what your usual prices are. We appreciate the help.

I travel a lot for my work, so I communicate best via email. I hope to hear from you soon. Yours,
ALIAS

Our approaches were deceptive in a number of ways. First, we used aliases rather than our own names. We associated the aliases with origin countries from which no emails actually originated. And we had no intention of actually incorporating with these firms.[3] Moreover, our subjects thought that these approaches were everyday business opportunities and so were not aware that this was part of a social science study. We thus used what Morton and Williams (2010, 502–504) referred to as "deceptive identities," although there are elements of "deceptive purpose" and "deceptive materials and information" as well.

So, why deception? Following the Belmont Report, Common Rule, and disciplinary ethical considerations (American Psychological Association 2002, Morton and Williams 2010), we addressed whether the study could be performed otherwise without bias. We considered basic concerns about the safety of the research team, as well as likely benefits to society and subjects, risks to society and subjects, and possible contamination of the pool of future subjects.

The first question we faced: Could we approach corporate service providers as researchers and use survey (or survey experiment) techniques to learn about compliance with international law? The answer to this question seemed simple. If asked whether they would act in accordance with international standards, we would expect most to say yes. People rarely admit to willful violations of law, especially to strangers. Thus, the sensitivity of the research area seemed to require more than a survey. While we might have been able to use list experiments or other techniques for sensitive questions, they likely would not have overcome poor response rates, selection bias, or a tendency for subjects to dissemble when asked if they would violate the law. To check this, we decided to employ a survey experiment at the end of the field experiment; we contrast the results of the two studies below. A lab experiment set up at a global conference of corporate service providers asking for volunteers to participate would likely have faced similar self-selection and social desirability biases.

Subjects in the field experiment first chose whether or not to respond to the inquiries from the aliases. In the international subject pool of 4,365 inquiries to firms from nearly every country, 47.9% responded to the field experiment inquiry, and in the United States we received responses to 19.8% of the 2,986 inquiries, for a combined response rate of 36.5% in the field experiment. In contrast, only 8.8% of all firms in the subject pool responded to the survey—less than one fourth the response rate from the field experiment. What is more, the set of firms that answered the survey were not a representative sample of the subjects that answered the inquiry in the field experiment (see Findley, Nielson and Sharman 2013a). This is the well-known phenomenon of response-rate or selection bias, and it can produce very misleading results.

The survey experiment sent after the field experiment was concluded made no mention of the prior field experiment, and subjects were never informed they were otherwise part of an experiment (i.e., they were not debriefed prior to the survey). We judged that, given the minimal costs of the field experiment, a full debriefing would cause more harm than good for subjects. Although the survey was the first contact they were aware of, we transferred the treatment condition they received in the field experiment into a "hypothetical scenario" in a survey-experiment instrument to gauge whether they would behave consistently with the field experiment in which they did not know they were being studied. To avoid detection, we changed background language when "piping in" the experimental treatment information, but we nonetheless provided the same basic scenario.

In both the field experiment and the survey, subjects responded to various treatment conditions that provided different information about law, financial incentives, or the identity of prospective clients. They could require no photo identity documents at all, coded non-compliant; they could insist on photo documentation but not demand that it be notarized, categorized as part-compliant; they could require notarized photo ID, coded compliant; or they could refuse service altogether. What did we learn about the differences between the behavioral outcomes in the field experiment and the survey-experiment responses?

Table 10.1 is a cross tabulation showing how subjects behaved in the experiment vs. the survey. The rows represent the outcome in the experiment, whereas the columns represent the outcome in the survey. This shows that, for example, of the 173 noncompliant subjects from the experiment on international CSPs, only 9 were non-compliant in the survey (5.2% of the 170), 22 part-compliant, and so forth. Panel 10.1A contains the results for the international sample and panel 10.1B shows the US results. Also note that this comparison considers subjects that received the same treatment in both experiment and survey.

Table 10.1 displays the results for subjects with matched conditions across survey and field for both the international (Panel A) and US samples (Panel B). Although highly aggregated, the findings are incredibly telling and reflect what we observe across all conditions almost uniformly. (Full results separated by treatment condition reported in Findley, Nielson and Sharman 2013a.)

First, non-compliance in the field experiment is much higher than in the survey. This confirms our intuition that signaling to providers that they are being studied alters their behavior, causing most of the incorporation scofflaws to dissemble. The raw rate of non-compliance goes from 1.3% in the survey experiment to 8.5% in the field, an implied increase of nearly 600%. However, if we scale the non-compliance rate by the response rate—considering only the proportion of subjects in non-compliance as a share of those responding (these results reported in Findley, Nielson, and Sharman 2014), which is the typical approach employed in survey experiments—the difference is increased a bit proportionally. Just under one fourth, or 23.5%, of responding firms asked for no photo ID whatsoever in the field experiment, thereby signaling their willingness to provide anonymous shell companies. However, only 3.5% of firms indicated that they would offer anonymous shells in the survey experiment—a non-trivial decrease.

The policy implications of these two contrasting findings are significant. The field experiment suggests that anonymous shell companies are widely available—nearly one in four responding firms offered untraceable corporations. Given that most international financial criminals involved in money laundering, tax evasion, sanctions busting, transnational corruption, and terrorist financing use anonymous

TABLE 10.1 Comparison of Responses With and Without Deception

Panel 3A: International

Experiment Outcome	Non-compliant	Part-compliant	Survey Outcome Compliant	Refusal	Non-response	Total
Non-compliant	9 (5.2%)	22 (12.7%)	8 (4.6%)	3 (1.7%)	131(75.7%)	173
Part-compliant	4 (1.3%)	40 (12.9%)	9 (2.9%)	4 (1.3%)	254 (81.7%)	311
Compliant	3 (0.9%)	26 (7.7%)	30 (8.9%)	8 (2.4%)	272 (80.2%)	339
Refusal	2 (0.9%)	10 (4.7%)	7 (3.3%)	3 (1.4%)	192 (89.7%)	214
Non-response	13 (1.2%)	39 (3.5%)	17 (1.5%)	10 (0.9%)	1033 (92.9%)	1112
Total	31	137	71	28	1882	2149

Panel 3B: United States

Experiment Outcome	Non-compliant	Part-compliant	Survey Outcome Compliant	Refusal	Non-response	Total
Non-compliant	10 (6.3%)	11	1 (0.6%)	3 (1.9%)	134 (84.3%)	159
Part-compliant	0 (0.0%)	6 (22.2%)	1 (3.7%)	1 (3.7%)	19 (70.4%)	27
Compliant	0 (0.0%)	0 (0.0%)	1 (16.7%)	0 (0.0%)	5 (83.3%)	6
Refusal	2 (1.1%)	5 (2.7%)	1 (0.5%)	3 (1.6%)	173 (94%)	184
Non-response	6 (0.4%)	15 (1.1%)	3 (0.2%)	6 (0.4%)	1356 (97.8%)	1386
Total	18	37	7	13	1687	1762

shells, the finding implies a substantial danger to citizens globally. On the other hand, the survey result suggests that anonymous incorporation is a less significant problem. Of course, both studies suggest meaningful implications for public policy, but it is likely that policymakers would also be sensitive to the naturalism of the field experiment compared to the contrived nature of the survey experiment and discount the latter even further. Indeed, our informants in the advocacy community have reported that the results of our field experiment, after they were made public in October of 2012, contributed to significant tightening of incorporation laws in the United Kingdom and the European Union.

If the findings proved valuable to policymakers, the question naturally arises as to why law-enforcement officials themselves did not adopt such a "secret shopper" approach and obviate the need for the study. We have had brief discussions with officials at the Financial Action Task Force, but they reiterated their commitment to assessing only the statutory compliance of member countries with international standards, which they maintained was more in line with their intergovernmental mandate. The approach we adopted, they noted, was politically untenable for them. This suggests a role for academic research even in domains where governments and international organizations have strong policy interests. Researchers possess independence and flexibility envied by the policy community.

The scientific implications of the differences between the studies are also large. If society values social science for its ability to provide valid and reliable evidence about the social world, the benefits of social research increase concomitantly with the quality and accuracy of the research findings. In this example, a strong case could be made that the field experiment, due to its enhanced ecological validity, provides much more valid and accurate evidence about a pressing global problem than the survey experiment. Therefore, the benefits of the deceptive field experiment are significant and the value of the survey experiment—performed without deception—is less so. In Findley, Nielson and Sharman (2013*a*), we discuss a full set of lessons learned. But we note here that had we not used an experiment with deception, the inferences drawn and conclusions made would have been very different.

But could we have used an experiment, say with confederates, and lowered the levels of deception? In the early design phase, we considered the possibility of identifying confederates from different possible origin countries who could send sincere requests, thus allowing us to avoid deception to a great extent. We even went so far as to put out an initial call for applications. The response was rather paltry.

But before we could press much further, our university legal counsel's office instructed us to use aliases given that no incorporation would actually occur and therefore no laws would be broken. They reasoned that research assistants would be protected with their identities safe behind aliases. Thus, the use of deception was partly taken out of our hands in the interest of legal protection for our student research assistants. But it proved to be a good choice scientifically as it also allowed greater control in our deployment of experimental conditions. Indeed, we were able to match origin countries with specific treatments in better ways. All of this suggests unbiased findings would have been difficult—if not impossible—to obtain without deception.

While there is a clear argument about why this study could not have been completed without deception, it does not therefore imply that the research was worth doing. We thus considered costs and benefits of the research both to the subjects and to society. First, consider the individuals. The research entailed more costs than benefits for the individual. This is not ideal based on the principle of beneficence outlined in the Belmont Report. However, we note that the costs were still very minimal. We estimate that response to our requests likely took between 5–15 minutes of their time to answer. This is based on the fact that the vast majority of subjects responded with canned language they likely used repeatedly with customers. The responses were thus part of their everyday business activities, which involve many inquiries that never ultimately pan out. Of course, it would strain credulity to argue for too many individual benefits to subjects. We note, however, that if subject firms follow the dissemination of the research (which many have done, actually), then they may be better informed about international standards and best practices.

The benefits to society, however, outweigh the costs that individuals incur. As Baumrind (1979) discuss, estimating benefits to society is difficult to do. In our case, however, we had strong reason to expect larger societal benefits given that the Financial Action Task Force is concerned about combatting terrorism financing and corruption, the World Bank is concerned about combatting corruption and crime financing, and so forth.

Indeed, as the experiment was being set up, we made many stakeholders aware (Financial Action Task Force, Department of Homeland Security, Senate Permanent Subcommittee on Investigations, Global Witness, etc.) and they signaled to us their interest in drawing on lessons learned to improve international incorporation law and enforcement of such standards.

Since the conclusion of the study and public release of findings, as noted, we have received feedback from a number of these stakeholders confirming that the findings were used to improve statutory and enforcement standards in the United Kingdom, the European Union, the British Virgin Islands, and a number of other countries, and even perhaps the United States. We thus had reason to expect societal benefits and are actually seeing the improvements come to fruition.

A final consideration, drawing on the concerns of economists, is whether the experiment will spoil the pool of future subjects. For those that learn of the study, which so far is a reasonable number, the difficulty of studying them in the future may be compounded. That said, corporate service providers will continue to go about their daily business addressing large numbers of inquires;

identifying inquiries as social science experiments will likely prove impractical and will probably not significantly influence their decision calculus. So, under some circumstances, such as the case of anonymous incorporation, it appears that the benefits of deception substantially outweigh the costs. Nevertheless, the costs of the study would decrease if a method could be found that eliminates (most of) the deception.

10.7 The Case for Confederates: Microfinance Confirmation Bias

A potential alternative to deception in field experiments therefore recruits confederates that would sincerely undertake the critical actions at the center of the study. These might be firms, non-governmental organizations, or individuals who express a genuine interest in receiving products or services provided by subjects or otherwise engaging the subjects as a part of their normal practices. In confederate designs, researchers might contact subjects on behalf of their confederates and then relay information from the communication with the subjects to the confederates for use in their normal affairs.

For example, in one confederate design undertaken with Nathan Jensen, we formed a consulting company to represent an actual manufacturing firm with which we have a formal, legal agreement seeking information on tax incentives that it might use to inform its anticipated decision to relocate to a new city (see Findley, Jensen and Nielson 2013). The firm is genuinely interested in the market research we provided as consultants, and, among other treatments, it was willing to allow us to randomly assign the projected announcement date for the relocation for two months before or one month after the next municipal election to assess the effects of electoral concerns on offered tax incentives.

In another confederate design, as representatives of BYU's Political Economy and Development Lab, we approached 1,700 non-governmental organizations (NGOs) first in Uganda for Experiment 1 and then 14,000 NGOs worldwide for Experiment 2 to assess their interest in a research partnership (see Bakow et al. 2013). In the interest of full disclosure, Daniel Nielson is director of the Political Economy and Development Lab, so in this case our organization in essence served as its own confederate in the associated research. But similar designs would be exportable to settings where there is real separation between the researchers and the confederate.

We asked the NGOs to provide estimates of the personnel costs required to task staff members to the joint project. PEDL's interest in finding potential partners is fully sincere, so the primary deception in the research involved withholding the fact that subjects were participating in an experiment. The inquiry was indeed genuine, and we have followed up on promising responses by sending to the NGOs additional information and ideas for potential joint projects.

We randomly assigned whether or not we mentioned (1) that all of our projects are audited, (2) that we have worked often with other NGOs and are familiar with standard costs, (3) that we sent the same inquiry to many NGOs (implying competition for partnerships), and (4) that past projects have been supported by more than \$3 million in grants and contracts from foundations and international financial institutions. The control condition contained only the PEDL introduction and invitation without the additional treatment information. The experiment, conducted in line with PEDL's partnership interests, will allow the estimation of treatment effects on reimbursement requests of the different information conditions and therefore enable assessment of causes of opportunism among NGOs.

In a similar design, discussed here at greater length, we again sought to recruit partners for PEDL to perform impact evaluations of microfinance institutions' (MFIs) effectiveness (see Brigham et al. 2013). The project represented a sincere effort to engage possible collaborators in randomized evaluations, which was a key underlying motivation for the research. With the experiment we sought to probe the possibility that development organizations may ignore the high-quality scientific findings emerging from the burgeoning randomized evaluations of international development programs. The microfinance sector presented a nice confluence of conditions: Many see microfinance as an anti-poverty panacea, and high-profile researchers have performed several rigorous field experiments randomizing access to microcredit.

The design was relatively simple. We sent emails to 1,400 MFIs inviting them to receive more information about a potential partnership with PEDL to perform an impact evaluation of their program. We collected the contact information from an online database of MFIs intended for research purposes. To the subjects we emphasized that any future partnerships would depend on prior commitments, availability, and funding, and we cautioned that this was not an invitation for immediate collaboration. But we did invite them to express interest and request additional information (which we provided to all willing MFIs after the experiment was concluded along with an invitation to pursue collaboration further).

The control email contained only the introduction to PEDL and the invitation to receive additional information about an impact evaluation. Two treatment conditions added an additional paragraph after the introductory statement. First, a positive treatment stated, "Academic research suggests that microfinance is effective." It then went on to cite a 2010 article by Dean Karlan and Jonathan Zinman in the *Review of Financial Studies* and provide a short synopsis of the results, which reported positive effects of microcredit on income, subjective outlook, and women's empowerment. Second, a negative treatment stated, "Academic research suggests that microfinance is ineffective." It cited a different article by Karlan and Zinman published by *Science* in 2012 and summarized the findings, which suggested null effects of randomly assigned microcredit for business growth, subjective well-being, and women's empowerment. Wording for the positive and negative treatments was otherwise very similar.

The positive treatment induced an acceptance rate for the invitation of 9.8%, the control 7.5%, and the negative treatment 5.0%. The positive and negative treatment groups were statistically distinct in a difference-of-means test at the .01 significance level (and in a variety of robustness checks using logit, multinomial probit, and a selection model). The research suggests that the randomization revolution overtaking development economics may face larger-than-expected challenges in persuading development organizations to use the findings from the research to update their practices.

It also has implications for the use of confederates in field experiments. A survey experiment on microcredit institutions may have achieved a similar response rate compared to the field experiment. This may have especially been the case given that BYU and PEDL in particular are relatively unknown institutions globally, and some MFIs may already be working with third-party evaluators (or have great confidence in their own evaluation practices). But if the interest of researchers is behavior rather than attitudes, the field experimental design is preferable. We strongly suspect that representative of MFIs would be less sensitive to negative information in a survey format compared to a field experiment where they are acting in behalf of their organization without knowledge they are being studied. Again this gets to the point of ecological validity.

We note here that this design did not avoid deception completely. Subjects were not told they were part of a social science experiment. And information was presented to subjects selectively. While all of the material presented was entirely truthful, the information omitted regarding alternative randomized studies of microcredit withheld key information. Nevertheless, subjects did potentially benefit from the information about impact evaluations of microfinance that we sent to them after the experiment. Thus, there were minor benefits to subjects that balanced against the minor costs of answering the email. But again, the email was from an actual organization with a sincere invitation, so it was very much in line with the normal day-to-day activities of subjects. With the confederate design the deception was especially minimal and therefore the costs of the study quite low compared to the benefits of learning about the challenges that randomized evaluations face in motivating development organizations to update.

10.8   The Case for Informed Consent: Behavioral Support for Aid

Our decisions to employ varying degrees of deception are rooted in the ethical principles outlined in the Belmont Report and Common Rule. Of course, many research questions do not require deception or do not warrant the associated costs. Indeed, in a recent study of ours gauging recipient perceptions of foreign aid, we informed participants fully and obtained their consent. The question at hand did not warrant deception, and neither the benefits nor the costs were substantial enough in either direction.

In the study we conducted an experiment on a nationally representative sample of more than 3,500 Ugandan citizens, approximately 400 village council leaders and district governors, and about 300 members of the Ugandan parliament. The field experiment provided information about actual foreign aid projects jointly funded by bilateral and multilateral donors that were slated for disbursement. And we observed a set of attitudinal and behavioral responses to this information. We further added a companion survey to the experiment to learn about possible causal mechanisms driving the results.

At the outset of the study we provided a brief oral statement, which identified us as researchers and discussed our goal of understanding economic development in their area. Rather than obtain a written signature as is common in many contexts, we obtained oral consent. Following that, we asked a variety of baseline questions, then presented randomly assigned information about which donor was funding a given project (as well as the sector purpose of the project), and then asked them about their support (or opposition) for the project. We asked them to supply simple attitudinal responses, followed by the opportunity to respond behaviorally through a petition to the funder as well as by sending a text (SMS) to a public platform that would be communicated to the donor.

The full results are reported elsewhere (Milner, Nielson and Findley 2013, Findley et al. 2013), and we will not discuss them all here. We note, however, that we uncovered substantial differences between the attitudinal and behavioral responses, suggesting that researchers should pay close attention to the types of outcomes measured. While we cannot know for sure whether the use of deception would have altered the results substantially, we have little reason to suspect that informing the subjects biased their responses in ways that would require deception.

One might still contend that there was deception in this study. We did not inform the subjects that we would present them with a petition or ask them to send a SMS. To the extent that the full set of intentions and requests should be apparent at the outset of a study, we may still have some deception in here. But we wonder—and indeed would be quite surprised—whether an approach that fully disclosed all intentions, purposes, and procedures up front could learn much of use, and without introducing its own set of biases.

10.9 Conclusion

In this chapter we presented an argument in favor of using deception under certain circumstances in international field experiments. We provided a rule of thumb that researchers might use as a self-check whereby they sincerely estimate the benefits and costs of the research, divide the expected benefits in half, double the costs, and then move forward with the research only if the halved benefits exceed the doubled costs. This informal screening mechanism is not in any way foolproof. But it might help guard against researchers' built-in tendency to justify scientific benefits and rationalize human costs.

We also presented three examples of research using different levels of deception from the very deceptive use of aliases, misinformation, and misrepresentation; to confederate designs withholding the fact that subjects are participating in a social science experiment; to designs employing informed consent. We argued that different circumstances might justify any of the alternative designs, but researchers should opt for deception only when alternatives have been exhausted and only after the half-doubled threshold is cleared.

We do not believe we have settled the debate over deception by any means. Lying is morally wrong, and we do not claim otherwise. But we do argue that deception can be justified on moral grounds under particular circumstances, and some contexts obligate people to deceive others in order to avoid greater immoral actions than lying. We argue that social science can sometimes be one such setting, and we attempted to provide guidelines and examples that researchers might use to navigate the challenges posed by competing ethical principles. Undoubtedly greater awareness to ethics in experiments, including that promoted by this edited volume, will provide clearer guidance about the appropriate use of deception in international field experiments.

Notes

1 The same Swedish authors also pursued a study where rental applications from fictitious heterosexual and lesbian couples were replied to over the Internet (Ahmed, Andersson and Hammarstedt 2008). Again, they found significant evidence that the lesbian couples were discriminated against by renters. And similar to the labor market experiment, another 2003 study used the same fabricated resume framework to test for discrimination against lesbians in the labor market, finding that identical resumes with a "lesbian" applicant were significantly less likely to receive a callback than "non-lesbian" resumes (Weichselbaumer 2003).

2 We also note that some have begun to suggest that the Internet may create a new world for research that requires a broadening of our definition of ethics (Whiteman 2007). This new medium of communication requires us to challenge traditional definitions of when, for example, deceit is inappropriate or when it is both beneficial and necessary. As Internet research evolves, more flexibility is necessary.

3 Once the experiment was underway, we began batting around the idea of setting up a corporation through one of the providers. We have not yet incorporated but still have plans to at the conclusion of the overall research. If we do incorporate, however, it will be in our own legal names and thus will be in full conformity with international and domestic law.

11

CONSIDERING THE POLITICAL CONSEQUENCES OF COMPARATIVE POLITICS EXPERIMENTS

Joshua R. Gubler and Joel S. Selway

Imagine you are an American citizen with strong preferences for the Democratic Party. You are actively involved in grassroots political mobilization to elect leaders you believe will adopt policies to benefit your local community. You receive word that Chinese academics with funding from China's equivalent of the National Science Foundation (i.e., Chinese government money) plan to run an experiment in your electoral district to "identify the determinants of support for Republican candidates." Their previous research suggests that certain interventions will increase support for Republican candidates. They plan to test these same interventions in your district, raising the possibility that the experiment might affect voting outcomes. Is such an experiment ethical? Why or why not?

How might your answer change if these were United Kingdom academics instead, or what if their funding was from a private organization? Would you see things differently if the academics were Americans from a leading research university in the United States, or even a colleague from your own department who also lives in your electoral district? Would it matter if said colleague's political beliefs differed from your own? Finally, would your answer change if certain aspects of the research design were different? For example, what if the experiment favored your political party instead? And what if the experiment were to be run in every single electoral district across the United States?

As comparative political scientists, these types of questions about ethics should accompany any experiment we conduct in a foreign setting. They arise from the very nature of our experimental work, which inescapably affects politics to some degree in the societies under study. As the foregoing thought experiment indicates, when considering questions of ethics from the point of view of individuals within these societies, who we are as researchers matters; our citizenship matters; our funding matters; our assumptions about "good" and "right" matter; our political leanings matter. And even if we could somehow keep all of the aforementioned personal characteristics out of our research by remaining completely neutral and objective (note: we do not think this is possible), our research design would still matter. Our intention in this chapter is not to tell researchers what is ethical or not. We begin with this thought experiment simply to note that to ignore such questions is to naively work under the Star Trek "Prime Directive" assumption, that it is possible to intervene in a society without affecting the natural development of that society.[1] We suggest that experiments always leave some trace—by design—and it is the ethical responsibility of those conducting political science experiments to directly assess whether that trace is acceptable, and specifically whether the risks of affecting social and political outcomes in these societies (sometimes against the will of individuals within those societies) outweigh any potential benefits.

In what follows, we do not present an argument that experimenters should always seek to minimize political effects, immediate or downstream, of their experimental treatments. Some political scientists may explicitly desire such political effects for normative reasons, especially in their own countries where they have citizenship and a personal stake. To be sure, there are many actors with less virtuous motives than the pursuit of knowledge engaged in attempts to affect political outcomes. Rather, we argue that regardless of one's motivations, manipulations from political science experiments have political consequences and we are best served in answering the necessary ethical questions about these particular consequences if we are able to consider them, and their costs and benefits, systematically. The political consequences we invite readers to consider arise both from the effects of the treatments *and from the effects of disseminating the findings.* The guidelines we propose not only consider the political consequences of the treatments, as is most commonly done, but also potential consequences of the findings.

This language of costs versus benefits should seem familiar to those who have worked with the Institutional Review Board (IRB) and its founding document, the Belmont Report. In what follows, we briefly review the Belmont Report and provide an overview of traditional IRB assessment procedures to highlight how at present they do not invite careful, systematic consideration of political risks to participants. We then sketch three questions we think should be addressed— both by IRB boards and researchers themselves—to fully consider these risks. Finally, we briefly illustrate the utility of these questions by evaluating our own experimental research as well a prominent comparative politics experiment, and conclude with a summary explaining how heightened attention to these three questions might better protect subjects from potentially harmful political consequences.

11.1 The Belmont Report

Local review boards work under the guidelines of the Belmont Report, which formulates two general rules for assessing harm: 1) do not harm and 2) maximize possible benefits and minimize possible harm. While seemingly redundant, these two rules separate two types of harm that are applicable to comparative politics experiments. The first point is an injunction to avoid direct and immediate (or short-term) harm to participants. The second point is a directive to consider unintentional, indirect, or potential long-term harm to participants and to weigh this against potential benefits. This harm is more conjectural in nature (what "might happen") and, as such, is often where researchers and the local review board put most focus.

The Belmont Report itself offers minimal guidelines to help local review boards and researchers assess what constitutes "minimal harm" and when benefits outweigh harm. Rather, it simply reminds researchers to consider the tradeoff between learning about what will potentially benefit subjects (and society more generally) and when the benefits should be "foregone because of the risks" (The National Commission for the Protection of Human Subjects of Biomedical and Behavioral Research 1979, Part B: Section 2, Para. 2). The report urges researchers to ponder the "longer term benefits and risks" from any potential improvement in knowledge (*ibid.*, Para. 3).

Most local review boards offer more detailed guidelines, often listing particular types of harm for reviewers to consider. For example, at Brigham Young University's IRB, researchers and reviewers are asked to consider "physical, psychological, social and economic harm" that "could reasonably place the subjects at risk of criminal or civil liability, or be damaging to the subjects' financial standing, employability, or reputation" (Part D, Section 8). It also adds the following question: "Are there cultural attitudes/beliefs that may affect subjects in this study?" (Part B, Section 7). These IRB-specific additions to the Belmont Report provide a checklist of particular risks that should be given special consideration.

Certainly, implied in this checklist, perhaps under the "social" or "economic" risk categories, is the concept of political risks, or potential negative consequences that could result from the experiment's use for political competition within a country. Political competition is multi-faceted and nuanced: It could be the struggle within a society over "who gets what, when, and how" (Lasswell 1936), the "monopoly of the legitimate use of violence" (Weber, Mills and Gerth 1918), or the "authoritative allocation of values" (Easton 1953). This competition can be between social groups, such as ethnic or religious groups, administrative units, socioeconomic classes, and the like. Intervening in any way that affects the balance between groups within a society, their values, economic possessions, legitimacy, or their sense of who has a monopoly over violence can have potentially harmful consequences, whether intentional/unintentional, direct/indirect, or immediate/

long-term. This may be especially true in contexts of developing countries where the rule of law is weak and the state does not have a monopoly over the use of violence, or may be compliant in such violence; where traditional values take precedence; and where economic inequality is high and often group-based. Regardless of the form it takes, risks to experimental participants stemming from political competition are never explicitly identified as a type of risk to consider in the Belmont Report.

While researchers might be most sensitive to the short-term effects of their experiments, political competition is a long-term phenomenon that extends beyond immediate, formal assessments of political preferences, such as at election time or during party conferences. Political competition within a society is a prime example of an iterated, multi-player game, with long-range strategies at play. As such, we should expect that any experiment that manipulates factors that change these strategies will likely have implications for the long-term game outcome. This is particularly true of experiments that manipulate political factors because political benefit for one group almost always entails political harm to another, *whether both groups participate in the experiment or not*. In other words, in most contexts, any change in resource allocation (whether financial, physical, psychological, cultural, or otherwise) to one group will necessarily have implications for the political chances of one group versus another; political competition is zero-sum. For example, if an experimenter gives one village money around the time of elections for participation in an experiment, perhaps a political party that would otherwise have bought that village's votes will no longer have as much influence. Likewise, if an experiment gives evidence that a particular institution, such as an electoral rule, is harmful for society, advocates of a change to the electoral rules (who might be advocating something worse!) are potentially given a political advantage. Thus, social experiments are prone to Orwell's Time Machine *butterfly effect*: Touch anything in the local environment and it will likely generate political repercussions.

Of course, these effects are not limited to political science, nor even just social scientific experiments. For example, epidemiologists conducting experiments that test different vaccination dissemination programs in Africa, but who ignore how this might play into local political competition, may put participants in their programs at political risk. In many parts of Africa, *iatrophobia*—distrust of Western medical workers (Washington 2007)—has been heavily politicized. In 2004, an outbreak of polio in the Nigerian state of Kano stemmed from local Muslim clerics preaching that the polio vaccination was a Western plot to depopulate Africa by rendering girls infertile or giving its recipients AIDS. This political discourse by militant clerics was part a larger struggle for political power that has since grown into a full-scale Islamic insurgency against the government. In such a context, a Western-led epidemiological experiment can put not only its participants in danger, but can also be seen as empowering one side of this competition either through resource distribution or simply through the publication of research findings. Less extreme examples of political consequences from epidemiological experiments might simply be the political distribution of health care provided as part of an experiment. Is the intervention truly going to the most needy, or simply to government supporters? Is the experiment being used by the incumbent government as evidence of its efficacy? Scientific disciplines need to better consider the potential political consequences of experimental interventions.

Although both the Belmont Report and IRB-specific guidelines hint at the importance of assessing these political effects, they do not provide clear direction on how political risks to participants should, or could, be evaluated. This direction is important, particularly given that most members of a local review board are untrained in the intricacies of the political processes of a particular country (or set of countries, depending on the experiment), the relationships between social groups within that country's context, the history of the area under study, and the cultural idiosyncrasies that shape worldviews and interactions within these contexts. In what follows, we suggest three sets of questions that will help both researchers and IRB board members consider the political consequences of social science experiments.

11.2 Three Sets of Questions

We propose three sets of questions that researchers and review boards, both local and foreign, should consider when assessing political risks from their experiment. They fall under three topics: 1) political generalizability, 2) political resources, and 3) political identity. While there is some overlap between these categories, we suggest that attention to all three will result in a more thorough exploration of political risks from experiments in comparative politics and beyond than we find at present.

The first question asks about *political generalizability* and starts with the basic question: "Are your research subjects drawn from a national sample, or a subset of groups within the country?" The following sub-questions follow:

- If from a national sample, are small groups oversampled to enable greater confidence in generalizations across all social groups?
- If from a subset of society, from which groups have you sampled?
- What is the universe of groups to which your sample belongs? (Ethnic; religious; political ideology; socioeconomic; geographic, including regions and urbanization; etc.)
- Will this sampling procedure mean that results cannot be generalized across all groups in society? What are the potential political implications of this sampling procedure? Could a particular group or groups benefit/harm from this sampling procedure?

- Does your research question constitute support for a particular ideology or policy that divides the country politically in any way? Is your sample reflective of the breadth of opinions and preferences across these spectrums?

The purpose of the first set of questions is to make the researcher and review boards aware of how their proposed sampling procedure may have implications for groups in society. It asks them to place subjects into one of a number of salient social, cultural, economic, and political groups and to assess if there is a bias in the sample toward any such group or groups. This awareness will aid in their exploration of the two remaining topics. These questions do not suggest that all experiments must always be perfectly balanced across all such groups. Indeed, focus on a single group may be the very purpose of the research. Instead, these questions help the researcher consider groups and their associated political interests, with particular focus on whether their research may be related to a particular ideology, policy, organization (party, NGO, interest group, ministry, etc.).

Building on the first set of questions, the second set of questions asks about political resources, beginning with the following question: "Does your research intervene in the balance of political resources in any way?" These subquestions follow:

- Will participation in the experiment provide (or take away from) any group's political resources (financial, physical, psychological, social, political organization, legitimacy, etc.), whether they are participating in the experiment or not?
- Does your research question constitute support for a particular ideology or policy that divides the country politically in any way?
- Could the results implicate either participants or non-participants in any type of behavior that could give advantage to their own or a competing political group?

Among other things, this set of questions asks the researcher to think particularly about the difference between groups included and those omitted from participation in the experiment as a result of the sampling procedure. It asks the researcher to systematically consider the potential effects on both those included and excluded, given the relationship between groups in society.

The third and final set of questions asks researchers and review boards to consider the potential effects of the experiment on *political identity*, starting with the question: "Could your research subjects be identified with a particular political or social group just by participating in the experiment?" It then invites individuals to ask the following subquestions:

- Could participants become a target of another political/social group because of participation (or non-participation) in this experiment?

- Are you working with an organization, governmental or non-governmental, supported by or identified with a particular political group?
- Are there local cultural (national, ethnic, religious, or other) beliefs or traditions that could enable non-participants to associate participation in this experiment with the breaking of cultural mores or beliefs, or as a breach of group-based solidarity?

In certain contexts, open participation in an experiment funded by or affiliated in any way with the United States can cause social problems for participants. This set of questions ask the researcher to consider the effects of these types of issues not just on external validity/generalizability, but on the participants themselves. Could participants become a target of another political/social group (either local or international) because of participation (or non-participation) in your experiment?

11.3 Three Questions Applied

Each of these questions, if asked at the research design and IRB assessment stage, would invite researchers to pay particular attention to the potential political consequences of their experiments. In this section, we review two experiments that we separately conducted in India and Israel as well as a prominent experimental study published in the discipline's leading journal, the *American Political Science Review*, by Malesky, Schuler and Tran (2012) in Vietnam, to illustrate the utility of these questions.

In summer 2010, Selway was a co-PI on a series of experiments investigating the impact of crosscutting identities on prejudice in Chennai, India. Due to financial limitations, the principal investigators decided to sample from amongst the lower castes in urban slums of the largest city of Chennai. Following a review of the literature on caste identity in the state of Tamil Nadu, this sampling decision was justified as representing a stronger test of the theory. Specifically, Selway and his co-author argued that evidence for crosscutting ties reducing prejudice among the lower castes—where average levels of prejudice are supposed to be lower than between upper and lower castes—would convincingly show that crosscutting identity had the effect hypothesized by their argument.[2]

Halfway through the experiment, one of the local research assistants expressed a desire to quit the project. His surprisingly emotional response was that, now that he better understood the purpose of the project, he was afraid that the upper castes would use it as evidence that caste prejudice was simply a phenomenon of the lower castes. This rhetoric is commonplace in the politics of Tamil Nadu. Because the inclusion of castes into the four official government categories provides increased access to jobs and a host of other benefits, the upper castes use any information possible to fight against lower class inclusion.

The project had passed the local review board in the United States with no flags raised on this issue. As part of that process, moreover, an academic in a different social science department who has written and travelled extensively in India raised no flags. The host institution in India also agreed to the project with no objections. And one of the PIs had himself lived in Chennai for several years. However, one simple sampling decision had the potential for unintended political consequences unforeseen by all involved.

That same summer, Gubler ran a series of experiments in Israel designed to identify what differentiates individuals who support and engage in outgroup aggression from those who do not. Due to the nature of the project (its focus on individuals within groups) as well as the difficulty of obtaining a diverse sample of Palestinian citizens of Israel (PCIs), the experiments focused on just one group, including just Jewish-Israeli participants.[3]

As with the India experiment, these experiments were approved by a US-based IRB as well as by an on-site ethics board (in this case, the board at a leading Israeli university). However, similar to the India experiment, some participants expressed concern over the political risks their participation might engender, with some participants noting that those groups who agreed to participate might be labeled by international or other local political groups as "aggressive" simply because we now had data on them, whereas we lacked similar data for other groups (PCIs, specifically) that did not participate.

Thus, in experiments in both countries, the limited sampling procedures—fully justified by Belmont and other traditional standards of ethical review—had important implications for political competition. These political risks were not flagged in either the local or foreign ethical review processes, conducted by country experts and social scientists, nor were they anticipated by the PIs. To be sure, the papers stemming from these projects emphasize the limited nature of the findings, how other groups within these countries might also exhibit similar characteristics, etc. However, these experiences highlight the importance of fully addressing potential political risks for the type of experiments that dominate comparative politics as well as the inadequacy of the current review process in identifying these risks.

In the case of these experiments, walking through the first set of questions could have attuned our research teams and the IRB board to the potential political consequences to participants from what was deemed a non-political issue: our participant recruitment strategy. In particular, an answer to the question, "Could a particular group or groups benefit/harm from this sampling procedure?" might have spurred a different sampling method. These oversights do not mean that conducting these experiments was unethical. We both might have proceeded anyway, deciding to provide appropriate cautions in the write-up of the results (as we did), or to sample from the omitted groups in a future study. However, clear answers to these questions might also have spurred changes to our sampling methods in ways that would have benefited participants.

Next we turn to a discussion regarding how these three questions might have aided Malesky, Schuler and Tran (2012) in their recently published study, "The Adverse Effects of Sunshine: A Field Experiment on Legislative Transparency in an Authoritarian Assembly." Although we have briefly discussed this article with Malesky (whom we thank for this discussion), we are not fully familiar with all the details of the IRB applications for this experiment. And as emphasized above, identifying potential political consequences does not mean that the experiment in this study was necessarily unethical. We use this as another example to highlight how considering these issues beforehand would have made the authors aware of a broader range of possible political consequences, inviting them to either make adjustments to the experimental design or to appropriately respond in other ways.

Malesky, Schuler and Tran (2012) test the effect of a transparency intervention on a random sample of Vietnamese legislative delegates. The authors published a scorecard on the website of the country's largest online newspaper, *VietnamNet*, providing information on the quantity and content of legislative speeches and queries that the selected delegates made. The content included information on degree of criticalness of government policies, and relevance to the interests of the delegate's constituents, province, and profession. The scorecard also compared delegates' performance to the highest, average, and lowest delegates. The results of the experiment were significant and surprising: Delegates either curtailed their participation in the legislative query sessions or were more likely to be punished through removal from office in the next election or a lack of promotion to higher office.

Malesky, Schuler, and Tran's experiment thus had clear political consequences. How would our set of questions have aided in anticipating these and other possible political consequences? The first set of questions would have led to identifying the universe of groups to which the sample belongs. Possible groups include all legislative delegates, national leaders, all political elites (local and national), Vietnamese Communist Party members, and Vietnamese citizens. The authors could then begin considering the implications for their sample in relation to the unselected portion of each universe.

Will participation in the experiment provide (or take away from) any group political resources (financial, physical, psychological, social, political organization, legitimacy, etc.) they otherwise would not have had? This question might have prompted consideration of the reaction of other national politicians to the experimentally induced behavior, and thus might have prompted the authors to explore what has happened in the past to delegates who critique the government. It could have led to this question: "Might the experiment aid party leaders in identifying possible troublemakers?" Given that top-level party leaders select who runs for legislative elections, a discussion would have almost certainly ensued regarding re-election prospects. The authors then would have assessed this risk and decided whether it was something with which they felt comfortable.

Alternatively, the added exposure certain delegates received from the experiment might have given them unfair political advantage over other national leaders. What if the selected delegates were more corrupt or less educated than the current leaders and the experiment provided them resources that propelled them to the top of the party? The authors would thus have had to think about the nature of the delegates and the likelihood of this scenario.

Does the research constitute support for a particular ideology or policy that divides the country politically in any way? This question would have caused the authors to think about pro- and anti-democratic elements within the country and how they might react to this experiment. Could it help them by providing a tool for voters to hold their delegates accountable? Might it hinder them by outing the most outspoken delegates who might otherwise bring about real change? Could it lead to conflict anyway, putting the delegates in the path of physical harm or leading to broader protests or riots in society?

Are you working with an organization, governmental or non-governmental, supported by or identified with a particular political group? This question would have led the authors to think about the political orientation of *VietnamNet*, with whom they partnered. Who owns and operates the company? Is it generally associated with any particular individual, faction of the party, or opposition group? Would selected delegates be unhappy about their exposure seek to close the company down?

These are just a sample of the considerations that would have likely been spurred by systematic consideration of our three questions. These questions would almost certainly have identified re-election prospects as a possible political consequence of the experiment. In our own discussions of these questions regarding this experiment, we arrived at this potential issue starting from several of the questions and sub-questions in our list. We also identified several potential political consequences of the experiment that, as far as we can tell, did not come to fruition, but that nevertheless would have caused the researchers to better investigate their likelihood and prepare accordingly.

As the three foregoing examples have illustrated, our three questions are helpful in the systematic identification of potential political effects of experiments in comparative politics. The questions alone, however, do not provide a set of parameters to determine whether the experiment was ultimately ethical. Like the Belmont Report, we make no attempt to provide such parameters or weigh in on this issue for any of the above experiments. Questions of ethics are ultimately normative questions based on individual beliefs about "good" and "right" in particular contexts, and as such are not easily captured by a general set of guidelines. Consider, as an example, Milgram's obedience to authority experiment in which participants believed they had (sometimes fatally) electrocuted other participants. In response to this experiment, no single set of guidelines emerged to prevent similar unethical occurrences within the field of psychology. Instead, we received the Belmont mantras of "do no harm" and "benefits outweigh the costs." Why?

Because these general guidelines are likely the best available. Equivalents in comparative politics to the harm induced by Milgram's experiment might include increasing corruption or supporting "oppressive" politicians, parties, or policies. But just as the discipline of psychology post-Milgram has not agreed on a set of parameters for what constitutes ethical levels of psychological or emotional harm in all contexts (beyond the general principles of the Belmont Report), we likewise do not attempt to establish parameters for what constitutes ethical levels of political harm. To do so might be even more difficult than in psychology, as it is quite difficult to agree on what constitutes political harm. While there is some degree of agreement among psychologists about what constitutes psychological and physical harm, such agreement on political issues is much harder to find, especially cross-nationally. To return to our thought experiment at the outset of the paper, some Democratic-affiliated Americans reading this piece likely bristled at the thought of a Chinese research team conducting experiments that might benefit Republicans in US elections. Yet even Republicans would be empathetic to opposing such research, fearing that future studies could affect them. Do we think equally hard about the sensibilities and opinions of the societies in which we conduct our research?

11.4   Conclusion

This paper presents an argument for the importance of systematically considering the unintended political consequences, or risks, of social science experiments, with particular focus on experiments in comparative politics. As our examples illustrate, these consequences arise both from the potential effects of treatments themselves on participants and also from the publication of the findings from the experiment. Although not directly addressed in this chapter, the failure to systematically consider these risks also raises the potential of political consequences for the discipline. Groups aggravated by such experiments in their societies might successfully reduce research funding, ban future experiments, or (in the extreme) prosecute or jail scientists conducting research on important topics within the country.

We suggest that political risks are not considered systematically enough in the experimental design and IRB assessment phases of research. We then highlight three sets of questions to aid researchers and IRB boards in the assessment of potential political risks and provide evidence for the utility of these questions with a brief discussion of their application to recent research in political science. We expect that all experiments that assess social outcomes of interest to political science come with some political risks. As such, we do not argue that experiments that entail potential political risks should not be conducted. Rather, as the Belmont Report suggests, these potential risks should be weighed against potential benefits. Given the recent explosion of experiments in comparative politics, and the relative newness of this methodology in cross-national research, if these risks are not carefully considered, then, at worst, Milgram-like consequences may occur and, at best, the risk-benefit analysis will be incomplete. Our three questions provide a framework to systematically assess the potential political consequences of these experiments.

Notes

1 We thank Scott Desposato for this analogy. The beginning scene of the most recent Star Trek movie sees Captain Kirk violate the Prime Directive in his attempt to save the "primitive" inhabitants of the planet Nibiru.
2 See Bossuroy and Selway (2011) "Cross-cutting Cleavages, Discrimination and Inter-Personal Financial Transfers—A Lab Experiment in Chennai, India" and Selway, Davidson and Bossuroy (2011) "Inter-Ethnic Civic Engagement and Discrimination" for a presentation of results.
3 See Gubler's (N.d) "When Humanizing the Enemy Fails" for a presentation of the results.

12

INFORMATION AND POWER

Ethical Considerations of Political Information Experiments

Brigitte Zimmerman

12.1 Introduction

A growing body of political science research today involves three things: human subjects, experiments (field, survey), and fieldwork (Druckman et al. 2006, Brady 2000, Kapiszewski, MacLean and Read 2015). This chapter considers a particular body of political science research: experiments providing information to citizens in democracies about their government. Experiments providing information address compelling research questions that relate to the core of political science literature. As many dependent variables in political science are behavioral (e.g., voting, corruption, declaring war, engaging in protest), and behavioral change is challenging to set in motion, the interventions associated with information experiments are often designed to be as strong as possible.

The strong interventions involved in this body of research have unique characteristics: 1) they often affect group-level outcomes, making them highly likely to incur spillover effects; 2) they often cause lasting harm to at least one person or group;[1] and 3) the positive and negative outcomes from these interventions are ambiguous in time horizon, causal relationship to the research, and normative value. These characteristics are particularly salient when the information is executed in the context of an election, as incumbent officials rarely have the turnaround time or monetary resources to respond to the information, which subsequently affects voters' actions at the polls and, sometimes, the results of the election.

These attributes pose corresponding ethical challenges regarding calculating the costs and benefits of this research and obtaining consent from those affected. Because these attributes are not present in the medical trials that heavily influence most IRB processes, they are not often addressed in obtaining IRB approval. As an initial attempt to mitigate this gap, I suggest a framework for evaluating the ethics of these experiments in the research design phase. Using my own proposed audit experiment as a case study, I offer concrete ideas for assessing the costs and benefits of information experiments, disseminating information about the research to affected parties, and obtaining consent from participants and non-participants.

In what follows, I first delineate the scope of experiments considered in this chapter. Then, I discuss the unique ethical considerations associated with these experiments. I next revisit the original Belmont Report (The National Commission for the Protection of Human Subjects of Biomedical and Behavioral Research 1979) and its ethical guidelines for human subjects research, considering its implications for the unique body of experiments considered in this chapter: those which provide information to citizens in democracies about their government. Finally, I suggest a framework for evaluating the ethics of information experiments and develop a case study in applying the framework. Throughout the discussion, I draw on my experience considering the ethics of my own research: a citizen survey, a survey of government officials (with embedded survey experiment and behavioral games), and a national transparency experiment with top-down and bottom-up components.[2]

12.2   Scope: Citizen Information Experiments

This chapter focuses on a particular body of research in political science: that involving interventions that provide information to citizens in democracies about their government. For the purposes of this discussion, this category of experiments includes anything that provides a message to a group of citizens by any means. The defining characteristic of the experiments considered in this chapter is that they are designed to answer research questions about the effect of information in democracies, where there is a chain of accountability from citizens to government officials via elections.

Experiments that fall under the scope of this discussion may provide information about corruption (Banerjee et al. 2010, Chong et al. 2011, Ferraz and Finan 2008), violence (Collier and Vicente 2014), government performance (Björkman and Svensson 2009, Gottlieb 2012), government policies (Obradovich and Zimmerman 2015, Wantchekon 2003), government spending (Chong et al. 2011), or voting (Ferree et al. 2011, Gerber, Green and Larimer 2008). Information can be provided through survey experiment (Obradovich and Zimmerman 2015), in-person canvassing (Chong et al. 2011, Collier and Vicente 2014, Ferree et al. 2011), campaigns (Wantchekon 2003), community meetings (Banerjee et al. 2010, Björkman and Svensson 2009, Collier and Vicente 2014, Gottlieb 2012), media (Ferraz and Finan 2008), written reports (Ferraz and Finan 2008, Gerber, Green and Larimer 2008), or community theatre (Collier and Vicente 2014). Finally, this information can be expected to affect turnout (Chong et al. 2011, Collier and

Vicente 2014, Ferree et al. 2011, Gerber, Green and Larimer 2008), vote choice (Banerjee et al. 2010, Chong et al. 2011, Ferraz and Finan 2008, Gottlieb 2012, Obradovich and Zimmerman 2015, Wantchekon 2003), public opinion on issues (Collier and Vicente 2014), public opinion on government (Chong et al. 2011, Obradovich and Zimmerman 2015), or other forms of political action (Björkman and Svensson 2009, Collier and Vicente 2014, Gottlieb 2012, Obradovich and Zimmerman 2015).

Examples of political science research that does not fall under the scope of this discussion are:

- Affecting information flow between citizens and government in a context without elections (e.g., Malesky, Schuler and Tran (2012))
- Opinion polling without providing them information (e.g., Gibson and Long (2009), Stokes (2005))
- Affecting the experience (either before, during, or after) of engaging in protest or war (e.g., Fearon, Humphreys and Weinstein (2009), Blattman (2009))

I steer clear of these types of interventions not because they do not have analogous ethical considerations, but because their possible effects and the affected individuals or groups are more challenging to anticipate, making the decision regarding whether to engage in these interventions less clear. I believe limiting the scope of this discussion in the way delineated above will allow me to develop an applicable framework for a large body of political science research.

This discussion deliberately pertains to both field and survey experiments. Field experiments provide information via a variety of means and study the effects of the information on real world behavior. Survey experiments provide information via "vignettes" in a survey and study the effects of the information on reported behaviors in the survey. Although field experiments may have stronger or more real effects, both types of experiments can affect the relationship between constituents and government through the provision of information. This discussion is structured to consider all interventions that affect this relationship in order to develop a framework for separating those worth pursuing from those that are not.

12.3 Ethical Considerations

As mentioned earlier in this chapter, there are three characteristics of research involving information experiments in democracies that set this body of research apart: 1) They often affect group-level outcomes, making them highly likely to incur spillover effects; 2) the interventions often cause lasting harm to at least one person or group; and 3) the positive and negative outcomes from these interventions are ambiguous in time horizon, causal relationship to the research, and normative value.

The first set of ethical challenges in this body of research arises from the group-level outcomes that often accompany these interventions. When information is provided to citizens in a democracy, the affected individuals are not only those participating in the research, but also those who bear the consequences or reap the benefits of government actions (which, in a democracy, is likely all citizens in the area). For example, a get-out-the-vote intervention hopes to affect individual voters, but it can change the landscape of political competition or even the outcome of the election. A transparency intervention providing information about corruption hopes to inform individual citizens, but it can change the distribution of public goods. A survey of citizens can prime them to think about a different set of issues when communicating policy preferences to government officials. The key is that each of these downstream outcomes is like a public good: It is non-excludable because it affects everyone without regard to who participated in the research and who didn't, and it is non-rivalrous, because it cannot be "used up" by one group so that others are not affected.

Another way to think about the group-level effects is that this kind of research is particularly prone to spillover effects. Setting aside issues of whether these spillover effects are measurable or anticipated, the mere presence of such spillover effects poses two ethical challenges for researchers. First, consent from individuals affected by the research is challenging to obtain in the presence of spillover effects, as it may not be clear which individuals will be affected by the research in advance, and even if clear, it may be costly, time-consuming, and otherwise challenging to contact all of these individuals. However, perhaps the effort in obtaining consent from non-participants should be proportional to the magnitude, longevity, and spread of the effects of the research, rather than have a standard applied to all research projects uniformly. For example, my current research involves a transparency intervention conducted at the level of district government of Malawi. I plan to select a small number of citizens and officials to participate in the intervention, and I will obtain consent from these participants. However, my unit of analysis is actually the district, and all district citizens and district officials, whether sampled or not, could be affected by the research, either bearing costs or receiving benefits. Adjusting consent procedures to provide these non-participants with information about the research and allow them to opt in or opt out is challenging.

The second challenge posed by spillover effects is that the costs and benefits of the research are more challenging to forecast. Currently, many IRB applications require an analysis of the costs and benefits of the research for participants, but very few require an analysis of the costs and benefits of the research for those who may be affected by the treatment but who are not participating in the research. For example, although the IRB required me to delineate the costs and benefits of a recent survey providing information about corruption to citizens, I was not compelled to delineate the costs and benefits of the research to the sampled citizens' government officials or to non-sampled citizens, even though these individuals might be affected by the survey.

Another set of ethical challenges in this body of research arises from the fact that the interventions almost always cause great harm to at least one individual or group. Some scholars have asserted that electoral politics is a zero-sum game (see, for example, Cox and McCubbins (1986), Weingast, Shepsle and Johnsen (1981)). Even if this is not absolutely true, it is definitely the case that information interventions have winners and losers: a person or group who "looks better" in light of the information and a person or group who "looks worse." This stands in stark contrast to the gold-standard biology intervention, where one person's benefit rarely results in another's downfall. For example, providing information about one candidate's good performance decreases the chances of another, but no other individual bears a significant cost when chemotherapy saves a cancer patient's life.

One reason there is potential for great harm in conducting experiments with information interventions, especially when conducting research in low income environments, is that researchers are often relatively wealthy and powerful compared to the participants and non-participants under study. Perhaps more precisely, it is often the case with information interventions that the researcher's "willingness to pay" for giving information to a participant is greater than the participant's willingness to pay for not receiving that information. For example, a get-out-the-vote campaign run by a research team in a rural, low-income setting is likely more costly than many low-level government officials' campaigns. The intended outcome of both activities is to mobilize voters, but the research team is much more empowered to achieve this outcome, and may significantly shift the body of voters mobilized and therefore the outcome of the election. This discrepancy means that it is possible for researchers to execute activities with persistent and far-reaching effects but not possible (at least, not realistic) for officials or citizens to counteract these effects. In other words, researchers have "undue influence" over the political outcomes in a system. If information is truly the "currency of democracy," then researchers are entering many democracies to distribute this "currency" and possibly change the course of various political processes. This ethical concern will not be accounted for in the framework proposed in this chapter, but can be considered by the researcher separately.

Much of evaluating the ethics of a research project involves weighing costs against benefits. However, because the costs and benefits for each individual are not uniform across the individuals affected, comparing the outcomes for different individuals results in an apples-to-oranges calculation. Even if the costs and benefits of the research can be anticipated, valuing the costs and benefits for individuals affected by the research is incredibly challenging. For example, how would I place a value on a politician being removed from office as a result of my research? Does this cost borne by five officials outweigh the benefit of making 10,000 citizens more informed or opening an opportunity for 10 non-incumbents? Would it make a difference if 100,000 citizens were informed instead of 10,000?

Not only are the effects challenging to anticipate and compare across affected parties, they are often ambiguous in time horizon, causal relationship to the research, and normative value. Anticipating the likelihoods of different outcomes is nearly impossible, partially because many of these outcomes are persistent effects of the intervention that won't be realized until far into the future. For example, an anti-corruption information campaign may not overturn an election in the near future, but it could affect the kinds of candidates citizens support for years to come.

Further, in information experiments, it is challenging to causally link outcomes to the research. Even when convincingly demonstrated, the causal mechanism is typically not understood. This is partially because other pressures in conducting research place an emphasis on measurable outcomes, but there are often unmeasurable (and therefore often not mentioned) outcomes of the research. For example, my research considers the effect of transparency increases on politician *choices* in office. Choices can be observed and measured. However, politician and citizen *attitudes* may also shift as a result of the intervention, but if I don't focus on attitudes as part of my research strategy, I would likely never anticipate this effect.

Finally, some effects are challenging to categorize as costs or benefits. The literature frames certain outcomes as normatively positive, but it isn't clear that this is always the case. We can envision situations where benefits are actually costs. For example, it may not be a "benefit" to an individual that she was compelled to vote in an election by a get-out-the-vote campaign if the opportunity cost of her doing so was earning a wage. Similarly, increased knowledge about government responsibilities may not be a "benefit" if individuals with this knowledge bear the psychological consequences of dissatisfaction or cognitive dissonance. In designing information experiments, researchers must scrutinize the prevailing assertions about the normative value placed on the effects of their research.

Before continuing on to discuss how these challenges could be addressed, I want to consider whether these challenges might be even more pressing in "field" research, research in which the researcher is not from the area under study. It seems possible to me that non-native researchers might be at a disadvantage when it comes to foreseeing all the potential outcomes of a research intervention, especially those that are highly unlikely but still possible. Furthermore, it may be inappropriate for non-native researchers to normatively evaluate these outcomes. Finally, because foreigners typically hire local enumerators to assist with research, this adds another category of individuals who should be considered when evaluating the benefits and costs of the research, even though many IRB application processes do not require this. Enumerators can both reap benefits (e.g., professional experience, networking, payment) and incur costs (e.g., retribution) from assisting with information experiments.

12.4   Review of Belmont Report Principles

To develop a framework for addressing these unique characteristics, I return to the Belmont Report (The National Commission for the Protection of Human Subjects of Biomedical and Behavioral Research 1979) that is often cited regarding ethical considerations for research involving human subjects. This report poses three considerations to guide such research: respect, beneficence, and justice. Based on Sieber and Tolich's 2012 interpretation of the Belmont Report and my experiences with IRB proposals in the past, I interpret each of these principles and discuss how current IRB procedures have distorted them. First, the principle of "respect" refers to protecting the autonomy of persons and treating them with courtesy. Over time, the discussion about this principle has generally been reduced to a discussion about signed, informed consent. However, this principle is more broadly about informing individuals about the potential benefits and costs of the research in terms they understand, and then upholding and reinforcing their individual autonomy to make a voluntary decision about whether they want to participate.

The principle of "beneficence" refers to maximizing positive outcomes and minimizing risks and harm associated with research involving human subjects. On most IRB applications, this principle has similarly been reduced to a review of the costs and benefits to each individual participating in the research. However, this principle is not only about the costs and benefits the participants incur as a result of their participation, but the costs and benefits the participants and non-participants incur as a result of the research occurring in their environment, both in the short-term and in the long-term. It is important to note that neither the principle nor current IRB proposals typically consider the cases in which a benefit for one party is a harm to another, as is the case with many interventions that provide political information.

Finally, the principle of "justice" refers to ensuring reasonable, non-exploitative and carefully considered procedures and their fair administration, as well as the fair distribution of costs and benefits among persons and groups (i.e., that the bearers of the costs should be the bearers of the benefits). In the words of Sieber (1992), "It is unjust that some should be left to suffer as a result of their yielding valuable knowledge that may benefit others" (Sieber and Tolich 2012). Here, the common thread when designing procedures or distributing outcomes is fairness, or the principle that these things should be done in an unbiased way. I would argue that current IRB application processes focus more on procedural justice than on outcome justice: whether the research procedures are fairly executed rather than whether the resulting benefits and costs of the research are fairly distributed. However, when the outcomes of research can be as strong, far reaching, and persistent as those arising from the research discussed in this chapter, justice in outcomes is also important. Specifically regarding the body of research considered in this chapter, it is not enough that the information provided in campaigns is accurate and all human subjects protocols are followed. The outcomes of the information campaigns should be distributed fairly as well.

In the next section, I introduce a framework within which to evaluate research involving information experiments in democracies, keeping the core meaning of each of these principles in mind.

12.5 Suggested Framework for Considering the Ethics of Information Experiments

There are two extreme responses that could result from this discussion (and the other discussions arising in this edited volume). First, researchers could decide to do nothing, refraining from research interventions of the sort considered in this chapter for fear of the ethical challenges. Second, because most of these interventions are legal for regular citizens to execute, political science researchers could simply do anything allowable by law, without regard to the ethical considerations that might constrain them as scholars. Realistically, the discipline will probably continue to find some middle ground, and the goal in proposing this framework is to assist in guiding the particular point of the middle ground found by scholars who execute information experiments in the future.

This framework reviews my thinking in designing my own research and makes suggestions based on this process, but does not prescribe a particular procedure. I do not propose that this framework should be included in formal IRB processes, but rather suggest a tool to informally guide researchers in designing their interventions. I envision an ethical analysis such as the one I undertake in the next section being published on researcher websites or in pre-analysis plans along with surveys, datasets, and other research materials.

There are two components of the framework I suggest. First, I suggest a more comprehensive cost-benefit analysis than what is currently mandated in most IRB processes. Second, I suggest more creative approaches to obtaining consent from non-participants who are nonetheless affected by the research.

The first suggestion is to engage in a more comprehensive cost-benefit analysis. Following the beneficence principle in the Belmont Report means considering all possible effects in deciding whether to pursue a research project, regardless of whether the effects are direct or indirect, certain or uncertain, short-term or long-term, or imposed on participants or non-participants. Following the justice principle in the Belmont Report means ensuring those who bear costs of the research also receive benefits. Combining these principles, any cost-benefit analysis evaluating the ethics of a given experiment that provides political information should evaluate:

- Costs and benefits to participants of participating in the research
- Costs and benefits to different groups of citizens of the research

- Costs and benefits to different groups of political elites of the research
- Costs and benefits to society surrounding research (considering factors such as political and economic development)
- Costs and benefits to research assistants and enumerators of the research
- Costs and benefits to the academic literature of the research

This analysis should be iterated for different time periods and for any and all outcomes of the research that might occur with a non-negligible probability. Given the growing literature involving information interventions, a thorough cost-benefit analysis should include a literature review. Outcomes, positive or negative, from others' work can provide a baseline for expectations regarding interventions in the design phase.

Perhaps the most appropriate tool for analyzing costs and benefits in this way is an expected value analysis. I would not suggest mandating (for example, in an IRB application) that researchers assign probabilities and monetary values to outcomes. Nonetheless, even independently executed, qualitative expected value analysis would enable researchers to more holistically consider the effects of research. Such an expected value analysis could be executed separately for each intervention in a research project. I provide an example of what I envision in the next section. When calculating the expected value of the research, I think it is important to base this evaluation on conservative estimates of likelihood for benefits and generous estimates of likelihood for costs, on the assumption that it is better to fail to do ethically questionable research that would have turned out well than to follow through on ethically questionable research that results in disaster. In other words, when it comes to ethically questionable research, I assert that Type I error is preferable to Type II error.

Based on my previous experiences and discussions in considering these issues, I want to forestall one danger that could arise in this process. I think it is important that this kind of analysis remain free of judgments directed towards the individuals affected. If one person bears a great cost for the research, this would only be balanced by a great benefit. It is irrelevant whether the former individual is a corrupt politician or an honest one; a wealthy, powerful citizen or an impoverished, disenfranchised one. Researchers sometimes laud efforts to help citizens remove poor performing officials from office or mobilize resources around a common goal. I would argue that it is not our mandate as researchers to advance an agenda such as these. A life negatively affected by our research is a life negatively affected, regardless of whose life it is. This cost is only justified if outweighed by comparable benefits.

After completing this analysis and presenting the costs and benefits of the potential research design clearly, an important last step is to apply the Belmont Report's principle of justice in considering the distribution of outcomes. In the body of experiments considered here, this often means ensuring costs and benefits of information are distributed equally across citizens, candidates, parties, and electoral units. There is rarely a compelling reason to target information campaigns at only one person, group, or geography. Often, sampling strategies and treatment arms can be adjusted for a more just allocation of outcomes. For example, in a recent experiment providing information to voters in Malawi's 2014 election (co-authored with Nicholas Obradovich), we took care to provide information about the four major parties equally, and to focus on positive information rather than negative.

The second suggestion is to go back to the core idea behind the Belmont Report's respect principle: that respecting individuals means informing them of the research occurring in their world that might affect them and allowing them to opt in or out. In experiments involving information interventions with indirect and far-reaching effects, this practically means we must develop creative methods by which to inform both participants and non-participants of the risks/benefits of the research to all parties and afford them an opportunity to ask questions or object to the research. In the body of research considered in this article, consent of participants is sometimes de-prioritized for practical reasons. However, consent procedures do not have to be cumbersome. Researchers could be more creative about obtaining consent from participants. For example, researchers planning an intervention that would post information about government performance in public spaces could obtain consent from the business managers or community (non-government) authorities proximate to the spaces. With some innovation, waivers of informed consent need occur in a minority of cases.

Consent can also be obtained from non-participants. One option for updating the informed consent procedures to reach non-participants would be to provide them with information and opportunities to ask questions, especially where allowing them the opportunity to opt in or out of the research is not possible. For example, researchers planning to conduct an information campaign during an election could announce their plans on the radio months in advance and provide a phone number and meeting time for citizens or political officials to ask questions and voice their concerns. Similarly, researchers planning to survey political officials could send the theoretical population a letter months in advance and allow them to call or email with questions or feedback.

Of course, these ideas might affect the validity of the research, especially for certain types of information in certain locations, and perhaps such measures are not always necessary, given their costs and benefits. These suggestions are simply creative alternatives to the straightforward informed consent process intended to alleviate some of the predominant ethical objections to this research. I see these types of actions as critically important when the research activities have the potential to affect group-level outcomes persistently, as they do for the class of interventions discussed in this chapter.

12.6   Case Study Demonstrating Framework

In this section, I apply the framework suggested above to a case study: specifically, to evaluate the ethics of a transparency intervention I plan to conduct in Malawi. This is a simplified version of the ethics evaluation and is intended to illustrate the use of the framework rather than give a full analysis of the ethical issues involved.

My research considers how political officials strategically shift their corrupt behavior in response to increases in transparency. Depending on the level of accountability among citizens and political superiors in a given area, I argue bottom-up and top-down transparency interventions should have differential effects on the forms of corruption politicians choose as part of their corruption portfolio. Working in local government in Malawi, I examine this relationship between transparency, accountability, and corruption using three research instruments: 1) a citizen survey (n=600) to measure citizen perceptions of corruption and test their willingness to hold politicians accountable via a survey experiment; 2) a politician survey (n=250) to gauge baseline levels of different corruption forms and test the relationship between corruption and transparency via a survey experiment; and 3) a randomized transparency intervention with top-down and bottom-up treatment conditions. The top-down treatment condition includes an audit of local government accounts executed by the National Audit Office of Malawi and then dissemination of the findings of the audit regarding the level and forms of corruption in local government to political superiors. The bottom-up treatment condition includes dissemination of the findings of the audit regarding the level and forms of corruption in local government to citizens via written materials, radio broadcast, and community meetings. In this case study, I focus on the bottom-up treatment condition of the transparency intervention.

The first step in the framework I'm suggesting is to more thoroughly consider the potential costs and benefits of a given research project as an expected value analysis. I include a table of anticipated costs and benefits for the bottom-up treatment condition of the transparency intervention in Table 12.1. The table includes a list of costs and benefits across different actors and different periods of time. Based on the existing literature using similar treatments and contextual factors in Malawi, I have made qualitative estimates of the probabilities of each outcome and the number of individuals affected. Each line of the table can be read as follows (example from first two lines of Table 12.1): "About 300 participants will face a medium risk of incurring an immediate low opportunity cost." Or "About 200 participants will face a low chance of receiving the long-term small benefit of improved understanding of government accountability structures."

This expected value analysis does not raise any ethical issues that we wouldn't have anticipated. However, it does organize the costs and benefits for evaluation. If the costs and benefits balanced less well or if some of the most adverse effects were more likely, this table would clearly highlight the issue. The exercise of more

TABLE 12.1 Expected Value Analysis of Bottom–Up Transparency Treatment

Affected Party	Number of Individuals Affected	Cost or Benefit	Description	Magnitude	Probability of Occurrence	Timing
Participants—Officials	180	Benefit	Financial compensation	Medium	Certain	Immediate
Participants—Officials	180	Cost	Opportunity cost of time	Small	High	Immediate
Participants—Officials	180	Benefit	Pride in contributing to good governance	Small	Low	Short–Term
Participants—Officials	180	Cost	Shame in contributing to poor governance	Small	Very Low	Short–Term
Participants—Officials	180	Cost	Immediate retribution	Large	Very Low	Short–Term
Participants—Officials	180	Cost	Downstream retribution	Large	Low	Long–Term
Participants—Citizens	500	Benefit	Financial compensation	Medium	Certain	Immediate
Participants—Citizens	500	Cost	Opportunity cost of time	Small	High	Immediate
Participants—Citizens	500	Benefit	Pride in contributing to good governance	Small	High	Long–Term
Participants—Citizens	500	Cost	Anxiety over pressure to contribute to good governance	Small	Low	Long–Term
Non-Participants—Citizens in Treated Districts	200	Cost	Political officials less available during intervention	Medium	High	Immediate
Non-Participants—Political Officials in Ruling Party	25	Cost	Renewed focus on corruption: unpleasant experiences	Small	Very Low	Short–Term

Non-Participants—Political Officials in Ruling Party	13	Cost	Renewed focus on corruption: loss of income	Medium	Very Low	Long-Term
Non-Participants—Political Officials in Ruling Party	3	Cost	Renewed focus on corruption: legal action	Large	Very Low	Long-Term
Non-Participants—Political Officials in Ruling Party	100	Benefit	Renewed focus on corruption: opportunities to take office	Large	Low	Long-Term
Non-Participants—Political Officials in Opposition Party	100	Benefit	Renewed focus on corruption: opportunities to take office	Large	Very Low	Long-Term
Society	NA*	Benefit	Corruption becomes more difficult	Medium	Low	Long-Term
Society	NA	Cost	Corruption becomes more hidden	Medium	Low	Long-Term
Research Assistants	3	Cost	Blacklisted with District Commissioners	Large	Very Low	Long-Term
Research Assistants	3	Benefit	Networking	Medium	Medium	Long-Term
Research Assistants	3	Benefit	Work experience	Medium	High	Long-Term
Academic Literature	NA	Benefit	Improved understanding of mechanisms behind corruption	Small	Medium	Short-Term

*Not applicable

thoroughly considering the effects of the research over time and across parties provides an opportunity to consider, document, and resolve ethical issues that may not come to light in an IRB process.

The second step in the framework is to develop creative options for informing participants and non-participants of the research and providing an opportunity to opt out. In the case of my research, I did or will obtain informed consent from the subjects recruited to participate in the citizen survey and the politician survey, as well as every local government official in a district treated with the transparency intervention and every citizen recruited to participate in the bottom-up transparency intervention. The informed consent procedures I use convey the relevant costs and benefits of participating in the research, as well as the costs and benefits of the research more generally. It also explains the subject selection process, something many subjects I have encountered ask for.

Informing non-participants requires more proactive creativity. In the case of the citizen and politician surveys, I informed the District Commissioner of the research in advance, overviewed the selection procedures, and allowed him or her to ask questions or object to the research on behalf of his or her citizens or other officials in the district. In the case of the transparency intervention, I plan to announce the intervention on the national radio in advance, stating the objectives of the research, overviewing the sampling procedure, and providing contact information for local partners.[3] This announcement will not afford the politicians enough time to change the actions that will be detected in the transparency intervention, but it will give citizens and politicians alike enough time to ask questions and raise issues with those executing research in their country. I see it as critically important to allow the affected parties to voice their concerns about the research.

12.7 Conclusion

One concern I have with the framework proposed in this chapter is that it might incentivize political scientists to randomize interventions with more moderate outcomes, or in other words, those with a narrower gap between the winners and the losers of the interventions. Perhaps interventions with extreme outcomes, such as changing the loser of an election to the winner of an election, would no longer be attempted under this framework. There are those who would argue that this would be a positive shift, and ethically, perhaps it would be. However, it seems like such a shift might occur at the expense of pursuing valuable research questions. One important criterion in deciding what research projects to pursue (and, by extension, how to allocate precious research time and funds) should always be the contribution of the research to academic literature.

This framework might also incentivize political scientists to avoid generating original data via experiments, exempting them from considering the ethical issues associated with executing such research. Perhaps this shift would result in increased use of pre-existing datasets, laboratory experiments, natural experiments, or even partnerships with other types of organizations. This is not necessarily a bad thing. It might be valuable to discourage the use of ethically challenging designs and encourage substituting more ethically straightforward methods wherever possible. Nonetheless, limiting experiments in political science research means severely limiting the data available for research. Research understanding the effect of information would likely be a casualty of this shift; studying the effects of artificially generated information about hypothetical government institutions or individuals on anticipated outcomes is not as convincing as the real-world information experiment equivalent.

This chapter has considered experiments that provide information to citizens in democracies about their governments, their unique characteristics, and their corresponding ethical issues. I have proposed a framework and offered some initial concrete suggestions for better addressing these ethical issues in the research design process. It is my hope that the discipline increasingly considers these issues in the research design phase, and that any strategies and tools for doing so are widely disseminated and applied.

Notes

1 There is a prevailing norm of treating political elites as different from other human subjects. Rather than weigh in on the circumstances under which this is acceptable, I treat them as any other human subject for the purposes of this discussion.
2 Throughout this chapter, "top-down" transparency interventions are those that intervene in the relationship between a government official and his political superiors (e.g., party bosses, higher level elected officials, central government institutions), whereas "bottom-up" transparency interventions are those that intervene in the relationship between a government official and the citizens in his area.
3 Note that I have yet to obtain permission to execute this idea from my local implementing partners.

13

CONDUCTING RESEARCH WITH NGOS

Relevant Counterfactuals From the Perspective of Subjects

David W. Nickerson and Susan D. Hyde

Some field experiments in comparative politics are designed to test hypotheses derived from social science theories, and are created and implemented entirely by researchers. Other field experiments explore the effects of existing interventions undertaken by non-academic organizations, such as Intergovernmental Organizations (IOs), Non-Governmental Organizations (NGOs), or government bodies. These interventions may be intended to reduce poverty, boost political participation, encourage development, promote democracy, or curb the spread of disease. The interventions may be well designed, have positive effects, and be cost effective. They may also have unintended consequences, adverse effects, or no effects whatsoever. Determining the effects of these interventions is important for public policy, intellectually rewarding, and socially desirable.

In evaluating the ethics of research, the difference between researcher-led interventions and studies of interventions initiated by third parties like IOs and NGOs is a critical factor. The crux of the ethical question depends on the cause of the intervention (or the "treatment") evaluated in the field experiment, so we distinguish between "the intervention" and "the research," and focus on counterfactual comparisons between the world with and without the research. Does the researcher cause the intervention to happen? Or would the intervention happen even if the researcher were not working with the organization? In cases where the intervention itself would not occur in the absence of the research, then the ethical questions involve both the intervention and the research, as is typical in human subjects cases. The relevant counter-factual involves the benefits of and costs of both the intervention and the research: Both would not occur in the absence of the study. However, in cases where the field experimental treatment would occur even if the study of it did not, then the ethical questions primarily concern the research component, and should be less concerned with the intervention itself, as we detail below. If an NGO, foreign government, or other third party will pursue the intervention independently, then the relevant (ethical) counter-factual comparison is between a world in which the treatment occurs and a world in which the treatment occurs and its causal effects are (at least in principle) better understood.

Questions about the ethics of collaborative field experimental research are relevant to both scholars and Institutional Review Boards (IRBs), which are housed at all US-based universities and from which scholars must seek approval for all research involving human subjects.[1] Many questions about the ethics of field experiments are addressed by IRBs, which are charged with protecting human subjects from unethical conduct by university researchers. The Federal Policy for the Protection of Human Subjects (FPPHS) provides guidelines and rules for IRBs across universities in the United States. These rules focus on three actors: subjects, researchers, and government departments. Although this focus is understandable, given outrage over infamous research conducted by governments (e.g., the Tuskegee Syphilis study) and researchers (e.g., Milgram's obedience to authority experiments), an increasing amount of contemporary research is produced by scholars working in conjunction with programmatically focused non-governmental organizations (NGOs). This essay offers practical guidelines for evaluating the appropriateness of collaborative experiments between researchers and NGOs, both for IRBs specifically and for the scholarly community more generally.

In particular, this essay argues that when researchers work with organizations already engaged in programmatic activity, IRBs and observers interested in the ethics of field experiments should focus less on the nature of the intervention and more on the changes introduced by the researcher's involvement in the project. The intervention made by the NGO (or that would be made by the NGO even in the absence of the researcher) should be taken as the baseline state of existence for subjects in the study and the IRB should ask whether the research-driven component adheres to the principles of the Belmont Report such as autonomy and beneficence. Even if a study falls outside of IRB scrutiny, researchers should be particularly concerned with the ethics of research when they cause an intervention to happen in the real world, even if they are working in cooperation with an organization or government entity.

This chapter is concerned both with how IRBs view field experimental research when scholars collaborate with NGOs and with the more general ethical relationships surrounding researcher–NGO cooperation. It considers IRB approval of a field experiment as a special case of the more general ethical concerns for cooperative research. It then explains why government studies are typically viewed as exempt from IRB oversight. The heart of the chapter then discusses the middle ground occupied by cases where researchers partner with NGOs rather than governments, which concludes with a set of practical questions that researchers and IRBs should ask about research conducted in conjunction with NGOs. These points are then illustrated by a case study of an academic–NGO research study in Cambodia and working with a partisan political campaign in the United States.

13.1 Standard Paradigm

The most common scenario for an IRB to consider is one in which the researcher is acting directly on the subjects in the experiment. In these instances, the FPPHS provides very clear guidance. The IRB should give the design careful scrutiny under three broad principles: autonomy, beneficence, and justice. *Autonomy* advances the claim that subjects should have the right to decide whether or not they participate in the experiment. Regardless of the scientific merits of the study, subjects should be informed of the costs and benefits of participating in the study and pro-actively opt into the study of their own free will. Just as a researcher should not surreptitiously slip a drug into a person's coffee without her consent, nor should they reveal sensitive information about friends or construct roadblocks to make voting in an election more difficult without the explicit approval of the people involved. The requirement for informed consent is not absolute. The FPPHS makes exceptions for studies of "minimal risk," which is how many social psychology experiments are allowed (e.g., Cialdini, Reno and Kallgren 1990, Norton et al. 2012), but the researcher needs to make a clear and compelling statement about why subject autonomy is being violated.

The principle of *beneficence* holds that the researcher has a duty to minimize the amount of harm (or risk of harm) that a subject in the study faces and maximize the amount of benefit. While assiduously adhering to this principle involves a great deal of effort and careful planning, the intuition behind the dictum is straightforward. If a researcher is going to intervene in a subject's life, the researcher has an obligation not to cause harm to the subject unnecessarily. Even if the risk of harm is low, the researcher should take every reasonable precaution to prevent the harm and rectify the situation quickly should harm occur. When someone is under your care or observation, playing roulette with their well-being is not acceptable. For instance, an intervention distributing new energy efficient stoves to villages (Ludwinski, Moriarty and Wydick 2011) should verify that the stoves will not increase the risk of house fires, create noxious fumes, or be misused in a manner that harms subjects in a way that is foreseeable. The principle of beneficence also precludes the researcher from denying subjects basic goods to which they have a reasonable expectation of enjoying. For instance, while a researcher may not have a moral obligation to construct bridges in remote areas, they cannot prevent the usage of existing bridges by residents for the purpose of research. Participating in the study should be as beneficial and as harmless as possible.

The principle of *justice* mandates that the costs of the study are borne by people who will eventually benefit from the results of the study. The goal of science is to benefit humanity, but if the costs of doing science are inflicted on subgroups who have no reasonable expectation of ever gaining the benefit of the results, the principle of justice forbids this asymmetry. The canonical example of this dynamic is with drug testing in developing countries. Recruiting human subjects for drug trials is much less expensive in poor countries, so drug companies may be tempted to run human trials in these locales. Once the treatment is proven safe and effective, the company could then release the drug in developed markets where insurance companies and patients can afford the newly developed and proven drug. Meanwhile, the residents of the poor country where the drug was tested are unlikely to be able to afford the new drug, even though they provided a collective benefit to the rest of the world while shouldering the cost. The principle of justice forbids this unequal dynamic.

The purpose of this chapter is not to explore these three principles of evaluation. Instead, this chapter identifies the locus where these principles apply and examines the consequences for academic studies where researcher involvement is not direct. One way to think about the relationship is by considering counterfactual circumstances from the point of view of subjects in the experiment.

The subjects exist in some sort of status quo. They have an expected level of psychological, physical, and emotional well-being. The researcher is not responsible for this status quo and is under no obligation to improve the situation of potential subjects. However, the researcher is directly responsible for the effect of his or her intervention on the subject. When the researcher acts on a subject—no matter how innocuously—it shifts the subject from her status quo to a state at least partially created by the intervention. The change is often desirable: Subjects are often compensated for their time, sometimes learn something from the experience, and may have been exposed to a beneficial treatment. However, it is the role of the IRB to determine that the intervention does not worsen the state of subjects in the experiment and require that the researcher take reasonable steps to minimize risks to subjects. As noted in the first row of Table 13.1, the effect of the intervention on the subject is the key area for scrutiny.

The situation is markedly different when a researcher studies a US government program. According to the FPPHS §46.101 b5, as long as an agency head approves

TABLE 13.1 Focus of Ethical Questions About Experiments

Cause of Treatment	Intervention	Research
Researcher	Full review	Full review
Government	Exempt	Exempt
NGO	Minimal scrutiny	Full review
Hybrid Researcher–NGO Model	Minimal scrutiny/Full review if researcher causes treatment	Full review

the project, the research is considered "exempt," and it suggests that IRBs provide the most minimal levels of scrutiny. There are five primary reasons for this reduced level of scrutiny. The first and foremost is that the government represents legitimate authority. The autonomy principle is important, but the government's monopoly on the legitimate use of force subordinates the autonomy principle on a daily basis. Given that governments have the authority to arrest and jail citizens (or even use deadly force), seize property, and wage war, the right to research the effect of policies is minor in comparison.

The second is that public accountability provides a presumption of goodwill on the part of the government. Researchers within universities are largely insulated from public scrutiny. Not only is the public unaware of researcher activities, but it has no mechanism for removing researchers who engage in unethical behavior. In contrast, the public observes government policies and pilot tests, and processes exist by which objections can be noted. While the heads of government agencies are rarely directly elected, the people appointing the heads are elected. The desire of elected officials to avoid controversy causes agency heads to self-censor and pursue only those policies and tests that they think will enhance the public well-being. Government abuses can occur (e.g., Tuskegee Airmen; internment of the Japanese) and some policies have negative consequences (e.g., the construction of high density public housing), but the vast majority of activities are pursued with the public interest explicitly in mind. Unlike agency heads, university researchers have neither public accountability nor a presumption of good will.

Third, the government agencies have to make collective decisions and enact policies over the objections of some individuals. Nearly every government action creates winners and losers, so a set of people is likely to object to the new policy implemented by the agency. Governing by its very nature entails violating the autonomy of certain individuals when implementing policy. Even the act of doing nothing (i.e., adhering to the status quo) is a decision with winners and losers, so there is no path where government actions can engage in behaviors that benefit everyone. The exemption for the evaluation of government policies recognizes this reality.

Fourth, policy evaluation is something that a government agency may legitimately desire. Although a government policy may be intended to advance the public welfare and accomplish particular policy goals, there is no guarantee that the policies will be successful. Careful and rigorous evaluation of policies can help to inform future policy decisions, so agencies can view research as an integral part of the policy-making process rather than as a peripheral activity that deserves special and isolated scrutiny.

Finally, researcher evaluation of government agency policies is a public service that should be encouraged. Although policies implemented by government agencies are public relative to the inner workings of universities, many members of the voting public will be unaware of the decisions and their consequences. Allowing researchers to partner with government agencies provides unusual transparency into operations. Not only can researchers document the activities of the agencies, but they can also measure their effectiveness. Much as the media is considered the "watchdog of the government," researchers can ensure that the government is behaving appropriately and effectively.

Underlying each of these justifications for the exemption enjoyed by research involving government agencies is the notion that the government has the legitimate authority to act on its own even if its programs are not systematically evaluated, but that understanding the consequences of government policies is important. This assumption is much more problematic in non-democracies, and does not guarantee that government actions are ethical or harmless. Again, let us approach the possible counterfactuals from the perspective of subjects in the experiment. The government agency is implementing a policy. This policy (with or without research) moves subjects from the status quo to a new position under the intervention being studied. The presence or absence of the researcher has nothing to do with this shift. Moreover, as noted earlier, research and evaluation can be considered a part of the policy changed being imposed by the government agency. That is, any involvement by the researcher is completely subsumed by the actions of the government agency. From the perspective of the subjects in the study, the researcher is irrelevant to their well-being and autonomy. Thus, research of policy interventions undertaken by US government agencies is already deemed exempt under human subjects guidelines, even when the introduction of research of an ongoing program influences which individuals receive the treatment (see Table 13.1, row 2).[2]

13.2   Hybrid Model With Interventions by NGOs[3]

In the space between research involving interventions made directly by the researcher and interventions undertaken by a government agency lies research involving interventions made by non-governmental organizations. NGOs differ from governments in a few key respects. Chief among these differences is that NGOs can claim no legitimate authority over and are not directly accountable to subjects in an experiment. Re-examining the justification for government research enjoying exempt status from IRB oversight, these differences in authority and accountability mean that the goodwill of the NGO cannot be assumed.

Of course, it is possible to argue that goodwill cannot be assumed on the part of many governments, particularly those that are willing to run harmful "experiments" on their citizens, and non-democratic governments may lack the type of legitimacy discussed above. In practice, some well-established NGOs may have significantly greater accountability and goodwill than some "bad" governments. Nevertheless, the goodwill of an NGO cannot be taken for granted, and the starting point for research conducted in collaboration with an NGO should be whether an intervention by an NGO (absent the research) is manifestly undesirable.

What is meant by manifestly undesirable? The IRB, when evaluating the researcher's role in the study, should ensure that researchers are not participating in programs that clearly violate the rights of the individuals involved, but that is a lower threshold than ensuring all principles of the Belmont Report are adhered to. NGOs are created to accomplish programmatic goals (e.g., reduce poverty, improve health, educate the public) and pursuing those goals requires taking action. There will be instances where the NGO commits to a course of action without knowing the ultimate consequences of the decision. The world is sufficiently complicated that it is impossible to know *a priori* the outcomes of all interventions—hence the need for research. NGOs implement policies that they think will further their programmatic goals, but may be mistaken. The goal of the IRB should not be to judge the efficacy or wisdom of the intervention.

For instance, voter intimidation campaigns where citizens are threatened, beaten, and otherwise coerced into abstaining from elections are clear violations of the basic rights of the people subjected to such campaigns of terror. Although understanding the effects of such intimidation campaigns is interesting and important, one of the roles of IRBs should be to ensure that researchers are not involved in morally repugnant behavior. Although the researcher may not be directly intimidating voters, her presence and active involvement offers a tacit endorsement of the activity.

In contrast, suppose the researcher is working with an anti-corruption campaign that distributes information on which candidates have been convicted on corruption charges and which candidates are "clean" (e.g., Banerjee et al. 2011, De Figueiredo, Hidalgo and Kasahara 2011). The campaign is intended to allow voters to cast a more informed ballot and increase participation by highlighting clean politicians. Of course, it is possible that the anti-corruption campaign could have negative consequences such as decreasing voter turnout by highlighting corrupt politicians or serving as a catalyst for street fights among partisans. But such consequences are not clear ex ante, and whether the outcome of the intervention is positive or negative is an empirical question and part of the reason that the experiment is interesting.

The outcome of the anti-corruption experiment is also irrelevant to the review by the IRB. The intervention will happen regardless of whether the researcher participates or not. From the perspective of the human subjects involved in the research, the researcher is not harming the subjects by observing precinct-level electoral returns for the number of votes cast and support for clean candidates. If the researcher were directly implementing the anti-corruption campaign, then she would need to demonstrate that she had taken precautions to minimize the possible risks posed by the intervention. However, because the intervention is taking place anyway, the IRB's question about the intervention outcome should be

"Could a reasonable person believe that this intervention would be helpful, or is it clearly designed to harm subjects?"

This "reasonable person" standard only applies to the intervention itself. The IRB should apply all the usual criteria about how the researcher involvement affects subjects in the proposed study. However, it is important to note that the baseline for comparison is not the status quo but the change in the conditions for subjects under the NGO's intervention with and without the activity of the researcher.

This change in baseline does not give researchers a free pass to conduct experiments. Researchers can often analyze human subjects data after an NGO has finished a program under the "found data" provision. However, if the researcher is active in the creation of the data, the found data clause does not apply. The autonomy and beneficence principles must be adhered to, but it is the researcher component rather than the intervention component that is the relevant consideration. Returning to the anti-corruption campaign example from above, if the NGO is going to intervene with the anti-corruption materials, then the subject autonomy to be exposed to the campaign or not has already been compromised and the researcher is irrelevant. However, autonomy applies just as strictly to the pure research component. The subjects should be free to decline interviews, survey instruments, blood pressure readings, or any other measurement that the researcher seeks to apply. Just because the NGO plans to intervene does not mean that the researcher has carte blanche to do as she sees fit.

The application of the beneficence principle when an NGO is staging the intervention is similar. The risks associated with the intervention planned by the NGO may not be relevant to the IRB's consideration, but risk is still a consideration because the presence of the researcher may introduce risks for subjects. For instance, surveying residents of neighborhoods where an anti-bribery intervention is taking place could potentially link illegal behaviors to particular individuals and put them at risk of being arrested. The IRB should demand that the researcher develop and implement strategies to assure the anonymity of survey responses and protect the identity of people surveyed. In some areas the mere presence of survey teams in a neighborhood can attract unwanted attention from local gangs and put residents at risk—even if they decline to answer the survey themselves. Researchers need to openly discuss any possible risks associated with the research component and explain how they plan to minimize such risks. However, the risks associated with the intervention conducted by the NGO are not the responsibility of the researcher (assuming that the manifest purpose of intervention is not to impose harm on individuals). From the perspective of the subjects involved in the study, the introduction of the researcher is the only relevant change. Thus, the intervention should receive limited scrutiny, while the major ethical question concerns the addition of the research component (see Table 13.1, row 3).

The application of the justice principle to research changes very little from this perspective. Research testing new policies that were unlikely to ever be implemented in the experimental setting simply to save money (e.g., measuring the effect of television advertising campaigns in regions with very low television penetration into the market) remains in potential violation of human subjects protections. However, the partnership with an NGO should generally ameliorate concerns about justice. NGOs implement pilot programs in settings where they plan to roll out the full-scale versions of programs. Given all the difficulty, local knowledge, and infrastructure required to implement sizable field experiments, it would make little sense to conduct pilots in irrelevant settings. Thus, questions about justice should continue to be asked about the research, but the partnerships with NGOs actually help to address these concerns.

This shift in the baseline for the purposes of IRB review is predicated on the fact that the NGO is in fact separate from the researcher. However, there are cases where the line between researcher and NGO is blurry. Some researchers are principals in consulting firms and not-for-profit organizations. A few NGOs like the Poverty Action Lab exist for the sole purpose of conducting research. When the researcher also has decision-making authority over the NGO, there is effectively little difference between the researcher and the NGO. From the point of view of subjects in the study, the NGO is acting as an extension of the researcher rather than as an independent intermediary. In these instances, the relevant point of comparison is between the status quo pre-intervention and the intervention with the research component. IRBs should apply the full battery of criteria to the intervention itself, not just to the research component.

This paradigm means that IRBs should inquire about the nature of the relationship between the researcher and NGO performing the intervention. There is no bright line standard, which is why we added the bottom row of Table 13.1 to address these hybrid situations. The researcher's relationship to the NGO and the NGO's decision-making process will have to guide the IRB in determining the extent to which the NGO is acting independently. Serving the as the CEO of the NGO probably grants the researcher a large degree of authority over the NGO's activities and completely muddies the line between researcher and NGO. In contrast, acting as an advisor to the NGO will probably not be sufficient to trump all decision-making authority. Serving on the board of directors to an NGO most likely falls into a middle ground that the researcher will have to explain carefully and the IRB should consider. The core concept of interest is who makes the final decision to authorize and implement the program.

Funding of the program is a related issue. If the researcher supplies funds for implementing the intervention (apart from the separate cost of the research), then she is responsible for the intervention and the relevant point of comparison is the status quo versus risks under the intervention. She is responsible because the intervention would be unlikely to occur on its own without funds from the researcher.

Money is not a smoking gun, however. If the researcher supplies funds for just the research component of the intervention, then the intervention sans research may have been possible and the intervention should be treated as exogenous to the researcher. The researcher could also help write grants for the organization; lending expertise to the organization to raise money or improve proposals and operations is not the same thing as making decisions on behalf of the NGO. The key decision is programmatic. If the NGO has capacity to execute the intervention and the program is within the broader mission of the NGO, then there is no particular reason to be suspicious that the researcher is dictating the terms behind the scenes. However, the researcher should clearly address her relationship with the NGO.

To summarize our core argument, Institutional Review Boards (and those interested in ethics of experiments more generally) should approach the beneficence and autonomy criteria from the point of view of the subjects in a study. When an NGO is planning to implement a new program and the researcher is not directly the cause of that program, then the effect of the program becomes the baseline for comparison. The subjects have already lost their choice on whether they are exposed to the program and its consequences. The relevant question is whether researching the program crafted by the NGO compromises autonomy or beneficence independently. The proposed research needs to adhere strictly to these two principles, but the nature of the intervention should not be the focus of the review board because the intervention by the NGO was going to happen even if the research did not.

One potential objection to this line of reasoning is that researchers would be passing the buck to NGOS, and the dynamic will lead to a slippery slope in which researchers coerce NGOs into providing cover for ethically questionable actions. At the extreme, a researcher could create a fake NGO in order to dodge the ethical standards that academic research normally faces. Although this is possible, it is unlikely because it assumes NGOs are very malleable and researchers are devious. Not only are these traits likely to be rare, it is far from clear that IRB oversight will mitigate these two problems. Ethically compromised scholars and unprincipled, profit-seeking NGOs are likely to do other ethically objectionable things: falsify results, lie about funding sources, harass their staff, or otherwise violate the spoken and unspoken norms of the academic profession. Overall, the "fake NGO" or "coerced NGO" possibility is a very labor-intensive way of avoiding IRB approval to conduct research and unlikely to be the normal state of affairs.

Perhaps more likely is the possibility that researchers would take on work as consultants or advisors to an organization and then use that relationship to create opportunities for field experimental research. This can be a grey area, but should be governed by the same general principle. If the researcher, even when acting outside his or her "day job" as a university professor, causes something to happen in the world that would otherwise not occur *and* relies on that intervention for field experimental research, the full intervention should be subject to human subjects review. If a researcher is working with an NGO in a capacity that is not at all related to field experimental research, does the researcher still have an obligation to bring up concerns that might arise in the course of university IRB review? In this type of case, the researcher may feel obligated to bring up concerns related to the intervention, and they are more than welcome to do so, but it is not necessarily their role to bring up IRB standards in all aspects of their life. The central ethical concerns, as we view them, mainly arise if the researcher is involved in using the NGO's work for their own research.

To summarize our argument and make the proposed considerations more concrete, when IRBs and researchers are confronted with proposed research evaluating the effects of NGO interventions, we suggest the following questions as a helpful starting point:

1) Would the intervention occur without the researcher?
    a. What role does the researcher play in the organization (i.e., does she have decision-making authority?)?
    b. Who is paying for the intervention?
2) Is the intervention obviously harmful or otherwise unethical such that a university should not tacitly endorse it?
3) Does the research component respect the autonomy of the subjects?
    a. Do subjects have the ability to opt out?
    b. Is any information being collected directly from individual subjects?
4) Does the research component comply with the demand for beneficence?
    a. Are subjects put at risk by researching the intervention?
    b. What steps are being taken to protect the welfare of the subjects?
5) Does the research component comply with the justice requirement?
    a. Will the subjects benefit from the results of this research?

Although these questions will not address every potentially problematic relationship or troublesome dynamic, they provide a framework for discussing the major ethical concerns that will commonly occur. Additionally, we recommend that any researcher engaged in a cooperative relationship with an NGO for field experimental research provide a clear explanation of the nature of the relationship between the researcher and the organization, including who pays for what, in the first footnote to any related publication. Researchers should also define whether they were paid to conduct the study (and research for which the cooperating organization pays the researcher for their work should potentially be discounted, as in other fields).

13.3   Case Study #1: Cambodia

To illustrate the proposal in this chapter, this section describes a democracy assistance intervention studied by one of the authors (hereafter the "researcher") and then answers the questions proposed in the preceeding sections. The goal of the section is to illustrate how the principle of relevant counterfactuals can be practically applied.

Democracy assistance is a common component of foreign policy, and democracy assistance activities are funded by dozens of governments, implemented by numerous NGOs, and have been carried out in more than one hundred countries in the world. At its core, democracy assistance is a targeted intervention aimed at encouraging democracy in target states. Democracy assistance organizations most often have permission for their work from host governments, but in some cases they do not. As highlighted by a 2008 report from the National Research Council, most US-funded democracy assistance activities are carried out absent the type of evaluation that would provide "compelling evidence of whether those projects had their intended effects" (Goldstone et al. 2008, 5). The same is true for most actors in democracy assistance, and it is relatively standard practice for NGOs to intervene within sovereign states without systematically evaluating the consequences of these interventions.

Motivated by the 2008 report, several NGOs receiving USAID funding were mandated by USAID to conduct rigorous impact evaluations of some of their democracy assistance programs. The program that was ultimately one of the pilot studies had been run by an International NGO (NGO) in Cambodia since 2004. Although it had been documented in periodic reporting and anecdotal evidence suggested that the program had positive effects, it had not previously been evaluated using rigorous methods for impact evaluation.

The program brings elected Cambodian Members of the National Assembly (MNAs) to rural villages in their district for multiparty town hall meetings. Once elected, it is rare for MNAs to visit rural parts of their districts. It is even more uncommon for rural villagers to be exposed directly to any situations in which opposition political parties share the same stage, and are on more or less equal footing, with the ruling Cambodian People's Party. The specific aims of the program are to encourage the MNAs to be more accountable to their constituents and to educate rural villagers about their roles and responsibilities as voters with the broader aim of encouraging them to hold their elected MNAs accountable.

The intervention in Cambodia consists of a town hall meeting designed to bring national representatives face to face with their constituents in a question and answer session. These town hall meetings are held in rural villages, are open to the public, and attended by 400 to 1,000 community members. The town halls are advertised using a loudspeaker on the back of a motorbike, which travels around all accessible roads and paths in the area surrounding the village, thereby reaching most villagers. The meetings are conducted with the permission of national, district, and local officials, who typically help publicize the events.

Each meeting begins with remarks by the senior program officer or director of the NGO, who explains the purpose of the meeting to the audience. Each introduction includes a statement that Cambodia is a democracy and that they, the audience, have elected their representatives and have a right to share their concerns with them; that the purposes of their elected representatives are to form policies and exercise oversight on the government, but not to provide gifts or personal favors; that these representatives must represent the interests of their constituents and that they work for and are accountable to their constituents; and a reminder that everyone, including the audience, has the right to speak and be heard and to criticize and disagree with the policies or positions on any issue.

Participating Members of the National Assembly (MNAs) are seated at a table in front of the participants and offer brief opening remarks to the audience. The floor is then open to participants to voice their concerns, raise questions directly to members of the National Assembly, and request that actions be taken to resolve problems. During their allocated response time, MNAs use the opportunity to update citizens on the activities of the legislature and government and provide other information relevant to their constituents. The dialogues encourage two-way communication and are unscripted, allowing for sometimes challenging questions and demands from citizens.

To ensure equity and neutrality and foster constructive dialogue, each town hall meeting follows a format and requires that MNAs, participants, and moderators follow a code of conduct.[4] The code specifies such items as the allotment of speaking time, appropriate and inappropriate topics for discussion, and the rules regarding audience participation. Local authorities such as commune councilors, village chiefs, and district and provincial officials are often present at the town halls, and in 2010, at the request of the parties, time was allotted for local authorities to speak at the end of the dialogues as well. Citizens who attend the town hall meetings are given water and bread, but no other remuneration or incentive to attend.

The town hall meeting program is explicitly designed to promote citizen interaction with multiple parties, and to demonstrate to citizens that opposition parties in Cambodia do exist and that debate between them is a normal part of multi-party democracy. Representatives from five parties in the National Assembly have been involved in the meetings, including the Cambodian People's Party (CPP), the Sam Rainsy Party (SRP), FUNCINPEC,[5] the Human Rights Party (HRP), and Norodom Ranariddh Party (NRP).[6] For each town hall meeting, each party that has one or more elected Member of the National Assembly in that province is invited to the meeting. Thus, fewer than five parties are represented at each town hall event.[7] In addition, town hall events are not held in provinces where the ruling CPP party is represented in the National Assembly, which excludes half of the provinces in Cambodia.[8]

The forum provides a rare opportunity for policy debate and showcases the distinctions between legislators from different parties and their approaches to both local and national concerns. Citizens interact with their elected MNAs, and see MNAs from multiple political parties interact with one another. The meetings provide an opportunity to enhance MNAs' knowledge of and relations with their constituencies and educate citizens on the roles and responsibilities of MNAs in a democracy. Citizens, through their attendance in the town hall event, have an opportunity to learn about their form of government, including not only the roles of the MNAs but also their own roles and rights as citizens. In theory, through their participation or the participation of others, citizens may also be motivated to take part in politics either through political party activity or other political behavior. The research component of the study involved helping to randomize where the community meetings took place. The randomization created communities that were on average identical and differed only with respect to the occurrence or non-occurrence of the meeting. The researcher could then conduct public opinion surveys in treatment and control communities to determine whether the meetings made residents more informed, more likely to participate, feel more efficacious, value democracy as a form of government, and support the regime. These questions are routinely asked in comparative public opinion surveys and no extremely sensitive questions were asked.

The first set of questions to consider about the research is whether the intervention would have occurred in the absence of the researcher. In this case, the Constituency Dialogue program would have taken place regardless of the researcher's involvement in the impact evaluation, and had been ongoing for several years. The (donor-mandated) addition of the impact evaluation to the program added a pre- and post-test survey to the existing programmatic activities, and expanded and systematized a focus group activity that took place the day before each Constituency Dialogue.

The researcher helped implement and analyze the results from the impact evaluation. As further evidence that the researcher did not "cause" the intervention, the researcher does not otherwise work for the NGO and is not a decision-maker in the organization. She chose not to be paid as a consultant on this project in exchange for access to the data, although travel expenses for the researcher were paid for by the NGO. The intervention itself was, critically, paid for by the NGO, not the researcher. In this particular case, the research component was also paid for by the NGO, although this, in our view, would not make an important ethical difference.

Second, is there evidence that, *ex ante*, the intervention would be judged by a reasonable person to be obviously harmful? In this case, the answer in advance of the study was no, as most of the anecdotal evidence was positive. Note that negative findings about the program as a result of the study were possible, but it was not clear before the evaluation the program was obviously harmful or unethical.

Third, IRBs should also consider whether the research (not the intervention) compromises the autonomy of subjects. The central added component introduced by the research was the survey. The survey contained a standard introduction and respondents could opt out. Respondents were also free to skip any questions that they preferred not to answer. In short, while subjects were unable to opt out of the intervention implemented by the NGO (i.e., the presence or absence of the community meeting in their region), they were free to participate or not in the research component of the study.

The fourth set of questions focus on beneficence in relation to the research component. The researcher-introduced component of the experiment is the survey, so an evaluating IRB should run through the questions it applies to most comparative survey research. Most surveys are deemed "minimal risk" and exempt under FPPHS guidelines except when surveys involve vulnerable populations or sensitive questions. In this instance, none of the questions were sensitive and answering would never put a respondent at risk. Furthermore, personal information was separated from the survey results, so although the data were individual in nature, they are anonymous. Because the survey constitutes minimal risk, the next question regarding beneficence requires weighing the gains from the research. Given that the intervention is likely to continue to occur even in the absence of the study (and that any risks that apply to the research would likely apply to the intervention), and the research component adds significant knowledge about the effects of the intervention, the added value is not trivial and could lead to future modifications of the program that make it more beneficial to participants.

The fifth and final questions relate to justice, and whether it is likely that the subjects would benefit from the research. Because the participating NGO was conducting this study with an eye toward future implementation of the program in Cambodia, there is little question that subjects in the experiment would be the ones to directly benefit from the added knowledge about the effects of the program provided by the research.

In short, the researcher involvement in the Constituency Dialogues experiment in Cambodia should be a relatively easy case for outside observers to deem acceptable. Objections that people may have about the overall program (e.g., exposing community residents to partisan violence or potentially affecting electoral outcomes) do not apply to the purely research component. Helping to randomize the intervention and implementing a survey to measure the attitudes of community residents are minimally intrusive and help to make the entire enterprise more valuable by measuring the effects of the program with an aim of improving future iterations of the project.

13.4   Case Study #2: Michigan

To illustrate that the same issues can arise in the developed world, we describe an experiment conducted by a political organization in the United States in conjunction with a team of researchers. In 2002, the Michigan Democratic Party was interested in measuring the effectiveness of mobilization efforts aimed at younger voters. The ability to engage people under the age of 35 was a priority for the party leadership and they wanted to ensure that traditional methods of mobilizing voters (i.e., door hangers, volunteer phone calls, and door knocks from volunteers) were effective on this younger target group (for a full description see Nickerson, Friedrichs and King 2006). The scripts and campaign literature employed in the mobilization effort were relatively anodyne persuasive appeals encouraging voting for the entire Democratic ticket. While subjects in the experiment (i.e., targeted young voters) would not be offended by the scripts, they also had no opportunity to opt out of either the experiment or the outreach effort by the party.

The 2002 election in Michigan was close up and down the ballot. For instance, the gubernatorial election was decided by 4 percentage points, the Democrats received more of the US Congressional vote but won only 7 seats compared to 9 seats won by the Republicans, and the Attorney General race was decided by a mere 5000 votes. In such a competitive environment, it was a bold decision by the party to work with a team of researchers in order to conduct a fully randomized experiment with a control group that would not be mobilized by the coordinated campaigns.

This decision was made somewhat easier by the fact that one member of the research team raised a considerable sum of money to fund the experiment. While the state party contributed the funds for the printed materials (flyers, door hangers, and scripts), the researcher raised funds from private donors to conduct the experiment. Most of the money went to paying for staff to oversee the experiment, but this had the additional effect of increasing the capacity of the campaign itself. A major job of the staff to manage the experiment was volunteer recruitment, retention, and oversight to assure that the hangers were hung, phones were called, and doors were knocked. This effort probably resulted in a larger volunteer outreach effort aimed at youth than would have been possible otherwise. The researchers also improved efficiency of the mobilization by assisting with the targeting and managing databases. So while the researchers did not have the power to authorize or initiate the mobilization experiment on their own, their efforts did change the nature of the youth engagement by the Michigan Democratic Party in 2002.

After Election Day passed, the researchers collected information on the turnout behavior of the subjects in the experiment by referencing official voter turnout records maintained by the Michigan Secretary of State and publicly available (for a nominal fee). The researchers also conducted a post-election survey (funded by an academic institution) via telephone to measure the vote choice for both the treatment and control groups. The survey was extremely brief and asked questions typical of political surveys, such as who the respondent voted for and whether they recalled any campaign outreach (see Nickerson (2005) for a full description).

If the researchers had attempted this experiment on their own, it would have potentially run afoul of ethical guidelines for research. The biggest concern is that the autonomy principle is violated because subjects have no choice of whether to participate in the experiment. Subjects were not forced to read the door hangers or engage in conversation with volunteers—indeed, many threw out the hangers, hung up the phone, or refused to answer the door in the first place—but there was no option to opt out of the study.[9] Some people might also object to conducting a mobilization experiment in an environment where it is possible that the outreach could decide the election. Whether or not Democratic victory would be a positive or negative consequence of the election is a matter of opinion and it is not up to researchers to make that decision for voters (but see Chapter 11 in this volume on the political consequences of experiments by Gubler and Selway). Given that the intervention involves minimal risk, such a researcher-initiated experiment would likely be approved, but it would deserve careful consideration.

If the Democratic Party shouldered the costs of the entire program, then the intervention would require less scrutiny and the study would be easy to approve. Campaigns have a right to engage in their electioneering, which means that residents do not have a right to not be targeted by the campaign. The mobilization effort may affect electoral outcomes; in fact, that is the entire point from the perspective of the political party studying its outreach. The question for the researcher and an IRB, then, is whether the intervention is inherently inappropriate. A reasonable person could believe that the mobilization tactics in question would pose no risk to the subjects in the experiment. Campaigns around the world utilize similar tactics without incident. Because the intervention is harmless to individual well-being and well within the programmatic goals of the organization, the intervention would not be a relevant factor in considering the appropriateness of the experiment.

The ethical question would be whether the research component adheres to the standards outlined in the Belmont Report. The research component consists of three primary components and each is unobjectionable.[10] First, the researchers randomized the state party's list. Just as political parties have the right to target whom they think appropriate, they also have the right not to target individuals. The control group is not being deprived of any expected right or benefit. Other groups may still knock on their door or make phone calls. Second, the researchers referenced public databases to determine who voted in the treatment and control groups. Although it is true that subjects cannot opt out of this data collection exercise, researchers are merely referencing publicly available data and not forcing individuals to give up information. Finally, the researchers attempted to survey subjects in the experiment. This survey was entirely voluntary and subjects could easily opt out of this part of the experiment by declining to take the survey or answering particular questions. Thus, the purely research component of the experiment poses no cause for concerns and would be approved quickly.

The actual experiment, however, fell between the two extremes of researcher-initiated invention and the organization lead experiment. Understanding this relationship in some degree of depth is necessary to determine the degree of scrutiny the intervention itself should receive. A key question is whether the organization chose to engage in the experiment independently or whether the researchers made the decision for them or exercised some form of coercion. The power dynamics in this case are relatively straightforward. Two graduate students can propose the experiment to a state party chair, but there is no way that they have the authority to force her/him to act in a certain way. So in this case, the locus of the ultimate decision-making authority squarely lies with the organization making the intervention and not the researchers.

The next question is whether the intervention would have taken place without the researchers. While it is true that the idea for the experiment originated with the researchers and not the organization, the proposed experiment manipulated outreach that was taking place regardless of researcher intervention. Given that the question is whether the intervention should receive full scrutiny, the fact that the researchers are not greenlighting the intervention is the key detail.

That said, the researchers did increase the scope of the operations. By hiring dedicated staff and assisting with technical details, the researchers allowed the organization to apply the treatment to more individuals than would otherwise have been possible. And this is an excellent example of why bright line standards may be impossible to apply in settings where NGOs and researchers collaborate and split costs. It is relatively obvious that if the researchers are the proximate cause of the lion's share of the outreach, then the experiment should be treated as if the researchers are responsible for the intervention. One could adopt a "one drop" rule where any researcher contribution taints the experiment and the intervention must receive full scrutiny, but that would preclude the researcher from supplying any labor to see that the research occurs, which strikes the authors as unreasonable. So how much labor and expense sharing can the researcher do before the intervention flips from full to minimal scrutiny? We do not think there is a good one-size-fits-all answer to this question, although the questions we outlined above should help IRBs and individual scholars work through important questions associated with researcher collaboration with real-world entities.

13.5 Conclusion

Researchers and Institutional Review Boards should be focused on the welfare of the human participants in research. This chapter argues that the effect of research should be evaluated from the perspective of the human subjects whose welfare and dignity are being protected. When a researcher assists an NGO in evaluating the effectiveness of a program, it is the researcher's activities and not the NGO's that should receive the most careful scrutiny. From the perspective of the subjects in the experiment, the NGO program is being implemented regardless of whether the researcher participates or not. The relevant question is whether the research component respects subject autonomy and adheres to the principles of beneficence and justice.

As with nearly all ethical questions, there will be gray areas and reason to debate. For instance, it may not be possibly to cleanly separate the research component from the program implemented if the program is altered to accommodate the research. In these cases, the review board should focus on the effect of the change in the program introduced by the research compared to the pure program rather than a counterfactual where no program took place. The goal of this essay is to provide a framework for asking these questions and focusing the discussion on the most ethically relevant component of the research.

Notes

1 In general, when we reference IRBs in this chapter, we are referring to the one at the researcher's home institution.
2 Of course, there may be government programs that a given researcher deems to be unethical, and individual researchers should not use the study of government programs as a blanket excuse to avoid thinking about any ethical considerations. The fact that an activity is allowed or legal or sanctioned by a government does not mean it is laudatory. Researchers should always follow their moral compass.
3 Note that NGOs are not subject to IRB approval. All discussion of IRBs pertains to their oversight over researchers who are based at universities in the United States and in other countries that have similar bodies governing academic research with human subjects.
4 A code of conduct was developed in 2008 to clarify misunderstandings and avoid confusion about the town hall process and allegations of bias. It also serves to prevent verbal attacks and personal insults during the dialogues. This method of preventing and resolving disputes was agreed to by the five political parties represented in the program. The code is regularly reviewed with the parties to ensure its relevancy and make modifications, if necessary.
5 FUNCINPEC is an acronym for the National United Front for an Independent, Neutral, Peaceful, and Cooperative Cambodia. It represents the party name in French, "Front Uni National pour un Cambodge Indépendant, Neutre, Pacifique, et Coopératif."
6 From 2004 to March 2008, only three political parties—the Cambodian People's Party (CPP), the Sam Rainsy Party (SRP), and FUNCINPEC—had seats in the Assembly. With two new parties, the Human Rights Party (HRP) and Norodom Ranariddh Party (NRP), gaining seats in the 2008 elections, five parties have now participated.
7 Each party chooses which representative will attend the town hall event. Through conversation with the NGO director, it appears that MNAs are trained for attendance to the town hall event.
8 These provinces are excluded from this program because the NGO elected not to work there for a variety of reasons, including that there are no elected representatives from multiple political parties representing those provinces eligible to participate in the events.
9 Exceptions can be made to the mandate to obtain informed consent when informed consent is impossible and the risk to subjects is minimal.
10 Volunteers recorded the disposition of their attempts to contact subjects in the treatment group, but this would occur in the absence of the experiment. The disposition of attempts to contact voters is valuable information for campaigns for volunteer oversight and better understanding the electorate. Care needs to be taken, however, to ensure that the research does not cause this information to become public.

14

MANIPULATING ELITES

Edmund J. Malesky

Research involving the use of educational tests (cognitive, diagnostic, aptitude, achievement), survey procedures, interview procedures, or observation
of public behavior that is not exempt under Category 2. Research involving these procedures is exempt, **only if: a) the subjects are elected or
appointed public officials or candidates for public office.**

(45 CFR 46.101(b) Exemption Category 3)

A brief scan through recent political science and economic journals reveals a
growing trend in social science research—experiments in which the subjects of
investigation are elite government actors, including parliamentarians, civil servants,
and local government leaders.[1] The trend makes sense. Political science theory has
a great deal to say about the impact of different accountability mechanisms, participatory norms, and information on the behavior of elected officials. And in most
of the extant literature, the empirical confirmation of these mechanisms leaves
readers wanting more. Sometimes, theories are tested at too aggregate a level to
establish confidence that the hypothesized mechanism has been confirmed. And
even when individual behavior can be observed and analyzed, there are serious
concerns about causal identification. Certain politicians may be both more interested in serving their constituents and opening up channels for communication
and information. Alternatively, officials with something to hide are more likely
to put up barriers to detection. The randomized assignment of participation and
transparency interventions has provided rigor to the empirical testing of these
foundational theories. We are starting to make progress and the momentum is
exhilarating.

To date, ethical considerations about experiments on public officials have not been as serious a concern as those on students or the broader public. Indeed, as the quote above indicates, experimental research on public officials can even be exempted in many cases from Institutional Review Boards (IRBs). IRB regards public officials as less vulnerable than other subjects (McClendon 2012*b*). These officials have chosen a life in the public eye, and expect their constituencies to carefully evaluate their actions and decisions. Consequently, their expectations about privacy and confidentiality differ dramatically from the average subject. Moreover, as experimenters have often pointed out, the voting public has a right to know whether their elected officials perform their jobs adequately, fulfill their campaign promises, and avoid malfeasance.

It would seem, therefore, that randomized experiments on public officials are in the sweet spot for academic research: They resolve critical empirical problems in the extant research, and they are less subject to the ethical concerns that complicate experimental research in other settings.

Although I believe this conclusion is generally correct, this is a new research agenda, so we are swimming in uncharted waters. Many questions remain. In this chapter, I reflect on two of the most immediate:

1) Who counts as a public figure? Campaigning, national politicians seem obvious, but where do low profile, subnational leaders or village chiefs fit? Because of scale, this second group is the more likely target for RCTs, but many of them are only one step removed from the citizenry they serve. Do they deserve more protection?

2) Academic research requires crisp operationalization of outcome variables. In the pursuit of academic rigor, do our interventions manipulate public officials into forms of representation that are measurable? The conceit is that we are simply measuring outcomes that are of interest the public, but how do we know that is the case?

I conclude by discussing how the "do no harm" criterion should be applied to public officials. Our choices influence the career prospects and livelihood of politicians, as well their ability to represent citizens. How should we account for this in our design?

14.1 Who is a Public Official?

The questions asked regarding transparency experiments and the impact on delegate performance and responsiveness are generalizable to all levels of government. Correspondingly, the empirical testing of the hypothesis has all taken place at all levels. Hix, Hagemann and Frantescu (2011) operate at the supranational level, others experiment at the national level (Humphreys and Weinstein 2012, Malesky,

Schuler and Tran 2012), and many others test their theories at the subnational level (Banerjee et al. 2010, Enemark et al. 2013).

Testing at the very local level has a number of advantages, particularly on the logistical side. Travel and monitoring costs are minimized for research teams, the experiment can be conducted within the field of operation of local partners, permissions can be more easily obtained, and it is far easier to obtain the number of observations for statistical power. There are also theoretical and methodological advantages. Socio-cultural, historical, and institutional differences that can complicate national-level research designs can be minimized when the testing is done among villages in one province or district. Enemark et al. (2013) is an excellent example of an experimental design on officials at the lowest level of the political hierarchy in Zambia.

Ethically, however, the more we drill down to local levels, the less likely we are dealing with "public officials" in the sense envisioned by the IRB exemption quoted above. Village chiefs, commune heads, and city council members all would currently fall under the rubric, but is that reasonable? It is not clear that the subjects of the experiment want or seek the public profile on which the exemption is premised.

In many cases, the officials being evaluated are only one or two steps removed from the constituencies they serve. In my experience in Vietnam, Cambodia, and Indonesia, village heads may not aspire to higher office and may not even want the job they currently have, but serve because their arms were twisted by higher-level (often Party) authorities, or because someone was needed to play the thankless job of local hall monitor, collecting "contributions" for village projects (i.e., new roads), policing illegal construction, and organizing for local cultural and political events. It is worth remembering that one of the most important findings from the Olken (2007) road construction experiment in Indonesian villages was that local participatory councils were not effective at reducing corruption, because they failed to resolve the collective action problem. In a detailed analysis of how much construction material was lost in World Bank road projects, participatory councils were significantly less effective than the threat of an audit and had roughly the same result as the control group. In other words, no member of the participatory councils truly was willing to personally absorb the opportunity costs (to their other activities and leisure) that it would take to adequately monitor the construction.

Often the representatives serve only part time. In Vietnam and China, for instance, the full body of all elected assemblies (National Parliament, and Provincial, District, and Commune People's Councils (Congresses)) meet only twice a year. Each of these bodies has a standing committee with fulltime members, but most of the delegates spend 50 weeks out of the year in other professions (civil servant, leader of a mass organization, small business owner, teacher, or farmer). Very few local delegates on local councils will seek higher office. Their goals are multifarious: They want to build connections with local policy-makers, they wish to have an influence over local policy or expenditures, or they believe they have a civic duty to serve. It is not clear how often they intend to seek public offices beyond the immediate setting.

The bottom line for experimenters in political science is that we need a better definition of public official that takes into account the true level and aspiration of the actors under investigation. The test needs to go beyond the official title and take into account: 1) the level at which they serve, 2) the footprint of their public profile, 3) the share of time devoted to their duties, 4) and their aspirations for public careers.

14.2 Operationalization Versus Job Performance. Do Our Interventions Manipulate Public Officials Into Forms of Representation That Are Measurable?

> As someone who relies strongly on survey research, it's good for me to be reminded that some surveys are useful, some are useless, but one thing they almost all have in common is . . . they waste the respondents' time.
>
> Andrew Gelman (2010) on his blog,
> "Statistical Modeling, Causal Inference,
> and Social Science"

A second ethical challenge that has emerged with the new experimentation on public officials is more subtle, but potentially more pernicious. Academic research requires clean operationalization of outcome variables. The more closely the measurement is tied to the theoretical concept under investigation, the greater the degree of validity. Clean measurement also reduces measurement error that can create noise, reducing the efficiency of the estimations, or worse, creating bias in the results themselves. The danger, however, is that what is measurable may not be what is most important for evaluating elite responsiveness and accountability to their constituencies.

First, it is important to consider the politician's time and energy. Richard Fenno famously observed in his masterpiece *Home Style* (1978) just how little flexibility there is in a congressman's schedule. Days are packed with legislative review, committee meetings, constituency meetings, and strategic outreach (including visiting interest groups, media, and special events). Recently, two slides from a PowerPoint presentation for freshman Democrats were leaked to the *Huffington Post* (see Figure 14.1). Days remain as jam-packed as when Fenno observed them, but now fundraising plays a critical role, accounting for 40% of the average freshman congressman's day.

The most immediate conclusion from this observation is that a public official's time is highly valuable. When we distract them from their duties, public resources are at stake. As McClendon (2012b) asks, should treasuries and public funds be replenished for the time and resources used during our experiment?

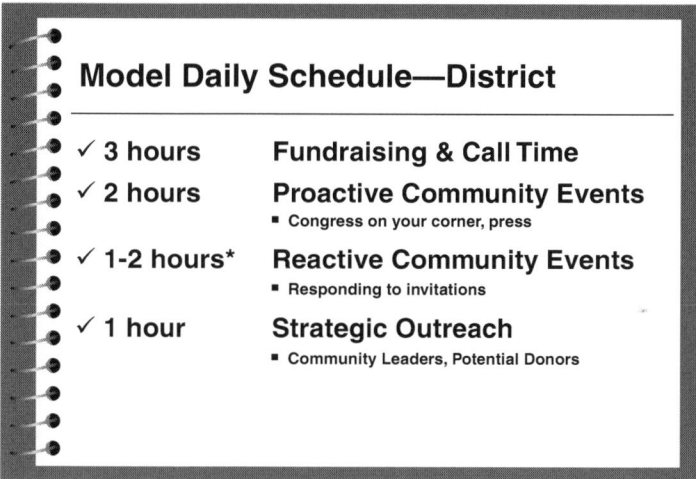

Figure 14.1 Daily Schedule of United States Congressman

Source: Grimm and Sidiqqi 2013

Beyond aggregate costs, there is a question of opportunity costs, as officials redirect their energy toward the outcomes incentivized in the experimental interventions. After years of research, there is still a great deal of uncertainty about which specific activities are most important for public officials to represent citizens' interests. Would we rather our officials be highly active in sponsoring bills and driving legislation through to fruition? Or would the constituency be better served by a delegate who spent less time working on legislation, but paid more attention to backroom deals and networking that delivered pork to their neighborhoods? In the US context, the question of fundraising is paramount. Reflecting on the amount of time spent fundraising, the *Huffington Post* article observed:

> Congressional hearings and fundraising duties often conflict, and members of Congress have little difficulty deciding between the two—occasionally even raising money from the industry covered by the hearings they skip. It is considered poor form in Congress—borderline self-indulgent—for a freshman to sit at length in congressional hearings when the time could instead be spent raising money. Even members in safe districts are expected to keep up the torrid fundraising pace, so that they can contribute to vulnerable colleagues
>
> (Grimm and Siddiqui 2013)

A US Congressman focused on fundraising would do poorly on some of the outcome measures highlighted by researchers. Their attendance and voting records would be spotty, they would have comparatively little legislation to their names, and their responses to constituent mail would incomplete and perhaps selective. On the other hand, healthy fundraising might make them more likely to ensure them a return to office and more likely to win seats on important committees. Similarly, fundraising for others will win greater opportunities for leadership positions. At the end of the day, congressmen who invest in fundraising over more measurable activities may actually be more responsive to the specific needs of their voters, especially when it comes to pork and the delivery of selective goods and legislation.

When Butler and Broockman (2011) sent letters to local legislators, grading them on whether they answered letters to constituents with minority names, they learn an important lesson, but is it the right lesson about responsiveness to minority voters? Most directly, staff resources were used to respond to the mail requests, which may have distracted them from other important activities. Further, the opportunity costs of the responses are not distributed equally. Better-resourced offices, measured by the household income of the population, were more likely to respond to all constituent leaders ($10,000 led to a 4% increase in the probability of responsiveness (Appendix A1). Consequently, it was the offices representing poorer areas that struggled to deal with the request. There is a good chance that trade-offs needed to be made in the office about staff resources (i.e., constituency service versus legislative research). If low household income is associated with the share of minorities in the district, there is a chance that responding to constituency mail may have actually led to worse representation of minorities in ways that really mattered (helpful legislation, improved public service delivery, fund-raising, selective benefits to the district).

McClendon (2012a), who engaged in a similar evaluation in South Africa, responded to critics of deception in her research design by arguing that it was the exact same research strategy employed by authors in the economics and business literature who wanted to study racism or sexism in hiring practices (see Anderson, Fryer and Holt 2006 or Bertrand and Mullainathan 2004). Rather than changing the signatures on constituency mail, they changed the names at the top of resumes. As a rebuttal to the use of deception, it is fair response. Nevertheless, it is worth noting that there is a critical difference between the two projects. In the Bertrand and Mullainathan resume project, the dependent variable was very closely aligned with the underlying research concept. There is a direct pathway between call-backs for job applicants and racial composition in the workforce. This cannot be said of constituency mail. A politician might never respond to a single constituent letter and still be a faithful servant of constituent interests in the legislature. In fact, the opportunity cost of the response could actually impede their ability to be helpful. Rather than constituency letters, the more interesting outcomes would have been voting on legislation beneficial to minorities after the treatment.

Outside of the United States, the time constraints faced by public officials are different, but no less important. In parliamentary systems, more emphasis may be placed on back-benchers assisting in the achievement of party programmatic goals than interacting directly with constituencies. In other environments, using parliamentary office to network with high-ranking officials may be far more important for bringing public investment and jobs back to local constituencies than open debate on the assembly floor. Clientelistic behavior is an entirely common form of responsiveness in democracies, ranging from Italy to Japan to Thailand.

In our own project with Vietnamese legislators, we faced a similar dilemma (Malesky, Schuler and Tran 2012). The goal of the project was to assess the impact of transparency on the performance of delegates in parliamentary query sessions. Cooperating with a major online newspaper, we created a "Know Your Delegate" website for a randomly sampled group of delegates. Ultimately, we found that transparency had no direct effect on delegate performance, and in provinces with high Internet penetration, delegates actually chose to speak and criticize top officials less. By posting scorecards of delegate performance in the biannual query sessions in the National Assembly, were we incentivizing delegates to take time preparing and giving speeches, when their constituents would be better served by backroom caucusing or the study of legislation? Ultimately, we decided that the limited timespan of the two-week query and legislative debate session made the project more reasonable. For these two weeks, speeches were the primary activity of delegates. They could go back to doing other work after the query period.

We did not resolve a separate issue, however, which also haunts such interventions—specialization. Parliamentary representatives are not created equal. Some delegates are gifted orators, others are policy wonks with great knowledge of legislative detail, others are better at the wheeling and dealing of legislative compromise, others excel at fundraising, and still others are equipped for the nuance of constituency service. The successful creation and implantation of legislation draws on all of these talents, but it does not mean that all delegates must excel at each element. When we publish scorecards that incentivize one of these behaviors over others, do we motivate individual legislators to behave in activities where they are less talented and consequently less useful to their voters? And ultimately, by creating an incentive structure that benefits conformity over specialization, do we impede the overall functioning of national and local legislatures?

Humphreys and Weinstein (2012) handle these problems most effectively. Their scorecard emphasizes attendance, which is hard to argue against. Successful representation has to begin with actually showing up for work. But they also collect data on all sorts of legislative behavior from debate participation, to influence in the creation of legislation, to bill sponsorship. More than any other project, they provide a balanced incentive structure that allows delegates to specialize in areas where they can make the biggest contribution. Empirically, the strategy also allows them to measure substitution from one activity to the next that results from the intervention. Other projects need to be as careful. Nevertheless, even in this well-executed project, formal metrics for representation were explicitly valued over informal approaches, which are harder to measure. What remains unknown is whether the informal approaches are actually more effective at achieving constituency goals in such settings. Without that information, we cannot truly assess the opportunity costs of the intervention.

14.3 Conclusion

All experiments are ultimately judged by two ethical norms: 1) informed consent and 2) do no harm. Others in this forum deal with the question of informed consent, but the "do no harm" criterion remains ill defined when it comes to public officials.

What does it mean to do no harm in the context of elite experiments? Public officials serve in the public eye, they are trustees and public servants, and they deserve to be carefully scrutinized by voters. Some might argue that providing information to citizens about the performance of public officials should be considered a virtue and admirable public service. If an RCT makes such information available to voters and they choose to act on it by voting out an official, what actual harm has been done?

In many ways, experimental interventions are simply more rigorous extensions of transparency and accountability mechanisms that already exist. Many interest groups provide ready-made mailers, email scripts, and phone lists for voters to contact their representatives without any regard for the opportunity costs of the representative and his/her staff. Similarly, media and interest groups publish score-cards on delegate voting from every possible direction. US representatives are ranked on their first and second amendment voting records, alignment with party leadership, women's rights, and other scales.

Annual national and subnational rankings also manipulate the incentive structure of politicians in important ways, and these projects have even less ethical precautions. State government officials are ranked on public service delivery, business climate, safety, and environmental standards.

Indeed, Ferraz and Finan (2008), Chong et al. (2010), and Malesky, Schuler and Tran (2012) simply took readily available information that was already published and reported in the media. The experimental intervention was not the creation of the information, but simply its packaging and redistribution. In this light it is not clear that RCTs should have any special experimental considerations that do not apply to these other accountability mechanisms.

I would argue, however, that the above discussion reveals three areas where we should proceed with caution.

First, electoral repercussions for public officials seeking a return to office or contemplating higher do not seem to be violations. These officials chose to seek higher office, were aware of their own record and the mechanisms for accountability, and put themselves at risk of not being re-elected. We should not be embarrassed by these consequences. We should, however, be very concerned about local and part-time officials who did not seek a public profile, were thrown by chance into higher office, and will need to provide for themselves or their family after the intervention is over. Our interventions should not place their external career prospects or safety in danger.

Second, the "do no harm" criterion must extend beyond the individual to the broader constituency they serve. Do our interventions create an incentive structure that distracts officials from activities that best serve their constituency, either by raising opportunity costs, or incentivizing behavior for which the delegate is ill suited? This is not an easy question to answer, because we must: 1) contemplate the secondary and tertiary effects of our experimental designs, 2) consider the general equilibrium effects on the ultimate legislation and not simply the partial effect on a single legislator, and 3) address the very real possibility that normatively ambiguous activities (clientelism, networking with elites, subservience to authoritarian elites) may provide the best representation possible in the research context.

Third, one lesson that we learned from our own RCT is that sometimes even the best political science theory is not an appropriate guide for understanding the short-term and long-term effects of our interventions, especially when applying accountability mechanisms from democratic theory to authoritarian contexts. When we designed our Vietnamese legislative transparency intervention, we were aware that there was a possibility that delegates could behave in a conformist manner (Naurin 2007, Prat 2005). This possibility had been well documented in the literature, and our application to IRB cited it. That said, we did not believe it was the most likely finding. We, along with other political scientists and development practitioners, expected the positive benefits of transparency to overpower the negative. We were as surprised as others by the outcome.

At the end of the day, political science experiments on public officials must continue. We need them to resolve key debates in the literature and understand exactly how officials respond to the participatory, accountability, and transparency interventions we envision. We are making great progress, but now may be a good time to step back and identify the ethical precautions needed to do this work most effectively.

Note

1 In some cases, the experimental intervention targets public officials directly (Wantchekon 2003, Butler and Broockman 2011, McClendon 2012a, Loewen and MacKenzie 2011, Loewen and Rubenson 2011, Enemark et al. 2013). In other cases, the officials are affected indirectly, as voters are informed about their activities (Banerjee et al. 2010, Besley, Pande and Rao 2012, Chong et al. 2010, De Figueiredo, Hidalgo and Kasahara 2011, Ferraz and Finan 2008, Humphreys and Weinstein 2012, Malesky, Schuler and Tran 2012).

15

FIELD EXPERIMENTS ON ELECTED AND PUBLIC OFFICIALS

Ethical Obligations and Requirements

Christian R. Grose

Field experimentation in political science has primarily been conducted on citizens. In some instances, field experiments examine the effect of treatments such as get-out-the-vote messages on public behavior, where the messages to voters provide essentially no risk to subjects and may even be normatively beneficial (De Rooij, Green and Gerber 2009). In these and other instances in which scholars study ordinary people, a university's Institutional Review Board (IRB) approves studies, giving the official stamp of approval to a study.

Less frequently, field experimental work has examined decision-making, responsiveness, and representation in political institutions (Butler 2014, Grose 2014). Scholars conducting field experiments of elected or public officials have no requirement to garner IRB approval for their studies. Elected officials as subjects are simply exempted by IRB guidelines. This provides efficiency in terms of getting a project off the ground, but it also has the potential to create difficulties for researchers concerned about the ethical obligations to their subjects (public officials).

I argue that scholars studying public officials should consider ethical obligations to their subjects above and beyond the minimum required due to exemption. Research exemption exists for public officials because nearly all of their behavior is, by definition, public. However, behavior of public officials has important gradations and the ethical obligations for the protection of public officials should increase as their behavior becomes less public. There are important distinctions between, for instance, town meetings by legislators, messages sent to constituents by public officials, and private behavior by public officials. Others have focused on the ethical components of studying public officials with a focus on minimal risk, time intrusions to subjects, and deception (e.g., Butler 2014, McClendon 2012b).

While I also consider these ethical considerations, my focus is on delineating how to protect elected officials as subjects when their behavior differs in its level of "public-ness" in order to provide guidance to researchers.

Finally, I argue that these ethical considerations should apply to field research broadly construed, and not simply to field experiments. Perhaps the relative novelty of field experiments has led some scholars to subject field experiments to greater ethical scrutiny; while the ethical considerations of other, more frequently practiced, modes of field research have been less common in recent years (e.g., this book is devoted to *the ethics of experimentation*, although perhaps it should be devoted to *the ethics of field research*). The guidelines I outline may apply to all field work examining elected officials. Any time scholars enter the field—whether it is through randomized and systematic delivery of treatments to elected officials, through interventions such as participant observation of elected officials, or by surveying elites—we must remain cognizant of our ethical obligations to our subjects. In addition, we must remember that academic freedom is also an important component of our ability to study subjects in the field. Particularly when we study elites, who are public officials, it is important to consider what is ethically acceptable. The ethical study of public officials engaging in public activities is essential to our understanding of political behavior and political institutions.

15.1 Research on Public Officials and Candidates: Exempt Categories in Current Regulations

In the regulations governing federally sponsored research (typically used by university IRBs) to cover generalizable research broadly, elected officials, public officials, and candidates for office are exempt categories in human subjects research. The regulations (45 CFR 46.10(b)(3)) state that if "the human subjects are elected or appointed public officials or candidates for public office," then the research is exempt. This exempt category means that research on public officials is not subject to the review and approval typically required of human subjects research on ordinary people. At most if not all universities, research on public officials is nevertheless submitted by researchers to IRBs so the IRBs verify the research is on public officials and therefore exempt (Seligson 2008). In contrast, interventions on ordinary people typically require IRB review and approval—and not simply a declaration of exemption.

There are very good reasons that public activities of public officials are exempt categories of human subjects research regulation. The ability for researchers and scholars to independently theorize about and empirically investigate individuals working in political institutions is a worthy subject of academic inquiry (Schrag 2009). The key to an open society is the ability for citizens (including scholars) to inquire with and about their elected and government officials. For scholars, the ability to systematically study behavior that is open and available to any citizen is essential to understanding political representation, political institutions, and the behavior of political elites. It would be unusual and counterproductive to the enterprise of the accumulation of academic knowledge in a democracy to allow citizens to petition their government non-systematically while not allowing academic researchers to systematically intervene and investigate the government as well.

According to one account, public official exemption was part of a broader attempt to exclude most research in social science (including surveys) from IRB regulation (Schrag 2009), as nearly all social science research—especially in the realm of political and related social sciences—was viewed as having very minimal risk to subjects (in contrast to medical trials on humans). When the current US IRB regulations were being proposed and discussed, Ithiel de Sola Pool and other colleagues wanted nearly all researcher interactions with anyone engaging in public activities to be exempted from IRB regulation (Schrag 2009). They particularly were opposed to extensive federal regulation of scholarly activities in which scholars interacted with public officials, candidates for office, and political elites.

Ultimately, after HHS sought public comment from Pool and other social scientists, public officials and candidates were made an exempt category not requiring human subjects review (Schrag 2009). As the subjects are not vulnerable and are in fact powerful populations, Pool argued that there is almost always minimal risk to subjects from scholarly interventions. Even if there was risk to political subjects, Pool argued that any proposed regulations on research about political elites was "an attack on free speech and the concept of a university" (quoting Schrag 2009, 18).

To some researchers, an advantage of studying public officials is that the exemption of public officials allows a relative efficiency in the IRB process relative to other studies with ordinary individuals that must be approved instead of exempted. However, there is a potential disadvantage to exempt categorization for researchers as well. There is little guidance in regards to what is considered ethical on the part of researchers and essentially no discussion of when interventions with public officials are warranted by the importance of the research question. Thus, it would be useful to begin a discussion among scholars about the ethical considerations facing those who choose to conduct field research, field experiments, and field interventions with this powerful and substantively important group of research subjects.

15.2   The Public Behavior of Public Officials: An Ethical Framework

I suggest a framework for determining when a field intervention or field experiment with public officials is not ethically challenging and when scholars should think more carefully about the ethical ramifications of proposed research. Because

the IRB guidelines provide a near-blanket exemption of research on public officials, scholars should use their best judgments and balance the ethical obligations
we have as researchers to public officials and candidates with the need to answer
interesting and important research questions about politics, behavior, institutions,
and society.

One key criterion for ethical evaluation is that interventions by researchers
should be done on what is truly public behavior by public officials or candidates,
and not essentially private actions by public officials. But what does *public activity*
mean when we study public officials? One of the reasons that public officials are
exempt human subjects is because almost everything they do is already under the
public eye. Especially in democracies, the behavior and actions of public officials
are not only public, but there is a legal and ethical expectation that citizens—
including researchers—can access, observe, and even intervene in the actions and
decisions of their government, their officials, or candidates for government office
(without the prior consent of those in government).

For instance, if decisions or actions of public officials are not already available,
the Freedom of Information Act (FOIA) in the United States allows a citizen or
researcher to access and request government information (Barnes 2004, 10). Given
this expectation of access to government information and the first-amendment–
guaranteed ability to contact and intervene with the US government, the definition of public behavior of government officials is quite broad. One reason field
interventions and field experiments with public officials are so useful for scholars
is that they can allow for more systematic empirical examinations of questions
using techniques that are not only ethical and legal, but that are often considered
normatively desirable (e.g., constituents contacting elected officials, monitoring
the behavior and choices of government agencies, and seeking greater transparency in how public officials make decisions about public policy).

Treatment email messages from constituent confederates to their elected officials (e.g., Butler 2014, Butler and Broockman 2011) or researchers intervening by observing members of Congress and their staff at events in their districts
(Fenno 1978, Grose 2011) are ethical because the official is already engaging in
these activities in public view. These interventions by the researchers also do not
put the elected officials at risk, a key criterion of evaluating the ethical implications of research interventions. In addition, the legal expectations of FOIA suggest
that any electronic or written communications from a federal public official are in
fact public information (Wood and Lewis 2015).[1]

When elected officials' actions and behaviors are clearly public, there are fewer
ethical considerations for researchers in terms of the protection of their subjects.
When legislators speak publicly on an issue or cast a roll call, these are obviously
public acts. There are already significant interventions from the general public,
challengers, the media, and interest groups in regards to public acts such as legislators' decisions on roll calls. Most researcher interventions (be it through field

experimentation or participant observation) are unlikely to be a significant burden to legislators or other public officials in general, but this is especially so when contrasted to other interventions that regularly occur in the normal political environment from constituents, parties, interest groups, and other influential actors.

However, other activities and behaviors of elected officials are technically public but may have an expectation of privacy to the elected officials as a component. At the most extreme, when legislators engage in private actions with family and close confidantes—especially when not related to public affairs—there is a much greater ethical obligation to protect the privacy of public officials and in most instances the costs of intervention to the public officials would likely outweigh any potential benefits from the research.

There are four categories of behavior by public officials in which scholars may be interested: (1) public behavior that is universally accessible to the general public, (2) public behavior that is less accessible but still accessible to the general public, (3) nominally public behavior that is only public due to legal requirements for disclosure, and (4) private behavior of public officials.

As the actions of public officials tend toward the private sphere, scholars should be wary of extensive intervention without consent and all the usual human subject protections for ordinary people should be considered. When the actions of public officials tend toward the public sphere, scholars should be more comfortable engaging in field interventions as allowed under the exemption criterion. These public activities that are part of or related to their jobs as public officials or candidates need scholarly examination and intervention in order for us to increase our understanding of the political and social world. One rule of thumb would be that if a citizen can intervene with an elected official as part of the normal, democratic process of civic engagement, these are also areas of inquiry where scholars face fewer ethical challenges when conducting field experiments or interventions.

(1) *Public and universally accessible activities.* If we study ordinary citizens, the distinctions between public and private activities are clearer. A citizen's decision to turn out to vote is public and generally ethically suitable for field experimentation. A legislator's roll-call voting record, by the same token, is also public. These are activities that I call *public and universally accessible*, as they are easily and readily available for all to observe. Field experiments conducted on these types of activities by legislators, public officials, and candidates should face few ethical objections because the data are already public and fully accessible for any citizen to access (and any citizen can also ethically contact and inquire with public officials as well).

There are fewer significant ethical considerations so long as there is no deception involved in the experiment and the intervention is relatively unobtrusive.[2] These activities can be ethically subject to experimental manipulation if the interventions are minimal risk, as all information is public. Similarly, if a researcher is able to partner or consult with an existing organization that is already intervening with public officials engaging in public activities, more extensive interventions may also be ethical when the outcome variables of interest are public behavior.

In addition, there is no harm in attaching names and identifying information to datasets collected as part of field experimentation on these publicly accessible activities, such as roll-call voting. For example, some researchers have conducted field experiments where a legislator is contacted by a constituent, interest group, or researcher as the treatment. The treatment typically consists of a letter or email, relaying information to the subjects. The outcome variable in these studies has been the decision on specific roll calls (Butler and Nickerson 2011, Bergan 2009, Richardson and John 2012); or the frequency of roll-call participation by public officials (Grose 2013, Malesky, Schuler and Tran 2012). Other field experimental studies might examine an official's willingness to publicly take a position on an issue following a minimal intervention. In these studies, there is no requirement to protect the identities of subjects because everything they are doing is public information. In addition, retaining identifying information on public officials increases the ability to conduct replication studies. There may be other ethical obligations regarding the time involved to react or respond to the treatment, but I will discuss that later in the essay.

(2) *Public and less accessible activities.* Legislators also engage in a number of activities that are part of their duties as public officials that are public yet not systematically accessible to the general public. I call these *public and less accessible* activities. An excellent example of this type of activity is when legislators and staff members respond to constituent correspondence about issues and/ or requests for service. These behaviors are public in the sense that they are directly related to the legislators' public duties; the legislators know that there is a chance that their message to a specific constituent could find its way into the hands of other constituents, interest groups, and even the media. Furthermore, internal government communications not initially made public are subject to FOIA requests. However, it is possible that correspondence from a public official to a constituent as part of his or her duties may never be read by anyone other than the recipient of a legislator's communication.

The data for these types of activities are not immediately available to any interested observer or researcher. A systematic data collection of correspondence from a legislative office to constituents may only be available well after the person is no longer in office via archival sources or via freedom-of-information requests. In field experiments on public and less accessible activities of public officials, it may be ethically wise for the researcher to consider de-identifying some information related to the subjects in study replication materials. While not a requirement because of IRB exemption, this allows what are public but less accessible communications to constituents or other actors to be treated with some modicum of privacy. De-identification means the public officials and candidates will be placed at minimal risk.[3]

There is very little risk to legislators in treating them with constituent contacts, if the legislators (as subjects) are de-identified or even partially de-identified from the raw data. In a study that co-authors and I recently completed (Grose, Malhotra and Van Houweling Forthcoming), we were interested in learning whether legislators communicate differently to constituents who agree and disagree with legislators' issue positions and how the legislators explain their positions to constituents. Using constituent confederates, we sent one identical letter (from constituents) taking one side of a policy issue to all US senators and a second identical letter (from constituents) taking the other side of the policy issue to all US senators (a between-subjects experiment). We were interested in assessing and testing theoretical expectations regarding legislator explanations to both agreeing and disagreeing constituents. One of our key findings is that senators tailored their letters to constituents based on the positions of the constituents.

While we made the dataset for the file publicly available (including names of the subjects, US senators), we did not widely release the actual letters written by US senators to their constituents with the senators' names attached.[4] We are certainly willing to share these letters with researchers, but at this time are not putting them publicly on a website. Thus, the raw text data are available for researchers, but are not "google-able" by anyone who might be interested in suggesting a specific senator "flip flopped" on an issue in correspondence with different constituents. It is possible, although very unlikely, that if the texts of the letters were revealed to the general public, the senators could face some embarrassing news coverage.

This is one model for the ethical treatment of human subjects who are public officials when studying public but less accessible behavior. Because they are elected officials, scholars are not required to de-identify their names from datasets (and in fact, such de-identification may make replication and extension studies more difficult). However, scholars should make an effort to keep raw, archival documents that emerge due to field experimental interventions with elected officials in the domain of scholars at least in the short run following the experiment. This allows for a balance between protections of human subjects who are elected officials and maintaining standards of replicability.

In addition, in some instances, scholars may want to fully de-identify their datasets on public officials to reduce risk to subjects, even though this protection of subjects is above and beyond that required by simple IRB exemption. For instance, audit studies examining whether legislators systematically are less likely to respond to people of different racial and ethnic backgrounds (Butler 2014, Butler and Broockman 2011, Broockman 2013, Mendez and Grose 2015) do not put the elected officials at risk if their names are de-identified from the dataset. It is an important theoretical and empirical question to find out if legislators differentially respond to constituents not of their own races and ethnicities. However, the goal of these studies is not to name and shame individual legislators but is instead to examine the theoretical question as to whether there are responsiveness biases among elected officials. The data from Butler and Broockman (2011), for instance, are available for download, but they have redacted the names of the state legislators in order to maintain legislator privacy and protection.

On the other hand, if there is minimal or no risk to the public officials by releasing names of subjects, then researchers should release subjects' names along with other data when the officials' activities are public and less accessible. Public officials are exempt categories of research because their activities as part of their job require them to interface with the public regularly. In fact, in democracies, we would not want to limit minimal-risk systematic interventions with public officials by academics when concerned citizens also can (and should) intervene non-systematically with their elected officials.

(3) *Nominally public activities.* The third example of behavior by public officials is a *nominally public* activity. In this category, for instance, I would include some information elected or public officials must disclose by law revealing their private data. For example, US members of Congress, federal judges, and some executive branch officials are required to disclose addresses of the home(s) they own in their financial disclosure reports. The amount of information that is part of the public record for most public officials is astounding, and suggests why there is an IRB exemption of public officials: public officials, especially at the federal level in the United States, are often an "open book."

In this particular category of nominally public activities, some interventions in the field to public officials may create risk to public officials and possibly invade privacy. A scholar who may want to directly contact legislators could use the data listing officials' private residences. While technically public information, these are public officials' personal addresses. Unless, for instance, a legislator uses his or her home address as a legislative office (which happens in some low-professionalization state legislatures where it is expected that legislators can be contacted at homes), I would suggest that scholars should not personally visit legislators' homes to engage in interventions. While the IRB exemption criterion may technically allow such interventions, a researcher will want to carefully weigh the costs and benefits of engaging in experimentation of these nominally public activities. Here consent of subjects prior to intervention would be much more important when there is intervention compared to the earlier examples of public activities where it is not always feasible. In this example, while the officials are public and the information is nominally public due to disclosure requirements, the setting (a private home) is more in the private than the public sphere. When legislators and public officials have offices, it will rarely if ever be ethically appropriate to intervene with the legislators at their personal residences.

(4) *Private activities by public officials.* Finally, there are *private activities by public officials* that should not be considered public because they are not publicly disclosed. Personal relationships and any information that is not in the public realm that the official is not required to make public and chooses not to make public should be considered private. In theory, the IRB rules may exempt research in this area too, but scholars are ethically obligated to think carefully about any research we conduct on private activities of public elites. In the instance of private behavior of public officials that has no bearing on their jobs as public servants, I would caution strongly against researcher interventions on ethical grounds.

This private–public distinction is critical to developing ethical guidelines for researchers conducting field experiments of elected and public officials. The more public a public official's activity, the more ethical the field intervention will likely be, and the more private a public official's activity, the more important the scholar very carefully consider whether the intervention is a good idea. In some instances of private behavior of public officials, field experimental intervention may not be ethically warranted without prior consent.

15.3   What About Time Costs to Subjects?

In addition to the private–public continuum of behavior of public officials, some observers of field experimentation where elected officials are contacted by researchers, constituents, or other groups have suggested that officials' time is valuable and these interventions could burden legislators and other public officials by taking too much time (McClendon 2012b, 15–16). Time costs to elected officials are important, but as long as the written messages or other interventions to elected officials and their staffs do not subject the officials to substantial time costs and the officials are not put at risk, then the intervention is likely ethically acceptable.

For example, in a recent year, the US Congress received over 200 million emails and letters from citizens (Fitch and Goldschmidt 2005). If each individual senator and representative received an equal number of emails and letters, this means that each legislative office received more than 370,000 messages in one year (200 million divided by 535). Hypothetically, if 100 scholars conducted field experiments in which a constituent contacted a legislator, the proportion of communications to this legislator from field experiments would be 0.00027 of all correspondence to the legislator (370,000 messages per legislative offices divided by 100 messages).[5] Mathematically, it is unlikely that short email interventions to elected officials are creating a significant time burden for legislators and their staffs. Nevertheless, scholars should ethically design these message interventions to be unobtrusive and to require little response time for public officials or candidates.

To compare these field experimental interventions and time costs to individuals, it is useful to consider field research with elites. In some ways, field experimentation on the public and official activities of legislators is "soaking and poking" for the 21st century (Fenno 1978). Interviews by scholars conducted with public officials, like field experiments, yield important insights on elite behavior. Like field experimentation, the act of observing elected officials as a researcher may induce changes in behavior (through the Hawthorne effect or through intentional intervention by the scholar interviewer/observer). I have conducted participant observation and interviews with multiple members of Congress and their staffs for the book *Congress in Black and White* (Grose 2011). The amount of time I spent with each staff member or member of Congress ranged from 30 minutes to multiple days for the participant observation of members in their districts. This is a substantial amount of time for these public officials to devote to an academic researcher, and these time costs should be considered when we interview or observe any public official (or any person, for that matter).

When we conduct field experimental treatments of elected officials and legislators, we should consider that the time commitment is not particularly onerous. Relative to field interviews and participant observation, the time commitment needed by legislators to respond to a short email with a minor request is quite small. If the intervention requires a substantial time commitment by legislators or other elected officials, researchers should weigh the costs of time to the subjects relative to the benefits of the knowledge gained by conducting the study.

If interventions with public officials might incur more than minimal time costs, it then becomes ethically important to partner with real-world organizations and groups when conducting field experiments (e.g., Kalla and Broockman Forthcoming). If an academic can partner with a lobbying or advocacy organization, there is no significant increased time burden placed on the elite subjects caused by researcher intervention as the group would have intervened anyway (likely without randomization).

In fact, these same concerns about time burdens were raised decades ago for other methods of research, and many of the concerns still remain unsettled. But scholars today rarely consider the time costs to public officials when conducting interviews or participant observation. The difference is that there is no longer novelty to these interview and participant observation methods. An article written over fifty years ago by Lewis Dexter (1964) raised ethical concerns regarding the use of interviewing with elites and public officials. Reading his article recently, none of his suggestions have been implemented (e.g., one was for the American Political Science Association to create a "clearinghouse" of information, including past interview data, about members of Congress and other elites that can be consulted prior to scholarly interviews so as not to waste the time of members of Congress in asking questions to which there are already answers). In one passage of his article lamenting that too many graduate students were wasting the time of elected officials, I am glad that a Harvard graduate student at the time (Dick Fenno) was not discouraged from "burdening" members of Congress through his own field interventions (Fenno 1978). Field experimenters on elites should more carefully consider the ethical obligations to their subjects, but so too should scholars who intervene with elites through interviews, participant observation, field experiments, and other field research. We should also not forget the benefits to academic knowledge that come from field research with political elites.

15.4   What About Deception?

Others have discussed whether it is appropriate for scholars to engage in deception of public officials (e.g., McClendon 2012b), so I will not dwell on it here. However, from an ethical perspective, I would suggest that researchers seek to eliminate deception of public officials when feasible. For instance, if scholars want to send messages to legislators, a best ethical practice may be to recruit actual constituents to serve as confederates (such as done by de Vries, Dinas and Solaz 2015, Grose, Malhotra and Van Houweling Forthcoming). Using actual constituent confederates to write or contact a public official reduces deception of officials.

   This recommendation of not using fictitious confederates is not practicable in all areas of study. For instance, experimental studies of racial and ethnic discrimination by elites may require fictitious constituents because of the difficulty of finding actual constituents in every district studied and also because of the potential harm to confederates. For instance, Mendez (2015) examines under what conditions legislators may be more responsive to undocumented immigrants via a field experiment. He finds that, even though undocumented immigrants cannot vote and are in the shadows of society, some legislators nevertheless are responsive to the needs of undocumented immigrants. He tests this by examining legislator responses to an undocumented immigrant constituent relative to citizen and "control" constituents who contacted legislators with a minimal intervention. In this case, it is ethically much better to use fictitious constituents when contacting elected officials, as one confederate group (undocumented immigrants) is a vulnerable population, while the subject group (elected legislators) is one of the least vulnerable populations in society. Of course, when deception is used, debriefing is important.

15.5   Conclusion

I have presented a framework for considering the ethics of examining public officials as subjects in research involving field experimentation, and have also considered other ethical issues that may arise when studying public officials. This framework requires the researcher to consider just how public the activities of public officials are. In some instances, researchers may feel ethically obligated to de-identify their subjects' names even though this is not a technical IRB requirement as public officials are exempt categories in human subjects regulations. In addition, other ethical considerations toward subjects are important and should be balanced against the increased knowledge offered to the scholarly community.

These ethical obligations should not be considered only by scholars conducting field experiments on elected officials. They should also guide field research in general, particularly field research of public officials engaging in public activities. It is also important to reiterate that the study of political elites—through field experimentation or through other field interventions—is unlike almost all studies that examine human subjects. Public officials are probably the least vulnerable subjects that one could study, yet we should still be particularly cognizant of the ethical challenges when studying public officials and candidates for office.

Finally, I hope this essay is the beginning of a conversation in which scholars consider the ethical obligations to public officials, elected officials, and candidates. It is certainly not the definitive or final word on this subject, and the community of political and social scientists must ethically engage in field interventions to learn about political representation, political institutions, and the political behavior of elites.

Notes

1 See the "Frequently Asked Questions" section of FOIA Advocates at http://www. foiadvocates.com/faq.html (accessed September 24, 2015).
2 In some instances, when appropriate, it is likely ethically preferable for the researcher to partner with existing organizations when conducting field experiments or interventions on public activities such as legislative roll-call voting. For instance, scholars wanting to examine the effects of interest group influence on legislative roll-call voting outcomes should work with interest groups and have the groups embed field experiments within their lobbying campaigns to legislators.
3 De-identification of the constituent confederate names, who are private citizens, is also a very good idea.
4 Replication data for this study are available at http://thedata.harvard.edu (accessed September 24, 2015).
5 There are only a few scholars doing these types of field experiments on political elites at this time (Grose 2014), so the estimate of 100 scholars is much higher than the actual number of scholars.

PART IV

Strategies for Moving Forward

16

HUMAN SUBJECTS PROTECTION AND LARGE-N RESEARCH*

When Exempt is Non-Exempt and Research is Non-Research

Mitchell A. Seligson

Social scientists are well aware of the unintended consequences of public policies. The protection of human subjects regulations, which emerged in response to a serious problem in the medical community, provides an ideal example of such unintended consequences; to paraphrase an old aphorism, "the road to bureaucratic hell is paved with well-intentioned public policies." In this chapter, I will seek to make three points. First, the protection of human subjects by federal regulation was long overdue. Second, this benefit to society has, in its application, ignored another widely accepted regulatory principle, namely that the costs of regulation should not outweigh its benefits; a combination of "bureaucratic creep" and litigation phobia has resulted in intrusive and counterproductive regulation of social science research, such that the cure has become worse than the disease. Third, ironically, because of institutional review boards' definition of what is and what is not research, the protection of human subjects is denied to subjects who actually could be at risk.

Protection of Human Subjects Long Overdue

The horrors of medical experiments performed on captive populations in World War II were so egregious and became so well known that it is surprising that regulation was so long in coming. The Nuremberg Code, emerging from the post-war trials, set standards for judging physicians and scientists involved in those experiments on concentration camp internees. Subsequent to Nuremberg, the 1964 Declaration of Helsinki was issued, providing further ethical guidelines for research.[1] But it was the Tuskegee case that finally motivated action in the United States. That study began with the reasonable intention of determining if the treatments for syphilis then in

---

*This is a revised version of a paper that originally appeared in *PS: Political Science and Politics*, July 2008, pp. 477–482.

use, which were often very dangerous, were better off not being used. Nearly 400 largely illiterate African Americans, however, were not given informed consent, were not told that they had the disease, and, most importantly, were not treated for the disease even after penicillin was shown to be safe and effective in 1947. The Tuskegee study ended when the press exposed it in 1972. In the United States, the National Research Act was signed into law in 1974, nearly 30 years after the end of the war.[2] The act created the National Commission for the Protection of Human Subjects of Biomedical and Behavioral Research. It was not until 1979 that *The Belmont Report: Ethical Principles and Guidelines for the Protection of Human Subjects of Research*, was issued, which begins by making explicit reference to the biomedical experiments carried out during the war, to the Nuremberg War Crime Trials, and to the Tuskegee project. Finally, in 1981 the Department of Health and Human Services (DHHS) of the Food and Drug Administration (FDA) approved a set of regulations that are known as the Code of Federal Regulations (CFR), Title 45 (public welfare), Part 46 (protection of human subjects) and 56 (institutional review boards). It was not until 1991 that this regulation was widely adopted by other agencies of the federal government—17 in all—and became known as the Common Rule.

One wonders why it took so long for the US Congress to establish the protection of human subjects involved in research studies. No doubt there is an interesting story here, linked to the power of medical schools and the pharmacology industry, but that subject is beyond the focus of this chapter. Fortunately, despite the long delay, a nationwide system has come into place that protects human subjects in research. Moreover, the US rules have sparked similar rules in many other countries, including some developing countries.[3] Violations will always occur, but one can be confident that those violations are the exception, and are likely to be quickly detected, reported, and corrected. It is inconceivable that anything like the Tuskegee study could be repeated today.

Today, human subjects research at US colleges and universities (and all other institutions, for that matter) in the United States is governed by CFR Title 45 Part 46. It is commonplace, however, to hear social science and humanities researchers working on non-federally funded human subjects research, or research that has no funding of any kind (such as small-scale studies) expressing great surprise (and not a little irritation) that their work is subject to the Common Rule. Although some universities of late have taken the position that such nonfederal research is indeed not covered by the regulations, most, on advice of their risk-management attorneys, insist on universal compliance irrespective of the source of funding.[4]

An argument can be made that non-federally funded research is not covered by the rules. Any reading of these regulations makes it clear that they *do not apply* to research that is not funded by the US government. The very first section of the CFR, "To what does this policy apply," states:

> this policy applies to all research involving human subjects conducted, supported or otherwise subject to regulation by any federal department or

agency which takes appropriate administrative action to make the policy applicable to such research. This includes research conducted by federal civilian employees or military personnel, except that each department or agency head may adopt such procedural modifications as may be appropriate from an administrative standpoint. It also includes research conducted, supported, or otherwise subject to regulation by the federal government outside the United States.

In other words, the human subject regulations apply *only* to research on human subjects that is conducted or supported by the federal government. It does *not* apply to research that is not conducted by or supported by the federal government. The great majority of all colleges and universities in the United States have extended the regulations to apply to *all* human subjects research, supported by the federal government or not. The reasoning often used to make this blanket expansion of the application of federal human subjects research standards is that federal grants to a given college or university make research on human subjects at that institution *as a whole* subject to such regulation, just as colleges and universities apply nondiscrimination rules to all aspects of hiring and student admissions even when the particular employees or students are not receiving federal funds.

Even though the case can be made that nonfederal research should be exempt, this exemption is groundless if one is serious about the basic principle of protection of human subjects. If one accepts the fundamental principle that human subjects should be protected, then it is easy to argue that the issue of the source of support, or indeed the presence or absence of support, should be irrelevant. Consider a small-scale medical study involving only a handful of patients carried out by a private hospital and not supported by any grant, federal or otherwise. Human subjects in such a study most certainly deserve to be protected, and the source of the funding, if any, should have no bearing on their rights as patients.

In sum, nearly all research on human subjects is now regulated, as it should be, and patients (and subjects) are now, quite literally, "safe in their beds." Yet this does not mean that all is well with the protection of human subjects when it comes to the social sciences, and in particular to the area of survey research, the methodology I use in my own work. In the sections of this chapter that follow, I contend that while researchers all need to be aware of the principles and regulations for protecting human subjects and apply them rigorously in their own research, it is also important take a close look at the risk/reward equation in the way in which the regulations are being applied and enforced.

16.2 The Belmont Report: Problems of Assessing the Risk/Reward Ratio

The regulations that govern the operationalization of human subjects protection provide for the establishment of campus-based institutional review boards

(IRBs) rather than a centralized, federal-level board. In effect, the government outsourced to campuses and other research institutions the regulation of human subjects protection, a policy that, at the time it was implemented in 1981, seemed like a very wise decision. The argument in favor of such decentralization was that the regulations would become, in effect, self-policing, with each campus being able to respond to the particular and local conditions of the research. The idea was to avoid a big brother police officer for the protection of human subjects and to simultaneously recognize the enormous diversity of research designs, methods, objectives, and settings.

Decentralization of the regulation of human subjects protections, while a good idea in theory, has run into serious problems in practice. One problem is the lack of uniformity in the way the IRBs at each campus interpret and enforce the regulations, all of which derive from the three "basic ethical principles" established in the Belmont Report (The National Commission for the Protection of Human Subjects of Biomedical and Behavioral Research 1979): (1) respect for persons, (2) beneficence, and (3) justice. Each of these principles confronts problems in their application. For example, the respect for persons provision has given rise to excessive and erroneous interpretations. The Belmont Report notes that some individuals have "diminished autonomy," such as children and prisoners, and when those groups are objects of studies they receive intensified scrutiny from IRBs, as they should. But this principle has also been applied to pregnant women (Subpart B of Title 45, Part 46), such that some IRBs have insisted that in surveys the first question that must be asked of females is: "Are you pregnant?"[5] Given the multitude of difficulties that survey researchers face in persuading subjects to respond to surveys, it is easy to see why a question such as this one would have a chilling effect on many female respondents, encouraging them to terminate the interview.

Similarly, the Belmont Report justice principle, designed to protect the poor and various minorities from having to bear more than their fair share of the costs of experimentation, has been poorly interpreted by some IRBs. Investigators are asked to justify why some individuals are not included in a survey of public opinion, and provide detailed explanations for why they were excluded. For survey research based on sampling, this is an absurd standard. How does one attempt to explain to randomly non-sampled individuals why they were not chosen to answer a survey? However, the mere requirement imposed by these IRBs to explain non-inclusion in a study could open the door to class action lawsuits formed by groups of those excluded.

But no component of the Belmont Report has been more troublesome than the beneficence requirement. This principle finds its applied dimension in the report in the section on "The Nature and Scope of Risks and Benefits." Here we face "The requirement that research be justified on the basis of a favorable risk/benefit assessment . . . Accordingly, so-called risk/benefit assessments are concerned with the probabilities and magnitudes of possible harm and anticipated benefits." Belmont goes on to correctly recognize, however, that, "Only on rare occasions will quantitative techniques be available for the scrutiny of research protocols." Nonetheless, even though risk can only rarely be measured, the Belmont Report requires that "the idea of systematic, nonarbitrary analysis of risks and benefits should be emulated insofar as possible." In other words, even though it cannot really be done, it must nevertheless be done and the calculation of a project's benefits outweighing its risk is one of the three elements that must be used to determine if an IRB will approve or reject a protocol.

Much of the critique of this component of the Belmont Report and its impact on IRB decision-making has been on assessing the risk side of the equation, but it is appropriate to look first at the benefit side, for if there is no benefit, it would seem that no risk, however infinitesimal, could be justified. How might one go about determining benefit? Few IRB protocols are brash enough to suggest that the study promises to revolutionize the field of study. Indeed, many protocols are based on research grant proposals in which overstatement of promised findings is almost surely to be met by disbelief from the funding committee. This would sharply reduce the chances for funding (which would, of course, obviate the need to submit an IRB protocol in the first place), and therefore it is quite likely that the principal investigator (PI) will make only minimalist claims for the potential benefit of the research. But does the PI really know, or even have a good hunch? No doubt oncologists hope that their research will produce *the* breakthrough that will finally unlock the dark secrets of a cure for cancer, just as democracy experts hope that their research will yield the holy grail of explaining why some nations democratize and others do not. Yet the reality is that not only is the probability slight that a single research project will transform the researcher's field, it is almost certain that nobody would know *before* the research is done, and sometimes for many years after, just how important a given discovery might be. After all, Nobel Prizes are usually awarded years, if not decades, after the research is carried out.

Risk, which is the measurement of the cost side of the equation, is likely easier to measure in the medical sciences than are the potential benefits. Enough may be known from animal studies, or prior human studies, to be able to estimate the probability of serious harm. But in the social sciences, how can we assess risk? In social science experimental studies, there is the chance of risk, as the infamous Stanley Milgram obedience to authority experiments at Yale demonstrated, in which subjects thought that they were giving powerful electric shocks to those who would not obey (Miller 1986). However, the problem of assessing risk is especially vexing for all of those who rely on large-N studies, typically in the field of survey research. Ironically, when only a handful of subjects are used in a campus laboratory-based experiment, the IRB is likely to approve the project with no objection. But survey research, which invariably relies on large-N studies, is viewed with suspicion by many IRBs simply because the risk, however small, is seen as being replicated 1,000 or more times, given that most samples strive for confidence intervals of ± 3% or better. Protocol analysts, who are used to seeing laboratory experiments and focus groups with samples of fewer than 100, are often taken aback when they confront the large sample sizes inherent in most survey research. And when they do, they question why such a large sample is needed. As a result, it is not at all uncommon to have IRB protocol analysts ask survey researchers to cut down their sample sizes.

The risk/benefit ratio has been addressed from the perspective of academic freedom in a detailed study published recently by the American Association of University Professors (AAUP) that states: "What is deeply troublesome is the fact that research on human subjects must obtain IRB approval whether or not it imposes a serious risk of harm on its subjects" (American Association of University Professors 2006). The concern has to do with the extensive information that those seeking exempt status often request that goes far beyond assurance to the respondents that they will not reveal their identities and that they have the right to refuse to answer or terminate the study at any time. The AAUP goes on to make the following recommendation:[6] "We recommend that research whose methodology consists entirely of collecting data by surveys, conducting interviews, or observing behavior in public places be exempt from the requirement of IRB review."

16.3   When Research Is Non-Research

Perhaps one of the most perverse consequences of the regulations governing human subjects research is that while they closely regulate social science studies that have an extremely low risk of producing harm, they leave unregulated studies that have a far higher (but still immeasurable) risk of producing harm to human subjects. Note that I refer here to *studies* rather than *research* because it is that very term, *research*, that is the source of this perversity of consequences.

The federal government understandably had to delimit what is covered and what is not covered under the regulations. In those regulations, the government made the unfortunate decision, however, to regulate research rather than studies. It then found itself in the position of defining research, and in CFR 46.102 it did so in the following manner: "Research means a systematic investigation, including research development, testing and evaluation, designed to develop or contribute to generalizable knowledge."

This definition of research is unfortunate because of two key words in the definition quoted above: *systematic* and *generalizable*. When a study is conducted that is not systematic, and is not designed to produce generalizable knowledge, the study is not considered research from the point of view of the government.[7] Much of what political scientists do is indeed both systematic and aimed at producing generalizable knowledge, even if it does not end up doing so, and so when human subjects are involved, the work comes under the aegis of human subjects protection regulations, as it should. But what of other styles of research that are less systematic, or not systematic at all? A classic case would be Fenno's "soak and poke" approach to his studies. Richard Fenno (1996, 18) describes this method, which has led to so many important findings, this way:

> there is much . . . to be learned on the campaign trail. And much of what an observer learns is gleaned from the kind of informal, disjointed, meandering, event-stimulated conversation I shall call "travel talk." It is a form of conversation more open-ended, more expansive, and more unpredictable than the structured, inhibited interviews conducted in the cocoon of Capitol Hill.

Does this mean that for the purposes of IRBs that Fenno's work is not research? Those who elected him to the presidency of the American Political Science Association and to the National Academy of Sciences apparently have no problem calling his studies research.

Some studies in political science, especially case studies, do not aim to produce generalizable knowledge. Some monographs written in the area studies tradition (e.g., "The Politics of Paraguay") may not have been aiming for the production of generalizable knowledge, but others may have. Which authors of such monographs would be required to undergo an IRB review and which would not? And what of an author who began the research with no intention of producing generalizable knowledge, but after the fieldwork was complete suddenly saw that the work was indeed generalizable? IRBs strongly discourage, and in most cases refuse to grant, retroactive approval. Would this author, after having the light bulb go on and seeing generalizable knowledge emerging, be forced by the IRB to jettison the entire project?

The great irony in all of this is that in the humanities, or indeed in the humanistic areas of the social sciences, many scholars have little or no knowledge of human subjects regulations, and when told about them argue strongly that they are not subject to them. Indeed, should they hear of them and should they approach their own IRBs, they are often quickly told that because their studies are not systematic and/or are not aiming for the production of generalizable knowledge, they are not doing research as defined by CFR 46 and therefore need not apply, not even for exempt status. From the point of view of the federal regulations, because humanistic studies are not classified as research, they do not represent any risks to human subjects. This perspective has been reinforced by the American Historical Association, which has formally declared that "oral history interviewing activities, in general, are not designed to contribute to generalizable knowledge and therefore do not involve research as defined by the Department of Health and Human Services regulations at 45 CFR 46.102(d) and do not need to be reviewed by an institutional review board" (Townsend 2004). This position was officially accepted by the Department of Health and Human Services in a letter in 2003.[8]

These rulings and positions create two different sets of problems. First, and most important from the point of view of human subjects research, the risks of such studies in my view is no less than the large-N research that political scientists do. Long before human subjects regulations and the invention of IRBs, survey researchers in all fields instinctually knew that by guaranteeing anonymity they would encourage frankness on the part of respondents. After all, voters know that they have a "secret ballot," so why should they give up that right to an interviewer? As a result, political scientists who carry out surveys have been aware for decades of the importance of guaranteeing anonymity to their subjects. Once human subjects regulations were established, little changed in the administration of surveys other than the addition of informed consent statements at the outset of each interview, which more or less told respondents what they already knew, namely that they could refuse the interview or refuse to answer questions. The positive impact of the IRB regulations on survey research is to ensure that everyone in the community is aware of the ethics and regulations.

But what of humanistic research where the tradition of anonymity is not the norm? In the field of oral history, as well as in the newer *testimonio* literature popularized in Latin American literature, many authors use the real names of those interviewed, which can present serious risks for those respondents. Historians are not only exempt from IRB control, they have no requirement or even need to take human subjects protection training and pass tests on their knowledge of the principles and rules. Literature faculties often have no knowledge at all of human subjects protection.[9] As a result, unlike social science departments in which knowledge of human subjects protections is widespread, some humanists may be naive about the risks involved in disclosing names of subjects. One can imagine many kinds of risk to respondents. One such risk is dismissal of employment from an employer who either might not like the views expressed in the oral history or testimonio or deems them harmful to the company's welfare. Potential employers might look at the oral history information and deny a position based on the statements contained therein. Another risk could be ostracism at work or in one's neighborhood for expressing politically unpopular views. One can even imagine law enforcement officials using oral histories to prosecute individuals for revelations that suggest criminal behavior.

A second risk of such studies is to the humanists themselves. Tenure decisions and pay raises are based at many institutions, to varying degrees, on research. What of the faculty member who is in a field that the federal government has declared, and the professional association has agreed, does not conduct research? Deans and provosts alike could take the position, "Because you don't do research, you can't get tenure here." Of course the individual and department could turn around and say, "but of course I do carry out research," at which point the institution's IRB could begin an investigation into noncompliance with the federal regulations. That is, if an individual had in fact carried out research and had not gotten IRB clearance, this could spell real trouble for that person. IRB decisions cannot be appealed, so once a process of this nature begins on a given campus, it would be the responsibility of the local IRB to protect the institution from the dreaded cut-off of federal funds to the entire institution, as is provided under 45 CFR 46.123, and take action against the humanists who have circumvented their policies by first having declared that they do not do research and then declaring that they do. Far fetched? Federal whistleblower regulations, as augmented by the Sarbanes-Oxley Act in 2002, and state rules create precisely the environment in which such a nightmare could occur.

16.4 When Public Behavior Becomes Private

When one reads the "observation of public behavior" forms on many university websites, it is hard not to imagine that they were heavily influenced by George Orwell. In common parlance, public behavior is just that, something we do with the knowledge that others out there can and do observe us. If we did not want it to be observed by others, we would not do it in public. Town councils, regulatory agencies, and courts frequently hold open hearings, in many cases televising them on community TV stations. C-SPAN broadcasts several channels of TV and 24-hour radio programs that provide very public views of these activities. When a member of the general public attends council meetings or flicks on C-SPAN, no approval is required. When a political scientist does so, then the long arm of the IRB comes into play. Researchers who decide to utilize any of these sources for their research (presuming that the purpose is to attempt to develop generalizable knowledge) need first to apply to their IRBs for permission. Of course, we have other public behaviors, such as when we take a walk, go to the mall, pray in church, or dine in a restaurant. Individuals are not intending to provide their personal information under those circumstances, but because their names are not public, only a genuine effort to invade their privacy would produce that information, which is clearly a violation of IRB rules as well as probably many federal, state, and local statutes.

Under most circumstances, requesting permission to observe public behavior represents only a small hardship for the investigator, but what happens when such behavior emerges serendipitously? Consider the researcher carrying out a study in a foreign country when suddenly a protest march occurs, or a coup d'état is attempted. What is one to do? Observing the event(s) without first obtaining IRB approval would potentially jeopardize one's research career. On the other hand, IRBs are not set up to provide instantaneous approvals of protocols, even if the researchers had the wherewithal to download the proper forms and submit them without being distracted from observing the history being made in front of their eyes.[10]

Can IRBs take their responsibility to regulate to the extreme? A quick perusal of the web will reveal countless horror stories of ones that have. Anecdotes abound, but I cannot resist one of my own. A very senior IRB official at one university, in order to impress upon a political science faculty member his omnipotence, asked, "Do you ever use the library to read books about President Bush?" When the response was affirmative, he said, "Unless you file for IRB approval *before* opening those books, you will be held in violation, since Bush is a human, is living, and the books almost certainly contain personal information."

16.5   Added Difficulties in Comparative Politics

Some IRBs make life especially difficult for those who do studies abroad. One IRB has the following language on its website:

> When studies are conducted in foreign countries, written authorization to conduct the research at that location must be attached to this application. If identifiers are collected as part of that research activity, the investigator has the responsibility to ensure that responses to questionnaires or interviews about political, economic, cultural, or religious topics will not affect the participant's reputation, employability, or financial standing. This may require additional documentation from someone with firsthand familiarity with the country's laws and mores.[11]

Consider the difficulties this requirement places in the path of researchers. First, one needs written authorization to carry out the research. Who would grant such authorization? In countries where IRBs exist, presumably they could do so, which means having the study authorized by two IRBs. Then there would be the potential for conflicting and irresolvable differences in the way human subjects must be protected because there is no prior guarantee that the two sets of regulations would be compatible. In countries where such IRBs do not exist, who can authorize the research? Consider the United States prior to the establishment of human subjects regulations. What authority could have granted permission to a foreign political scientist wishing to carry out a survey of public attitudes in this country? Who would de Tocqueville have asked for approval of his research? In foreign environments, just as in the United States, there are almost always multiple and conflicting jurisdictions that could conceivably approve or deny research studies. Does one ask the central government, the local government, or both? Finally, the quotation above requires, in addition to permission, a statement that will attest that "responses to questionnaires or interviews about political, economic, cultural, or religious topic will not affect the participant's reputation, employability, or financial standing." Who could provide such assurances? The mayor of the town, the governor of a state, the president of the country? And what if it is a sample to be carried out in several dozen locations? Does each mayor, town council, and governor need to grant permission?

16.6   Exempt Status: Guilty Until Proven Innocent

The Kafkaesque nature of the human subjects protection regulation as they are being implemented nationwide today is that the authors were wise enough to exempt many of the kinds of research political scientists undertake. Regulation 46.101(b) states quite clearly that exempt from IRB regulation is:

> Research involving the use of educational tests (cognitive, diagnostic, aptitude, achievement), survey procedures, interview procedures or observation of public behavior, unless: (i) information obtained is recorded in such a manner that human subjects can be identified, directly or through identifiers linked to the subjects; and (ii) any disclosure of the human subjects' responses outside the research could reasonably place the subjects at risk of criminal or civil liability or be damaging to the subjects' financial standing, employability, or reputation.

Survey researchers, as already noted, have a long tradition of unlinking (or not even recording) the identities of the respondents, and I can think of no book or article in which that tradition has been violated. One anticipates, therefore, that surveys should be exempt from IRB control.[12] Indeed, that is how IRBs ruled for many years, but, according to Katz (2007, 799), "Procedural immunity from IRB oversight was progressively effaced and then decisively abolished around 2000, as campuses came to reflect a view communicated by federal human subjects administrators that 'self-exemption' was contaminated by conflicts of interest."

In effect, even though political scientists conducting educational tests and surveys are exempt from federal regulation, they are not, after all, exempt because the federal government believes we cannot be trusted. What is so strange here is that in countless other important ways, we are trusted by that same federal government. When we grade tests taken by our students, we are not allowed to discriminate on the basis of race, creed, national origin, sexual preference, etc. Yet we are not asked to sign a statement saying that we will not discriminate *before* (or indeed after) we grade each exam or before we determine final grades. We hold office hours, but are not asked to submit an application prior to each office hour, not even prior to the start of each term, to the affirmative action offices on our campuses that we will not sexually harass students. We submit articles to conferences but are not asked to submit signed statements saying that we did not plagiarize the material. Beyond our lives as professors, we have many obligations to obey the laws, and breaking them can have severe and immediate consequences. Thus we take driving license tests showing that we know the rules of the road and are competent to drive, but each time we turn on the ignition, we are not asked to certify that we will obey the traffic laws. Failure to do so, of course, annually results in most of the over 40,000 annual deaths from automobile accidents. These accidents produce a fatality rate of about 14 per 100,000, more than twice the current national murder rate, a level of real risk that wildly exceeds any imaginable harm that surveys could possibly be causing, regulated by IRBs or otherwise. Bus drivers and train operators take great responsibility in their hands when they transport passengers, but do not need to recertify themselves each and every time they begin a new journey. Yet that is what political scientists are being asked to do. We cannot be trusted to have studied the rules, to have passed examinations proving that we know the rules, and to have regularly been retested to make sure that our knowledge has not faded over time. Rather, we must take the additional step of submitting a protocol for each and every study we carry out.

Equally troubling is the ongoing control that IRBs have over the evolution of a study. Consider the problem of the survey researcher. Almost all surveys undergo many refinements and revisions as pretests and trials produce responses that cause us to make changes in questionnaire wording and/or coding. Many IRBs, however, demand that "amended protocols" be submitted when even a single comma is changed in a questionnaire. Consider the implications for this hypervigilance on the real world of survey research, especially in a foreign context. A surveyor could be in the field and discover that in a certain region a different word is used for a local institution. In order to change that single word, the PI would need to call a halt to the survey, submit an amended protocol explaining the reason for the change and attach a revised questionnaire, and then await the decision of the IRB. If no snags emerge, the survey might be able to resume with only a week's delay. Of course, during that week, salaries and per diem are paid, and given the lean budgets that most of us work under, this would of necessitate cutting down the fieldwork by a week, thus reducing the sample size. This would now require another protocol modification, but it will also increase Type II errors because the reduced sample size would increase the chance that a true finding will emerge as statistically insignificant.

The risk/reward ratio is clearly entirely out of whack. Once IRBs nationwide began making the assumption that social scientists cannot be trusted to act ethically and protect human subjects from harm, then the full weight of the regulatory burden has fallen on their shoulders. What are the benefits for applying for exempt status for each and every survey? What are the benefits of requesting permission to make changes in questionnaires? What are the risks that are being minimized by this scrutiny?

16.7 Conclusion

The roadmap to the future should be clear. The IRB regulations need to be modified in two important ways. First, the dysfunctional definition of research needs to be dropped. IRB regulations need to cover all studies of any kind that obtain data on living humans. This would immediately require faculty members in a broad range of institutions to familiarize themselves with the IRB regulations and to take the tests to demonstrate their knowledge of same. Second, the exemptions that are provided for in the regulations need to be enforced as written and not as artificially and unnecessarily subverted by overzealous bureaucrats, both federal and on campuses.

More generally, campus-based IRBs need to take a hard look at the risk/reward ratio. If regulations remain unchanged, and if federal misinterpretation of those regulations continues, the local IRBs could become far more creative by providing blanket exemptions to survey researchers once they have demonstrated that they understand the Belmont principles and the governing regulations. A university might provide for a biannual review of such blanket exemptions, but would stop requiring each new project to undergo a protocol submission and review. If that objective cannot be achieved, certainly the requirement that changes in questionnaires need approval ought to be dropped.

Finally, attitudes at the federal and campus level need to be altered, and those who operate those bureaucracies need to be retrained. They need to stop assuming, as the prevention on self-exemption does, that we are all guilty of violations of human subjects rights unless we can prove otherwise.

Notes

1 Among other things, the Helsinki statement argued for the establishment of independent committees to review research prior to its initiation, a requirement of informed consent from participants in studies, and that risks should not exceed benefits.
2 Prior to this act, the Kefauver Amendments to the Food, Drug and Cosmetic Act were passed into law in 1962 as a result of the Thalidomide disaster, in which pregnant women who took this sedative, a nausea-control drug, gave birth to thousands of babies born with severe deformities. These rules, however, had less to do with research and more with clinical practice.
3 Most of the human subjects protection in developing countries is focused on medical and drug research. An up-to-date compilation of the worldwide picture can be found at: www.hhs.gov/ohrp/international/intlcompilation/intlcompilation.html
4 According to a report from the AAUP, 164 institutions, including Harvard, Princeton, University of Chicago, and UC Berkeley, have not agreed to requiring non-federally funded research to adhere to IRB rules even though in practice apparently many of them do (American Association of University Professors 2006).
5 The IRB regulations for pregnant women, Subpart B, 46.201(b) specifically exempt surveys that collect information in which the subjects cannot be identified.
6 The AAUP says that its recommendation applies only to "autonomous adults," and therefore does not apply to children and prisoners, population groups for which they make no recommendation.
7 It is less clear what the government's position is on research that meets one of these criteria but not the other. That is, systematic studies that are not designed to produce generalizable knowledge or studies that are not systematic that are nonetheless striving for such knowledge. An example of a systematic, non-generalizable study could be a history of a political party in which the investigator systematically interviewed all

living elected officials from that party. A nonsystematic but nonetheless generalizable study could involve an entirely random, indeed even haphazard, set of elite interviews that produces a coherent theory of the bureaucracy.

8 The link to the letter can be found at the end of the American Historical Association's press release: www.historians.org/publications-and-directories/perspectives-on-history/march-2004/exclusion-of-oral-history-from-irb-reviews-an-update (accessed November 11, 2015).

9 The Modern Language Association's "Statement of Professional Ethics" includes a footnote: "Scholars should inform themselves of and observe institutional regulations and guidelines on the use of human subjects in research." Available at www.mla.org/repview_profethics (accessed September 28, 2015).

10 Some IRBs have gone to web-based submissions, and while this could ease the problem, it would require web access in the field, something not always possible, especially in foreign settings. It is more common, however, for IRBs to insist on original signed copies of the protocols, a virtual impossibility under the circumstances described here.

11 http://www.irb.pitt.edu/content/chapter-23-site-research-activities (accessed November 11, 2015).

12 The exemption by the regulations of public behavior unless the data are de-identified is inexplicable. Again, if behavior is public, one's right to anonymity is at the least compromised, and quite typically lost. Citizens who stand up at televised meetings and register complaints have little expectation that their faces will not be easily known to many. Moreover, at many public meetings, those who speak are required to identify themselves. So it is unclear to me, at least, as to why the exemption of public behavior is qualified in the regulations.

17

ETHICS AND RESEARCH IN POLITICAL SCIENCE

The Responsibilities of the Researcher and the Profession

Elizabeth J. Zechmeister

As the use of experiments of varying types and in varying locales propagates, how should political scientists address issues related to ethics in research involving human subjects? In particular, how should we respond to the increasing use of experiments by US-based researchers operating in foreign countries? In response to these questions, this chapter argues for approaching issues related to ethics in experiments abroad with emphasis on the central role of the individual researcher and on the political science profession as a whole.

I advance two core theses. First, ethical research necessitates a high burden for due diligence by the researcher. This applies to all researchers engaged in studies of human subjects, but is particularly pertinent in the case of studies located abroad because of insufficient expertise on domestic IRB review teams. Engaging local communities and undergoing local reviews (where possible) are useful steps that can be taken to help minimize risks to human subjects and reduce the likelihood that the research produces public backlash. At the same time, I argue that any emphasis on local review must be balanced by recognition of its own limitations and the fact that adherence to ethical conduct is ultimately the responsibility of the individual researcher(s). Second, so that researchers are adequately prepared to assess issues of ethics and research, it is important for political science as a discipline, and not just islands within the discipline, to commit to more extensive training and discussion on topics of ethics in research and the protection of human subjects.

In developing these points, I first draw attention to the importance of broadening considerations of risk when navigating ethical issues in research. I then present the case for an emphasis on the individual researcher(s) against the backdrop of limitations inherent in the capacities of domestic and foreign review boards. Finally, I argue for an extension of curricula and resources related to ethical research in the profession. I note that the discipline of psychology provides important models for such an expansion in focus on ethics in political science research, including with respect to research abroad.

17.1 Broadening Considerations of Risk

A standard procedure in the teaching of ethics in human subjects research is to focus attention on risks to those recruited into the research study. This is an appropriate starting point, in particular given the tendency of many neophyte researchers to state "blithely . . . that no [such] risk is involved" (Sieber 1992, 79). It is also an appropriate starting point because federal guidelines focus attention on the research participant, to whom the researcher is principally responsible.

However, it is imperative that ethical researchers also consider the broader risks that may stem from their research, even research that successfully minimizes risks to participants and accomplishes valuable short-term objectives (benefits). In considering broader risks, I have in mind the downstream consequences of research to both researchers and populations. One important type is the backlash that can occur when a study's procedures are deemed insensitive or offensive to a degree that threatens future research with a given approach or population. The obvious examples involve cases in which the participant incurred clear harm. Exemplars of this class of examples are the Tuskegee syphilis studies in the United States and their counterparts in 1940s Guatemala, in which research subjects from vulnerable populations were not consented into the studies with sufficient information and, worse, were exposed to reprehensible risks and harms by researchers who intentionally infected individuals with disease (Ove 2011). These studies not only inflicted harm on the subjects being studied, but also on their families and two additional populations: potential research participants whose consequent distrust of medical research induced them to opt out of research studies that might have returned benefits (see Tuskegee Syphilis Study Legacy Committee 1996) and researchers and scholars who consequently confronted socially imposed barriers to conducting research.

While purview of an IRB does not typically extend to these downstream consequences, they must be considered as part of the calculus of the ethical researcher. Sieber (1992, 78) refers quite clearly to this facet of ethical research when she writes that "no researcher would want to invite the destruction that can result from offending local sensibilities."

Thus, an ethical approach to social science research in the field of comparative politics and experiments—and any other subfield or discipline conducting research on human subjects—involves consideration of whether a particular study's protocol could be viewed as insensitive or offensive in such a way as to invite criticism and backlash to a degree that harm is incurred on future generations of potential research subjects and scholars. One way to mitigate against these risks is to present studies for local review, whether through an established IRB and/or through inviting review by local officials and communities.

17.2   Understanding the Limitations of Domestic (US) IRBs in Reviewing Research Conducted Abroad

Too often I have heard a researcher (without wanting to offend a particular population, I will note that these statements often come from student researchers) indicate that she will ensure her research is conducted in an ethical way by subjecting the research to review by an Institutional Review Board (IRB). Yet, as noted in the above section, not all ethical considerations are part of the established scope of the IRB's federally derived charge. Moreover, there are two additional problems with leaning on the IRB to certify a research study as ethical. In the first place, reviewers acting for IRBs often lack even basic knowledge of the countries, settings, and subjects at the core of a proposed research project. In the second place, IRBs, like any bureaucracy, are prone to mission creep; their purpose is distorted away from original objectives. In both cases, these limitations tend to impose unfortunate delays and bureaucratic red tape on researchers, without bringing any benefit to the research subject. In short, responsibility for ethical research ultimately rests with the researcher, who should be given training and take precautions that go beyond the scope of local university IRB requirements.

Let me draw on my own experiences to provide several anecdotes illustrating situations in which problems have surfaced, with the first two examples speaking to the problem of a lack of even basic knowledge of the countries, settings, and subjects at the core of a proposed research project and the third speaking to mission creep. Each of the anecdotes draws on an experience with a different university, so that collectively they suggest these issues are common and not unique to one particular IRB.

Anecdotes 1a and 1b

Anecdote 1a. Lack of knowledge of political climate in foreign country. The PI proposes to conduct a small, quasi-experimental research study on political ideology in a Latin American country that transitioned to democracy three decades prior and has maintained high Freedom House scores ever since. The PI intends to recruit subjects from a university population. Prior to submitting the IRB application, the PI has fully designed the study's protocol and instrument (designed to ensure subject anonymity) and has secured institutional affiliation and approval for the study from a private, elite college in the capital. Due to under-staffing, the PI's application for exemption to her university's IRB is re-routed from the social science division to the medical division, where it is reviewed by a physician whose research focuses on medicinal uses of marijuana in the United States. The physician denies the request for exemption under the (erroneous) grounds that the dictatorial, authoritarian climate in Argentina makes it too sensitive to ask questions about partisanship to research subjects in this country. The PI appeals and, ultimately, the decision is reversed.

Anecdote 1b. Lack of knowledge of standards of living among subject population in foreign country. The PI proposes to conduct a quasi-experimental research study on political ideology in a Latin American country characterized by democratic party politics and a mid-level of per capita income. The PI intends to recruit subjects from a university population. Prior to submitting the IRB application, the PI has fully designed the study's protocol and instrument (designed to ensure subject anonymity) and has secured institutional affiliation and approval for the study from a private, elite college in the capital. The protocol calls for compensation valued at the equivalent of a can of soda. The PI's application for exemption to her university's IRB is denied on grounds that the (trivial) amount offered to subjects as compensation is, in that country, so very substantial as to be coercive. The PI appeals and, ultimately, the decision is reversed.

Anecdote 2

Anecdote 2. Improper intrusion into study protocol (mission creep). The PI proposes to conduct an experimental research study on threat and public opinion in a democratic Latin American country, recruiting subjects from an opt-in Internet panel administered by a professional research firm. Prior to submitting the IRB application, the PI has fully designed the designed the study's protocol and instrument (designed to ensure subject anonymity) and has had the study's documents translated and reviewed by natives of that country with advanced graduate training. The PI's IRB application is returned with a request that translations are adjusted in order to reflect the IRB reviewer's (American) understanding of the Spanish language. The PI appeals and, ultimately, the request is withdrawn.

The above anecdotes need to be considered at a level beyond the irritating but not insurmountable (in the cases described above) obstacles that were placed on the researcher. Rather, and more importantly, they need to be considered for what they reveal about the inadequacies inherent in reviews conducted by analysts who lack sufficient training, experience, and knowledge of different countries and, in the case of the last example, federal guidelines.

One potential remedy to these issues is to bring more expertise into the domestic review process in university IRBs, but given the myriad different settings in which individuals can conduct studies of varying topics abroad, a more efficient set of solutions might be found in encouraging local review and by fostering discussion and training in ethical research within the discipline so that scholars—new and old—consider the IRB as only one small element in the set of considerations they must make in order to satisfy the objective of conducting research in an ethical manner.

This is all the more important because it is typically the researcher, with a nuanced understanding of a particular region and research method, who is best equipped to identify potential risks. Here is one example, which I'll call anecdote 3 in keeping with the structure of this section.

Anecdote 3

Anecdote 3: IRB underperformance in assessing real risks. The PI proposes to conduct an experimental research study on threat and public opinion in a democratic foreign country, recruiting subjects to be interviewed in their households via a representative sample combined with quota methods developed and administered by reputable local survey firms. At the core of the study is the fact that treated participants are asked to read one of several news stories, some of which contain information about security threats. Prior to submitting the IRB application, the PI has fully designed the study's protocol and instrument (to ensure subject anonymity). The PI's IRB application is approved. The PI re-considers the protocol, realizing that poor eyesight and literacy problems may result in study instruments (news stories about threat) being read aloud to the interviewee. The PI considers that household interviews may mean children are present. The PI independently adjusts the protocol for the study administration and training of interviewers in order to minimize risk to minors who might be in the vicinity of the interview. The new protocol is submitted and approved by the IRB and the study proceeds.

The point is that it is the researcher's obligation to work to anticipate risks that might not be anticipated by IRBs. In the field of comparative experimental research, ethical research means doing research ahead of time into culture and conditions on the ground. For example, if a researcher is going to distribute significant amounts of money to research participants, the researcher should have an understanding of what community and domestic relations are like in that setting so as to anticipate the potential responses that other members of the community or household could have to a payment to study participants.

17.3 Local Review Is Only a Partial Remedy

The question has been raised by scholars and by IRBs as to whether and how a researcher conducting a study in a foreign country should acquire and certify local review. I want to suggest that, while this process should be encouraged, it is important to recognize that mere bureaucratic requirements alone are not sufficient to ensure a comprehensive local review.

To illustrate this, I offer another anecdote. In this case, as part of a newly introduced stipulation by a university IRB, the PI was required to have the IRB at the foreign institution supporting the research project review and approve the study. The problem was that, as is often the case, there was no local IRB. The PI's IRB then required the institution to pledge its adherence to the principles established in the Declaration of Helsinki. Without clear direction on who can be considered to speak for the "institution," the PI approached the chair of the academic department that had extended affiliation and support for the research study. The chair admitted a lack of significant familiarity with the Declaration of Helsinki but, upon reviewing and approving the study, submitted a statement that his institution adheres to the principles established in the Declaration of Helsinki. The PI's IRB application was approved.

The key points here are that a) there are often no established IRBs at institutions abroad supporting research and b) attempts to operate "as if" those IRBs and related training exist are likely to result only in superficial review statements. If local review is to be required, then guidelines need to be established that take into consideration the varying realities of IRBs and related training (or lack thereof) at foreign institutions. This requires a commitment on the part of the IRB and the researcher to move together beyond an attempt to appear compliant and, instead, toward an attempt to understand, for example, local norms relevant to the conducting of research.

Finally, I note there does seem to be an increasing number of IRB or "ethics boards" at universities in other countries. Especially given that this is a changing landscape, finding relevant information about submission and review procedures and navigating these institutions can be difficult. It would be highly valuable for researchers knowledgeable about these institutions to pool together that information in a common online resource.

17.4   Broadening Consideration of Human Subjects Research

The last point I want to raise is that I find it impossible to consider issues related to ethics in experimental research in the comparative context in isolation. We know, for example, that experimental methods in general are becoming more commonplace in political science (see Kam, Wilking and Zechmeister 2007). My intuition, seemingly backed up the available evidence and discussion, is that increasingly scholars in the discipline of political science are interacting with human subjects as they collect their research. And yet training and discussions of ethical approaches to research involving human subjects seem comparatively limited.

In searching for discipline-wide statements on the subject of ethics in human subjects research, I consulted APSA's website. The discipline offers a "Guide to Professional Ethics in Political Science." The most recent version I found online is dated 2012. In no part of that document is there a discussion of the importance of training researchers in ethical approaches to social science investigation. Contrast this with the discipline of psychology. The American Psychological Association

(APA) has established a well-known statement on ethics and code of conduct (see http://www.apa.org/ethics/code/index.aspx). Furthermore, research methods textbooks in the field of psychology give clear emphasis to and instruction on issues related to ethics in research (see Shaughnessy, Zechmeister and Zechmeister 2011). And, finally, the APA offers a guide to psychologists who "go abroad." It covers a range of topics, including a series of points relevant to conducting research abroad (see pp. 17–19): http://www.apa.org/international/resources/academics-abroad-2011-hi.pdf.

The broadening and increasing scope of human subjects research in political science justifies a discipline-wide response, so that we work toward uniformity in norms, training, and requirements. Often experimental research is singled out for examination, but we as ethical researchers should be just as concerned that scholars carrying out in-depth qualitative interviews with selected segments of a foreign population are asked to make the same set of considerations, provided with the same types of training and support, and subjected to the same types of requirements that are appropriately attached to experiment-based research abroad (see also Seligson 2008).

17.5 Conclusion

I want to conclude by returning to my call that, in discussing issues related to ethics and experimentation in the comparative context (and in simultaneously discussing issues related to ethics and human subject research in political science more generally), we put a strong emphasis on the researcher and the profession. The considerations that an ethical researcher must make reach beyond both the mandate and the capacity of IRBs (on this point, see also the discussion in Fujii 2012). This is not to say that local review should not be encouraged; in fact, I hope that it can be facilitated by way of a shared online database providing information relevant to local review processes. Rather, my point is that ethical approaches to social science research must recognize that the IRB application and review process, both domestic and abroad, is only one part of a broader set of considerations that the researcher should make. Finally, ethical research in the profession of political science can be advanced by increasing curricula, discussion, and resources related to ethics in research, possibly modeled after examples from outside the discipline of political science.

18

JOURNAL EDITORS AS ETHICS SHERIFFS

Rick K. Wilson, William Mishler, and John Ishiyama

What role should journal editors play in enforcing research ethics? Three editors from different general interest journals in Political Science were invited to comment on what might be done. The particular topic of concern is with possible ethics violations in laboratory and field experiments. With an increase in the number of manuscripts that use experimental designs and with the potential for violating human subjects especially possible in comparative research, the editors were asked about what the journals were doing, could do, and should do. All three editors noted that potential ethical violations, to this point, appeared rare. Still, the roles that editors and associations have with respect to potential violations are important concerns.

The most important ethical concern in experimental research is almost certainly violations of the rights of human subjects. Unfortunately, where there is a violation in this regard, the journals are typically left in the position where the "horse is already let out of the barn." The damage has been done; the breach of ethics occurred at the point when the research was carried out. The editors agreed that local Institutional Review Boards (IRBs) have the primary obligation to review research protocols before a researcher begins a project and to monitor compliance during the conduct of the research. Researchers, too, should self-regulate with respect to ethics. When the project is completed, there is little left for editors to do except to evaluate the work. Although all of the editors are willing to reject manuscripts that are known to violate ethical concerns, this is not easily done. Given that we already decline more than 90% of submissions, the sanction is a minor one as well. Moreover, as we note at the end, our attention to completed research is not ordinarily toward whether the research passes an ethics threshold, but rather whether it passes a high bar in terms of science. Even if we did attend more self-consciously to ethical concerns, manuscripts usually provide little information that would enable us to play a major role in this regard.

18.1   Problems

There are at least five problems faced by editors. First and foremost is that Institutional Review Boards (IRBs) differ a great deal across universities. Although the Common Rule elaborates the regulations overseeing the protection of human subjects, it is left to the local IRB to interpret and implement those protections. Different standards are applied and different aspects of human subjects protections are emphasized. Some IRBs emphasize the protection of subjects, while others intrude into the research design. Some IRBs are lenient, while others are quite strict. In the face of this variation, which standards should an editor enforce? Obviously, it is incumbent on authors to demonstrate that their experiment has been approved, but it is problematic to expect editors to choose one type of IRB over another. Worse, if a manuscript is published that falls into a gray area but is allowed by the researcher's local IRB, can other scholars complain? To what extent should editors be allowed to make comparative judgments across different types of IRB rulings?

A second problem is that journals are typically owned and overseen by an association. Most associations do not have an ethics statement. Consequently, editors again do not have an institutional standard by which to judge whether a piece of research is in compliance or not. In the absence of such standards, are editors subject to legal liability? If such standards exist, should an association's standards trump an IRB?

A third problem is that journal editors are typically over-subscribed. There is plenty to do on a daily basis just to ensure that manuscripts are reviewed in a timely manner. Adding ethics sheriff to editors' portfolios will increase their burden. It also will detract from the satisfaction of the job because confronting colleagues and friends on ethics "charges" is inherently conflictual and distasteful.

A fourth problem is that editors do not have any special knowledge or training with respect to research ethics or human subjects protection. Most editors have completed IRB training at their universities (and probably should be required to do so as a precondition for being selected), but they typically have not received the extra training required, for example, of IRB board members. Nor do they have any special knowledge or training regarding the myriad other ethical concerns that arise in social science research. Should policing (and training to police effectively) be added to the long list of things that editors are expected to do?

A fifth problem is what ethical issues should an editor prioritize? Here there may be little agreement. There are a number of major concerns on which the experimental community has not reached consensus. For example, most experiments require informed consent by subjects. Yet some types of experiments (many field experiments, for example) make getting informed consent difficult. Oftentimes the intervention needs to be masked so that the subjects are unaware of the treatment. Getting consent beforehand might ruin the effect of the treatment and debriefing a large number of subjects afterwards is impossible. Another issue concerns deception. Should an editor treat all instances of deception as ethical grounds for rejecting a manuscript? For some reviewers this certainly is the case; for many others, it is not. Editors vary in their views of deception, as well (in economics, for example, it is a rare editor who would not desk reject an experiment with deception).

Moreover, informed consent is just the tip of the ethical iceberg. Randomization raises ethical issues about providing services to one part of a needy community but not to other, equally needy, parts. It also risks provoking community discord. Providing compensation to needy subjects is tantamount to coercion in the eyes of some scholars, although not to others. The array of unsettled ethical issues is vast. Should editors be encouraged to exercise their personal ethical judgment in the absence of agreed-upon community standards?

18.2 Proposed Solutions

What might be implemented in the short run? A number of suggestions were offered but for which there was little agreement. First, can a journal require that an IRB be produced before it is reviewed? This is possible. This would require the author certify that the study had been cleared by their IRB and that editors check this when the manuscript arrives. This is required for numerous journals in the medical field (e.g., *JAMA*) and in the social sciences (e.g., *American Economic Review*). Implementing such a requirement raises two problems. First, why stop with lab and field experiments? Should this be insisted on for all observational data? Depending on the local IRB, even scholars who carry out secondary analysis on observational data must be reviewed. The second problem relates to foreign manuscripts. A number of foreign countries have no IRB equivalent or standards that are very different from those in the United States. Should those manuscripts be exempted from the requirement? Should this be left to editor discretion? Our general sense is that authors should produce evidence that they have complied with their IRB and the community, when reviewing, should be skeptical about the ethics when evidence about the IRB is missing from the manuscript.

As noted, editors have a lot of demands on their time, they are beholden to their own local IRBs, and they have little guidance from their sponsoring associations, which may or may not indemnify them if sued by adversely affected authors. One possibility would be for the development of an ethics in research and publication training program for editors. For example, EGAP (Experiments in Government and Politics) or the American Political Science Associations's Experimental Research Section could develop a training manual or even provide a training workshop for editors. Our guess is that a workshop would be more effective than a training manual. But which organization should have that responsibility? What would be its content? Why should associations forego implementing their own standards and making a clear statement about ethics? Should completion of such training be mandated for journal editors?

It has been suggested that editors require that all experiments be pre-registered. The goal is to ensure that experiments and the analysis are carried out as proposed. This may eliminate unreported "fishing" for results. It may also cure the p<.05 publication bias phenomenon. The editors argued that researchers should be encouraged, but not required, to register their experiments. Even within the experimental community the value of pre-registration is debated. If this is important for the community, then it will become the norm. Editors can highlight when research is pre-registered. During the review process, noting exactly where the project is pre-registered presents a problem for double-blind review. Knowing that a manuscript is pre-registered might be important for reviewers, although not knowing whether the reported research was faithful to the pre-registered design may give reviewers a false sense of the manuscript's rigor. For journals that maintain double-blind review, this can be problematic. Editors (and reviewers) are unlikely to read both the manuscript and the pre-registration and certify that the manuscript is consistent with its pre-registered plan.

Require that a protocol accompany any experiment. This is easy. If a reviewer is going to evaluate a manuscript, then the experimental protocol should be attached as part of the supporting information. The *American Journal of Political Science* has failed manuscripts at technical check for not including a sufficient protocol. However, increasing demands on the reviewer pool already are eroding reviewer cooperation. The trend toward more and longer online appendices, including robustness checks, survey sample details, and experiment protocols, among other worthy items, further burdens reviewers and threatens the viability of the peer review process. Expecting a protocol is commonplace in the experimental community, and authors should routinely make them available.

Finally, it is suggested that manuscripts that may have ethical problems be submitted to a special panel that reviews the manuscript. Two problems arise with this. First, what organization can sponsor and/or staff a panel that is capable of making ethical decisions? This could be a costly activity and further delay the review process. Second, it requires that editors recognize that an ethical problem exists. Given limits on editor training (as noted above) this may be problematic. Does this mean that the panel would vet all manuscripts with an experiment? This only leads to additional delays in review while creating a burden for the ethics panel.

18.3 Conclusion

Should editors be the sheriffs in policing ethics in experimental research? Our responses range from probably not to absolutely not. As noted above, editors lack the time, the incentives, and the training necessary to make clear ethical decisions—especially where the ethical standards are not shared by the community (experimental and not) and by local IRBs. As we read manuscripts when they arrive, our focus is first and foremost on whether the manuscript ought to be desk rejected. If so, it is usually on the grounds of the appropriateness of the manuscript for the journal. If deemed reviewable, then the focus turns to finding appropriate and willing reviewers. When the reviews are returned, the focus shifts mostly to the scholarly merits of the manuscript unless one or more of the reviewers raise ethical issues, which is a very rare occurrence. When a reviewer does identify a potential ethics concern, this is matter of serious concern for an editor and one for which the advice of the editorial board and association leadership usually will be sought. However, in our view it is the community that has the larger responsibility for ensuring that ethical standards are upheld. Organizations such as EGAP or the Experimental Research Section of APSA have an important responsibility for shaping the ethical standards in their communities and for building and enforcing norms. Editors can reinforce what the community does, but even sheriffs can only enforce those standards that their communities establish.

19

CONCLUSION AND RECOMMENDATIONS

Scott Desposato

19.1 Introduction

"What would happen if someone ran one of these experiments in the United States?" This was the question I posed to this volume's contributors towards the end of our conference in 2013. The origin of the question deserves some explanation. Many of our discussions focused on experiments being conducted in the developing world. Experimental research there might be described as a "Wild West" right now, where scholars have broad flexibility in the studies they run and how they run them for several reasons. IRBs have generously approved studies that seem inappropriate: committing traffic crimes, soliciting and paying bribes, and violating electoral laws. Researchers' budgets often go further in the developing world, making scholars much more powerful actors than they would be in the United States. Inequalities between researchers and subjects can breed deference and prevent subjects from speaking up about inappropriate interventions. If scholars are not deeply knowledgeable about the contexts of their experiments, they may be more likely to dehumanize their subjects. Scientific research requires some detached and dispassionate perspective, but one cost of that may be less empathy.

My question was thus designed to force scholars to think about the consequences of conducting a study in a context where they would have less power, where subjects and media would be more likely to detect the intervention and comment on it, and where scholars themselves might be the subjects or bystanders affected by the treatment. Would there be any negative consequences of running a typical comparative politics experiment—say, an intervention during a real election—in the United States, instead of overseas?

Recent news suggests an answer to my question. Since the conference, a number of experiments have generated public controversy in the United States. One was an experiment conducted during a judicial election in Montana, where researchers sent flyers to 100,000 registered voters.[1] The mailer provided information about the ideology of candidates based on their donor histories. The reported goal of the study was to see how providing information about candidates would affect participation (Stanford University and Dartmouth University 2014).

Though seemingly innocuous (what could be wrong with providing factual information about candidates to voters?), the study generated widespread criticism from scholars, politicians, and the press. The Montana Secretary of State filed a complaint against the researchers' universities for inappropriate election practices. Politicians, journalists, and researchers criticized the study.[2] Ultimately, the presidents of Stanford and Dartmouth sent letters to all subjects apologizing for the study and asking them to disregard the contents of the original mailer (Stanford University and Dartmouth University 2014).

It is especially ironic that this study generated so much controversy, because in many ways it used caution when compared with other field experiments conducted in other countries during real elections. The flyer provided factual and comparable information about all judicial candidates; in other studies, scholars made allegations against candidates, effectively sending negative or attack messages. The flyer self-identified as being part of a study, and included an Internet address where subjects could learn more about the candidate information provided. Other scholars have sent mailers with no notification that the recipients are part of a study, leading subjects to presume that real candidates sent the messages. Lastly, the Montana study was designed to increase turnout—presumably a normatively good thing. Other studies focus on changing vote share—which is of questionable normative value and, for some, implies direct harm to those candidates losing vote share.

The fracas over the Montana Study should be a wake-up call for political scientists. Even experimental treatments that are clearly common parts of everyday life and pose no obvious risk to subjects can prove controversial and ethically questionable. These types of controversy are new to our discipline because the widespread adoption of experimental methods is a recent phenomenon. Experimentalists are confronting many unexpected ethical issues, especially when operating internationally. My goal for this volume was to start a dialogue on some of these issues—identifying, debating, and proposing some practical strategies to avoid problems while still generating robust research.

In this conclusion, I will pursue two tasks. First, I will review what we have learned about the most important issues confronting experimentalists and will identify areas of consensus and controversy regarding ethical research design. In cases of controversy, I will attempt to identify and explain the positions on each issue and offer my own position. Second, I will offer suggestions on how the field might proceed to resolve disagreement and develop consensus about best practices.

19.2 Consensus and Controversy

At the start of this book, I identified three broad categories to organize the types of problems political scientists are encountering: contextual issues, local review, and field experiments. The first, contextual issues, refers to unexpected problems encountered when exporting designs to other cultural, religious, political, and legal environments. The second, local review, examines types of review procedures required in other countries, how to navigate them, and when and how to consider avoiding them. The third, field experiments, examines the challenges and promise of these studies' combination of real-world impact, deception, and a lack of informed consent.

19.2.1 Contextual Issues

Many of the contextual issues encountered herein appear to be "easy" issues. "Easy" means that there is clear agreement that the experiment has the potential to cause harm and we can easily avoid that harm with modest design changes. Contributors examined compensation and exclusion in very poor settings, treatments that affect or measure religion, and research in dangerous environments.

Dionne, Harawa, and Hondes' chapter focuses on problems with compensation plans in contexts of extreme poverty. They report on their experiments in Malawi, where even a low-value payment for participation—a bar of soap—was problematic in some experiments. Standard compensation plans led to conflict between subjects and non-subjects, and generated feelings of resentment and distrust toward researchers. For these authors, the solution involves educating subjects about compensation, anticipating and avoiding inequalities in that compensation, and developing beforehand a backup plan in the event that their original plan did not work. Lotteries and random assignment may be familiar and seem fair to researchers, but they may seem arbitrary and unfair in other contexts. The clear implication of this chapter is that researchers should be aware of this potential and educate subjects regarding the nature of random sampling and assignment—our motives for doing so, how the mechanisms are impartial and fair, and how non-participants may be compensated.

Nielsen's chapter examines the ethics of experiments involving religion, focusing specifically on experiments in which subject beliefs are either the dependent or independent variable. Drawing on his experience with religious communities in the United States and the Middle East, he argues that religion is problematic as an independent or a dependent variable, given its powerful role in many subjects' lives and its unverifiable truth claims. He concludes that experiments with religion should be limited to measurement exercises—those in which an experiment is used to measure the degree of religiosity, not to manipulate it.

Morton and Rogers's chapter also examines the contextual challenges posed by religion. When treating subjects in standard laboratory economic games, subjects may perceive the treatments to be a form of gambling, which is prohibited by some religions. When subjects are asked to perform taboo acts, the potential consequences include considerable stress and angst for subjects as well as a possible backlash from the community against subjects, assistants, researchers, and perhaps the discipline more broadly. This example can also be labeled as an "easy" case, because the harm is clear and because there are other ways to get the research done without gambling. Morton and Rogers suggest practical solutions. For example, by recasting the game about another stochastic event common in everyday life—traffic patterns—one can avoid violating religious norms while still testing exactly the same hypotheses.

Perhaps the most important unresolved contextual question is that of doing research in dangerous and violent places. Scholars increasingly conduct research in environments where violence is a serious risk to scholars, assistants, and subjects. Existing regulations offer little guidance. The Common Rule defines research as "minimal risk" if it poses no more risk than would be "ordinarily encountered in daily life" (US Department of Health and Human Services 2015, 46.102.i). This guideline has at least two limitations. The first is that it says nothing about ethics or responsibility for research assistants, graduate students, or others working on a project—it only applies to subjects. Second, "daily life" does not clarify the appropriate standard for acceptable risk in dangerous environments. Daily risk could be determined by the subjects, assistants, or researchers' daily lives. Unfortunately, no clear consensus exists on what "ordinary risk" means, or whether or how we should manage research differently in dangerous contexts. This creates a great deal of ambiguity regarding scholars' responsibilities.

Driscoll's chapter explores two tensions between professional incentives, on the one hand, and the risk and ethics of fieldwork in violent countries. The first is that scholars, especially those starting their careers, may be rewarded for bigger and bolder interventions, sometimes at great risk to themselves, their assistants, or their subjects. A second tension is the decision to cooperate or conflict with an authoritarian regime. In the cooperative case, scholars may find themselves legitimizing and supporting oppressive states with their research. In cases where scholars' research is in conflict with the regime, they may find themselves, their assistants, or their subjects at great risk of violence. Driscoll argues that solutions to these tensions are very personal, and he calls for self-awareness and self-examination; he also reminds senior faculty of their important role in constraining ambition-induced risk. Some scholars will take serious risks—and given the importance of the research, perhaps they should.

The question of fieldwork and interventions in violent places is much broader than the ethics of experiments and is clearly critically important. There is real risk of a tragedy involving a research team or a subject, and these risks should not just be chalked up to part of graduate school and growing up, with an expectation that the fittest will survive. I offer three recommendations for conducting research in dangerous places. First, regarding the safety of individual scholars, young research-ers need to be able to make informed and self-aware decisions about their toler-ance for risk. This implies a thorough understanding of the context where they are working, the incentives of the discipline, and the risks of momentum.[3]

Second, when others are involved—assistants and subjects—scholars have an additional responsibility to prepare a risk management plan. Bateson (2015) pro-vides a model of how to develop and implement such a plan, based on her time as a Foreign Service Officer and researcher in Guatemala. Such a plan should attempt to identify the main risks, propose strategies for mitigating them, and include steps for responding to some tragic event—the kidnapping of an assistant, for example. It is tempting to outsource all these judgments to our local assistants and subjects, as they certainly know the context better than we do. But they may be erroneously trusting our judgment and implied protection when they follow our instructions. Certainly our assistants' input will be valuable, but we will bear responsibility for the project and its consequences.[4]

Third, successfully complying with the preceding two recommendations will require knowledge and training. Because not all departments will have in-house resources, knowledgeable senior faculty and our professional associations should provide leadership in offering training, workshops, and publications to support and mentor those new to fieldwork in violent systems. It is easy to imagine mul-tiple conferences and books on this topic.

19.2.2   Local Review

The second set of questions we examined were those of local review. When con-ducting research in other countries, should we seek approval of our design from foreign agencies or scholars? Both the rules and the institutions overseas vary greatly. Some countries have strict legal frameworks governing research by for-eign scholars and mandating an in-country ethical review. The nature of these institutions varies widely across countries; some are professional and competent institutions with straightforward review processes, others are corrupt and incom-petent organizations that seem to exist only to defend the incumbent regime or to extract rents from foreigners. Still other countries have no apparent rules or institutions. The case studies of this volume reflect this diversity. There was no institutionalized review process in Mexico, although new legislation and efforts by scholars there are creating procedures for review of foreign research proposals. The Brazilian regulations are well developed, but the institutions were unresponsive to attempts to navigate their process. The Chinese case seems designed to protect the regime, not the subjects, and is vague and generally unfriendly to political research. Other cases not examined in this volume provide different challenges.

In Malawi, running an experiment is straightforward but has a list of manageable but demanding requirements, including hiring local staff, mentorship and training, data sharing, possible co-authorship, and paying 10% of the project budget to their review committee to cover costs (Harawa 2013). In the case of Vietnam, one scholar told us that the procedure would be simple—if one were to request permission to conduct research, it would almost certainly be denied (Tran 2015). Perhaps the only thing these diverse cases have in common is that most foreigners conducting research do not comply with local review requirements and do not have any local review of their research.

Should political scientists attempt to comply with foreign review procedures? On this question, I expect a partial consensus among political scientists. The easy cases are those at the extremes—where local review is easy, or where it is impossible. When local review is fast and painless, there seems to be little disagreement that it is appropriate to comply. At the other extreme, if local review is impossible and simply a mechanism to protect an authoritarian regime, then there seems to be little expectation that scholars will attempt full compliance. In addition, there is agreement that *some* form of local review is always appropriate. If the formal rules seem impossible, one should at a minimum ask a qualified colleague based in the target country to examine your design and provide feedback before you proceed. This is an easy and valuable way to receive feedback on the appropriateness of your experiment and identify any harms or risks of which you may not be aware.

The difficult cases are those where local review is possible, but hard, slow, or expensive. There are at least three arguments against local review. One is that it will, at a minimum, delay or, in a worst-case scenario, prevent the research. A second argument against full compliance in difficult cases is that review at our home institutions provides adequate safeguards. Most scholars conducting experiments internationally will have completed a human subjects review at their home institution. These reviews may be more than adequate and provide sufficient protections for subjects overseas. Lastly, in many cases, our home IRBs do not require that we complete a local review, and there are minimal consequences for scholars and subjects associated with noncompliance.[5]

Even so, there are at least three reasons to attempt some form of local review. The first is that a local review may help scholars identify problems in their research design that need adjustment and adaptation to local contexts. One may not anticipate all the cultural, legal, or contextual problems that a local review could identify. As discussed above, risk of violence is one area where scholars may be poorly equipped to gauge the risk of their designs when applying them overseas, and local review could be extremely useful. The second reason is that local review offers some legal cover in the event that something does go wrong. This is not about human subjects, but about protecting scholars, their assistants, and the field as a whole. In some countries, research without approval is illegal, and a scandal involving illegal experiments might lead to a general reaction against political science experimentation. There may even be diplomatic consequences to conducting experiments illegally overseas using government resources.[6] And as discussed in Lü's chapter on China, while international scholars may face little risk, their local collaborators may face serious consequences when governments discover research projects that lack local review.[7]

The third reason to comply with local review rules is that doing so signals respect for the host nation's sovereignty. Conducting research illegally in a foreign nation requires an attitude of superiority and imperialism. Yet most scholars conducting overseas experiments are not complying with host countries' rules, and our field seems to have our own unwritten version of "don't ask, don't tell"—we won't ask if there are any local rules, and we won't tell anyone that we are there doing research. Other disciplines—both STEM and social sciences—have much stronger and clearer norms of respect for local authorities and would never condone or publish research that was conducted without the approval of the host nation. Such compliance is not surprising from medical research, given NIH rules and the risks associated with experimental drugs. But it is also common in other social sciences. For example, anthropology publications provide detailed discussions of how they obtained local review before beginning fieldwork. I suspect that the field will look back at the many political science studies conducted illegally in other countries with embarrassment. Until we change our norms, I can only hope that no political science research generates any international incidents.

Questions about local compliance clearly beg for more discussion. Most likely, solutions will be country-specific. I have two recommendations for moving forward. In the hard cases—where legitimate but arduous review procedures exist—we should test the waters of local review and attempt to comply. With some practice and experience, we may be able to streamline review in other countries and at the same time help establish good research practices there. The Mexican and Brazilian cases both appear to be examples where review procedures are improving and may not pose an excessive burden on future researchers.[8]

Second, contributors in this volume have offered several possible shortcuts that will allow scholars to complete the research without breaking foreign law. One suggestion is that scholars use international Internet surveys for which scholars technically are not "in-country," and thus one can argue that local rules should not apply. The second is that we collaborate with third parties—NGOs, political actors, or government agencies—who take responsibility for the randomization, with the scholar acting merely as a consultant or advisor.

19.2.3   Field Experiments

I predict that the third topic, the ethical challenges of field experiments, will be the most difficult for social scientists. The design advantages of these experiments are clear: They allow us to capture causal effects on behavior without the shortcomings of laboratories or survey experiments. In laboratories, subjects are in an artificial environment and know they are being closely watched. In surveys, we measure expressed opinion or intended action. Field experiments improve on both designs, because we can directly observe behavior without the pollution of Hawthorne and other measurement effects. But their real-world nature and the lack of informed consent are also the source of controversy.

The contributors to this volume examine some of the most critical questions and provide practical advice that can resolve many issues. Findley and Nielson focus on designs where researchers interact deceptively with unknowing subjects—pretending to be potential clients, for example. They acknowledge the harm in deception, and argue that scholars must justify this harm with the social benefit of the research. They demonstrate how deception may improve measurement, and they propose a half-double rule to help scholars assess whether deception can be justified.

The chapters in this volume by Zimmerman (Chapter 12) and Gubler and Selway (Chapter 11) examine field experiments that have political effects. Zimmerman focuses on information interventions during elections. She sees potential problems with these designs as having three sources: 1) the normative ambiguity of treatments, 2) the lack of informed consent, and 3) the possibility of an experiment affecting election outcomes. She proposes a set of best practices to minimize these problems, including careful identification of all parties potentially affected by such an intervention and creative strategies for seeking informed consent. Gubler and Selway argue that ethical considerations of political experiments should address three issues: 1) the representativeness of the results, 2) the impact on political power and resources, and 3) the impact on political identity. They also provide a series of practical questions to guide scholars' ethical assessments.

Hyde and Nickerson focus on the appropriate rules governing research conducted by third parties with scholarly participation. If a third party (NGO, business, or other actor) is conducting the research, then it is exempt from IRB examination and the results are "fresh data." Hyde and Nickerson provide guidelines for self-examination as to whether the research deserves review, and what form that review should take. They propose that scholars fully disclose the nature of their relationship with third-party organizations in any publications that result from those types of partnerships.

Malesky and Grose each focus on the ethics of research on public officials. Regulations in the United States exempt research using public officials and their appointees as subjects from IRB review (US Department of Health and Human Services 2015, 46.101.b.3.i).[9] We generally accept that members of the US Congress and other elected office holders in the United States are public officials. But does that give researchers carte blanche to intervene in all aspects in their personal and professional lives? Alternatively, are village chiefs in Ghana public officials, or do they deserve some protection? Malesky proposes criteria to help separate public officials from private citizens and discusses the potential harms associated with treating elites. Grose argues that the Common Rule is not a blank check for any intervention in public officials' lives, and proposes that research be limited to public sphere activity, excluding the subjects' private lives from exempted research. He defends research on elites in terms of impact—noting that typical constituency response experiments on Members of Congress constitute a minuscule portion of their constituent contacts. Unclear from his discussion, however, is whether these experiments would have excessive impact in environments where constituents have much less frequent contact with representatives.

19.2.3.1   Field Experiments, Harm, and Consent

I conclude the discussion of field experiments by considering what we have learned about these interventions and the sources of disagreement about their appropriateness. In this section, I will examine the nature of risk and harm in these studies. I will focus largely on experiments where private citizens are subjects and are not informed about the study and where scholars, not third-party actors, control the intervention. I thus exclude studies of public officials or public institutions. I also ignore cases where some other actor—a political party, an NGO, or a government agency—administers the treatment and the scholar is merely an observer or advisor. Most of my examples draw on electoral field experiments, but I will consider other examples as well.

I will note that many of the disagreements about these experiments reflect differences in the calculation of harm. In particular, defenders of these studies focus on the very low individual risk of treatments, while critics often focus on the potential aggregate or social effects. More fundamental, however, is the question of informed consent. If subjects were fully informed and consenting, the problems of aggregate harm would have much less traction. This suggests two recommendations: 1) we should avoid deception and unconsenting studies whenever possible and 2) when using deception or operating without consent, we should consider both individual and aggregate harms and use designs that minimize both. Consideration of harm here will reflect both pure ethical considerations as well as practical empirical perspectives—namely, the opinion of our subjects and affected bystanders.

I proceed in four steps. First, I examine how individual and aggregate harm are the source of much controversy regarding field experiments. Second, I argue that the more important question is that of consent, and I review the diversity of views on informed consent. Third, based on recent controversies I consider factors that interact with deception to make a study more or less problematic. Finally, I discuss the implications these issues have for the design of field experiments.

1. Minimal Individual Harm, Costly Aggregate Harm?

Consider first individual-level harm from electoral field experiments. These often study whether interventions increase participation (GOTV, or "get out the vote" messages) or affect vote choice (persuasion messages). Typical treatments include providing reminders to vote or information about candidates via mailers, phone calls with recorded messages or live messages, television or radio advertisements, text messages, or Facebook posts.[10]

In all these designs, the risk of harm to an individual seems trivial and well within any definition of minimal risk. A mailer, robocall, or text message are everyday occurrences that subjects regularly encounter. Clearly, physical risk is difficult to imagine—a paper cut or finger fatigue from "liking" a Facebook status update. Information treatments are also very unlikely to cause any psychological harm: Subjects regularly receive mailers, status updates, and robocalls. One might even argue that the treatments and/or outcomes are normatively valuable—that providing GOTV messages, providing factual information about candidates, or increasing turnout are normatively good for subjects and society.[11]

Other types of field experiments may have slightly more consequential treatments, but at the level of the individual also seem to place only small costs on subjects. In some experiments, researchers interact deceptively with subjects. Researchers might test for discrimination in employment by sending fake resumes to employers or test for bias in constituency service by making false requests to legislators. Scholars may also test faculty by sending emails requesting information about graduate programs, pretending to be prospective PhD students. These types of designs are useful when investigating behavior that has strong social or legal norms attached to it.

The form of deception here is what I refer to as "deception with implied benefit." More than just information about a candidate or a reminder to vote, the interaction implies a direct and tangible benefit to the subject. Recruiters believe they are finding a new candidate for a position, faculty think they are recruiting a potential student, politicians think they will earn some support for constituency service, and businesses think they might have a new customer. In reality, however, the student, job candidate, customer, and constituent simply do not exist. The deception suggests that the expected value of the interaction is positive for the subject, when in fact it is negative.[12]

Proponents of field experiments defend these types of studies by arguing that the individual cost is very low and far outweighed by the knowledge gained from the study. Subjects may spend a few minutes reviewing a resume or talking on the phone with someone they believe to be a prospective client. A legislator's intern might spend a few minutes printing a standard constituency response letter. For individual subjects, the harm and risk of harm are minimal. There are other job applicants that will not accept an offered position and there are other prospective customers that will ultimately decide not to make a purchase. These are normal in everyday public interaction. One can argue, however, that these time costs are not zero and that they deserve some consideration. I will consider that position shortly.

While proponents of field experiments note their minimal individual risk, critics often focus on possible aggregate or social harm. Aggregate harm might simply be the sum of individual harms or greater, especially if there are spillovers beyond the subject pool. For critics of electoral field experiments, total harm imposed by a large field experiment might exceed acceptable levels given impacts on subjects and bystanders.

Consider a study where a researcher submits fake resumes to would-be employers or requests for proposals to small businesses. In these designs, the individual cost may be small—just a few minutes—but the social cost could be large. Deceiving 5,000 subjects into spending 5 minutes on some task—reviewing resumes or requests for bids for services—requires a total of 25,000 minutes, or over two months of full-time employment.

In electoral field experiments, while the impact of a mailer on an individual subject's life is trivial, a large study with many subjects could affect which candidate or party wins the election, thereby affecting thousands, or millions of citizens, depending on the jurisdiction. The probability of this event is small, but worthy of some consideration, especially when running an electoral field experiment during a close race or when one's research budget is much larger than candidates' campaign budgets.

Further, even if the winner of an election is unaffected by an experiment, there may be downstream consequences of even small experimental impacts on vote share. In some countries, parties' and candidates' allocation of time for television advertising is a function of their vote share in past elections, so any electoral impact affects future media access. Similarly, changing a candidate's vote share impacts her ability to raise funding for future campaigns, and may also affect whether she is nominated or runs again in the future.[13] Given that elections are zero-sum events, this implies that any impact of an experiment on election outcomes, including small shifts in vote share, might be considered harm, as discussed in the Zimmerman and Gubler and Selway chapters.

There is something not quite right, however, about this line of argument. In a strict causal sense, many types of research could influence outcomes without being called harm. An influential book or even a compelling lecture might directly and indirectly affect an election outcome. Many scholars' research agendas and publications directly reflect their political commitments, interests, and desire to have an impact, yet these efforts are not considered unethical and any impacts are not considered harm. Why is "impact" acceptable in some cases but not others?

2. Deception Without Consent as a Necessary Condition for Controversy

The missing variable here is informed consent. Complaints about aggregate impact have little traction when subjects are informed and consenting. Suppose several thousand citizens volunteered to be part of a study in which they learned about elections. As a result of something they learned during the study, further suppose they decide to vote on election day, or to vote for a different candidate than the one they originally supported. It is difficult to imagine a justifiable complaint against such a study.[14]

This discussion suggests that the most important question we need to consider is not the broad impact of a study, but the lack of informed consent. Are we justified in treating subjects without any consent, and then having an impact on the real world? Scholars in the United States rely on the Common Rule to support the lack of informed consent. However, the Common Rule is a set of federal regulations—not a set of ethical guidelines. Informed consent is more prominent in the three foundational documents on human subjects research: the Belmont Report, the Declaration of Helsinki, and the Nuremberg Code.[15] These guidelines were largely directed toward medical studies and were written in response to abusive experiments. Yet even within medicine, their scope and applicability have been widely debated for decades (O'Neill 2003, Kristinsson 2009). Opinions range widely; some argue that any form of deceit is harm and should always be avoided (Wendler 1996). Others decry the obsession with informed consent as a "fetish" that is stifling research, and call for public bodies to grant consent on behalf of others (Koenig 2014).[16]

Political scientists are looking for deep first-principle answers to their questions—but the questions are the same ones that scholars in medical and psychological ethics have been debating for over fifty years. We could join them in their quest, but it is not clear that such an exercise would provide practical solutions any time in the near future. For these reasons, I propose a different strategy for assessing whether our deceptive field experiments are ethical or not. Instead of arguing about whether or not the treatment harms our subjects, we should assess what our subjects think of our studies. This approach of "empirical ethics" (Salloch, Schildmann and Vollmann 2012) has grown in the medical ethics literature and may help resolve enduring debates at a practical, if not philosophical, level.

Although we have little systematic empirical evidence on our subjects' thoughts, a number of controversies suggest that many subjects do not like to be deceived, even when treatments are clearly minimal risk. Widespread anger erupted in response to a Facebook emotion study in which positive posts were removed from subjects' feeds to test for an impact on emotion (Kramer, Guillory and Hancock 2014). The Montana election field experiment generated similar anger, albeit on a smaller scale. Other types of field experiments have generated similar responses when the deception is revealed. For example, a Columbia Business School professor, conducting an experiment on vendor response, sent complaint letters to New York restaurants. When restaurant owners and staff learned the letters were fabricated for a study, they were furious. Given the ultra-competitive nature of the New York restaurant market, the negative messages caused the owners and staff great distress (Kifner 2001). And while researchers may defend the benefits of these studies, it's clear that they also do not appreciate being on the other side of the randomization. Faculty have complained about being the subjects of experiments without informed consent. These typically involve emails that appear to be from prospective students, with some feature of the student or their request randomly assigned across faculty. In other cases, scholars have complained about replication dataset requests that they spent 30 or more minutes answering, only to learn that the request was part of a deceptive study.

The treatments in all these cases were minimal risk and caused no physical harm. The Facebook study, for example, had extremely small effects on users: "the result was that people produced an average of one fewer emotional word, per thousand words, over the following week" (Facebook Post 2014). Despite their staffs' concerns, the restaurants' business was unaffected because the experiment was a hoax. Faculty lost a few minutes to a deceptive email from a fake student. Regardless, in each case people strongly objected to the deception.

A preliminary conclusion is that treatments administered with deception and without informed consent can make people angry. This implies two ethical considerations of harm. The first type of harm is simply that of angering or upsetting subjects. This form of harm may result even when subjects have consented to the study. The second ethical problem is that, if subjects are upset, it implies that our cost-benefit analysis was inaccurate. Further, we have inappropriately violated subject autonomy, because subjects would have preferred not to be in the study yet were forced into it by our deception. One can imagine that benefit might still outweigh harm in some cases and justify the research. But in many cases, we should be seeking other designs.

There are also two secondary negative consequences to running deceptive field experiments. First, research relies on public trust. Making many people angry in a large field study neither generates a constructive research environment nor helps the public understand the value of research. Indeed, it may lead to more regulation and restrictions on legitimate and safe activities and decrease financial support for research. Second, one can imagine another risk to field experiments—litigation. Could a class action attorney lead a suit against universities that run large, deceptive studies? With 100,000 subjects, a modest judgment per subject could generate a reasonable living for an underemployed attorney. Some of these studies may even qualify as negligent misrepresentation or fraud. These risks might seem far-fetched, but the restaurants treated in the Columbia study pursued litigation. A New York court eventually ruled that this was an actionable case for claims of emotional distress and other harms (Crohan June 2014). The case was eventually settled out of court (Gajda 2010).

3. What Don't Subjects Like About Our Studies, and Does It Matter?

If our treatments are minimally intrusive, have noble goals, and are typical of subjects' everyday life, then why do subjects and citizens sometimes get very upset with our field experiments? The answer to this question both matters and does not matter. Why subjects are upset does not matter for our immediate course of action: If subjects are angry about being forced or tricked into a field experiment or about being affected by study spillovers, then we simply should not run the study. Their reasons for not wanting to participate are generally (though not always) irrelevant. Yet, the answer to this question is critically important for the future of the field. Understanding what aspects of our experiments are offensive will help us adapt our designs to avoid angering subjects. We know little about what our subjects think of our studies, and we need empirical research on this topic. But recent controversies and ensuing discussion about field experiments suggest some hypotheses about how citizens and subjects feel about our research.

The first and most important factor is that human beings do not like deceptive behavior, especially when it has questionable or difficult-to-appreciate benefits. Human beings expect others to behave sincerely and they do not like it when we intervene insincerely, even when the individual-level costs are "minimal risk."

This does not mean that human beings never tolerate experiments, even when we are not aware they are happening. We are constantly experimenting and being experimented on in all of our daily actions, including our social relations. Most of these we accept without question. We accept that businesses constantly experiment to learn about us—they relocate toothpaste and ice cream in stores to maximize profits. We accept that the Obama campaign randomizes emails to learn about donation-maximizing messages. We expect Walmart to maximize profits and politicians to maximize votes and donations. Crucially, in these cases, agents are interacting with us in sincere and understandable ways, and their manipulations are extremely minor, with low to no individual and social cost. We do not know that we are being experimented on, but the investigator is not deceiving us—our interactions with the store and with the campaign are both sincere.

In under-the-radar field experiments, interventions do not reflect a sincere desire to get a job, form a partnership, or persuade a voter. They are simply scholars' attempts to "mess with" employers or scholars or voters to see if we can make them do something. The real purpose of the interaction is to satisfy our curiosity, further our research agendas, and advance our careers. People do not appreciate being treated like guinea pigs without their permission for these purposes.

The extent of anger over deceptive experiments varies with the nature of the study and the magnitude of the intervention. Small studies that do not burden subjects and have minimal spillovers will cause less harm than large treatments that impose burdens and that could have larger spillovers. Complaints about controversial studies often mention size as a factor in whether or not the experiment was ethical. Larger studies imply more deception and a greater social cost. One implication is that while we may only consider individual harm when preparing our IRB application, subjects' evaluations of our studies rely both on individual and social harm.

Deception in election field experiments is particularly problematic, even when the individual and aggregate risks are small. One reason is that elections are generally considered sacred and high-stakes rituals, even in less-than-perfect democracies. Citizens may dislike the rough-and-tumble of campaigns and politics, but the process and the act of voting are essential parts of identities and understandings of representation. Deceptive interventions in these sacred rituals seem profane and offensive to many. This is especially the case because the normative consequences of affecting election outcomes are ambiguous at best and because many political beliefs rest on unverifiable truth claims—similar to religious beliefs.

4. Recommendations for Field Experiments

This discussion suggests a way forward for field experiments. Most obviously, we should avoid deception whenever possible, and also strive for informed consent in every study. As we have learned, treatments that we believe have minimal risk may still be perceived as very harmful by subjects when administered with deception and without consent. As subjects do not like these designs, we should avoid them whenever possible. If fully informed consent is not possible, there may be other forms of consent we can use. One possibility is the use of panels of subjects who consent to a certain number of interventions in their lives and are compensated for their research participation. Faculty could volunteer to be on experimental panels where some of their interactions will be part of research studies. We already know that some of the emails we receive are fake and part of studies, so it is unlikely that the measurement problems are as large as one might imagine.

If the research question demands a field experiment without informed consent, do some due diligence. Justify the lack of informed consent by showing that an existing literature has exhausted the gains from alternative designs, leaving critical questions that require a surreptitious field experiment. Understand that you are running an experiment that your subjects might not have joined willingly. Acknowledge the potential individual and aggregate harm, and justify the choice in terms of the potential payoffs from your research. In so doing, I refer not to the rhetorical ballet that one might perform to convince an IRB to approve a study, but to honest self-examination as to the social value of the knowledge your research might produce.

Consider design features for field experiments that help make them more palatable to your subjects and community. In particular, we can minimize controversy with some simple norms: Do good, tread lightly, confess, and compensate. The first, "do good," means making sure that the treatment and dependent variable are normatively defensible at an individual and aggregate level. If subjects see the endeavor as low-burden with positive social consequences, this will reduce the probability of harm with the deception. In electoral field experiments, increasing turnout can usually be defended as normatively valuable, as long as treatments are not distributed with political bias. Information provision about candidates may be defensible. Persuasion messages are often the least defensible. A similar logic may be applied to other topics. However, the appropriateness of any one of these treatments will vary across context.

Part of doing good also means that if your experiment provides information about candidates, tell the whole truth. Make sure that the information you provide is factually accurate, balanced, and complete. Factually accurate but incomplete information can be unethically deceptive. For example, in one field experiment, scholars reminded voters that one candidate had been accused of crimes—without mentioning that charges had been dismissed. In another, the candidates' ideologies were compared on a graphical scale—but without confidence intervals or explanation as to whether the differences between candidates were significant.

Second, tread lightly. This implies minimizing the aggregate social costs and minimizing the amount of deception. An obvious first step is to conduct a power analysis and use the smallest possible sample size. If running an election field experiment, treading lightly also implies choosing an election where polling and history suggest that your treatment, in the worst-case scenario, will not affect the outcome. Further, don't be the biggest fish in the sea: For election studies, do not outspend or out-campaign the real candidates. One of the Montana judicial candidates raised about $6,000. The researchers in that study spent an estimated five to ten times that amount (National Institute on Money in State Politics 2014).

Third, confess. After the experiment, provide some form of debriefing to your subjects. If you had the resources to contact them once, you probably can find a way to contact them twice. Send information about the study, their role in it, and provisions for protecting their anonymity. Give them a chance to opt out, if appropriate. If your unit of analysis is larger—say, villages or precincts—without any contact with individuals, issue a press release, hold a community meeting, or otherwise inform your subjects.[17] Although infrequently employed, this is part of the Common Rule. The very same provision of the Common Rule that gives US scholars the freedom to skip informed consent also states, "(4) Whenever appropriate, the subjects will be provided with additional pertinent information after participation" (US Department of Health and Human Services 2015, CFR46.116.d.4).

Post-study debriefing has several benefits. One is that it provides a check on our career incentives. Knowing that we will be accountable to our subjects should temper some of the incentives provided by our curiosity and our ambition. Debriefing also provides an important opportunity for learning about how subjects perceive these studies. And clear explanation of our research may help to increase public trust and understanding of what we are doing and why it is valuable.[18]

Fourth, compensate. Pay your subjects for their time, directly or indirectly. When there is a minimal intervention—for example, just a piece of mail—we should provide some standard amount, perhaps $5 per subject. When our treatment is more burdensome, we should pay them at least the greater of our or their standard rate. For example, suppose a faculty member making $100,000 is running an experiment using deception in which subjects spend an estimated 15 minutes responding to an inquiry. That implies paying each subject at least $12, or more if subjects' annual income exceeds that of the researcher.[19] Compensation could be paid directly to subjects, as part of a debriefing discussed above. When it is impossible to identify individual subjects, compensation could be paid into some fund that provides public goods to the subjects. This could be an aid organization, a local government, or a local school or non-profit; the best choice will be a function of the setting and nature of the study.

Compensation has two advantages. One is that it shows respect for subjects and acknowledges the value of their time—time that we are effectively stealing when we deceive them into spending time on our task. The second is that it puts a natural constraint on the size of our projects, just as a prior distribution may keep a parameter estimate from heading off to infinity. Technology has made massive field experiments increasingly feasible and inexpensive. A norm of compensation will show some respect for our subjects and will also help reign in unnecessary N-maximization.

I conclude this section with some backpedalling. First, there is an exception to every rule. No doubt there will be contexts and settings in which aggressive interventions without any informed consent are entirely appropriate, whether or not subjects consider them harm. Perhaps there is a political system in which candidates and elites might never share any substantive information about policies. Voters may be grateful to receive the same informational treatments that might generate controversy in the United States. When one candidate has a history of corruption or worse, information provision or even attack messages might be normatively valuable. Second, I have based much of my argument on the assumption that subjects do not like being included in many studies without permission. Anecdotally, this seems to be the case, but representative data might prove me wrong. Empirical evidence to explore these questions is needed. Lastly, much more important than my thoughts, the broader community must continue to discuss these issues: The immediate, spillover, and downstream consequences of field experiments demand that we explore their ethics deeply and continue to do so.

19.3 Conclusion

This volume sought to identify and explore the most important emerging ethical issues for political science experiments. Certainly there are many other issues confronting researchers that were not addressed herein: deception in laboratory experiments, privacy, and big data, for example. But the ethical challenges of new types of interaction with human subjects through experimentation pose new and critical challenges. The goal here was not to have the last word, but to start a broader dialogue that will help us understand the stakes and the controversies and work toward norms and practices appropriate for a new era. Many of these conversations have started—at workshops and conferences, and with panels on ethics appearing at our major conferences.

Many of these conversations eventually turn to the idea of creating new constraints to prevent unwanted outcomes. How can we prevent "X" from happening? The answer is that we do not need major changes or new authoritarian institutions. The chapters by Zechmeister and Seligson demonstrate the limitations of regulation for solving ethical problems and protecting human subjects. Many IRBs are uninformed about the risks and non-risks associated with our research. Outsourcing difficult ethical judgments to a bureaucracy is not a solution and does not absolve scholars of responsibility for their research. Indeed, a rare point of consensus among scholars with whom I have discussed these topics is that we do not need more IRB oversight. Instead, scholars need to accept and retain ownership of the ethics of their research.

As political science transitions toward a normal science (Kuhn 1970), we can learn from other disciplines that have already confronted similar challenges. The lessons from these other cases are that modest changes in the way we operate as a profession should provide significant protections for subjects, researchers, and the field. Three minor changes that should help us adapt are norm development, new journal rules, and research on our profession and subjects.

Political science needs to promote norms by revising education and guidelines in the area of ethics. Other research disciplines that have regular interaction with human subjects have well-developed ethics training programs, especially for graduate students. Zechmeister's chapter reports on the standards for the field of psychology. Their leading professional associations have extensive codes of conduct for research, and standard methods training includes in-depth examination of ethical issues. Political science falls far behind this standard. APSA's ethics guide has a few vague sentences on human subjects (American Political Science Association 2012). My training in human subjects and ethics—which I understand was typical for political science—involved a lengthy online course exploring the history of regulation of research. As one example, Nestor and Phillips (2015) compared required coursework in top political science and psychology programs by examining departmental websites. They found that 90% of psychology departments surveyed had ethics as part of their core curriculum. In contrast, in political science, only one of the programs even mentioned ethics as part of a required course.[20]

As our discipline evolves toward normal science, we need more normal science practices. This means that as part of students' professionalization, they need to know more than basic trivia about the Belmont Report and the Nuremberg Code. They (and we) need training in the kinds of difficult issues unique to political science, with appropriate case studies and discussion. Other fields' professional associations have taken leading roles in addressing these challenges, with ethical guidelines for members that establish best practices. As a first step, our professional associations should provide leadership in proposing guidelines for human subjects research.

Changing the editorial policies of our journals can also generate greater adherence to ethical standards. One standard practice in other disciplines is that certification of IRB approval is a condition for publication. This is a minor but important institutional change. Reports suggest that a recent controversial case may not have had full IRB approval. Knowing that one must provide a certification will discourage scholars from skipping the review process and may improve their designs. At a minimum, it will provide more legal cover. The burdens to journals seem modest and the payoffs potentially significant.

Requiring IRB certification for publication is standard practice in other fields. Nestor and Phillips (2015) surveyed psychology and medical journals, and found that every journal required compliance with ethical standards. For psychology journals, this meant that every journal required authors to sign a form certifying that they complied with IRB, informed consent, compensation, and debriefing rules. Medical journals have similar standards. Nestor and Phillips's 2015 survey of medical articles found that every article fully complied with certification rules.

In political science, this practice is rarely adopted. Nestor and Phillips (2015) report that of political science journals surveyed, only three have any mention of IRB certification.[21] This is clearly an area where there is room for progress.

More than just footnoting an IRB procedure number, we should also acquire a habit of discussing ethical issues in publications, just as we discuss research design trade-offs. Anthropology articles regularly include discussions of the ethical trade-offs in their research and explain the decisions that they made. Political science should acquire the same norm. Doing so will force self-engagement and reflection on the ethics of our research, help build norms and guidelines for the field and for future research, and make these issues part of the public research debate.

I will offer one additional suggestion: We should archive IRB applications (as long as there are no privacy or security risks), just as some journals archive datasets. This would have several advantages. It would allow scholars to compare others' assessments of risk/benefit ratios, as part of an ongoing dialogue and consensus development. It could also provide ammunition when dealing with unreasonable IRBs that do not recognize the benefits or low risks of a proposed experiment. And it would encourage transparency and full disclosure in dealings with IRBs. This also imposes a small burden—especially for those journals that already have data archiving. The same IT infrastructure currently being used for data could also be used to archive IRB applications.

A third step is research on human subjects and ethics in political science. This is standard practice in psychology, medicine, and other fields that have regular interaction with human subjects. Scholars in those fields regularly report on difficult cases and how they adapted research designs, as well as on subjects' reactions to their studies. In political science, we know little about what our subjects think, especially in the case of field experiments where subjects are never informed that they are part of a study. In the few cases where subjects have discovered that they are in a surreptitious study, they do not seem to like it very much—but we do not have representative samples of subjects to gauge how widespread these opinions are. One idea would be to regularly debrief all or a sample of subjects and ask them what they thought of the study, if it made them upset, and whether they would voluntarily participate in such a study in the future. We also need surveys of scholars' opinions and more journal articles discussing designs that worked or failed.

Research on ethics also implies regular conference panels on ethics and publications on these questions. One benefit to publishing studies of our difficult cases is that they may provide guidance for future scholars and may help us develop norms and frameworks that can be applied to new situations. Building a consensus on practices from first ethical principles is difficult and unlikely to succeed in this millennium. But building a set of cases that we can look to for examples and comparisons could, over time, help us converge toward a common understanding about how we should conduct research.[22] Unfortunately, although we critically evaluate research design, data analysis, and even literature review framing, we are hesitant to discuss and criticize ethics. This is probably because talking about ethics implies some moral judgment of the researcher. But we need to acquire a norm of doing our best and accepting criticism—just as we do with research designs and data analysis.

I conclude with an unfair, but perhaps instructive, comparison. John Charles Cutler's obituary describes a career and a life to which many of us aspire. He was a respected scholar with a prestigious position at a good university. He was admired for his research and leadership. On his passing, a speaker series was named in his honor, and his colleagues recalled him working "tirelessly" to provide health care services to those who needed them (Ackerman 2003).

Of course, there were a few blemishes on his record. One involved a field experiment in Guatemala, where subjects were deliberately and illegally infected with syphilis without their consent. The subjects were never told they were ill and the disease was allowed to spread through their families for decades. His next assignment involved an observational study in Tuskegee, Alabama, where subjects were told they were being treated for "bad blood," when in fact they had syphilis. The doctors involved did not offer readily available treatment or even tell the subjects what the disease was, so that they could observe the effects of the disease. These studies, of course, are now considered two of the most infamous cases of subject abuse in US medical research.

Cutler's research has many of the features common in our designs today: deception, a lack of informed consent, significant spillovers into the broader community, illegal activities, and no local review. Further, there was clear awareness that the Guatemala study could not be done in the United States. Of course, the harm inflicted by the Guatemala and Tuskegee studies was immeasurably greater than in any of our experiments, at least so far.

What's most illustrative and useful for us is how Cutler responded to criticism. In an interview in 1993, he strongly defended the research in terms of the science: "It was important that they were supposedly untreated, and it would be undesirable to go ahead and use large amounts of penicillin to treat the disease, because you'd interfere with the study" (Strait 1993).

The lesson for all scientists is to be aware of the natural conflict of interest that we all face between ethics, on the one hand, and the combined forces of our curiosity, our career ambitions, and our research, on the other. Doing research carefully, with more respect for your subjects and with more consideration of consequences, will conflict with all of these goals. It will make research harder, will slow down your career, and will restrict your ability to ask questions. It is easy for us to construct convincing narratives about the merit and propriety of our work. Let's try to always be honest with ourselves about what we are doing, and be careful out there.

Notes

1 Additional flyers were sent to California and New Hampshire subjects.
2 Senator Tessler of Montana called the experiment "voter manipulation"(Dennison 2014). Some political scientists were also critical, calling the study "a lapse in judgement," "political science malpractice," "improper and unethical" (Scott 2014).
3 Bateson notes that once fieldwork has started, if a security situation deteriorates gradually, scholars are reluctant to pull the plug given sunk costs, and may gradually find themselves well beyond their risk tolerance (Bateson 2015).
4 For her dissertation fieldwork, Bateson implemented an elaborate risk management plan that included extensive pre-trip research on security, preparations for contact with vigilante and other irregular security forces, a budget for post-trauma counseling for her assistants, daily security protocols, and cues for abandoning the project.

She notes particularly the risk of momentum—once in the field with sunk costs, it is easy to rationalize increasing risk exposure rather than pull the plug on a project. Her solution was a set of benchmarks that would terminate part or all of the research. Bateson's model would not work for every situation. Some scholars might not have the resources for all security provisions. In other cases, the research might demand greater risk-taking and integration with a community, and a scholar might be willing to accept those risks.

5 Merolla and Madrid's chapter in this volume shows that there are few institutional incentives for local review and very few scholars seem to attempt it.

6 Thanks to an anonymous reviewer of this volume for pointing this out.

7 Recently, a research assistant in Tajikistan was imprisoned by the regime and charged with High Treason while working on a research projects for the University of Exeter. The assistant was a PhD student in Canada, but also a Tajikistani citizen.

8 See the Aguilar (Chapter 9) and the Cunow and Desposato (Chapter 8) chapters in this volume.

9 This exemption may not exist, of course, in other countries.

10 This literature is large. Examples include Arceneaux, Kousser and Mullin (2012), Bond et al. (2012), Gerber and Green (2000, 2001), Green, Gerber and Nickerson (2003), Green (2004), Gerber, Green and Larimer (2008), Arceneaux (2007), Cardy (2005), Clinton and Lapinski (2004), Green and Vavreck (2006), Hansen and Kosiara-Pedersen (2014), Nickerson (2005), Nickerson, Friedrichs and King (2006), Niven (2006), and Panagopoulos (2008).

11 Of course, there are always exceptions, and one can imagine environments where this is not the case. For example, in some contexts, voting might be dangerous and changing one's political allegiance very costly, so a treatment might be encouraging people to engage in risky behavior, which seems inappropriate. One might also argue, as Zimmerman's chapter points out, that because an individual's vote has a low probability of affecting an outcome, when we encourage people to participate, we are encouraging them to waste their time.

12 The expected and realized payoff for the subject are both negative, because the subject expends some cost but the benefit is guaranteed to be zero.

13 Thanks to Ken Sherill for discussing this point with me based on his experience in local party politics.

14 Teele (2014) examines the question of field experiments through the lens of the Belmont Report, and finds that they potentially violate all three principles embodied therein: respect, beneficence, and justice. I largely agree with her arguments, with two exceptions. The first is that the value of the research should be balanced against the harm caused by a lack of consent. That harm should be at least partly measured through subjects' own attitudes about the study. Second, I would argue that the questions of justice and beneficence are often secondary to the questions of respect for persons and informed consent, especially in field experiments.

15 Here are key passages from each of the three documents: "Respect for persons requires that subjects, to the degree that they are capable, be given the opportunity to choose what shall or shall not happen to them. This opportunity is provided when adequate standards for informed consent are satisfied" (Belmont Report, The National Commission for the Protection of Human Subjects of Biomedical and Behavioral Research 1979). The Declaration of Helsinki (2008 [1964]) states that "no individual capable of giving informed consent may be enrolled in a research study unless he or she freely agrees." The Nuremberg Code (1947) declares, "The voluntary consent of the human subject is absolutely essential." See Teele (2014) for a nice discussion of the relationship between respect for subjects' autonomy and informed consent, focusing on the Belmont Report.

16 Recently, even medical studies have implemented field experiments without informed consent in very limited settings, involving subjects with life-threatening conditions who are not able to provide informed consent, where treatments have been investigated to the extent possible using non-human subjects, and where there are clear potential benefits. Practically, these have been designed for situations including emergency room procedures where subjects are unconscious, there is not enough time for a careful and judicious informed consent, there is uncertainty as to the best practice, and there are significant possible improvements in medical care. These changes have been controversial and are not universally accepted. In other words, there are no easy answers to questions about research without informed consent.

17 Zimmerman's chapter has several suggestions on how to communicate with subjects in these types of cases.

18 It does seem that part of the anger against these projects reflects misunderstanding. Online discussions about the Montana study alleged right-wing conspiracies to intervene in elections.

19 The figure of 12 dollars is calculated as follows: 100,000 dollars per year divided by 52 weeks per year divided by 40 hours per week divided by 60 minutes per hour * 15 minutes per subject = 12 dollars per subject.

20 Some programs may have ethics training as topics within courses, but not list ethics in the course description.

21 The APSR "may require" IRB certification, the *Journal of Experimental Political Science* (*JEPS*) recommends reporting IRB certification, and only *Political Behavior* asks authors to include a statement on IRB approval. Since the time of their survey, *JEPS* has revised its procedures to require IRB certification or a reasonable substitute (*The Journal of Experimental Political Science* 2015).

22 Thanks to Matthew Hitt for this suggestion.

LIST OF CONTRIBUTORS

Rosario Aguilar
Assistant Professor, División de Estudios Polìticos, Centro de Investigación y Docencia Económicas

Saul Cunow
Senior Research Manager, Analyst Institute

Scott W. Desposato
Associate Professor, University of California, San Diego and the University of Zurich

Kim Yi Dionne
Five College Assistant Professor, Smith College

Jesse Driscoll
Assistant Professor of Political Science (IR/PS), University of California, San Diego

Michael Findley
Associate Professor of Government, University of Texas at Austin

Christian R. Grose
Associate Professor, University of Southern California

Joshua R. Gubler
Assistant Professor, Brigham Young University

Augustine Harawa
Senior Research Manager, Invest in Knowledge Initiative–Malawi

Hastings Honde
Research Manager, Invest in Knowledge Initiative–Malawi

Susan D. Hyde
Associate Professor, Political Science & Jackson Institute for Global Affairs, Yale University

John Ishiyama
Professor, Department of Political Science, University of North Texas

Xiaobo Lü
Assistant Professor, Department of Government, University of Texas at Austin

Raul Madrid Jr.
PhD Candidate, Claremont Graduate University

Edmund J. Malesky
Associate Professor, Duke University

Jennifer L. Merolla
Associate Professor, Claremont Graduate School

William Mishler
Professor, School of Government and Public Policy, University of Arizona

Rebecca Morton
Editor, *The Journal of Experimental Political Science*; Professor, New York University

David W. Nickerson
Associate Professor, Temple University

Daniel Nielson
Professor & Associate Chair of Political Science, Brigham Young University

Richard A. Nielsen
Assistant Professor, Massachusetts Institute of Technology

Jonathan Rogers
Visiting Assistant Research Professor in the Social Science Experimental Laboratory, NYU Abu Dhabi

Mitchell A. Seligson
Professor of Political Science and Professor of Sociology, Vanderbilt University

Joel S. Selway
Assistant Professor, Brigham Young University

Rick K. Wilson
Professor, Department of Political Science, Rice University

Elizabeth J. Zechmeister
Associate Professor, Vanderbilt University

Brigitte Zimmerman
Assistant Professor, University of North Carolina, Chapel Hill

REFERENCES

Ackerman, Jan. 2003. "Obituary: John Charles Cutler/Pioneer in preventing sexual diseases." February 12. http://old.post-gazette.com (accessed June 2014).

Adams, Jimi, Philip Anglewicz, Stephane Helleringer, Christopher Manyamba, James Mwera, Georges Reniers and Susan Watkins. 2013. "Identifying Elusive and Eager Respondents in Longitudinal Data Collection." Unpublished working paper.

Agger, Robert E., Miroslav Disman, Zdravko Mlinar and Vladimir Sultanovic. 1970. "Education, General Personal Orientations, and Community Involvement: A Cross-National Research Project." *Comparative Political Studies* 3(1):90–116.

Aguilar, Rosario. 2009. "The Political Consequences of Prejudice Among Mexicans and Mexican Americans." PhD thesis. University of Michigan.

Aguilar, Rosario, Saul Cunow and Scott Desposato. Forthcoming. "Choice Set, Gender, and Candidate Choice in Brazil." *Electoral Studies*.

Aguilar, Rosario, Saul Cunow, Scott Desposato and Leonardo Barone. 2015. "Ballot Structure, Candidate Race, and Vote Choice in Brazil." *Latin American Research Review* 50(3): 175–202.

Ahmed, Ali M., Lina Andersson and Mats Hammarstedt. 2008. "Are Lesbians Discriminated Against in the Rental Housing Market? Evidence from a Correspondence Testing Experiment." *Journal of Housing Economics* 17(3):234–238.

Ahmed, Ali M. and Mats Hammarstedt. 2008. "Discrimination in the Rental Housing Market: A Field Experiment on the Internet." *Journal of Urban Economics* 64(2):362–372.

Akay, Alpaslan, Goekhan Karabulut and Peter Martinsson. 2013. "The Effect of Religiosity and Religious Festivals on Positional Concerns—An Experimental Investigation of Ramadan." *Applied Economics* 45(27):3914–3921.

American Association of University Professors. 2006. *Research on Human Subjects: Academic Freedom and the Institutional Review Board.* Washington, DC: Author.

American Political Science Association. 2012. "A Guide to Professional Ethics in Political Science, Second Edition." *APSA Committee on Professional Ethics, Rights and Freedoms* pp. 1–30. http://www.apsanet.org/Files/Publications/APSAEthicsGuide2012.pdf (accessed March 5, 2015).

American Psychological Association. 2002. "Ethical Principles of Psychologists and Code of Conduct." *American Psychologist* 57:1–16.

Anderson, Lisa, Roland Fryer and Charles Holt. 2006. "Discrimination: Experimental Evidence from Psychology and Economics." *Handbook on Economics of Discrimination* pp. 97–115 William M. Rodgers III, Editor. Edward Elgar Publishing, Northampton.

Arceneaux, Kevin. 2007. "I'm Asking for Your Support: The Effects of Personally Delivered Campaign Messages on Voting Decisions and Opinion Formation." *Quarterly Journal of Political Science* 2(1):43–65.

Arceneaux, Kevin, Thad Kousser and Megan Mullin. 2012. "Get out the vote-by-mail? A randomized field experiment testing the effect of mobilization in traditional and vote-by-mail precincts." *Political Research Quarterly* 65(4):882–894.

Aronson, Elliot and Judson Mills. 1959. "The Effect of Severity of Initiation on Liking for a Group." *The Journal of Abnormal and Social Psychology* 59(2):177–181.

Attanasio, Orazio P., Costas Meghir and A. N. A. Santiago. 2012. "Education Choices in Mexico: Using a Structural Model and a Randomized Experiment to Evaluate PRO-GRESA." *The Review of Economic Studies* 79(1):37–66.

Augenblick, Ned, Jesse M. Cunha, Ernesto Dal Bo and Justin M. Rao. N.d. "The Economics of Faith: Using an Apocalyptic Prophecy to Elicit Religious Beliefs in the Field." http://faculty.haas.berkeley.edu/ned/WaitingForTheEnd.pdf (accessed April 23, 2013).

Baird, Sarah J., Craig McIntosh and Berk Ozler. 2011. "Cash or Condition? Evidence from a Cash Transfer Experiment." *Quarterly Journal of Economics* 126:1709–1753.

Baird, Sarah J., Ephraim Chirwa, Craig McIntosh and Berk Ozler. 2010. "The Short-Term Impacts of a Schooling Conditional Cash Transfer Program on the Sexual Behavior of Young Women." *Health Economics* 19(S1):55–68.

Baird, Sarah J., Richard S. Garfein, Craig McIntosh and Berk Ozler. 2012. "Effect of a Cash Transfer Programme for Schooling on Prevalence of HIV and Herpes Simplex Type 2 in Malawi: A Cluster Randomised Trial." *The Lancet* 379(9823):1320–1329.

Bakow, Ryan, Alex Egbert, Michael Findley, Daniel Nielson and Brian Reed. 2013. "A Field Experiment on Opportunism Among Non-Governmental Organizations." Typescript.

Baldwin, Kate. 2013. "Why Vote with the Chief? Political Connections and Public Goods Provision in Zambia." *American Journal of Political Science* 57(4):794–809.

Banerjee, Abhijit, Donald Green, Jennifer Green and Rohini Pande. 2010. "Can Voters be Primed to Choose Better Legislators? Experimental Evidence from Rural India." Presented at the Political Economics Seminar, Stanford University.

Banerjee, Abhijit V., Selvan Kumar, Rohini Pande and Felix Su. 2011. "Do Informed Voters Make Better Choices? Experimental Evidence from Urban India." Working paper, November 11.

Barnes, Jeb. 2004. *Overruled? Legislative Overrides, Pluralism, and Contemporary Court-Congress Relations*. Stanford University Press.

Bateson, Regina. 2015. "Risk Management During Field Research." Working Paper.

Batson, C. Daniel. 1977. "Experimentation in Psychology of Religion: An Impossible Dream." *Journal for the Scientific Study of Religion* 16(4):413–418.

Batson, C. Daniel. 1979. "Experimentation in Psychology of Religion: Living with or in a Dream?" *Journal for the Scientific Study of Religion* 18(1):90–93.

Baumrind, Diana. 1979. "IRBs and Social Science Research: The Costs of Deception." *IRB: Ethics and Human Research* 6:1–4.

Becker, Gordon M., Morris H. De Groot and Jacob Marschak. 1964. "Measuring Utility by a Single-Response Sequential Method." *Behavioral Science* 9(3):226–232.

Behrman, Jere R, Piyali Sengupta and Petra Todd. 2005. "Progressing Through PRO-GRESA: An Impact Assessment of a School Subsidy Experiment in Rural Mexico." *Economic Development and Cultural Change* 54(1):237–275.

Bergan, Daniel E. 2009. "Does Grassroots Lobbying Work? A Field Experiment Measuring the Effects of an E-Mail Lobbying Campaign on Legislative Behavior." *American Politics Research* 37(2):327–352.

Berns, Gregory, Emily Bell, C. Monica Capra, Michael J. Prietula, Sara Moore, Brittany Anderson, Jeremy Ginges and Scott Atran. 2012. "The Price of Your Soul: Neural Evidence for the Non-Utilitarian Representation of Sacred Values." *Philosophical Transactions of the Royal Society* 367(1589):754–762.

Bertrand, Marianne and Sendhil Mullainathan. 2004. "Are Emily and Greg More Employable than Lakisha and Jamal? A Field Experiment on Labor Market Discrimination." *American Economic Review* 94(4):991–1013.

Besley, Timothy, Rohini Pande and Vijayendra Rao. 2012. "Just Rewards? Local Politics and Public Resource Allocation in South India." *World Bank Economic Review* 26(2):191–216.

Bhat, S.B. and T.T. Hegde. 2006. "Ethical International Research on Human Subjects Research in the Absence of Local Institutional Review Boards." *Journal of Medical Ethics* 32(9):535–536.

Björkman, Martina and Jakob Svensson. 2009. "Power to the People: Evidence from a Randomized Field Experiment on Community-Based Monitoring in Uganda." *The Quarterly Journal of Economics* 124(2):735–769.

Blair, Graeme, C. Christine Fair, Neil Malhotra and Jacob N. Shapiro. 2013. "Poverty and Support for Militant Politics: Evidence from Pakistan." *American Journal of Political Science* 57(1):30–48.

Blattman, Christopher. 2009. "From Violence to Voting: War and Political Participation in Uganda." *American Political Science Review* 103(2):231–247.

Boas, Taylor C. 2012. "Vote for Pastor Paulo: Religious Ballot Names as Heuristics in Brazil." Paper Presented at the International Congress of the Latin American Studies Association.

Bohnet, Iris, Benedikt Herrmann and Richard Zeckhauser. 2010. "Trust and the Reference Points for Trustworthiness in Gulf and Western Countries." *The Quarterly Journal of Economics* 125(2):811–828.

Bond, Robert M, Christopher J. Fariss, Jason J. Jones, Adam D.I. Kramer, Cameron Marlow, Jaime E. Settle and James H. Fowler. 2012. "A 61-Million-Person Experiment in Social Influence and Political Mobilization." *Nature* 489(7415):295–298.

Bosch, Mariano, M. Angeles Carnero and Lidia Farre. 2010. "Information and Discrimination in the Rental Housing Market: Evidence From a Field Experiment." *Regional Science and Urban Economics* 40(1):11–19.

Bositis, David A. and Douglas Steinel. 1987. "A Synoptic History and Typology of Experimental Research in Political Science." *Political Behavior* 9(3):263–284.

Bossuroy, Thomas and Joel Selway. 2011. "Cross-Cutting Cleavages, Discrimination and Inter-Personal Financial Transfers—A Lab Experiment in Chennai, India." APSA 2011 Annual Meeting Paper.

Brady, Henry E. 2000. "Contributions of Survey Research to Political Science." *PS: Political Science & Politics* 33(1):47–58.

Brewer, Marilynn B. 2000. "Research Design and Issues of Validity." *Handbook of Research Methods in Social and Personality Psychology* pp. 3–16. Editors, Harry T. Reis and Charles M. Judd. Cambridge University Press, New York.

Brigham, Matthew, Michael Findley, William Matthias, Chase Petrey and Daniel Nielson. 2013. "Aversion to Learning in Development? A Global Field Experiment on Microfinance Institutions." Typescript.

Broockman, David E. 2013. "Black Politicians Are More Intrinsically Motivated to Advance Blacks' Interests: A Field Experiment Manipulating Political Incentives." *American Journal of Political Science* 57(3):521–536.

Burtless, Gary and Larry L. Orr. 1986. "Are Classical Experiments Needed for Manpower Policy." *Journal of Human Resources* 21(4):606–639.

Butler, Daniel M. 2014. *Representing the Advantaged: How Politicians Reinforce Inequality*. New York: Cambridge University Press.

Butler, Daniel M. and David E. Broockman. 2011. "Do Politicians Racially Discriminate Against Constituents? A Field Experiment on State Legislators." *American Journal of Political Science* 55(3):463–477.

Butler, Daniel M. and David W. Nickerson. 2011. "Can Learning Constituency Opinion Affect How Legislators Vote? Results from a Field Experiment." *Quarterly Journal of Political Science* 6(1):55–83.

Cammack, Diana. 2012. "Malawi in Crisis, 2011–12." *Review of African Political Economy* 39(132):375–388.

Campbell, David, John Green and Geoffrey Layman. 2011. "The Party Faithful: Partisan Images, Candidate Religion, and the Electoral Impact of Party Identification." *American Journal of Political Science* 55(1):42–58.

Cardy, Emily Arthur. 2005. "An Experimental Field Study of the GOTV and Persuasion Effects of Partisan Direct Mail and Phone Calls." *The Annals of the American Academy of Political and Social Science* 601(1):28–40.

Carlson, Allen, Mary E. Gallagher, Kenneth Lieberthal and Manion Melanie. 2010. *Contemporary Chinese Politics: New Sources, Methods, and Field Strategies*. New York: Cambridge University Press.

Carpusor, Adrian G. and William E. Loges. 2006. "Rental Discrimination and Ethnicity in Names." *Journal of Applied Social Psychology* 36(4):934–952.

Chong, Alberto, Ana De La O, Dean Karlan and Leonard Wantchekon. 2010. "Information Dissemination and Local Governments' Electoral Returns, Evidence from a Field Experiment in Mexico." Presented at the Annual Meeting of the American Political Science Association, Seattle.

Chong, Alberto, Ana De La O, Dean Karlan and Leonard Wantchekon. 2011. "Looking Beyond the Incumbent: The Effects of Exposing Corruption on Electoral Outcomes." Paper No. 17679, National Bureau of Economic Research.

Chong, Alberto, Ana De La O, Dean Karlan and Leonard Wantchekon. 2015. "Does Corruption Information Inspire the Fight or Quash the Hope? A Field Experiment in Mexico on Voter Turnout, Choice, and Party Identification." *The Journal of Politics* 77(1):55–71.

Christensen, Larry. 1988. "Deception in Psychological Research: When Is Its Use Justified?" *Personality and Social Psychology Bulletin* 14(4):664–675.

Cialdini, Robert B., Raymond R. Reno and Carl A. Kallgren. 1990. "A Focus Theory of Normative Conduct: Recycling the Concept of Norms to Reduce Littering in Public Places." *Journal of Personality and Social Psychology* 58(6):1015–1026.

Clinton, Joshua D. and John S. Lapinski. 2004. "'Targeted' Advertising and Voter Turnout: An Experimental Study of the 2000 Presidential Election." *Journal of Politics* 66(1):69–96.

Collier, Paul and Pedro C. Vicente. 2014. "Votes and Violence: Evidence From a Field Experiment in Nigeria." *The Economic Journal* 124(574):F327–F355.

CONEVAL, Consejo Nacional de Evaluación de la Política de Desarrollo Social. 2014. *La pobreza en la población indígena de México, 2012.* Technical report.

Congreso de la Unión. 2010a. "Ley Federal de Protección de Datos Personales en Posesión de los Particulares de México. Disponible para su consulta en el vínculo electrónico siguiente." http://www.diputados.gob.mx/LeyesBiblio/pdf/LFPDPPP.pdf (accessed March 10, 2013).

Congreso de la Unión. 2010b. "Reglamento de la Ley Federal de Protección de Datos Personales en Posesión de los Particulares de México." http://www.diputados.gob.mx/LeyesBiblio/regley/Reg_LFPDPPP.pdf (accessed March 10, 2013).

Congreso de la Unión. 2014. "Ley General de Instituciones y Procedimientos Electorales." http://www.diputados.gob.mx/LeyesBiblio/ref/lgipe.htm (accessed July 18, 2014).

Conselho Nacional de Saúde. 2000. *Normas para pesquisa envolvendo seres humanos (Res. CNS 196/96 e outras).* Brasília: Ministério da Saúde. http://conselho.saude.gov.br/biblioteca/livros/Normas_Pesquisa.pdf (accessed November 11, 2015).

Conselho Nacional de Saúde. 2015. "Apresentação." http://conselho.saude.gov.br/apresentacao/apresentacao.htm (accessed November 11, 2015).

Coppock, Alexander and Donald P. Green. 2013. "Assessing the Correspondence Between Experimental Results Obtained in the Lab and Field: A Review of Recent Social Science." Mimeo, Columbia University.

Cox, Gary W. and Mathew D. McCubbins. 1986. "Electoral Politics as a Redistributive Game." *Journal of Politics* 48(2):370–389.

Crohan, Robert J. June 2014. "United States: Subjects of Professor's 'Ill-Conceived' Research Project Can Pursue Claims For Intentional Infliction of Emotional Distress." *Mondaq Employment and HR Briefing.*

Cunow, Saul. 2015. "Vote Choice in Complex Electoral Environments." PhD dissertation. Department of Political Science, University of California, San Diego.

De Figueiredo, Miguel F.P., F. Daniel Hidalgo and Yuri Kasahara. 2011. "When Do Voters Punish Corrupt Politicians? Experimental Evidence from Brazil." Unpublished manuscript, University of California Berkeley.

De La O, Ana. 2013. "Do Conditional Cash Transfers Affect Electoral Behavior? Evidence From a Randomized Experiment in Mexico." *American Journal of Political Science* 57(1):1–14.

De La O, Ana and Leonard Wantchekon. 2011. Experimental Research on Democracy and Development. In *The Cambridge Handbook of Political Science*, ed. James Druckman, Donald Green, James Kuklinski and Arthur Lupia. New York: Cambridge University Press.

De Rooij, Eline A., Donald P. Green and Alan S. Gerber. 2009. "Field Experiments on Political Behavior and Collective Action." *Annual Review of Political Science* 12:389–395.

de Vries, Catherine E., Elinas Dinas and Hector Solaz. 2015. "You Have Got Mail! A Field Experiment on Legislator Responsiveness in the European Parliament." Paper presented at the Southern Political Science Association Miniconference on Field Experiments and Political Elites.

Declaration of Helsinki. 2008 [1964]. *World Medical Association Declaration Of Helsinki: Ethical Principles for Medical Research Involving Human Subjects.* http://www.wma.net/en/30publications/10policies/b3/17c.pdf (accessed September 28, 2015).

Dennison, Mike. 2014. "U.S. Sen. Tester Accuses Stanford, Dartmouth of 'Voter Manipulation'; Demands Funding Disclosure." *Independent Record*, October 24. http://helenair.com/ (accessed September 28, 2015).

Desposato, Scott. 2014. "Ethics and Research in Comparative Politics." www.washingtonpost.com/blogs/monkey-cage/wp/2014/11/03/ethics-and-research-in-comparative-politics/ (accessed November 11, 2015).

Dexter, Lewis A. 1964. "The Good Will of Important People: More on the Jeopardy of the Interview." *Public Opinion Quarterly* 28(4):556–563.

Dickson, Eric. 2011. Economics vs. Psychology Experiments: Stylization, Incentives, and Deception. In *The Cambridge Handbook of Political Science*, ed. James Druckman, Donald Green, James Kuklinski and Arthur Lupia. New York: Cambridge University Press.

Dionne, Kim Yi. 2014. "The Politics of Local Research Production: Surveying in a Context of Ethnic Competition." *Politics, Groups, and Identities* 2(3):459–480.

Dionne, Kim Yi. Forthcoming. "Social Networks, Ethnic Diversity, and Cooperative Behavior in Rural Malawi." *Journal of Theoretical Politics*.

Distelhorst, Greg and Yue Hou. 2014. "Ingroup Bias in Official Behavior: A National Field Experiment in China." *Quarterly Journal of Political Science* 9(2):203–230.

Doolittle, Fred and Linda Traeger. 1990. "Implementing the National JTPA Study." Manpower Demonstration Research Corporation.

Driscoll, Jesse. 2015. *Warlords and Coalition Politics in Post-Soviet States*. Series in Comparative Politics. New York: Cambridge University Press.

Driscoll, Jesse and Danny Hidalgo. 2014. "Intended and Unintended Consequences of Democracy Promotion Assistance to Georgia After The Rose Revolution." *Research and Politics* 1(1):1–13.

Driscoll, Jesse and Nicholai Lidow. 2014. "Representative Surveys in Insecure Environments: A Case Study of Mogadishu, Somalia." *Journal of Survey Statistics and Methodology* 2(1):78–95.

Druckman, James N., Donald R. Green, James H. Kuklinski and Arthur Lupia. 2006. "The Growth and Development of Experimental Research in Political Science." *American Political Science Review* 100(4):627–635.

Druckman, James N., Donald P. Green, James H. Kuklinski and Arthur Lupia. 2011. An Introduction to Core Concepts. In *The Cambridge Handbook of Experimental Political Science*, ed. James N. Druckman, Donald P. Green, James H. Kuklinski and Arthur Lupia.

Duffy, John-Charles. 2008. "Can Deconstruction Save the Day? 'Faithful Scholarship' and the Uses of Postmodernism." *Dialogue: A Journal of Mormon Thought* 41(1):1–33.

Dunning, Thad. 2010. "Race, Class, and Voter Preferences in Brazil." Manuscript, Department of Political Science, Yale University.

Dunning, Thad and Lauren Harrison. 2010. "Cross-Cutting Cleavages and Ethnic Voting: An Experimental Study of Cousinage in Mali." *American Political Science Review* 104(1):21–39.

Easton, David. 1953. *The Political System*. New York: Knopf.

Emanuel, Ezekiel J, David Wendler and Christine Grady. 2000. "What Makes Clinical Research Ethical?" *Jama* 283(20):2701–2711.

Enemark, Daniel, Clark Gibson, Matthew McCubbins and Brigitte Zimmerman. 2013. "The Effect of Holding Office on the Behavior of Politicians." Working paper.

Facebook Post. 2014. "Adam D. I. Kramer in Floyd, Virginia." https://www.facebook.com/akramer/posts/10152987150867796 (accessed April 7, 2015).

Fair, C. Christine, Neil Malhotra and Jacob Shapiro. 2010. "Islam, Militancy, and Politics in Pakistan: Insights From a National Sample." *Terrorism and Political Violence* 22(4):495–521.

Fassinger, Ruth and S. Morrow. 2013. "Toward Best Practices in Quantitative, Qualitative, and Mixed-Method Research: A Social Justice Perspective." *Journal for Social Action in Counseling and Psychology* 5(2):69–83.

Fearon, James D., Macartan Humphreys and Jeremy M. Weinstein. 2009. "Can Development Aid Contribute to Social Cohesion After Civil War? Evidence From a Field Experiment in Post-Conflict Liberia." *The American Economic Review* 99(2):287–291.

Fenno, Richard F. 1978. *Home Style: House Members in Their Districts.* Boston: Little Brown.

Fenno, Richard F. 1996. *Senators on the Campaign Trail: The Politics of Representation.* Norman: University of Oklahoma Press.

Ferraz, Claudio and Frederico Finan. 2008. "Exposing Corrupt Politicians: The Effects of Brazil's Publicly Released Audits on Electoral Outcomes." *The Quarterly Journal of Economics* 123(2):703–745.

Ferree, Karen, Robert Dowd, Danielle Jung and Clark C. Gibson. 2011. "Getting Out the Vote, Uganda Style: Social and Political Context and Turnout in an African Election." Working paper.

Festinger, Leon. 1957. *A Theory of Cognitive Dissonance.* Stanford: Stanford University Press.

Festinger, Leon and Elliot Aronson. 1960. Arousal and Reduction of Dissonance in Social Contexts. In *Group Dynamics,* ed. D. Cartwright and Z. Zander. 3rd ed. New York: Harper and Row.

Festinger, Leon, Henry W. Riecken and Stanley Schachter. 1956. *When Prophecy Fails: A Social and Psychological Study of a Modern Group That Predicted the Destruction of the World.* Minneapolis: University of Minnesota Press.

Findley, Michael G., Adam S. Harris, Helen V. Milner and Daniel L. Nielson. 2013. "Elite and Mass Perceptions of Foreign Aid in Recipient Countries: A Field Experiment in Uganda." Unpublished Manuscript.

Findley, Michael, Nathan Jensen and Daniel Nielson. 2013. "A Field Experiment on Incentives for Direct Investment: Research Registration Report and Data Analysis Plan." Typescript.

Findley, Michael and Daniel Nielson. 2014. "Obligated to Deceive? Aliases, Confederates, and the Common Rule in International Field Experiments."

Findley, Michael G., Daniel L. Nielson and J.C. Sharman. 2013*a*. "Deceptive Studies or Deceptive Answers? Alternative Global Field and Survey Experiments on Anonymous Incorporation." Unpublished Manuscript in Progress.

Findley, Michael G., Daniel L. Nielson and J.C. Sharman. 2013*b*. "Using Field Experiments in International Relations: A Randomized Study of Anonymous Incorporation." *International Organization* 67(4):657–693.

Findley, Michael G., Daniel L. Nielson and J.C. Sharman. 2014. *Global Shell Games: Experiments in Transnational Relations, Crime, and Terrorism.* Cambridge: Cambridge University Press.

Fitch, Brad and Kathy Goldschmidt. 2005. "Communicating with Congress." Congressional Management Foundation. CMF Report.

Fried, Brian J., Paul Lagunes and Atheendar Venkataramani. 2010. "Corruption and Inequality at the Crossroad: A Multimethod Study of Bribery and Discrimination in Latin America." *Latin American Research Review* 45(1):76–97.

Fujii, Lee Ann. 2012. "Research Ethics 101: Dilemmas and Responsibilities." *PS: Political Science & Politics* 45(04):717–723.

Gajda, Amy. 2010. *The Trials of Academe: The New Era of Campus Litigation.* Harvard University Press.

Gebauer, Jochen and Gregory Maio. 2012. "The Need to Belong Can Motivate Belief in God." *Journal of Personality* 80(2):465–501.

Geddes, Barbara. 2003. *Paradigms and Sandcastles.* Ann Arbor: University of Michigan Press.

Gerber, Alan. 2011. Field Experiments in Political Science. In *The Cambridge Handbook of Experimental Political Science*, ed. James Druckman, Donald Green, James Kuklinski and Arthur Lupia. New York: Cambridge University Press.

Gerber, Alan S. and Donald P. Green. 2000. "The Effects of Canvassing, Telephone Calls, and Direct Mail on Voter Turnout: A Field Experiment." *American Political Science Review* 94(03):653–663.

Gerber, Alan S. and Donald P. Green. 2001. "Do Phone Calls Increase Voter Turnout? A Field Experiment." *Public Opinion Quarterly* 65: 75–85.

Gerber, Alan S., Donald P. Green and Christopher W. Larimer. 2008. "Social Pressure and Vote Turnout: Evidence from a Large-Scale Field Experiment." *American Political Science Review* 102(1):33–48.

Gervais, Will M. and Ara Norenzayan. 2012. "Analytic Thinking Promotes Religious Disbelief." *Science* 336 (6080):493–496.

Gibson, Clark C. and James D. Long. 2009. "The Presidential and Parliamentary Elections in Kenya, December 2007." *Electoral Studies* 28(3):497–502.

Gibson, James L. 2008. "Group Identities and Theories of Justice: An Experimental Investigation into the Justice and Injustice of Land Squatting in South Africa." *Journal of Politics* 70(3):700–716.

Gneezy, Uri, Ernan Haruvy and H. Yafe. 2004. "The Inefficiency of Splitting the Bill: A Lesson in Institution Design." *The Economic Journal* 114(495):265–280.

Goldstone, Jack A., Larry Garber, John Gerring, Clark C. Gibson, Mitchell A. Seligson and Jeremy Weinstein. 2008. Improving Democracy Assistance: Building Knowledge Through Evaluations and Research. Technical report. Committee on Evaluation of USAID Democracy Assistance Programs, National Research Council of the National Academies.

Gosnell, Harold F. 1927. *Getting Out the Vote: An Experiment in the Stimulation of Voting.* Chicago: The University of Chicago Press.

Gottlieb, Jessica. 2012. "Can Information that Raises Voter Expectations Improve Accountability? A Field Experiment in Mali." Unpublished Manuscript. Stanford University.

Green, Donald P. 2004. "Mobilizing African-American Voters Using Direct Mail and Commercial Phone Banks: A Field Experiment." *Political Research Quarterly* 57(2): 245–255.

Green, Donald P. and Alan S. Gerber. 2002. Reclaiming the Experimental Tradition in Political Science. In *Political Science: The State of the Discipline*, ed. Ira Katznelson and Helen Milner. New York: W.W. Norton and Company.

Green, Donald P., Alan S. Gerber and David W. Nickerson. 2003. "Getting Out the Vote in Local Elections: Results From Six Door-to-Door Canvassing Experiments." *Journal of Politics* 65(4):1083–1096.

Green, Donald P. and Lynn Vavreck. 2006. Assessing the Turnout Effects of Rock the Vote's 2004 Television Commercials: A Randomized Field Experiment. In *Annual Meeting of the Midwest Political Science Association, Chicago, IL*, pp. 20–23.

Gries, Peter, Kaiping Peng and H. Michael Crowson. 2012. Determinants of Security and Insecurity in International Relations: A Cross-National Experimental Analysis of

Symbolic and Material Gains and Losses. In *Psychology and Constructivism in International Relations: An Ideational Alliance*, ed. Vaughn P. Shannon and Paul A. Kowert. Ann Arbor: University of Michigan Press.

Grimm, Ryan and Sabrina Siddiqui. 2013. "Call Time For Congress Shows How Fundraising Dominates Bleak Work Life." *Huffington Post*, January 18. http://www.huffingtonpost.com/2013/01/08/call-time-congressional-fundraising_n_2427291.html (accessed September 28, 2015).

Grose, Christian R. 2011. *Congress in Black and White: Race and Representation in Washington and at Home*. New York: Cambridge University Press.

Grose, Christian R. 2013. "Priming Rationality." Working paper.

Grose, Christian R. 2014. "Field Experimental Work on Political Institutions." *Annual Review of Political Science* 17:355–70.

Grose, Christian R., Neil Malhotra and Robert Parks Van Houweling. Forthcoming. "Explaining Explanations: How Legislators Explain Their Policy Positions and How Citizens React." *American Journal of Political Science*.

Guan, Mei and Donald P. Green. 2006. "Noncoercive Mobilization in State-Controlled Elections: An Experimental Study in Beijing." *Comparative Political Studies* 39(10):1175–1193.

Gubler, Joshua R. N.d. "When Humanizing the Enemy Fails: The Role of Dissonance and Justification in Intergroup Conflict." Under Review.

Hansen, Kasper M. and Karina Kosiara-Pedersen. 2014. "Cyber-Campaigning in Denmark: Application and Effects of Candidate Campaigning." *Journal of Information Technology & Politics* 11(2):206–219.

Harawa, Augustine. 2013. "Ethical Challenges Faced by IKI as a Research Organization and How US Scholars Should Operate Outside the US." Working Paper.

Harawa, Augustine, Hastings Honde and James Mkandawire. 2010. "MLSFH 2010 Field Notes." Unpublished dataset.

Harmon-Jones, Eddie and Judson Mills. 1999. *Cognitive Dissonance: Progress on a Pivotal Theory in Social Psychology*. Washington, DC: American Psychological Association.

Hartman, George W. 1936. "A Field Experiment on the Comparative Effectiveness of 'Emotional' and 'Rational' Political Leaflets in Determining Election Results." *Journal of Abnormal and Social Psychology* 31:99–114.

Hidalgo, Daniel, Miguel F. P. de Figueiredo and Yuri Kasahara. 2011. "When Do Voters Punish Corrupt Politicians? Experimental Evidence from Brazil." Working Paper.

Hix, Simon, Sarah Hagemann and Doru Frantescu. 2011. "The Effect of Transparency on Legislative Voting: An Experiment Using Members of the European Parliament." London School of Economics and Political Science. Unpublished manuscript.

Hoffmann, Robert and Jeremy Larner. 2013. "The Demography of Chinese Nationalism: A Field-Experimental Approach." *The China Quarterly* 213:189–204.

Holt, Charles and Susan Laury. 2002. "Risk Aversion and Incentive Effects." *American Economic Review* 92(5):1644–55.

Holz, Carsten A. 2007. "Have China Scholars All Been Bought?" *Far Eastern Economic Review* 170(3):36–40.

Humphreys, Macartan. 2014. "How to Make Field Experiments More Ethical." www.washingtonpost.com/blogs/monkey-cage/wp/2014/11/02/how-to-make-field-experiments-more-ethical/ (accessed November 11, 2015).

Humphreys, Macartan and Jeremy M. Weinstein. 2009. "Field Experiments and the Political Economy of Development." *Annual Review of Political Science* 12(1):367–378.

Humphreys, Macartan and Jeremy Weinstein. 2012. "Policing Politicians: Citizen Empowerment and Political Accountability in Uganda Preliminary Analysis." Working Paper.

Johansson-Stenman, Olof, Minhaj Mahmud and Peter Martinsson. 2009. "Trust and Religion: Experimental Evidence From Rural Bangladesh." *Economica* 76(303):462–485.

Kalla, Joshua L. and David E. Broockman. Forthcoming. "Campaign Contributions Facilitate Access to Congressional Officials: A Randomized Field Experiment." *American Journal of Political Science.*

Kam, Cindy D., Jennifer R. Wilking and Elizabeth J. Zechmeister. 2007. "Beyond the 'Narrow Data Base': Another Convenience Sample for Experimental Research." *Political Behavior* 29(4):415–440.

Kapiszewski, Diana, Lauren M. MacLean and Benjamin L. Read. 2015. *Field Research in Political Science.* New York: Cambridge University Press.

Katz, Jack. 2007. "Toward a Natural History of Ethical Censorship." *Law & Society Review* 41(4):797–810.

Kelsall, Tim. 2009. *Culture Under Cross-Examination: International Justice and the Special Court for Sierra Leone.* New York: Cambridge University Press.

Kifner, John. 2001. "Scholar Sets Off Gastronomic False Alarm." *The New York Times*, September 8. http://www.nytimes.com/2001/09/08/nyregion/scholar-sets-off-gastronomic-false-alarm.html (accessed April 7, 2015).

King, Gary, Jennifer Pan and Margaret E. Roberts. 2013. "How Censorship in China Allows Government Criticism but Silences Collective Expression." *American Political Science Review* 107(2):326–343.

King, Gary, Robert Keohane and Sidney Verba. 1994. *Designing Social Inquiry.* Princeton: Princeton University Press.

King, Gary, Jennifer Pan and Margaret E. Roberts. Forthcoming. "Reverse Engineering Chinese Censorship Through Randomized Experimentation and Participant Observation." *Science.*

Koenig, Barbara. 2014. "Have We Asked Too Much of Consent?" *The Hastings Center Report* 44(4):33–34.

Kohler, Hans-Peter, Susan Watkins, Jere Behrman, Philip Anglewicz, Iliana Kohler, Peter Fleming, Rebecca Thornton, James Mkandawire, Linda Kalilani-Phiri, Hastings Honde, Augustine Harawa, Ben Chilima, Chiwoza Bandawe, Victor Mwapasa and MLSFH Study Team. 2015. "Cohort Profile: The Malawi Longitudinal Study of Families and Health (MLSFH)." *International Journal of Epidemiology*, 44 (2):394–404.

Kramer, Adam D.I., Jamie E. Guillory and Jeffrey T. Hancock. 2014. "Experimental Evidence of Massive-Scale Emotional Contagion Through Social Networks." *Proceedings of the National Academy of Sciences* 111(24):8788–8790.

Kristinsson, Sigurdur. 2009. "The Belmont Report's Misleading Conception of Autonomy." *Virtual Mentor/ AMA Journal of Ethics* 11(8):611–616.

Kuhn, Thomas S. 1970. *The Structure of Scientific Revolutions.* Chicago: University of Chicago Press.

Kuklinski, James H., Michael D. Cobb and Martin Gilens. 1997. "Racial Attitudes and the 'New South.'" *The Journal of Politics* 59(2):323–349.

Lagunes, Paul. 2009. "Irregular Transparency? An Experiment Involving Mexico's Freedom of Information Law." *ISPS Working Paper*, May 2.

Larson, Edward J. and Larry Witham. 1998. "Leading Scientists Still Reject God." *Nature* 394:313.

Larson, Stephanie Greco. 1990. "Information and Learning in a Congressional District: A Social Experiment." *American Journal of Political Science* 34(4):1102–1118.

Lasswell, Harold Dwight. 1936. *Politics: Who Gets What, When, How.* London: Whittlesey House McGraw-Hill Book Company Inc.

Levitt, Steven D. and John A. List. 2007a. "Viewpoint: On the Generalizability of Lab Behaviour to the Field." *Canadian Journal of Economics* 40(2):347–370.

Levitt, Steven D. and John A. List. 2007b. "What Do Laboratory Experiments Measuring Social Preferences Reveal About the Real World." *The Journal of Economic Perspectives* 21(2):153–174.

Linardi, Sera, Rebecca Morton, Kai Ou, Gumilang Sadahewo and Xiandong Qin. 2014. "The Price of Religion: Altruism and Risk in Islamic Banking." Working Paper.

List, John A. 2006. "The Behavioralist Meets the Market: Measuring Social Preferences and Reputation Effects in Actual Transactions." *Journal of Political Economy* 114(1):1–37.

Loewen, Peter John and Michael K. MacKenzie. 2011. "Representation in a Federal System: a Field Experiment." Working Paper.

Loewen, Peter John and Daniel Rubenson. 2011. "For Want of a Nail: Negative Persuasion in a Party Leadership Campaign." *Party Politics* 17(1):45–65.

Lü, Xiaobo. 2013. "Equality of Educational Opportunity and Attitudes Toward Income Inequality: Evidence From China." *Quarterly Journal of Political Science* 8(3):271–303.

Lü, Xiaobo, Kenneth Scheve and Matthew J. Slaughter. 2012. "Inequality Aversion and the International Distribution of Trade Protection." *American Journal of Political Science* 56(3):638–654.

Ludwinski, Daniel, Kent Moriarty and Bruce Wydick. 2011. "Environmental and Health Impacts From the Introduction of Improved Wood Stoves: Evidence From a Field Experiment in Guatemala." *Environment, Development and Sustainability* 13(4):657–676.

Lund, Frederick Hansen. 1925. "The Psychology of Belief." *Journal of Abnormal and Social Psychology* 20:174–196.

Lyall, Jason, Graeme Blair and Kosuke Imai. 2013. "Explaining Support for Combatants During Wartime: A Survey Experiment in Afghanistan." *American Political Science Review* 107(04):679–705.

Malesky, Edmund J., Paul Schuler and Anh Tran. 2012. "The Adverse Effects of Sunshine: A Field Experiment on Legislative Transparency in an Authoritarian Assembly." *American Political Science Review* 106(4):762–786.

Manion, Melanie. 2012. A Survey of Survey Research on Chinese Politics: What Have We Learned? In *Contemporary Chinese Politics: New Sources, Methods, and Field Strategies*, ed. M. G. Allen Carlson, Kenneth Lieberthal and Melanie Manion. New York: Cambridge University Press.

McCauley, John. 2010. "Religious and Ethnic Conflict in Africa." PhD dissertation. ProQuest/UMI 3463911.

McCauley, John. 2013. "Measuring and Reducing Religious Bias in Post-Conflict Zones: Evidence from Côte d'Ivoire." *Political Psychology* 35(2):267–289.

McClendon, Gwyneth H. 2012a. "Co-ethnicity and Democratic Governance: A Field Experiment with South African Politicians." Working Paper.

McClendon, Gwyneth H. 2012b. "Ethics of Using Public Officials as Field Experiment Subjects." *Newsletter of the APSA Experimental Section* 3(1):13–20.

McCubbins, Mathew D. and Thomas Schwartz. 1984. "Congressional Oversight Overlooked: Police Patrols Versus Fire Alarms." *American Journal of Political Science* 28(1):165–179.

McDermott, Rose. 2002. "Experimental Methods in Political Science." *Annual Review of Political Science* 5:31–61.

Mendez, Matthew S. 2015. "Who Represents the Interests of Undocumented Latinos? A Field Experiment of State Legislators." Manuscript, University of Southern California.

Mendez, Matthew S. and Christian R. Grose. 2015. "Revealing Discriminatory Intent: Legislator Preferences, Voter Identification, and Responsiveness Bias." Working Paper, University of Southern California.

Merolla, Jennifer L. and Elizabeth J. Zechmeister. 2009. *Democracy at Risk: How Terrorist Threats Affect the Public.* Chicago: University of Chicago Press.

Milgram, Stanley. 1977. *Obedience to Authority.* Harper Collins.

Miller, Arthur G. 1986. *The Obedience Experiments: A Case Study of Controversy in Social Science.* New York: Praeger.

Miller, Candace, Maxton Tsoka and Kathryn Reichert. 2010. Impacts on Children of Cash Transfers in Malawi. In *Social Protection for Africa's Children*, ed. Sudhanshu Handa, Stephen Devereux and Douglas Webb. New York: Routledge.

Miller, Candace, Maxton Tsoka and Kathryn Reichert. 2011. "The Impact of the Social Cash Transfer Scheme on Food Security in Malawi." *Food Policy* 36(2):230–238.

Milner, Helen, Daniel L. Nielson and Michael G. Findley. 2013. "Which Devil in Development: A Randomized Study of Citizen Actions Supporting Foreign Aid in Uganda." Unpublished Manuscript.

Morton, Rebecca B. and Kenneth C. Williams. 2010. *Experimental Political Science and the Study of Causality: From Nature to the Lab.* New York: Cambridge University Press.

Moseley, J. Bruce, Kimberly O'Malley, Nancy Petersen, Terri Menke, Baruch Brody, David Kuykendall, John Hollingsworth, Carol Ashton and Nelda Wray. 2002. "A Controlled Trial of Arthroscopic Surgery for Osteoarthritis of the Knee." *New England Journal of Medicine* 347(2):81–88.

National Institute on Money in State Politics. 2014. "Follow the Money: Election Overview." http://followthemoney.org/election-overview?s=MT&y=2014 (accessed on March 5, 2015).

National Science Foundation. 2014. "NSF Award Database." http://www.nsf.gov/award-search/advancedSearch.jsp (accessed September 28, 2015).

National Statistical Office [Malawi]. 2011. "Malawi Demographic and Health Survey 2010 Preliminary Report."

Naurin, Daniel. 2007. *Deliberation behind Closed doors: Transparency and Lobbying in the European Union.* Colchester, UK: ECPR Press.

Nestor, Franchesca and Trisha Phillips. 2015. "Ethical Standards in Political Science: Journals, Articles, and Education." Working Paper.

Nickerson, David W. 2005. "Partisan Mobilization Using Volunteer Phone Banks and Door Hangers." *The Annals of the American Academy of Political and Social Science* 601(1):10–27.

Nickerson, David W., Ryan F. Friedrichs and David C. King. 2006. "Partisan Mobilization Experiments in the Field: Results From a Statewide Turnout Experiment in Michigan." *Political Research Quarterly* 34(1):271–292.

Nielsen, Richard A. 2013. "The Lonely Jihadist: Weak Networks and the Radicalization of Muslim Clerics." PhD thesis. Harvard University.

Niven, David. 2006. "A Field Experiment on the Effects of Negative Campaign Mail on Voter Turnout in a Municipal Election." *Political Research Quarterly* 59(2):203–210.

Norton, Michael I., Elizabeth W. Dunn, Dana R. Carney and Dan Ariely. 2012. "The Persuasive 'Power' of Stigma?" *Organizational Behavior and Human Decision Processes* 117(2):261–268.

Obradovich, Nicholas and Brigitte Zimmerman. 2015. "Climate Change Policy in Africa: A Political Toxin?" Working Paper.

Olken, Benjamin A. 2007. "Monitoring Corruption: Evidence From a Field Experiment in Indonesia." *Journal of Political Economy* 115(2):200–249.

O'Neill, Onora. 2003. "Some Limits of Informed Consent." *Journal of Medical Ethics* 29(1):4–7.

Ornelas Núñez, Lina. 2013. Características del modelo de la Ley Federal de Protección de Datos Personales en Posesión de los Particulares y su reglamento. In *La Protección de Datos Personales en México*, ed. José Luis Piñar Mañas. México, D.F.: Tirant lo Blanch.

Ove, Torsten. 2011. "Before Tuskegee, the Guatemala Experiment: A Pitt Legend's Research is Under Scrutiny." *Pittsburgh Post-Gazette*, June 12. http://www.post-gazette.com/opinion/op-ed/2011/06/12/the-next-page-before-tuskegee-the-guatemala-experiment-a-pitt-legend-s-research-is-under-scrutiny/201106120141 (accessed April 17, 2013).

Paluck, E.L. 2009. Crossing the Border, Changing Tactics: A Comparative Look at Fieldwork in Two "Post-Conflict" Zones, East DR Congo and Rwanda, 2005–2007. In *Surviving Research: Doing Fieldwork in Difficult and Violent Situations*, ed. C. Sriram et al. New York: Routledge.

Paluck, Elizabeth L. and Donald P. Green. 2009. "Deference, Dissent, and Dispute Resolution: An Experimental Intervention Using Mass Media to Change Norms and Behavior in Rwanda." *American Political Science Review* 103(4):622–644.

Panagopoulos, Costas. 2008. "Partisan and Nonpartisan Message Content and Voter Mobilization: Field Experimental Evidence." *Political Research Quarterly* 62(1):70-76.

Parra, Juan Carlos. N.d. "The Effects of Religion on Social Cooperation: Results From a Field Experiment in Ghana." http://www12.georgetown.edu/students/jcp29/ghana-exp3.pdf (accessed April 23, 2013).

Pepinsky, Thomas, R. William Liddle and Saiful Mujani. 2012. "Testing Islam's Political Advantage: Evidence From Indonesia." *American Journal of Political Science* 56(3):584–600.

Platvoet, Jan G. and Arie Leendert Molendijk, eds. 1999. *The Pragmatics of Defining Religion: Contexts, Concepts, and Contests*. Leiden: Brill.

Plott, Charles. 2013. "Risks and Harm: The Disciplines of Economics, Political Science, Game Theory, Judgment and Decision." www.tvworldwide.com/events/nas/130321/slides/Common%20Rule%20Workshop_Plott.pdf (accessed November 11, 2015).

Pollock, Philip. 2012. *The Essentials of Political Analysis*. 4th ed. Washington: CQ Press.

Prat, Andrea. 2005. "The Wrong Kind of Transparency." *American Economic Review* 95(3):862–877.

Rice, Stuart A. 1929. "Contagious Bias in the Interview: A Methodological Note." *American Journal of Sociology* 35:42–423.

Richardson, Liz and Peter John. 2012. "Who Listens to the Grass Roots? A Field Experiment on Informational Lobbying in the UK." *The British Journal of Politics & International Relations* 14(4):595–612.

Robinson, Amanda Lea. 2013. "Nationalism and Interethnic Trust: Evidence From an African Border Region." Unpublished working paper, Ohio State University.

Rogers, Jonathan. 2014. "Other Peoples' Money: Warm Glow and Risk Preferences." Working Paper.

Rooth, Dan-Olof. 2009. "Obesity, Attractiveness, and Differential Treatment in Hiring." *The Journal of Human Resources* 44(3):710–735.

Ruffle, Bradley J. and Richard Sosis. 2007. "Does it Pay To Pray? Costly Ritual and Cooperation." *The B.E. Journal of Economic Analysis & Policy* 7(1):18.

Salloch, Sabine, Jan Schildmann and Jochen Vollmann. 2012. "Empirical Research in Medical Ethics: How Conceptual Accounts on Normative-Empirical Collaboration May Improve Research Practice." *BMC Medical Ethics* 13(5).

Samii, Cyrus. 2013. "Perils or Promise of Ethnic Integration? Evidence From a Hard Case in Burundi." *American Political Science Review* 107(03):558–573.

Schrag, Zachary M. 2009. "How Talking Became Human Subjects Research: The Federal Regulation of the Social Sciences, 1965–1991." *Journal of Policy History* 21(1):3–37.

Scott, Dylan. 2014. "Profs Bumble Into Big Legal Trouble After Election Experiment Goes Way Wrong." *Talking Point Memo*, October 27.

Seligson, Mitchell A. 2008. "Human Subjects Protection and Large-N Research: When Exempt is Non-Exempt and Research is Non-Research." *PS: Political Science & Politics* 41(3):477–482.

Selway, Joel, Michael W. Davidson and Thomas Bossuroy. 2011. Inter-Ethnic Civic Engagement and Discrimination. *APSA 2011 Annual Meeting Paper.*

Shariff, Azim, Adam Cohen and Ara Norenzayan. 2008. "The Devil's Advocate: Secular Arguments Diminish Both Implicit and Explicit Religious Belief." *Journal of Cognition and Culture* 8:417–423.

Shaughnessy, John J., Eugene B. Zechmeister and Jeanne S. Zechmeister. 2011. *Research Methods in Psychology.* 9th ed. New York: McGraw Hill.

Sheikh, Hammad, Jeremy Ginges, Alin Coman and Scott Atran. 2012. "Religion, Group Threat, and Sacred Values." *Judgement and Decision Making* 7(2):110–118.

Sieber, Joan E. 1992. *Planning Ethically Responsible Research: A Guide for Students and Internal Review Boards.* New York: Sage Publications.

Sieber, Joan E. and Martin B. Tolich. 2012. *Planning Ethically Responsible Research.* Vol. 31. New York: Sage Publications.

Simtowe, Franklin, Mariapia Mendola and Julius Mangisoni. 2011. "Independent Project Impact Evaluation of the Community Based Rural Land Development Project (CBRLDP) in Malawi." Lilongwe: Government of Malawi.

Singer, Eleanor and Felice J. Levine. 2003. "Protection of Human Subjects of Research: Recent Developments and Future Prospects for the Social Sciences." *The Public Opinion Quarterly* 67(1):148–164.

Singleton, Royce Jr., Bruce C. Straits, Margaret M. Straits and Ronal J. McAllister. 1988. *Approaches to Social Research.* New York: Oxford University Press.

Spilka, Bernard, Jr. Ralph W. Hood, Bruce Hunsberger and Richard Gorsuch. 2003. *The Psychology of Religion: An Empirical Approach.* 3rd ed. New York: The Guilford Press.

Stanford University and Dartmouth University. 2014. *An Open Letter to the Voters and Citizens of Montana.* October 28.

Stokes, Susan C. 2005. "Perverse Accountability: A Formal Model of Machine Politics With Evidence From Argentina." *American Political Science Review* 99(3):315–325.

Strait, George. 1993. *The Deadly Deception.* Original broadcast January 26, 1993.

Sultana, Farhana. 2007. "Reflexivity, Positionality and Participatory Ethics: Negotiating Fieldwork Dilemmas in International Research." *ACME: An International E-Journal for Critical Geographies* 6(3):374–385.

Taleb, Nassim Nicholas. 2007. *The Black Swan: The Impact of the Highly Improbable.* New York: Random House.

Tan, Jonathan H.W. and Claudia Vogel. 2008. "Religion and Trust: An Experimental Study." *Journal of Economic Psychology* 29(6):832–848.

Tavris, Carol and Eliot Aronson. 2007. *Mistakes Were Made: But Not By Me*. New York: Houghton Mifflin Harcourt.

Teele, Dawn Langan. 2014. "Reflections on the Ethics of Field Experiments." *Field Experiments and Their Critics: Essays on the Uses and Abuses of Experimentation in the Social Sciences* p. 115–140.

The Journal of Experimental Political Science. 2015. "Instructions for Contributors." http://journals.cambridge.org/action/displaySpecialPage?pageId=5904 (accessed April 6, 2015).

The National Commission for the Protection of Human Subjects of Biomedical and Behavioral Research. 1979. *The Belmont Report: Ethical Principles and Guideline for the Protection of Human Subjects of Research Office* [Technical report]. US Government Printing Office.

The Nuremberg Code. 1947. www.hhs.gov/ohrp/archive/nurcode.html (accessed November 11, 2016).

Thorton, Rebecca. 2008. "The Demand for, and Impact of, Learning HIV Status." *American Economic Review* 98(5):1829–1863.

Todd, Petra E. and Kenneth I. Wolpin. 2006. "Assessing the Impact of a school Subsidy Program in Mexico: Using a Social Experiment to Validate a Dynamic Behavioral Model of Child Schooling and Fertility." *The American Economic Review* 96(5):1384–1417.

Townsend, Robert B. 2004. "AHA Council Reaffirms Position on Oral History and Institutional Review Boards." Press Release. American Historical Association.

Tran, Anh. 2015. "Ethical Issues in Conducting Political Science Research in Authoritarian Regimes." Working Paper.

Tsai, Lily L. 2010. Quantitative Research and Issues of Political Sensitivity in Rural China. In *Contemporary Chinese Politics: New Sources, Methods, and Field Strategies*, ed. M. G. Allen Carlson, Kenneth Lieberthal and Melanie Manion. New York: Cambridge University Press.

Turgeon, Mathieu and Lucio Rennó. 2010. "Informação política e atitudes sobre gastos governamentais e impostos no Brasil: evidências a partir de um experimento de opinião pública." *Opinião Pública* 16(1):143–159.

Tuskegee Syphilis Study Legacy Committee. 1996. "Final Report of the Tuskegee Syphilis Study Legacy Committee." *University of Virginia Health System*. http://exhibits.hsl.virginia.edu/badblood/report/ (accessed on April 17, 2013).

US Department of Health and Human Services. 2015. "Federal Policy for the Protection of Human Subjects." http://www.hhs.gov/ohrp/humansubjects/commonrule/ (accessed on April 1, 2015).

Wantchekon, Leonard. 2003. "Clientelism and Voting Behavior: Evidence From a Field Experiment in Benin." *World Politics* 55(3):399–422.

Washington, Harriet. 2007. "Why Africa Fears Western Medicine." *New York Times*, July 31.

Weber, Christopher and Matthew Thornton. 2012. "Courting Christians: How Political Candidates Prime Religious Considerations in Campaign Ads." *Journal of Politics* 74(2):400–413.

Weber, Max, Charles Wright Mills and Hans Heinrich Gerth. 1918. Politics as a Vocation. In *From Max Weber: Essays in Sociology*, ed. Hans H. Gerth and C. Wright Mills. New York: Routledge.

Weichselbaumer, Doris. 2003. "Sexual Orientation and Discrimination in Hiring." *Labour Economics* 10(6):629–642.

Weingast, Barry R., Kenneth A. Shepsle and Christopher Johnsen. 1981. "The Political Economy of Benefits and Costs: A Neoclassical Approach to Distributive Politics." *The Journal of Political Economy* 89(4):642–664.

Wendler, Dave. 1996. "Deception in Medical and Behavioral Research: Is It Ever Acceptable?" *The Milbank Quarterly* 74(1):87–114.

Whiteman, Ellen. 2007. "'Just Chatting': Research Ethics and Cyberspace." *International Journal of Qualitative Methods* 6(2):95–105.

Wood, Abby and David Lewis. 2015. "Measuring Agency Responsiveness: A Federal FOIA Audit Study." Paper presented at SoCLASS III: Regulation, Law, and Social Science conference, University of Southern California.

Wood, Elisabeth. 2006. "The Ethical Challenges of Field Research in Conflict Zones." *Qualitative Sociology* 29(3):373–386.

World Bank. 2015. "GINI Index (World Bank estimate)." http://data.worldbank.org/indicator/SI.POV.GINI?page=1

Wroe, Daniel. 2012. "Briefing: Donors, Dependency, and Political Crisis in Malawi." *African Affairs* 111(442):135–144.

Yanow, Dvora and Peregrine Schwartz-Shea. 2008. "Reforming Institutional Review Board Policy: Issues in Implementation and Field Research." *PS: Political Science and Politics* 41(3):483–494.

Yeatts, John R. and William Asher. 1979. "Can We Afford Not to Do True Experiments in Psychology of Religion? A Reply to Batson." *Journal for the Scientific Study of Religion* 18(1):86–89.

INDEX

Note: Page numbers in *italics* followed by *f* indicate figures. Page numbers followed by n indicate notes.

Abkhazia 87, 95n9
academic freedom 228, 246
academic mentors and regulators 82
accountability mechanisms 217
aggregate effects of political science experiments 17
aggregate or social harm 277
Aguilar, Rosario 19–20, 128, 139, 273, 290; *see also* countries without an Institutional Review Board
AJPS *see American Journal of Political Science*
American Association of University Professors (AAUP), human subjects protection 246, 253n4, 253n6
American Economics Review 86
American Historical Association 247–8, 254n8
American Journal of Political Science (AJPS) 5, 6, 105; journal editors and ethics 265
American Political Science Association (APSA):creating "clearinghouse" of information 236–7; Experimental Research Section 264, 266; "Guide to Professional Ethics in Political Science" (2012) 260; human subjects protection 247
American Political Science Review (APSR) 5, 6, 86, 105, 107, 177, 289n21

American Psychological Association (APA) 153, 161, 256, 260–1
anonymity of subjects 1, 3
anonymous incorporation (the case for deception) 151, 152, 159–66, 170n3
apostasy, religion and experiments 70
APSR *see American Political Science Review*
authoritarian governance regimes ("Prison States and Games of Chicken") 20, 81–96, 114, 126, 270; Abkhazia 87, 95n9; academic mentors and regulators 82; *American Economics Review* 86; *American Political Science Review* 86; anti-regime activism 90–1, 96n16; arming UN Peacekeepers 93, 96n18; background 81–2; "Black Swan" events 85, 91, 94n4, 95n5; comparative politics 81, 83, 91; computer and smartphone technology 86; conclusion and implications 93–4; confrontational activism 89–91; control groups 82; cooperation with NGOs 82, 84, 88, 90; cooperation with state authorities 82, 86–8; decentralized regulatory regime for experimenting 84–5, 93; the experimental frontier (2015) 82–4; experiments as positive-sum enterprises 82; fieldwork 83, 85,

86, 88, 95n13; generalized rule-set to incentivize good behavior 82; "going native" in comparative politics 91–3; graduate students 81, 83, 94; informed consent 87, 95n10, 95n11; inquiry into the ugly facets of politics 94; Institutional Review Boards (IRBs) 83–4, 85, 90, 94n3; language barriers 83; observational studies 86, 93; perpetuating bad governments 85–8; PhD programs 84; publishing non-findings 88–9; randomized control trials (RCTs) 90, 95n7; referee reports 94; scholarly work as diplomatic passport 89; search committees 83; social engineering projects of Soviet social scientists 93, 96n17; social mobilization 89–90, 95n15; Somalia 85, 95n6; tenure committees 83, 84; top-down, "eyes of the sovereign" perspective 87; transnational civil society linkages 94; volunteerism within the discipline 94; World Bank 86

belief as sacred, religion and experiments 69–72
Belmont Report 18, 278, 288n14, 288n15; in comparative politics experiments 103, 104, 172, 173–5, 181; countries without an Institutional Review Board 140, 142, 146; deception in international field experiments 152, 153, 157, 158, 161, 165; ethics of exclusion in impoverished settings 26–7; human subjects protection 242, 243–5, 253; learning from other disciplines 285; political information experiments 189–91; research with non-governmental organizations (NGOs) 199, 204, 214, 216n10
beneficence principle 140–1, 146, 200, 212, 244–5, 297
benefit/cost approach, religion and experiments 67–8, 79n2
"Black Swan" events 85, 91, 94n4, 95n5
bottom-up transparency interventions 184, 197n2
Brazil, local ethical review in comparative politics experiments 102, 105, 108, 111, 111n5
"Brazilian Black Box" see local review (the "Brazilian Black Box")

bribes 108
Brigham Young University, Political Economy and Development Lab (PEDL) 166–8
"bureaucratic creep" and litigation phobia 241

Cambodia 219
Cambodia (case study #1) 208–12
candidates for public office see public behavior of public officials; public officials, elected officials, and candidates
Cardenas, Sergio 143, 144
career prospects and livelihood of politicians 218, 220, 225
case study demonstration framework 193–6
censorship: comparative politics experiments in China 115, 116; recent censorship guidelines 127n7
Center for Research and Teaching in Economics 143, 148n9
CEPs see Committees on Ethics in Research
change manipulations in religion 46–57
China see comparative politics experiments in China
Chinese Communist Party 115, 116
citizen information experiments 184–5
Claremont Graduate University 101, 103, 104, 109
Cocker, Jarvis 93
cognitive dissonance 168, 188
collaborating with scholars within country 108
commercial marketing firms, collaboration with 120, 123–4
Committees on Ethics in Research (CEPs) 129, 130, 138n1
Common Rule 21n3; Code of Federal Regulations (CFR) 242–3, 246, 247; deception in international field experiments 152, 153, 157, 158, 161; local ethical review in comparative politics experiments 100, 111n1; recommendations for field experiments 282; religion and experiments 67
Community Based Rural Land Development Project (CBRLDP), Malawi research experiences 33
community theatre 184
Comparative Political Studies (CPS) 5, 6, 22n6, 105

Comparative Politics (CP) 5, 6, 105
comparative politics experiments 256,
267; local ethical review in comparative
politics experiments 103; *see also*
comparative politics experiments
in China; local ethical review in
comparative politics experiments;
political consequences of comparative
politics experiments
comparative politics experiments in China
113–27, 273; authoritarian regimes
114, 126; background 113–14; barrier
of entry in data collection 114, 120–1;
breaking the law 125–6; censorship
115, 116; Chinese Communist Party
115, 116; Chinese government's motives
114–16; collaboration with Chinese
academic institutions 123; collaboration
with commercial marketing firms 120,
123–4; collective action potential theory
of censorship 115; common practices
and their trade-offs 122–6; controlled
information environment 113, 126;
data-collection process 119–20;
diplomatic relations between China and
the United States 120; ethical issues 114,
119–22; experimental studies in China
120; experimental studies in political
science outside China 114, 127n2; field
experiments 114; foreign individuals
and entities 117, 127n5; foreign media
outlets 116; future collaborative
opportunities 114; government
documentation and statistics 120;
government maintaining regime
stability 113; high-level political elites'
corruption 115, 127n3; Hong Kong
127n5; inconsistency in government
enforcement 117; independent research
without government approval 124;
Internet censorship programs 115;
Internet use in studies 125; interviews
and ethnographic studies 120; language
skills 116; list of organizations approved
to carry out research with foreign
involvement 127n8; Macau 127n5;
market research 117, 122; *Measures for
the Administrative of Foreign Affiliated
Surveys* 117–18, 127n4; National Bureau
of Statistics of China (NBS) 117–18,
123, 127n6; need for local Chinese
collaborators 120–2, 123–4, 125, 126;

outcomes of studies 114, 115–16, 122;
papers not published in China 115–16;
permit to conduct future market
research and societal investigations 118;
political action 116; process of studies
114–16; public opinion research 115,
120; recent censorship guidelines 127n7;
research conducted in sensitive areas
115; researchers challenging the regime
116; research protocol 121; risks under
the Chines government regulations
116–19; safety of respondents and local
collaborators 126; scientific training 116;
selective enforcement of rules 118–19;
self-censorship 126; social media in
China 115, 116; societal investigation
activities 117; state critique theory of
censorship 115; studying contemporary
Chines politics 113, 127n1; Taiwan 115,
127n5; territorial integrity issues 115;
Tibet 115; traditional methods of data
collection 113–14; Xinjiang 115
compensating subjects 104, 129, 138n2,
141, 148n5, 283, 289n19
CONEP *see* National Committee for
Ethics in Research
confederates: constituents serving as
confederates in research 237; deception
in international field experiments 152,
164, 166–8
Congress in Black and White (Grose) 236
contextual issues 269–71
controlled information environment
113, 126
corporate service providers (CSPs)
160, 165
cost-benefit analysis, political information
experiments 180–91
counterfactual comparisons 198, 201,
203, 216
countries without an Institutional Review
Board 110–11, 112n10, 139–48, 273;
autonomy of subjects 147; background
139–40; Belmont Report 140, 142,
146; beneficence principle 140,
140–1, 146; biomedical issues 139;
Center for Research and Teaching in
Economics 143, 148n9; compensation
to participants 141, 148n5; conclusion
and implications 146–7; conducting
research in Mexico 140–53; conflict
zones 141; Confucian principle 142;

consent form 145; creating a curriculum to teach ethics in research 143; creating an ethics committee 143; destruction of data 146; developing countries with no ethical regulations 139, 147n1; Federal Institute for Access to Public Information and Data Protection 145; field experiments 141; finding potential reviewers 146; indigenous people 147; Institutional Review Boards (IRBs) history 139; journal editors 147; justice principle 141, 148n3; Law for the Protection of Personal Data (2010) 144–5; laws and ethics in Mexico 143–6; legal framework 139, 142; levels of inequality in Mexico 142, 148n7; literature review of recent research in Mexico 140; medical research 143; Mexican National Institutes of Health 143; National Electoral Institute 142, 143, 148n8; nationality 142; non-governmental organizations (NGOs) 142; participants in political science experiments 141, 148n2; phenotypes of participants 141, 148n4; power relation between researcher and participants 141–2, 148n6; privacy notice 144, 145, 148n10, 148n11; racial appearance 142; respect for persons 140, 146; risks versus benefits 140; role of ethics reviewers in Mexico 139; socioeconomic status 142; storage of data 146; type of data collected 144; Universidad Iberoamericana 143; vulnerable groups 147
CP *see Comparative Politics*
CPS *see Comparative Political Studies*
criminal or civil liability 173
cross-disciplinary partnerships and studies 3
C-SPAN 249
CSPs *see* corporate service providers
cultural differences 2, 103, 110, 175
Cunow, Saul 19, 128, 273, 290; *see also* local review (the "Brazilian Black Box")
Cutler, John Charles 286–287

"daily life" standard for evaluation 68
dataset of published experiments from 1990 to 2013 with limited sample of earlier years 4–11; distribution of published political science experiments

8, *9f*, 22n12; experiments versus observational data 10; field experiments 8, 22n9, 22n10; growth in published political science experiments *5f*; journals surveyed 5–6; methodological shift toward experiments 10; National Science Foundation experimental dissertation grants 8, *9f*; publishing outlets other than journals sampled 10; types and locales of research 6–7, *7t*, 22n7; *see also Ethics and Experiments,* background and history
Dawkins, Richard 75
debriefing: public behavior of public officials 237; recommendations for field experiments 282–3; religion and experiments 69, 75
deception: local ethical review in comparative politics experiments 110; public behavior of public officials 227, 237; public officials, elected officials, and candidates 223; recommendations for field experiments 281; religion and experiments 66, 71, 75, 79n4, 79n5, 80n6; without consent 276, 278–80, 288n12
deception in international field experiments 151–70; alternatives to deception 152; American Psychological Association rules about deception 153, 161; anonymous incorporation (the case for deception) 151, 152, 159–66, 170n3; appropriate use of deception in international field experiments 170; articulating conditions for waiver of informed consent 154; background 151–2; behavioral support for foreign aid (the case for informed consent) 152, 168–9; Belmont Report 152, 153, 157, 158, 161, 165; cognitive dissonance 168; Common Rule 152, 153, 157, 158, 161; comparison of responses with and without deception 162, *163t*; compliance with international incorporation law 159–60; conclusion and implications 168, 169–70; confederates 152, 164, 166–8; corporate service providers (CSPs) 160, 165; cost and benefit assessment 159; deception defined 152; deception in social science research 152–4; deception vs. bias in field experiments 155–7; Department of Homeland Security 165; discrimination

against lesbians 170n1; ecological validity
155–6, 164, 168; ethics of using aliases in
research 155; experimental psychology
155; Financial Action Task Force 151,
164, 165; financial transparency 159;
Global Witness 165; Guatemala syphilis
experiments 152; the half-doubled
rule 152, 157–9, 169–70; hiring
discrimination 154; incorporation laws
in the United Kingdom and European
Union 164, 165; informed consent
152, 157; international development
programs 167; International Monetary
Fund 151; Internet research 170n2;
Investigative Review Boards (IRBs)
157–8; justifications for deception
in research 156; legal liability 158,
164; microfinance as an anti-poverty
panacea 167; microfinance confirmation
bias (the case for confederates) 152,
166–8; Nazi medical experiments
152; non-governmental organizations
(NGOs) 166–7; "obese"-pictured
discrimination 154; oral and written
consent 169; petty ethics and "moral
rigorism" (Kant) 151, 156, 157;
policymakers 164; Political Economy
and Development Lab (PEDL), Brigham
Young University 166–8; pool of future
subjects 165; prominent research in
which aliases prove key 154–5; public
policy 156; racial discrimination 154–5;
rationalization and justification 152,
170; recipient perceptions of foreign
aid 168–9; renter discrimination 154;
response-rate or selection bias 161;
Review of Financial Studies 167; safety
of research team 161; *Science* (journal)
167–8; self-regulation on ethical matters
158; Senate Permanent Subcommittee
on Investigations 165; "sham" surgeries
on patients 156–7; third-party evaluators
168; Tuskegee sterilization experiments
152; types of outcomes measured 169;
World Bank 151, 165
Declaration of Helsinki 241, 253n1, 260,
278, 288n15
de-identification 232–3, 238n3
democracies 230
democracy assistance intervention 201–12
Desposato, Scott 1, 19, 128, 182n1, 267,
290; *see also Ethics and Experiments,*

background and history; *Ethics
and Experiments,* conclusion and
recommendations; local review (the
"Brazilian Black Box")
developing countries 3; experiments
conducted in 267; rules in 242, 253n3
Dexter, Lewis 236
Dionne, Kim Yi 18, 25, 269, 290; *see also*
ethics of exclusion in impoverished
settings
"do good" defined 282
Dominguez, Alejandra 143
"do no harm" criterions 218, 224, 225
double-blind reviews 265
downstream consequences of research to
both populations and researchers 256
Driscoll, Jesse 19, 81, 290; *see also*
authoritarian governance regimes
("Prison States and Games of Chicken")
drug testing in developing countries 201

ecological validity 155–6, 164, 168
elected officials *see* public behavior of
public officials; public officials, elected
officials, and candidates
elites *see* public behavior of public officials;
public officials, elected officials, and
candidates
emerging ethical issues for political science
experiments 284
ethical challenges 11–18; aggregate effects
of political science experiments 17;
Belmont Report 18; criticisms of the
dialogue 17–18; economic games and
gambling prohibitions 12; experiments
in new contexts 11–13; experiments
outside the United States 11–13, 22n13;
first-principles approach 18; impact,
deception, and informed consent issues
13–15, 22n16, 22n17; Institutional
Review Boards 15–16; local review
procedures 13, 22n14; normative value
of research 16–17, 22n16; origins
and nature of experiments generating
controversy 11–15; plan for progress
17–18; political science and powerful
people 16; risks to research 16–17; *see
. also Ethics and Experiments,* background
and history
Ethics and Experiments, background and
history 1–22; anonymity of subjects 1, 3;
Common Rule 21n3; cross-disciplinary

partnerships and studies 3; cultural differences 2; developing countries 3; dialogue about 2–3; the experimental revolution 1, 3–11; experiments defined 3, 21n2, 21n3; field experiments 1–2, 3; gambling 2; human subjects 1, 2, 3; Institutional Review Boards (IRBs) 2, 21n1; journals published 4, 5; laboratory experiments 1; legal environments 2; low-risk early experiments 4, 22n5; "make your own rules" environment 2; organization of the volume 18–21; political science and 1, 2, 3; professional associations 2; professional ethics 1; subjects informed and consenting 4, 21n4; survey respondents 1; *see also* dataset of published experiments from 1990 to 2013 with limited sample of earlier years (Desposato); ethical challenges

Ethics and Experiments, conclusion and recommendations 267–9; aggregate or social harm 277; background 267–9; Belmont Report 278, 288n14, 288n15; comparative politics experiments 267; conclusion 284–7; consensus and controversy 269; contextual issues 269–71; Cutler, John Charles 286–7; deception without consent 276, 278–80, 288n12; Declaration of Helsinki 278, 288n15; diplomatic consequences to conducting experiments illegally overseas using government resources 273, 288n6; emerging ethical issues for political science experiments 284; experiments conducted in the developing world 267; Facebook emotion study 278, 279; field experiments 273–84; "get out the vote" messages 276, 288n10, 288n11; Guatemala experiments 287; harm and consent 275–84; inequalities between researchers and subjects 267; informed consent 278, 289n16; international Internet surveys 273; litigation 279–80; local collaborators risking serious consequences 278, 288n7; local review 271–3; Montana judicial election experiment 268, 278, 282, 287n1, 287n2, 289n18; New York restaurants study 279–80; Nuremberg Code 278, 288n15; public trust 279; research in

dangerous places 271, 287n3, 287n4; responsibilities of scholars 284; starting a dialogue on ethical issues 268; subjects' attitudes about our studies 279, 280–1; third party collaboration 273; Tuskegee experiments 287; workshops and conferences 284; *see also* learning from other disciplines; recommendations for field experiments

ethics in core curriculum, learning from other disciplines 285, 289n20

ethics in political science research 255–61, 284; American Political Science Association (APSA), "Guide to Professional Ethics in Political Science" (2012) 260; American Psychological Association (APA) 256, 260–1; background 255–6; broadening consideration of human subjects research 260–1; broadening consideration of risk 256–7; comparative politics 256; conclusion and implications 261; Declaration of Helsinki 260; domestic (US) IRBs and research conducted abroad 257–9; downstream consequences of research to both populations and researchers 256; extension of curricula and resources related to ethical research in the profession 255–6; Guatemala research subjects (1940s) 256; improper intrusion into study protocol (mission creep) 257, 258–9; Institutional Review Boards (IRBs) underperforming in assessing real risks 259; lack of knowledge of political climate in foreign countries 257–8; lack of knowledge of standards of living in foreign countries 258; limitations of domestic and foreign review boards 255; local review only partial remedy 259–60; local reviews in foreign countries 255, 261; researchers pooling information in a common online resource 260; responsibilities of the profession 255, 260–1; responsibilities of the researcher 255; Tuskegee syphilis studies 256; US-based researchers operating in foreign countries 255

ethics of exclusion in impoverished settings 18–19, 25–41, 269; background 25–6; Belmont Report 26–7; National

Job Training Partnership Act Study 27; risk-benefit ratio for participants 25, 27; sample selection: randomization, fairness, and exclusion 26–8; selection bias 26, 40n1; types of experiments 25; *see also* Malawi research experiences; Zomba district rural areas study on ethnic identity and social networks

exclusion *see* ethics of exclusion in impoverished settings

exempt categories in current regulations 227, 228–9

exempt status 246, 247, 251–2, 253, 254n12

existing intervention undertaken by non-academic organizations 198

expected value analysis of bottom-up transparency treatment 193–6, *194t–5t*

expected value of the research 191

experimental manipulation of religion 19, 42–65, 269–70; an argument from interest in forming beliefs without manipulation 47–9; an argument from the ambiguity of religious harms and benefits 49–51; an argument from the impossibility of informed consent 53–6; background 42–3; change manipulations are generally unethical 46–57; ethical experiments that change religiosity 56; examples 57–63; a failed experiment proposal 58–60; hypothetical examples 51–3; implications and conclusion 63–4; importance of religion in politics 64; manipulations that change non-religious beliefs 56–7; measurement and change manipulations 43–6, *44f, 44t, 46t*, 64n1; measurement manipulation example 60–1; permanent change manipulations 62–3; religion defined 63, 65n8; taboo 63; temporary change manipulations 62

Experiments in Government and Politics (EGAP) 264, 266

experiments outside the United States 11–13, 22n13

experiments versus observational data 10

extension of curricula and resources related to ethical research in the profession 255–6

Facebook 133; emotion study 278, 279

Federal Institute for Access to Public Information and Data Protection 145

Federal Policy for the Protection of Human Subjects (FPPHS) 199, 200, 201

Fenno, Richard 237, 247; *Home Style* 220

field experiments 1–2, 3, 8, 22n9, 22n10, 273–84; *see also* deception in international field experiments

Financial Action Task Force 151, 164, 165

Findley, Michael 20, 151, 290; *see also* deception in international field experiments

first-principles approach 18

FOIA *see* Freedom of Information Act

foreign individuals and entities 117, 127n5

foreign media outlets 116

"found data" provision 205

FPPHS *see* Federal Policy for the Protection of Human Subjects

framework for considering the ethics of information experiments 190–2

framing questions and priming beliefs, religion and experiments 72–4

Freedom of Information Act (FOIA) 230, 232, 238n1

funding sources, human subjects protection 242–3, 245, 253n4

fundraising by public officials 222

Gelman, Andrew 220

generalizable knowledge 175–6, 246, 247, 249, 253n7

"get out the vote" messages 276, 288n10, 288n11

Global Witness 165

Green, Don 96n18

Grose, Christian R. 20, 227, 274, 290; *Congress in Black and White* 236; *see also* public behavior of public officials

Guatemala research subjects (1940s) 152, 256, 287

Gubler, Joshua R. 20, 171, 178, 274, 277, 290; *see also* political consequences of comparative politics experiments

half-doubled rule 152, 157–9, 169–70

Harawa, Augustine 18, 25, 269, 290; *see also* ethics of exclusion in impoverished settings

Hidalgo, Daniel 88

Hitt, Matthew 286, 289n22

HIV testing experiment in a longitudinal study 29–30, 40n2-n4

Home Style (Fenno) 220

Honde, Hastings 18, 25, 269, 290; *see also* ethics of exclusion in impoverished settings
Hong Kong 127n5
human subjects 1, 2, 3
human subjects protection 241–54; academic freedom 246; amended protocols submitted to IRBs 252; American Association of University Professors (AAUP) 246, 253n4, 253n6; American Historical Association 247–8, 254n8; American Political Science Association 247; anonymity guarantee 248; background 241; *The Belmont Report: Ethical Principles and Guidelines for the Protection of Human Subjects of Research* 242, 243–5, 253; beneficence principle 244–5; "bureaucratic creep" and litigation phobia 241; case studies 247; Code of Federal Regulations (CFR) known as the Common Rule 242–243, 246, 247; comparative politics and IRBs 250–251; conclusion and implications 252–3; costs versus benefits of regulation 241; C-SPAN 249; decentralization 244; Declaration of Helsinki 241, 253n1; definition of research by institutional review boards (IRBs) 241; definition of research by the Code of Federal Regulations (CFR) 246, 247; diminished autonomy 244; exempt status 246, 247, 251–2, 253, 254n12; Fenno's "soak and poke" approach 247; funding sources 242–3, 245, 253n4; generalizable knowledge 246, 247, 249, 253n7; horrors of medical experiments 241; institutional review board regulations need to be modified 252–3; institutional review boards going to web-based submissions 249, 254n10; justice principle 244; Kefauver Amendments (1962) 253n2; large-N studies 245–6, 248; long overdue 241–3; medical community 241; Milgram obedience to authority experiments 245; Modern Language Association 248, 254n9; National Academy of Sciences 247; National Commission for the Protection of Human Subjects of Biomedical and Behavioral Research 242; National Research Act (1972) 242, 253n2; Nobel Prizes 245; non-inclusion in a study 244; Nuremberg Code 141; Nuremberg War Crime Trials 242; oral history 247, 248; requesting permission to observe public behavior 249; respect for persons principle 244; risk/reward assessment problems 242–6, 252, 253; risks to researchers 248–9; risks to respondents 248; rules in developing countries 242, 253n3; Sarbanes-Oxley Act (2002) 249; self-exemption 253; survey research 243, 252; systematic nature of research 246, 253n7; *testimonio* literature 248; Thalidomide disaster 253n2; Tuskegee case 241–2; when public behavior becomes private 249–50; when research is non-research 246–9
Humphrey, Peter 127n9
Hyde, Susan D. 20, 198, 274, 291; *see also* research with non-governmental organizations (NGOs)

iatrophobia (distrust of medical workers) 174–5
impact, deception, and informed consent issues 13–15, 22n16, 22n17
impoverished settings *see* ethics of exclusion in impoverished settings
indigenous tribes 129, 135
Indonesia 219
information and power *see* political information experiments
informed consent 278, 289n16; deception in international field experiments 152, 157; political information experiments 192; public officials, elected officials, and candidates 224; recommendations for field experiments 281; religion and experiments 66, 69; research with non-governmental organizations (NGOs) 214, 216n9
Institutional Review Boards (IRBs) 2, 15–16, 21n1; amended protocols submitted to 252; authoritarian governance regimes and 83–4, 85, 90, 94n3; at Brigham Young University 173; countries without 139–48, 273; decentralized nature of 101; exemptions 217, 218, 219; expedited or exempt from review 109; experience of sitting on 102–3; going to web-based submissions 249, 254n10; government

studies exempt from IRB oversight 199, 201–3, *201t*; history 139; limitations of domestic and foreign review boards 255; local ethical review in comparative politics experiments 99, 100–1, 111n2; overzealous IRBs 104; political information experiments 183–4; public behavior of public officials 227, 229; regulations need to be modified 252–3; religion and experiments 67–8; reporting about the IRB process in journals 105–8, *105f*, 111, 111n6; requirement for publication and funding 99, 105–8; and research conducted abroad 257–9; research with non-governmental organizations (NGOs) 199, 200, 207, 216n1; underperforming in assessing real risks 259; at University of California at San Diego 131, 132, 135; at Vanderbilt 102; at Yale 106
international development programs 167
International Monetary Fund 151
International Organization (IO) 5, 6
Internet: censorship programs 115; and deception in international field experiments 170n2; international Internet surveys 273; and public officials, elected officials, and candidates 223; use in studies 125
IO *see International Organization*
Ishiyama, John 21, 262, 291; *see also* journal editors and ethics
Islam: *haram* (forbidden) to wager money in Islam 76, 77, 80n8; insurgency against the government 174–5
Israel's outgroup aggression experiments 178, 182n3

Japanese internment 202
JCR *see Journal of Conflict Resolution*
Jensen, Nathan 166
JOP *see Journal of Politics*
journal editors and ethics 147, 262–6; *American Journal of Political Science* 265; background 262–3; Common Rule 263; community standards 264; comparative judgments 263; comparative research 262; compensation to subjects 264; conclusion and implications 265–6; debriefing 264; deception 264; demands on journal editors 263, 266;

double-blind reviews 265; enforcing research ethics 262; ethics violations in laboratory and field experiments 262; Experimental Research Section of APSA 264, 266; Experiments in Government and Politics (EGAP) 264, 266; foreign manuscripts 264; human subject rights 262; informed consent 263–4; Institutional Review Boards (IRBs) 262, 263; learning from other disciplines 285–6, 289n21; pre-registration of experiments 265; prioritizing ethical issues 263–4; problems 263–4; professional associations 263; proposed solutions 264–5; protocol accompanying experiments 265; randomization 264; requiring an IRB before review of manuscript 264; reviewer pool 265; self-regulation by researchers 262; special knowledge or training 263; submissions declined 262; training program for editors 264–5, 266
Journal of Conflict Resolution (JCR) 5, 6, 22n8
Journal of Experimental Political Science 289n21
Journal of Politics (JOP) 5, 6, 105, 106
junior faculty 137
justice principle: countries without an Institutional Review Board 141, 148n3; human subjects protection 244; research with non-governmental organizations (NGOs) 200–1, 206, 212

Kant, Immanuel 151
Karlan, Dean 167
Kefauver Amendments (1962) 253n2
"Know Your Delegate" website 223

Laitin, David 81, 90
language barriers 83, 116
large-N studies 245–6, 248
Law for the Protection of Personal Data (2010) 144–5
learning from other disciplines 284–6; Belmont Report 285; ethics in core curriculum 285, 289n20; journal editorial policies 285–6, 289n21; legal cover 285; norm developments 284–5; Nuremberg Code 285; professional association code of conduct for research

284; research on human subjects and ethics in political science 286; *see also Ethics and Experiments*, conclusion and recommendations

legal cover 136, 285

legal liability 158, 164

letters of approval or permission 109

list of organizations approved to carry out research with foreign involvement 127n8

litigation 279–80

local collaborators risking serious consequences 278, 288n7

local ethical review in comparative politics experiments 99–112, 273, 288n5; alternative options 109–10; background 99–100; Belmont Principles 103, 104; biomedical research 100, 101, 111n3; Brazil 102, 105, 108, 111, 111n5; bribes 108; challenges of obtaining local ethical review 108–10; China 102; Claremont Graduate University 101, 103, 104, 109; collaborating with scholars within country 108; Common Rule 100, 111n1; comparative politics experiments 103; compensation to participants 104; conclusion and implications 110–11; cooperation with NGOs 107, 110; costs to obtain reviews 108; countries not having ethical review boards 110–11, 112n10; culture and customs 103, 110; decentralized nature of IRBs 101; deception 110; expedited or exempt from review 109; experience of sitting on an Institutional Review Board 102–3; government bureaucracies 108; Institutional Review Boards (IRBs) 99, 100–1, 111n2; journals and funding agencies 99, 105–8; less formal types of reviews 109; letters of approval or permission 109; level of risk 108, 110; list of journals reviewed 105; local ethical review defined 99; National Institutes of Health (NIH) grants 109; National Science Foundation (NSF) 100–1, 102, 109, 111; overzealous IRBs 104; participants put at risk 103; Principal Investigators (PIs) 100, 102, 111; protocols overseas 103; reasons for getting a local ethical review 102–5; reporting about the IRB process in journals 105–8, *105f*, 111, 111n6;

requirement for publication and funding 99, 105–8; researchers put at risk 103; the status quo 100–2; subject advocates 109–10; time window 109; Vanderbilt's Institutional Review Board 102; Yale's Institutional Review Board 106; *see also* authoritative governance regimes

local review (the "Brazilian Black Box") 128–38; attempting the full review process 136; background 128–9; backlash against all political science experiments in Brazil 136; basic review 130; Brazilian ethical rules 128, 129–31; Brazilian scholars' attitudes 137, 138n6; case for compliance 135–6; Committees on Ethics in Research (CEPs) 129, 130, 138n1; communication problems 133; comparative politics 137; consequences of violations of rules 130–1; constructive alternatives to compliance 136–7; domestic involvement of project 130; experiment and experience with the Brazilian review process 131–4; Facebook 133; foreign scholars conducting experiments in Brazil 128; graduate students 137; incentivizing behavior 129, 138n3; indigenous tribes 129, 135; issues at stake 134–6, 138n5; junior faculty 137; legal cover 136; lengthy delays in the Brazilian review process 134; local review by a Brazilian university committee 137; low-risk projects 128, 131, 137; medical studies 129; Ministry of Health 128, 129; National Committee for Ethics in Research (CONEP) 129, 130, 132, 135; National Council of Health 128, 129; prohibitions on compensating subjects 129, 138n2; return of results 130; scholars with short time horizons 137; technology transfer 130; third party interventions 137, 138n9; time limits 130, 138n4; timeline of Brazilian review process 132–3; types of experiments 137, 138n8; UCSD Institutional Review 131, 132, 135

local reviews: in foreign countries 255, 261; only partial remedy 259–60; procedures of 13, 22n14

Lu, Xiaobo 19, 113, 138n7, 138n8, 273, 291; *see also* comparative politics experiments in China

Macau 127n5
Madrid, Raul, Jr. 19, 99, 288n5, 291; *see also* local ethical review in comparative politics experiments
Malawi research experiences 28–35; behavioral economics experiments on the border 31–3, 41n7; Community Based Rural Land Development Project (CBRLDP) 33; conclusion and implications 39–40; HIV testing experiment in a longitudinal study 29–30, 40n2–n4; Malawi Social Cash Transfer Scheme (MSCTS) 34–5, 41n8; Zomba Cash Transfer Program 30–1, 40n5–n6; *see also* ethics of exclusion in impoverished settings; Zomba district rural areas study on ethnic identity and social networks
Malawi transparency intervention 193–6
Malesky, Edmund J. 20, 217, 274, 291; *see also* public officials, elected officials, and candidates
manipulating elites *see* public behavior of public officials; public officials, elected officials, and candidates
measurement and change manipulations 43–6, *44f, 44t, 46t*, 64n1
Measures for the Administrative of Foreign Affiliated Surveys 117–18, 127n4
Merolla, Jennifer L. 19, 99, 288n5, 291; *see also* local ethical review in comparative politics experiments
Mexico: conducting research in 140–53; laws and ethics in 143–6
Michigan (case study #2) 212–15
microfinance confirmation bias (the case for confederates) 152, 166–8
Milgram, Stanley 245; obedience to authority experiments 180–1, 182, 199
minimal individual harm, recommendations for field experiments 276–7
minimal risk 200, 212
minimizing controversy, recommendations for field experiments 282–3
Mishler, William 21, 262, 291; *see also* journal editors and ethics
mission creep 257, 258–9
Modern Language Association 248, 254n9
Montana judicial election experiment 268, 278, 282, 287n1, 287n2, 289n18
Morton, Rebecca 19, 66, 270, 291; *see also* religion and experiments

National Academy of Sciences 247
National Bureau of Statistics of China (NBS) 117–18, 123, 127n6
National Commission for the Protection of Human Subjects of Biomedical and Behavioral Research 242
National Committee for Ethics in Research (CONEP) 129, 130, 132, 135
National Institutes of Health (NIH) grants 109
National Job Training Partnership Act Study 27
National Research Act (1972) 242, 253n2
National Research Council 209
National Science Foundation (NSF) 100–1, 102, 109, 111; experimental dissertation grants 8, *9f*
Nazi medical experiments 152
New York restaurants study 279–80
Nickerson, David W. 20, 198, 274, 291; *see also* research with non-governmental organizations (NGOs)
Nielsen, Richard A. 19, 42, 269, 291; *see also* experimental manipulation of religion
Nielson, Daniel 29, 151, 166, 291; *see also* deception in international field experiments
Nobel Prizes 245
nominally public activities 234
non-democracies 201
non-governmental organizations (NGOs):in authoritarian governance regimes 82, 84, 88, 90; cooperation with 107, 110; initiatives in religion and experiments 74; *see also* research with non-governmental organizations (NGOs)
normative value of research 16–17, 22n16
norm developments, learning from other disciplines 284–5
Nuremberg Code 141, 278, 288n15; learning from other disciplines 285
Nuremberg War Crime Trials 242

Obradovich, Nicholas 192
"one-drop" rule 215
online resource, researchers pooling information for 260
oral history 247, 248
Orwell, George 249; Time Machine butterfly effect 174

PB *see Political Behavior*
peer review systems 79
plan for progress 17–18
Political Behavior (PB) 5, 6, 105, 107, 289n21
political competition 173–4, 178
political consequences of comparative
  politics experiments 171–82, 274;
  American Political Science Review 177;
  background 171–2; Belmont Report
  172, 173–5, 181; Brigham Young
  University's IRB 173; conclusion and
  implications 181–2; criminal or civil
  liability 173; crosscutting identities on
  prejudice in Chennai, India 177–8,
  182n2; cultural differences 175; economic
  equality 174; effects of disseminating the
  findings 172; effects of the treatments
  172; experiments in foreign settings
  171–2; *iatrophobia* (distrust of medical
  workers) 174–5; imagining/thinking
  exercise 171–2; Institutional Review
  Boards (IRBs) 172; Islamic insurgency
  against the government 174–5; limited
  sampling procedures 178; obedience
  to authority experiment (Milgram)
  180–1, 182; Orwell's Time Machine
  butterfly effect 174; outgroup aggression
  experiments in Israel 178, 182n3;
  political competition 173–4, 178;
  political generalizability 175–6; political
  identity 175, 176–7; political resources
  175, 176; publication of research findings
  175; resource allocation 174; risks of
  affecting social and political outcomes
  in societies 172; rule of law 174; Star
  Trek "Prime Directive" assumption
  172, 182n1; subjects' financial standing,
  employability, or reputation 173; "The
  Adverse Effects of Sunshine" (Malesky,
  Schuler, and Tran) 179–80; three
  questions applied 177–81; three sets of
  questions 175–7; worldviews 175
Political Economy and Development Lab
  (PEDL), Brigham Young University
  166–8
political information experiments 183–97,
  274; affecting voter turnout 184;
  background 183–4; Belmont Report principles 189–91;
  bottom-up transparency interventions
  184, 197n2; case study demonstration
  framework 193–6; citizen information
  experiments 184–5; cognitive dissonance
  188; community theatre 184; conclusion
  and implications 196–7; cost-benefit
  analysis 180–91; ethical challenges
  183–4; ethical considerations 185–8;
  executed in context of an election 183;
  expected value analysis of bottom-up
  transparency treatment 193–6, *194t–5t*;
  expected value of the research 191;
  experiments providing information
  to citizens in democracies about their
  government 183; field experiments 185;
  framework for considering the ethics
  of information experiments 190–2;
  great harm to at least one individual or
  group 187; group-level outcomes 185,
  186; incentivizing political scientists
  on ethical issues 196–7; informed
  consent 192; informing participants and
  non-participants of the research 196;
  in-person canvassing 184; Investigative
  Review Boards (IRBs) and 183–4;
  lasting harm to at least one person
  or group 183; literature review 184,
  191; local enumerators 188; Malawi
  transparency intervention 193–6;
  media 184; non-native researchers 188;
  outcomes ambiguous in time horizon,
  causal relationship, and normative value
  183, 188; political action 185; political
  elites 197n1; public opinion 185;
  real-world information 197; researchers
  having "undue influence" over political
  outcomes 187; respect, beneficence, and
  justice 189–91; spillover effects 185,
  186–7; survey experiments 184, 185;
  top-down transparency interventions
  184, 193, 197n2; topics of information
  experiments 184–5; Type 1 error and
  Type 2 error 191; vote choice 185;
  written reports 184
Pool, Ithiel de Sola 229
Poverty Action Lab (NGO) 206
power and information *see* political
  information experiments
pre-registration of experiments, journal
  editors and ethics 265
private activities by public officials 235
professional associations 2; code of conduct
  for research 284; journal editors and
  ethics 263
proselytization 71
protocol accompanying experiments,
  journal editors and ethics 265

public accountability 202
public activity 230
public and less accessible activities 232–4
public and universally accessible activities 231–2
public behavior and private behavior 249–50
public behavior of public officials 227–38; academic freedom 228; access to government information 230; American Political Science Association creating "clearinghouse" of information 236–7; background 227–8; conclusion and implications 237–8; *Congress in Black and White* (Grose) 236; constituents serving as confederates in research 237; correspondence from a legislative office to constituents 232; debriefing 237; deception 227, 237; de-identification 232–3, 238n3; democracies 230; and ethical framework 229–35; ethics of field research 228; exempt categories in current regulations 227, 228–9; federal level of officials 234; Freedom of Information Act (FOIA) 230, 232, 238n1; free speech 229; "Frequently Asked Questions" section in the Freedom of Information Act (FOIA) 230, 238n1; Institutional Review Boards (IRBs) 227, 229; interviews or participant observations 236, 237; minimal risk to public officials 234; minimal risk to subjects 229; nominally public activities 234; partnering with existing organizations in field experiments 238n2; private activities by public officials 235; protection of public officials 227–8, 231; public activity 230; public and less accessible activities 232–4; public and universally accessible activities 231–2; "public-ness" level 228; replicability standards 233; roll-call voting 231, 232; time costs to subjects 227, 235–7; US Congress 235–6, 238n5; *see also* public officials, elected officials, and candidates "public-ness" level 228
public officials, elected officials, and candidates 217–26, 274; accountability mechanisms 217; activities most important to represent citizens' interests 221–2; background 217–18; in Cambodia 219; career prospects and livelihood of politicians 218, 220,

225; conclusion and implications 224–6; congressman's schedule 220, *221f*; deception in research design 223; defining a public official 218–20; "do no harm" criterions 218, 224, 225; ethical concerns 218, 226; footprint of public profile 220; fundraising by public officials 222; *Home Style* (Fenno) 220; Huffington Post article 222; incentive structure 225; in Indonesia 219; information already published 225; informed consent 224; Institutional Review Boards (IRBs) exemptions 217, 218, 219; Internet and 223; "Know Your Delegate" website 223; levels of government 218–19, 220; literature review 217, 226n1; local level testing 219; operationalization versus job performance 218, 220–4; opportunity costs 221, 224; part-time representatives 219–20, 225; political science theory 225–6; privacy and confidentiality 218; responsiveness and accountability to constituencies 220; scorecards on 225; specialization 224; staff resources 222; time constraints outside the United States 223; time devoted to duties 220; transparency and accountability mechanisms 224–5; in Vietnam 219, 223, 225–226; World Bank 219; *see also* public behavior of public officials
public policy 156, 198
public trust 279
published political science experiments dataset 4–11, 8, *9f*, 22n12
publishing non-findings 88–9

randomized control trials (RCTs) 90, 95n7
RCTs *see* randomized control trials
"reasonable person" standard 205, 211
recommendations for field experiments 281–3; Common Rule 282; compensation to subjects 283, 289n19; debriefing (confess) 282–3; deception 281; "do good" defined 282; informed consent 281; minimal individual harm 276–7; minimizing controversy 282–3; social value of the knowledge from research 281; "tread lightly" defined 282; *see also Ethics and Experiments*, conclusion and recommendations
religion, *see also* experimental manipulation of religion; religion and experiments

religion and experiments 66–80, 168, 270; analytical thinking and religious disbelief 75; anonymity 69; apostasy 70; background 66–7; belief as sacred 69–71; benefit/cost approach 67–8, 79n2; biased or false political information 75; changing/manipulating religious beliefs 66–7, 70, 74–5; civil unrest and 66; collateral benefits 67; Common Rule (US Federal Regulations) 67; conclusion and implications 77–9; "daily life" standard for evaluation 68; debriefing 69, 75; deception by experimenters 66, 75; deception risk 71, 79n4, 79n5, 80n6; effect of religion on politics 66, 79n1; ethical issues in 67–9; experimental tasks variant with beliefs 76–7; framing questions and priming beliefs 72–4; government initiatives 74; *haram* (forbidden) to wager money in Islam 76, 77, 80n8; human subject committees 79; Implicit Association Test 75; incentivized measures of risk preference 76; indirect measure 71; informed consent 66, 69; Institutional Review Boards 67–8; lottery prohibition 76–7; measuring religious beliefs 66, 69–72; NGO initiatives 74; open debate on religion 74; participation in religious rituals 71; peer review systems 79; political economy versus political psychology 80n7; political psychology 72; possible risks to research team members 66; potential harms to subjects 66; proselytization 71; reconciliation programs 74; religious calendars 74, 76; subjects asked to engage in activities in conflict with beliefs 67

research and non-research 246–9
research on human subjects and ethics in political science 286
research with non-governmental organizations (NGOs) 198–216, 274; anti-corruption campaigns 204–5; autonomy (respect) principle 200, 202, 207, 211–12, 214; background 198–200; Belmont Report 199, 204, 214, 216n10; beneficence principle 200, 207, 212; Cambodia (case study #1) 208–12; Cambodian Members of the National Assembly (MNAs) 209–10; Cambodian People's Party (CPP) 209, 210, 216n6; changes introduced by researcher's involvement in projects

199, 216; collaborative experiments between researchers and NGOs 199; conclusion and implications 215–16; Constituency Dialogues experiment in Cambodia (case study #1) 208–12; counterfactual comparisons 198, 201, 203, 216; decision-making authority 215; democracy assistance intervention 201–12; distinguishing between the intervention and the research 198; drug testing in developing countries 201; evaluating effects of NGO interventions 208; existing intervention undertaken by non-academic organizations 198; Federal Policy for the Protection of Human Subjects (FPPHS) 199, 200, 201; focus of ethical questions about experiments 201–3, *201t*, 205, 206; "found data" provision 205; funding of programs 206–7, 215, 313; goodwill presumption 203, 292; government studies exempt from IRB oversight 199, 201–3; Human Rights Party (HRP) 210, 216n6; hybrid model with interventions by NGOs 203–8, 216n3; infamous research 199; informed consent 214, 216n9; Institutional Review Boards (IRBs) 199, 200, 207, 216n1; intimidation campaigns 204; Japanese internment 202; justice principle 200–1, 206, 212; manifestly undesirable 204; Michigan (case study #2) 212–15; Michigan Democratic Party 212–15; Milgram's obedience to authority experiment 199; minimal risk 200, 212; mobilization efforts aimed at younger voters 212–15; National Research Council 209; National United Front for an Independent, Neutral, Peaceful, and Cooperative Cambodia (FUNCINPEC) 210, 212, 216n5, 216n6; non-democracies 201; Norodom Ranariddh Party (NRP) 210, 216n6; "one-drop" rule 215; policy evaluation 202–3, 216n2; post-election survey 213; Poverty Action Lab (NGO) 206; public accountability 202; public policy 198; "reasonable person" standard 205, 211; researchers creating opportunities for field experimental research 207–8; Sam Rainsy Party (SRP) 210, 216n6; scripts and campaign literature 213; slippery slope 207; standard paradigm 200–3; town hall meetings 209–10, 216n4,

216n7, 216n8; traditional mobilizing methods 213; turnout behavior of the subjects 213; Tuskegee syphilis study 199, 202; volunteer outreach effort 213
respect for persons principle: countries without an Institutional Review Board 140, 146; human subjects protection 244; research with non-governmental organizations (NGOs) 200, 202, 207, 211–12, 214
response-rate or selection bias 161
responsibilities: of the profession 255, 260–1; of the researcher 255, 284
reviewer pool 265
Review of Financial Studies 167
risk-benefit ratio for participants 25, 27
risk/reward assessment problems 242–6, 252, 253
risks to research 16–17
Rogers, Jonathan 19, 66, 270, 291; *see also* religion and experiments

safety: possible risks to research team members 66, 161, 248–9; potential harms to subjects 66; of respondents and local collaborators 126, 248
Sarbanes-Oxley Act (2002) 249
Schelling, Thomas 89
selection bias 26, 40n1
self-regulation on ethical matters 158, 262
Seligson, Mitchell A. 21, 241, 284, 291; *see also* human subjects protection
Selway, Joel S. 20, 171, 177, 274, 277, 291; *see also* political consequences of comparative politics experiments
Semmelweis, Ignaz 21n2
Senate Permanent Subcommittee on Investigations 165
Sherill, Ken 288n13
social media in China 115, 116
social value of the knowledge from research, recommendations for field experiments 281
Somalia 85, 95n6
Star Trek "Prime Directive" assumption 172, 182n1
subjects: advocates for 109–10; attitudes about our studies 279, 280–1; financial standing, employability, or reputation 173
survey research 184, 185, 243, 252
systematic nature of research 246, 253n7

Taiwan 115, 127n5
testimonio literature 248
Thalidomide disaster 253n2
third party collaboration 273
third party interventions 137, 138n9
Tibet 115
top-down transparency interventions 184, 193, 197n2
"tread lightly" defined, recommendations for field experiments 282
Tuskegee case 241–2

Universidad Iberoamericana 143
University of California at San Diego Institutional Review Board 131, 132, 135
US Congress 235–6, 238n5; congressman's schedule 220, *221f*

Vanderbilt's Institutional Review Board 102
Vietnam 219, 223, 225–6
volunteerism within the discipline 94

Wilson, Rick K. 21, 262, 291; *see also* journal editors and ethics
workshops and conferences 284
World Bank 86, 151, 165, 219
worldviews 175

Xinjiang 115

Yale's Institutional Review Board 106

Zechmeister, Elizabeth J. 21, 101, 104, 147n1, 255, 284, 291; *see also* ethics in political science research
Zimmerman, Brigitte 20, 183, 274, 277, 289n17, 291; *see also* political information experiments
Zinman, Jonathan 167
Zomba district rural areas study on ethnic identity and social networks 35–9; data collection and participant earnings 37–8, 41n15; integrating local knowledge into study design 38–9; sampling: aiming for inclusion and transparency 36–7, 41n10-n14; *see also* ethics of exclusion in impoverished settings; Malawi research experiences